Cloth

As

Metaphor:

(Re)reading the Adinkra Cloth

Symbols of the Akan of Ghana, 2nd Edition

G. F. Kojo Arthur

**CLOTH AS METAPHOR: (RE)READING THE ADINKRA CLOTH
SYMBOLS OF THE AKAN OF GHANA, 2ND EDITION**

Cover Design: G. F. Kojo Arthur (based on initial first edition design by G. F. Kojo Arthur and Kwadwo Edusei)
Layout: G. F. Kojo Arthur

Photo Credits:
    Chapter 2
(a) National Museum of African Art, Smithsonian Institution, Washington, DC.
(b) Museum of Ethnology, Leiden, The Netherlands - Collection Nationaal Museum van Wereldculturen. Coll.no. RV-360-1700"

All other photos © G. F. Kojo Arthur

iUniverse books may be ordered through booksellers or by contacting:

iUniverse
1663 Liberty Drive
Bloomington, IN 47403
www.iuniverse.com
1-800-Authors (1-800-288-4677)

ISBN: 978-1-5320-2893-9 (sc)
ISBN: 978-1-5320-2894-6 (e)

Library of Congress Control Number: 2017915672

Print information available on the last page.

iUniverse rev. date: 11/30/2017

Dedicated to
Abena Otuwaa
    Abena Abasewa
      Esi Boama
        Efua Debiwa
         Efua Seguwa
           Ama Otuwa Hamah
            Nana Yaa Debra
              Kobina Boama Arthur
                Keep the touch aglow

CONTENTS

PREFACE

How have human beings throughout time communicated? The human brain is known to be capable of storing knowledge, but this ability is limited, so how have human beings stored knowledge throughout time? What visual strategies have humans developed to store knowledge for recall at a future date? What is writing anyway? Is all writing linear or there are some writing that is nonlinear? Does what my doctor write to the pharmacist on my prescription form constitute writing? What about scientific notations, road signs, music scores and the Indian wampum cloth that were woven to mark treaties signed between Indian nations and the European settler in the new world? Do all these things constitute writing?

Before exploring these questions, we need to remind ourselves of the three basic strategies that underlie writing systems. The strategies differ in the size of the speech unit denoted by one written sign: either a single basic sound (phonogram - eg, the alphabetic system for various languages), or a whole syllable, or a whole word or idea (ideogram). There are also pictograms that use picture units to represent ideas (whole sentences, perhaps themes). Writing systems are based on the use of arbitrary symbols that have semantic (meaning-centered) value and/or phonetic (sound-centered) value.

The most widespread strategy in the modern world is the alphabet, which ideally would provide a unique symbol — a letter — for every basic sound, or phoneme, of the language. This one symbol for one basic sound is not achieved in many alphabetic writing systems. (By the way, what sounds do the following symbols represent in the English language: *, ~, %, &, and ?). Also, the relationship between the visual and the auditory codes in the alphabetic writing system is arbitrary, e.g., c is pronounced differently in each of the following words in the English language that uses the roman alphabets for writing: _cent_, _cat_, _chair_ and _ocean_.

Another widespread strategy employs logograms, written signs that stand for whole words. Before the spread of alphabetic writing, systems heavily dependent on logograms were common and included Egyptian hieroglyphs, Mayan glyphs, and Sumerian cuneiform. Logograms continue to be used today, notably in Chinese and in kanji, the predominant writing system employed by the Japanese. Interestingly, the Japanese also have an alphabet-based writing system called hiragana.

One of the principal functions of all writing is to serve as a store of information. Another principal function of all writing is to convey linguistic meaning, but writing systems vary greatly in how they encode meaning. In purely phonetic transcription, access to meaning is mediated through sound representation, while a purely ideographic notation bypasses representation of sounds, encoding concepts instead. Actual writing systems belong to neither of these 'pure' categories, but are located somewhere along a continuum which ranges from sound-centered to meaning-centered.

By the way, what does the symbol 0 stand for – does it represent a sound or does it represent some meaning? The answer is both depending on the context in which it is used! Writing system is context based.

The book began as a short piece for the newsletter put out by the Office of International Student, Marshall University, Huntington, WV, USA in 1990. This increased my interest to examine more closely what the adinkra symbols were all about. I was awarded visiting scholar research grant by the African Studies Program, Indiana University in 1996. I initiated in 1997 the Akan Cultural Symbols Project Online. This was available on the Internet from 1997-2008 at http://www.marshall. edu/akanart. It is now hosted at http://www.cfiks.org. The Akan Cultural Symbols Project Online served as a resource base for teachers and schools interested in knowing more about the adinkra cloth and how to do adinkra print projects. This took me to schools in the tri-state area of Kentucky, Ohio and West Virginia close to Huntington, WV. I was awarded Ford Foundation research scholar grant in 2001 that enabled me to set up Centre for Indigenous Knowledge Systems (CEFIKS – http:// www.cfiks.org). The first edition of this book was published in 2001 by the Centre. I was awarded a Senior Research Fellowship by the Smithsonian Institution at the National Museum of African Art in 2007-2008 to undertake extensive research in Akan material culture, particularly wood carrvings, *adinkra* and *kente* cloths.

My research indicates that the Akan of Ghana developed *adinkra* symbols for writing. These symbols comprise mostly pictograms and ideograms. The *adinkra* symbols of the Akan of Ghana fall somewhere on the meaning-centered and sound-centered continuum, closer to the meaning-centered (ideogram) system. The *adinkra* symbols draw on the extensive Akan oral literature. The *adinkra* symbols are linked to proverbs, stories, songs, mythology, riddles and puzzles, as well as everyday expressions of the Akan of Ghana. What meanings these symbols encode form the subject matter of this book.

This second edition includes a comprehensive catalogue of symbols and the proverbs and maxims linked with each symbol. Chapters 1, 5, 6, 7 and 10 have been expanded extensively. Several photographs have been included in this edition. A very extensive bibliography and index are also provided.

ACKNOWLEDGMENT

Even after the seemingly endless solitary hours of writing, this book reflects the contributions and influences of many people besides the author. There are several people to whom I owe a debt of gratitude for the support and assistance they gave to me in the preparation and completion of this book. I would like to thank Ford Foundation, Smithsonian Institution, The National Museum of African Art and Marshall University for their generous financial and material support for the field research and preparation for publication. A very special acknowledgement goes to Dr. Betty J. Cleckley, former Marshall University Vice President for Multicultural Affairs and International Programs whose office provided the financial assistance for research. Her steadfast commitment to the infusion of diversity in Marshall University's curricula made it possible for me to receive research grants that enabled me to visit Ghana, and museums in England, Germany, Holland and Switzerland, and a number of libraries and museums in the United States to gather data. I would like to express my gratitude to the African Studies Program at the Indiana University, Bloomington for offering me the Ford Foundation Research Fellowship in the summer of 1996 to do further museum and library research in Bloomington and Indianapolis in order to revise the initial manuscript.

I am also grateful to Ford Foundation for awarding me a grant that made it possible for setting up the Centre for Indigenous Knowledge Systems in Ghana in 2001. This grant also partly supported the printing of the first edition of this book.

I would like to express my appreciation to all those whose stories, proverbs and anecdotes taught me Akan *mpanisɛm* (that is, the wisdom and knowledge of the past acquired through the elders). At the risk of offending some people, and I hope they will forgive me, I will have to acknowledge particular debts of gratitude to my father-in-law Rev. Joseph Yedu Bannerman a retired minister of the Methodist Church of Ghana (now deceased), and his wife and the extended family members; Nana Antwi Buasiako, Asanthene's Kyeame for allowing me to photograph his extensive collection of *adinkra* cloths; Rev. Peter Sarpong, Catholic Archbishop of Kumasi; and Mr. Owusu-Ansah, formerly of UST, Kumasi. Nana Antwi-Buasiako has transitioned to join the ancestors, and may his soul rest in peace. Special thanks go to Teacher Kofi Nsiah of Ntonso (who also has transitioned to join the ancestors), and Kwadwo Appiah of Asokwa, the cloth producers in the Kumasi Metropolitan area, for their support and encouragement when I carried out research in Ghana from 1992 on.

My gratitude is extended also to Professor Robert Bickel of Marshall University who read various drafts of the entire book with great care and made elaborate comments from which I benefited a great deal. My thanks go also to Professor Joseph Adjaye, formerly of Pittsburgh University, Dr Al Bavon, University of Arkansas, Professor Robert Osei-wusuh; Dr. Ed Piou of University of South Florida, Tampa; Professor Kwesi Yankah and Professor Kwame Karikari both of the University of Ghana, Legon, Ghana; and Dr. William Kojo Darley of University of Toledo, Ohio for their useful comments and suggestions.

Second Edition

In addition to all the people mentioned above, I would want to express my gratitude to Janet Stanley, Librarian, National Museum of African Art, Smithsonian Institution, Washington, D.C. She immersed me in the resources of the Museum's library and directed me to literature on semiotics. I also appreciate the support of the staff of the National Museum of African Art, particularly Christine Kreamer and Amy Staples during my tenure as senior research fellow of the Museum in 2007-2008. Doran Ross, formerly of the UCLA Fowler Museum was gracious in opening up to me to his Beverly Hills home and allowing me to drink deep from his fountain of knowledge, and to delve into his extensive documentation on Akan crafts people. I tremendously appreciate his support.

Last, but not the least, I am very grateful to Mr. Anthony Kweku Annan (Apollo) for making it possible for me to seize the opportunity to move to the US in the early 1970s, and for remaining a very good friend over the last half century. His comments and suggestions were very helpful to me as I toiled to complete the revisions for this second edition.

This work, however, is entirely mine, and I am responsible for its shortcomings.

CHAPTER 1

Kyɛmferɛ se ɔdaa hɔ akyɛ, na onipa ɔnwenee no nso nyɛ dɛn?
The potsherd claims it is old, what about the potter who molded it?

SIGNS AND SYMBOLS FROM GHANA: A WRITING SYSTEM?

INTRODUCTION

Pre-colonial African societies are believed to have depended entirely on oral communication because it has been generally assumed they had not developed a recognizable form of writing (Goody, 1977, 1986). Even after phonetically-based and other writing systems were introduced through contact with outsiders,[1] many African societies are believed to have continued to rely mainly on oral communication. Such critics of pre-colonial Africa tend to assume that writing takes only one form — the phonetically-based form of writing, an example of which is the alphabetic system, and that all writing is linear. Non-linear and non-phonetically-based writing systems have come to be seen as inferior attempts at the real thing and, thus have been marginalized. In relatively recent years the narrow view of writing as visible speech and the correspondingly limited view of literacy as the ability to read and write in alphabetic script have increasingly come under scrutiny and attack. In recent years it has been recognized that many writing systems in West Africa, the best known being those of the Vai in Liberia (Scribner and Cole, 1981; Pilaszewicz, 1985) and Mende (Bledsoe and Robey, 1986), for example, were developed outside of the Western context.

Societies throughout Africa have preserved knowledge about their societies through verbal, visual, and written art forms. From Ghana's *adinkra* symbols that are centuries old, to geometric decorations painted on the walls of houses by Frafra women in Northern Ghana as well as women in South Africa, through the ancient Ge'ez alphabetic system of early Christians of Ethiopia, to the patterns of wax fabrics worn in West Africa, the African continent is filled with writing systems

---

[1] The Portuguese are believed to be the first to have introduced the alphabetic (Roman) writing system to the Akan in the fifteenth century. The importance of Akan (Mfantse/Twi) in West Africa forced missionaries, and later, the colonial administration to set about standardizing and providing an alphabetic writing for the language.

of its own. However, most of the scholars who think and write about writing consider writing to be alphabetic writing. Indigenous African systems of writing were considered to be either at the beginning of or outside the writing development sequence.

Recent research into art forms and other material culture of various African societies has revealed that some societies including the Akan did indeed develop and maintain certain forms of writing prior to contact with Europe (Hau, 1959, 1961, & 1964; McLeod, 1976; McGuire, 1980). Hau, in a series of articles that appeared in the French journal, Bulletin d'IFAN, uses the ivory carvings and other art work to make the claim that writing pre-dated Islam and the Europeans in certain parts of West Africa. McLeod (1976, p. 94) notes "that images in use" in Asante and "elsewhere in Africa also have a verbal component: proverb images are found among the Bawoyo, possibly among the Barotse and, as Biebuyck has shown in great detail, many of the figurines used among the Bwami are used to call to mind certain aphorisms and, most importantly, the form of these images can vary within wide limits while still having the same aphorism as their basic referent." McGuire (1980, p. 54), to cite another example, describes how the Woyo people of Cabinda used pot lids to create "a pictographic language to convey their feelings about specific situations."

The development of writing in Africa seen as a whole certainly predates the histories of European colonialism and Islamic conquest. Among Africa's ancient script traditions are the world's oldest known scripts, including the Egyptian "sacred carvings," the hieroglyphs (since ca. 3000 BCE), and the other scripts and literacy/literary traditions found in the old Nile Valley civilizations, including Hieratic, Demotic, Coptic, Old Nubian, and Meroitic (Baines 1983). Those ancient scripts that are still (or again) in use today, include Ge'ez, Nsibidi and Tifinagh. In the Horn of Africa syllabic Ge'ez developed since 500 BCE as the liturgical language and holy script of the Ethiopian Orthodox Church and survived until today as the common script for Amharic and Tigrinya in Ethiopia and Eritrea (cf. Hailemariam 2002; Asfaha 2009; Ashafa, Kurvers and Kroon 2008).

Niangoran-Bouah (1984) and Asante (1992, p. 73) distinguish three writing systems in Africa: (1) pictographs or pictograms, used in such areas as Zaire, Gabon, Cameroon, and the Central African Republic; (2) ideograms or ideographs such as the *adinkra* and *abramoɔ* (or *djayobwe*) systems in Ghana and La Côte d'Ivoire (the Ivory Coast), the *nsibidi* system of east-central Nigeria, and the *sona* and *lusona* systems in Angola and Zambia; and (3) phonologically or phonetically-based scripts (phonograms or phonographs) used in places such as Ethiopia (the Ge'ez system), Liberia (the Vai syllabic system), Guinea, Sierra Leone, and Cameroon. Dalby (1986) provides extensive examples of various writing systems that have been developed in Africa from the ancient pictograms and ideograms, which form the root of all writing, through to the contemporary indigenous and international efforts to represent the sound system of African languages syllabically and alphabetically.[2]

The recent exhibition – *Inscribing Meaning: Writing and Graphic Systems in African Art* – developed by the Smithsonian National Museum of African Art, Washington, D. C. in association with the Fowler Museum at UCLA, together with accompanying book of the same title (Kreamer, et al, 2007), recognizes Africa's long engagement with written and graphic systems as part of the broader global history of writing and literacy. *Inscribing Meaning* highlights how Africans use scripts comprising interrelated symbols as writing and graphic systems to encode and transmit meaning. Some of these scripts are phonetic alphabets, while others are ideographic (Kreamer, et al, 2007).

It appears that almost all the scholars who have seriously examined writing systems have

---

[2] The computer technology has made widespread, the use of various font software to facilitate the alphabetic writing of various African languages. Some of the adinkra cloth symbols have been developed into a font for the computer (see for example, http://new.myfonts.com/fonts/akofa/adinkra/).

defined writing as spoken language that is recorded or referenced phonetically by visible marks. Many of these scholars are linguists, and it would seem natural for them to tie writing to speech. Gelb (1963) reserved the term "full writing: to designate the "vehicle through which exact forms of speech could be recorded in permanent form" (Gelb, 1963, p. 121). Archibald Hill (1967), Walter Ong (1982, 1977), and anthropologist Jack Goody (1987, 1986, 1977, 1968), too, consider writing as recorded speech, as do historians like Michael Camille (1996) and M.T. Clanchy (2012), who have examined the writing system phenomenon. DeFrancis has been perhaps the most adamant on this point. His "central thesis is that all full systems of communication are based on speech, Further, no full system is possible unless so grounded," and he dismisses all non-speech-based writing as "Partial/ Limited/Pseudo/Non-Writing" (DeFrancis, 1989, p.7 and p. 42).

Writing systems are generally believed to be successors of the so-called proto-writing, i. e., early ideographic or mnemonic symbols. Gelb (1963), followed by Coulmas (1989), DeFrancis (1989), and others, distinguishes "full writing" systems from their "forerunners" as having gone beyond pictures/icons and mnemonic devices to a firm relation between symbol and sound. According to Gelb,

> "A primitive [picture/icon] writing can develop into a full system only if it succeeds in attaching to a sign a phonetic value independent of the meaning which the sign has as a word. This is phonetization, the most important single step in the history of writing. In modern usage this device is called 'rebus writing'" (Gelb, 1963, p. 193-194).

Gelb attaches a developmental directionality to writing systems (p. 210) starting from picture writing through 'word-syllabic', and 'syllabic' to 'alphabetic' systems. With racist overtones, he considers alphabetic writing to have 'conquered the world' (pp. 183-189).

Writing is a system of conventional signs which can be used to store and transmit a specific content. Fraenkel (1965, p. 7) defines writing as "an acquired arbitrary system of visual marks with which people who know the represented language can communicate." Street and Besnier (1999) indicate that there are three major writing systems recognized as logographic (or ideographic), syllabic, and alphabetical writing systems. Hunter and Whitten (1976, p. 409), on the other hand, view writing as "communication by means of a system of conventional graphic symbols which may be carved, incised, impressed, painted, drawn, or printed in a wide variety of media." According to Hunter and Whitten (1976), writing systems may be grouped as those that are based on pictographs (pictorial signs or pictograms), ideographs (or ideograms), and phonographs (or phonograms). While pictographic and ideographic writing systems tend to be non-linear, phonographic writing systems tend to be linear.

Pictographic writings are recognizable pictorial representations. Although they may be highly stylized, there is a clear representational link between the symbol and the meaning. Pictographs represent things, not linguistic forms. Pictographs have a semantic rather than a phonetic value. If the conventions are understood, they can be read in any language (Hunter and Whitten, 1976, p. 409). In that respect, pictographs can be used conveniently to store and communicate information to a multilingual public or in environments where reliance on alphabetic-based writing is impractical (see Table 1).

Table 1: Some Examples of Pictograms and Ideograms

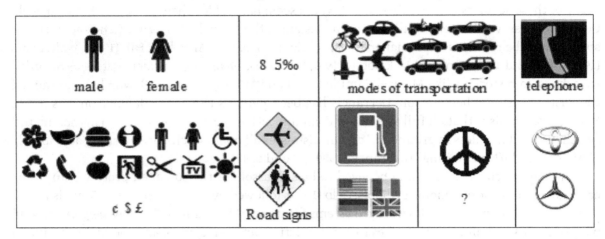

Ideographs or ideograms represent things or ideas, though not necessarily pictorially. Ideographic signs may be pictographic in origin, but they usually have broader ranges of meaning. Ideograms involve a closer relationship with language than pictograms in that the extensions of meaning assigned to the symbols follow the semantic domains of a language (Hunter and Whitten, 1976). Since their association with meaning is not mediated by the representation of sounds, they can be pronounced in any language. The numeral 5, for example, stands directly for an idea - a number, but does not have a phonetic value. It can be represented by a tally — ///// or by V or the fingers (digits) on a hand. It can be pronounced *cinque* or *cinq* or *anum* as well as *five*. The word *five* is a phonetic symbol, while the numeral 5 has a semantic value. The musical notes, mathematical symbols such as infinity (∞[3]) and greater than or equal to ($\geq$), some aspects of Egyptian hieroglyphic and cuneiform are often given as examples of writing systems that make use of pictographs and ideographs. Rock art and cave paintings and stained glass paintings are also well known examples of pictographic and ideographic writing systems. M. Màle (1919) is said to have viewed the medieval cathedral with its stained glass paintings, "as a book of stone in which were recorded for the ignorant all teachings of the Church in natural science, philosophy, morals, and history..." (Cited in Read, 1973, p. 24).[4]

Phonologically-based script follows not ideas but the spoken linguistic forms (sounds of speech) for them. Phonological script has an intimate relationship with a language. It is focused on the minimal units of representation, that is, the graphemes of the system. Rebus writing, syllabic systems (e.g., logographs), and alphabetic writing systems are examples of phonologically-based scripts (Hunter and Whitten, 1976).

In an alphabetic system of writing, for example, one symbol or one letter is used to represent each significant sound (phoneme) in a language. The relationship between the visual and the

---

[3] ∞ is the ancient Roman symbol for 100 million.

[4] According to Màle (1919, p. 456-7 as cited in Read, 1973), "by means of statues and windows in a church, the clergy in the Middle Ages tried to teach their flock the greatest possible number of truths. They fully realized the power of art on souls still innocent and vague. For the immense body of illiterates, for the crowd which had neither psalter nor missal, and who only grasped in Christianity what they actually saw there, it was necessary to materialize the idea, to clothe it in a perceptible form."

auditory codes in the alphabetic writing is arbitrary[5]. The letter does not have any inherent meaning on its own; it only represents a sound.

Most alphabetic systems of writing do not actually achieve the one sound to one symbol principle but do represent most of the sound system of the language with a combination of letters from a very small set of symbols. The English language, for example, has 26 letters that are used in combination to produce 45 phonemes. The symbol "c", for instance, is used to represent the following distinct sounds: [s] as in cent, center or census; [k] as in calm, college or cost; and [tʃ] as in church, chin or chapel. The combination of letters of the alphabet is best understood when it is in a linear form to be read from left to right (or vice versa) and up and down. But even that does not explain the logic behind spelling in the alphabetic system of the English language. As Diamond (1994) illustrates, what is the logic for spelling the word "seed" as we do instead of "cede" or "sied?" Or why the sound "sh" cannot be written as "ce" (as in ocean), "ti" (as in nation), or as "ss" (as in issue)?

Literacy on a mass scale is much enhanced in a writing system that uses very few symbols. It is in this sense that one may say the alphabetically-based system of writing facilitates mass literacy. On the other hand, in Mandarin Chinese, the logographic system of writing that utilizes syllables requires the use of over 1500 basic characters. Literacy based on the logographic system of writing was, therefore, in the past limited to the elites (known as the *literati*) of the society.

The writing systems, according to the orthodox view (e.g., Goody, 1977, 1986, 1987; Goody and Watt, 1963; Ong, 1982), follow an evolutionary order from pictographs through logographic through syllabic to the alphabetic system. It needs to be pointed out, however, that the pictographic, ideographic, and phonographic forms of writing do not represent inevitable stages in the development of writing as no direct evolutionary line can be drawn from the pictographic to the phonographic writing system (Fraenkel, 1965). As Coulmas (1996, p. 334) points out:

> The principal function of all writing is to convey linguistic meaning, but writing systems vary greatly in how they encode meaning. In purely phonetic transcription, access to meaning is mediated through sound representation, while a purely ideographic notation bypasses representation of sounds, encoding concepts instead. Actual writing systems belong to neither of these 'pure' categories, but are located somewhere along a continuum which ranges from sound-centered to meaning-centered.

Thus writing utilizes codes that may be put on a continuum of pictograms on one end through ideograms to phonograms on the other end. Most writing systems utilize some combination of the principles involved in each of the forms of writing. For example, in writing the English language

---

[5] The arbitrary nature of the relationship between the auditory and the visual codes in alphabetic writing systems may be illustrated with the letter "b" in the Roman alphabetic writing system and the Cyrillic alphabetic writing system. The sound, in English, which typically goes with the visible arrangement of marks making up the Roman alphabetic character "b" involves closure of the vocal chords, or "voicing" (Ladefoged, 1975). This sound is broadly invariant across different spelling contexts – bat, table, combine, comb, perturb. The sound a reader of Russian would make in response to the same visual arrangement "b" in Cyrillic alphabet is quite different, involving the tongue and the roof of the mouth, something like the way these are used when saying the italicized part of the English word "onion." And whereas, in the Roman alphabet the visible arrangement of "b" and "B" are the lower and upper case versions of the same character (hence pronounced identically), the visual shape of "B" in Russian represents a different character as compared to "b" and is pronounced like "v" in English (Folomkin and Weiser, 1963).

with Roman alphabets, use is made of symbols such as "?" ; :, ! and "." for punctuation. These symbols do not represent sounds in the language. They have semantic value as they enhance meaning in the context in which they are used. Also, in order to facilitate international travel through airports, phonologically-based writing is often combined with pictographs to indicate telephones, access for handicapped people, and to direct people to toilet facilities on the basis of gender. Road signs[6] often incorporate all three systems of writing.

Andrew Robinson (2009, pp. 142-143) sums it up succinctly thus:

> Contrary to what many people think, all scripts that are full writing operate on one basic principle. Both alphabets and the Chinese and Japanese scripts use symbols to represent sounds; and all writing systems mix such phonetic symbols with logograms. What differs between writing systems – apart from the forms of their signs, of course – are the proportions of the phonetic signs and the logograms. Many scholars of writing today have an increasing respect for the intelligence behind ancient scripts. Down with the monolithic 'triumph of the alphabet', they say, and up with Chinese characters, Egyptian hieroglyphs, and Mayan glyphs, with their hybrid mixtures of pictographic, logographic, and phonetic signs. Their conviction has in turn nurtured a new awareness of writing systems as being enmeshed within societies, rather than viewing them somewhat aridly as different kinds of technical solution to the problem of efficient visual representation of a particular language. While I personally remain skeptical about the expressive virtues of pictograms and logograms, this growing holistic view of writing systems strikes me as a healthy development that reflects the real relationship between writing and society in all its subtlety and complexity.

All writing is information storage. While human memory can serve as a storage of information, throughout time, human memory has been found inadequate in storing all information. Writing system serves not only as adjunct to human memory for the storage of information. It also serves to broaden the scope and amount of information to be stored, and also facilitates the utilization of more efficient and independent storage media that enhance timely retrieval and transmission of the information by all those who can consult and decode it. If all writing is information storage, then all writing is of equal value. Each society stores information essential for its survival (Gaur, 1992).

Writing as a means of communication has been constantly evolved, particularly due to the development of new technologies over the centuries. The pen, the printing press, the computer and the mobile phone are all technological transformations which have altered what is written, and the medium through which the written word is produced. More so with the advent of digital technologies, for instance the computer and the mobile phone, characters can be formed by the press of a button, rather than making the physical motion with the hand.

---

[6] International road signs, computer icons, mathematical notation and musical notations constitute a writing system called semasiography - writing with signs - such writing is not tied to speech, works through symbolic means to communicate a variety of kinds of information (Sampson, 1985).

THE ADINKRA SYMBOLS OF THE AKAN

The Akan

The term Akan has been used to cover a wide variety of ethnic groups who occupy a greater part of southern Ghana and the south-eastern Ivory Coast. The groups constituting the culturally and linguistically homogenous Akan ethnicity include the Asante, Fantse, Akuapem, Akyem, Okwawu, Bono, Wassa, Agona, Assin, Denkyira, Adansi, Nzima, Ahanta, Aowin, Sefwi, and Baoulé (see Map). Together, these groups constitute over 40 percent of the country's population (Dolphyne and Kropp-Dakubu, 1988; Bodomo, 1996); and they dominate about two-thirds of the country's land area as Ashanti, Brong Ahafo, Central, Eastern, and Western Regions, and parts of the north of Volta Region (see map below). What is believed to have been the first modern day Akan empire, Bono, was established in the western area of present day Brong-Ahafo Region of Ghana before 1300 AD (Boahen, 1966; 1977). The Akan have unique cultural traits and institutions that set them apart from the other ethnic groups in the country in particular and Africa in general. The most significant traits and institutions include, as Adu Boahen (1966; 1977) points out, a common 40-day calendar (*adaduanan*), common religious beliefs, marriage institutions, naming ceremonies, matrilineal system of inheritance, and an identical exogamous matrilineal clan system.

Fig 1: Map of Ghana showing the Area of Akan Speaking People

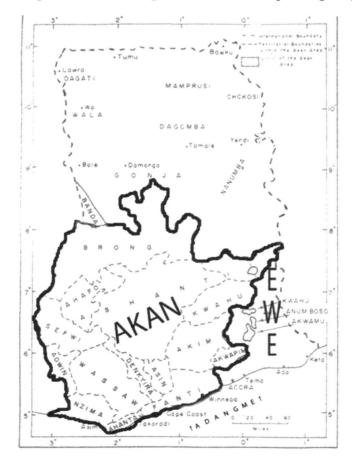

The Akan of Ghana and La Côte d'Ivoire incorporated the ideographic and pictographic writing systems in their arts in such media as textiles, metal casting, woodcarving, and architecture. The Akan use of pictographs and ideograms reached its most elaborate forms in the king's court. As Kyerematen (1964, p. 1), has written about the Asante, for example:

> the regalia of Ghanaian chiefs have been of special significance in that they have not been merely symbols of the kingly office but have served as the chronicles of early history and the evidence of traditional religion, cosmology and social organization... [and] it has been customary for the regalia to be paraded whenever the chief appears in state at a national festival or durbar, so that all who see them may read, mark and inwardly digest what they stand for.

Among the Akan of Ghana, the regalia of the kingly office included wood-carvings (e.g., stool - *adwa*, umbrella tops – *kyiniie ntuatire*, and staffs - *akyeamepoma*), swords (*akofena*), and clothing (e.g., *kente, akunintam* and *adinkra*). These items in the king's regalia made use of pictograms and ideograms. The sets of pictograms, ideograms and signs encoded in the Akan cloths (*kente, akunintam* and *adinkra*), gold weights (*abramoɔ*, singular, *mmramoɔ*, plural), wood carvings (e.g. stools and staffs), pottery, and architectural designs are used as a store of information, and are clearly understood, as they have meanings commonly shared by the masses of the population. These art forms carry proverbs, anecdotes, stories, and historical events through visual form.

In this book a neglected area in the study of Akan cloths — their function as a writing medium[7] (Tsien, 1962; Mason, 1928) and thus, a storage and communicative device - is discussed. The book takes the view that mutually interpretable significant symbols need not be limited to spoken and written alphabets and syllables which eventually are strung together in sentences and paragraphs. Instead, communication can be accomplished through the use of discrete graphical representation of commonly held ideas and views. In this way, ostensibly, "non-literate" societies may produce, through the use of their symbols and signs, a literature which pervades their environment by being emblazoned on their clothes, tools, and other common material artifacts.

The arts of a people offer an illuminating view of its culture, and hence of its thought processes, attitudes, beliefs, and values. The art of a particular culture can reveal ever-changing human images and attitudes, so awareness of a people's indigenous art, visual and cultural symbols can become an important medium for cross-cultural understanding. "Just as written documents [that utilize phonographs] materialize history in literate communities," as pointed out by Fraser and Cole (1972, p. 313), "so in traditional societies, art forms make the intangible past more real." Some of these art forms like the *adinkra* cloth of the Akan utilize pictograms and ideograms (see Table 1), and are pregnant with text that symbolizes ideas on several levels of discourse. The focus of this book is to utilize the writing system of pictograms and ideograms encoded in the *adinkra* cloth to decode some aspects of the history, beliefs, social organizations, social relations, and other ideas of the Akan of Ghana.

---

[7] Cloth as medium for writing is believed to have been invented by the Chinese who wrote on fabric made of silk (Tsien, 1962). In the U. S., one of the most noted and successful attempts at using pictograms and ideograms in cloth to write is the famous Penn Treaty *wampum* belt now in the possession of the Pennsylvania Historical Society in Philadelphia. This belt was given by the American Indians to William Penn as their record of the signing of the famous treaty at Schackamaxon on the Delaware in 1682 (Mason, 1928, p. 98).

SYMBOLS: A FRAMEWORK FOR ANALYSIS

Clothes are used all over the world not only for protection and modesty, but also for the purpose of constructing socially meaningful messages about oneself. Clothes may also be worn by certain people to make ideological, political, and other kinds of socially relevant statements. In effect, clothes constitute a nonverbal language system and thus are of obvious relevance to semiotic inquiry, revealing how connotation operates in one specific domain of material culture. As Kathryn Sullivan Kruger (2001. p. 11) explains in *Weaving the Word*:

> The relationship between texts and textiles is, historically, a significant one. Anthropologists have long been intrigued at the various ways in which cloth embodies the unique ideas of a culture. They can trace the history of a culture through the record of its textiles, "reading" cloth like a written text. Indeed, this cloth transmits information about the society which created it in a manner not dissimilar from a written language, except in this case the semiotics of the cloth depend on choice of fiber, pattern, dye, as well as its method of production.

To this end, numerous researchers have approached clothing (and cloths) as a semiotic, cultural, and emotive phenomenon involving communication and meaning (Simmel 1957, Finkelstein 1991, Gonsalves 2010). Indeed, clothes and adornments are a significant cultural form through which our bodies relate to the world and to other bodies (Roach and Eicher 1965, Storm 1987, Craik 2005). Further, in every society and culture, clothing and dress is a form of projection through which signs and meanings are expressed and contested (Robson 2013). Here then, dress is a sort of sociocultural syntax that may be "read" for connotative meanings and alternative systems of interpretation.

This book draws its theoretical perspective from studies of semiotics[8] (and/or semiology) and metaphoric analysis. In general terms, *semiotics* is the science of signs and symbols and how we use them in our lives to infer and communicate meanings. Meanings and identities do not exist only as mental phenomena 'inside' people. They always arise and develop by the mediation of material tokens or signs of some kind: words, images, sounds or other perceptible external marks organized into various forms of artefacts, texts, works, genres and discourses. The science of semiotics encourages a systematic awareness of how meanings are expressed and interpreted from the vast amount of available data to which we are regularly exposed. Semiotics can help to make us aware of what we take for granted in representing the world, reminding us that we are always dealing with signs, not with an unmediated objective reality, and that sign systems are involved in the construction of meaning (Chandler, 2001).

Communication in the form of writing is based on the use of arbitrary symbols. Every society - be it pre-literate, literate, or post-literate - uses symbols and signs as a complement to spoken language and adjunct to human memory. Symbols have evolved to the point of universal acceptance in such areas as music, mathematics, computers, travel, and many branches of science. It now appears that in some important areas there is an increasing need for an adjunct to sophisticated speech, and the

---

[8] The two terms, "semiotics" and "semiology," have often unfortunately been confused. Semiology is of the Saussurean, structuralist, poststructuralist, continental study of the sign. Semiotics follows the Peircean concept of the sign. Semiotics, or semiology, is the study of signs, symbols, and signification. It is the study of how meaning is created, not what it is. Nowadays the term 'semiotics' is more likely to be used as an umbrella term to embrace the whole field.

use of new (and in some cases, the revamping of old) symbols and icons to ease communication and facilitate international understanding.

Symbols provide the means whereby human beings can interact meaningfully with their natural and social environment. Symbols are socially constructed, and they refer not to the intrinsic nature of objects and events but to the ways in which human beings perceive them. Ott (1989, p. 21) says the following about symbols:

> Symbols are signs that connote meanings greater than themselves and express much more than their intrinsic content. They are invested with specific subjective meanings. Symbols embody and represent wider patterns of meaning and cause people to associate conscious or unconscious ideas that in turn endow them with their deeper, fuller, and often emotion-evoking meaning.

Symbols are important as they create, change, maintain, and transmit socially constructed realities. Charon (1985) and Ritzer (1992) identify several functions of symbols. Symbols allow people to deal with the material and social world by allowing them to name, categorize, and remember the objects that they encounter. Symbols also improve a people's ability to perceive the environment. They improve a people's ability to think. Symbols greatly increase human beings' ability to solve problems. While lower animals depend primarily on instinct and trial and error, human beings can think through symbolically a variety of alternative actions before actually taking one. The use of symbols allows people to transcend time, space, and even their own persons, that is, symbols allow people to imagine alternative realities (Charon, 1985; Ritzer, 1992). These functions of symbols imply that symbols can be manipulated (symbolism) and, thereby, can be used to create or impede social change.

In politics, for example, a number of scholars have written about how political symbols are utilized to maintain established power, status, and resource differentials (Edelman, 1964, 1971, 1988; Evans-Pritchard and Fortes, 1967; Elder and Cobb, 1983; and Hayward and Dumbuya, 1984). It is not so much the symbols themselves that are significant in politics, but the meanings that people attribute to them. A national or party flag is more than a piece of cloth; it is used to evoke feelings of great loyalty, hostility, support or resentment. In India's political struggle for independence from British rule, Mahatma Gandhi was portrayed as the semiotician who used clothing as a metaphor for unity, empowerment and liberation from imperial subjugation (Gonsalves, 2012; Tarlo, 1996). How one dressed was very closely related to Gandhi's vision not only of the means Indians should use to achieve independence but also of the type of nation India should become. Central to that vision was homespun cloth known as *khadi*. Gandhi believed that making *khadi* would provide employment for many Indians, and contribute to the country's self-sufficiency, and eventually result in *swaraj* or self-rule. He worked very hard to get every Indian to spin his or her own cotton thread and to weave *khadi*. He often stated that wearing *khadi* was moral duty, a sign that a person had transformed his or her life and was now devoted to "self-sacrifice," "purity," and "fellow feeling with every human being on earth" (Tarlo, 1996). In other words, Gandhi's appearance in home spun cloth put forth two important political messages - the message of self–sufficiency and liberation from British colonialism.

Social life can proceed only if the meanings of symbols are largely shared by members of society. If this were not the case, meaningful communication would be impossible. The survival of human life is facilitated by communication. The means of communication and its constant improvement and development have been a major factor in the growth of human civilization. Communication among individual members of a social group enhances mutual understanding as individuals convey ideas, mental pictures, and concepts among themselves by verbal and non-verbal means. Language, the most complex form of the use of symbols, has become the primary medium through which a society's concepts, elements, values, and beliefs are communicated. Semiotics is thus useful for analyzing both verbal and non-verbal communication.

Even though communication within and among social groups comprises verbal and non-verbal means, over time human communication has increasingly concentrated on verbal means. With the development and increased use of alphabetized writing, verbal expression has become fixed as visual marks that represent sounds and meanings, and has come to be seen as a rationalized method of communication. This visible form of communication, that is, writing, used to be the preserve of the privileged few in many societies - for example, the clerical elite in many societies and the *literati* of the ancient Chinese civilization. With the development of printing and mass production of texts using the alphabetic system of writing, the visible form of communication has been democratized. The development and expansion of formal schooling has further stressed the importance of phonetically-based forms of writing as the hallmark of literacy. Despite the popularity of phonetically-based forms of writing, "signs and pictograms are still under development and will in future become an absolute necessity for the fixing and transmission of a world-wide fund of knowledge" (Frutiger, 1989, p. 342) for their utility lies in their independence from language.

In Akan art, verbal and non-verbal signs are used to produce meaning, which leads to the creation of social relationships, systems of knowledge, and cultural identity (Bezuidenhout, 1998). But when one refers to 'adinkra cloth' of the Akan the word assumes the status of a symbol. It is laden with connotations that far exceed the meaning of the arbitrary sign 'c', 'l', 'o', 't', 'h'. It is culturally and historically specific. It is even given a name: *adinkra (or ntiamu ntoma)*. Its meaning does not easily fit the connotations attributed to, let us say, the cloth used in the Maoist or Zairian clothing revolutions. In course of time, this connotative specificity of symbols gives rise to a variety of possible interpretations, both within and without the culture of origin.

The first recorded account of the existence of Adinkra symbols is from a drawing of an Akan celebration in Thomas E. Bowdich's book *Mission from Cape Coast to Ashantee*, published in 1819. The British government sent Bowdich to Ghana in 1817, and his book that came out of his expedition was the first European account of the Ashanti people. The drawing from the book does not explain the origins of the *adinkra* symbols, but it does illustrate that the Adinkra symbols and their adornment on clothing was already an established practice of the Ashanti people by the early 19th century, if not much earlier.

Understanding the semiotics in the Akan *adinkra* cloth must strongly take into cognizance the Akan worldview. This is because for the Akan, there is no happenstance, and life is one continuous whole without any break. The Akan believe in the cosmic realms of the world (*wiase*) and the great beyond (*asamando*) across which the human soul transmigrates respectively in body and spirit in processes of birth, death and reincarnation.

AKAN CLOTH SYMBOLS

In the days before printing and formal schooling as we know them now, the Akan society in Ghana was believed to have utilized only oral methods of communication for the transmission of knowledge and ideas. The Akan must have placed emphasis on the ability to influence by verbal skills and through the art of public speaking. This does not mean that they did not appreciate and did not utilize some visual markers as forms of writing. The Asantehene, for example retained the services of Arabic scribes (*ɔhene krakye*), yet honored the orator (e.g., the *ɔkyeame*) more than the scribe. In addition, the royal court retained several crafts people who created various symbols and designs to store information in media such as wood carvings, textiles, ceramics aand pottery, architecture and metal casting.

In this book an attempt is made to show how the "pre-literate" Akan of Ghana used their textiles (*adinkra* cloth in this book) as one of the media in a highly complex system of fixing, storing and transmitting that which was thought or spoken with pictures, symbols, signs, and signals. Not only are the symbols and patterns in the Akan textiles (*adinkra*) regarded as aesthetically and idiomatically traditional; more importantly, the symbols and patterns in the textiles constitute a code that evokes meanings: they carry, preserve, and present aspects of the beliefs, history, social values, cultural norms, social and political organization, and philosophy of the Akan. As Patton (1984, p. 72) notes: "The verbal element of these cloths makes them visual metaphors. The application of a phrase or word to an object it does not literally denote, to suggest comparison with another concept, is a recurring aspect of traditional Akan art. During important public occasions such as durbar, this visual metaphor reinforces traditional leadership roles." Metaphor, in this context, is much more than a figure of speech. As Hermine Feistein describes it:

> Metaphor... is now considered to be an essential process and product of thought. The power of metaphor lies in its potential to further our understanding of the meaning of experience, which in turn defines reality. In art and language, metaphor urges us to look beyond the literal, to generate associations and tap new, different, or deeper levels of meaning. The metaphoric process reorganizes and vivifies; it paradoxically condenses and expands; it synthesizes often disparate meanings. In this process, attributes of one entity are transferred to another by comparison, by substitution, or as a consequence of interaction (Feinstein, 1982, p. 45).

Like symbols, metaphor is integral to our communication systems and is equally shaped by its context. Metaphor carries concepts and is essential to language and the communication of abstract thoughts. In viewing the *adinkra* cloth as metaphor, it enables us to make sense of how the Akan use the *adinkra* cloth and its symbols as visual markers to express their beliefs, attitudes and thoughts. This perspective makes it possible for us to see how the Akan link words and images or how the Akan construct meaning by metaphorically transforming words into visual images.

The seminal work by Rattray (1927, pp. 220-268), based in part on an earlier work by Bowdich (1819), identified names and the symbolic meanings of several of the symbols and patterns in the *adinkra* and *kente* cloths[9]. Rattray, however, failed to recognize that these cloths served as a medium for communication. McLeod (1981, p. 143) recognized that each of the cloths, "and the way in which each was worn, served to communicate a distinctive message, and the subtleties of its significance

---

[9] See Appendix D for the fifty-three symbols that Rattray identified from the *adinkra* cloth. It must be pointed out that Rattray failed to include some symbols that could be found in the samples of cloth that Bodwich had collected in 1817. Apparently, Rattray did not get to study samples of *adinkra* and *kente* cloths that the British took away as war booty from Kumasi during the 1874 and the 1900 Asante-British wars.

were widely understood." However, he failed to elaborate on the communicative functions of the *adinkra* and *kente* cloths.

Other people who have written about *adinkra* cloth and its symbols continue to provide an elaborate catalog of hundreds of *adinkra* symbols yet fail to address the ideas, events, and beliefs of the Akan that these symbols encode. Mato (1986), for example, provides an extensive number of symbols in the *adinkra* cloth and the proverbs and meanings associated with these symbols. He points out that

> As an art of public display *adinkra* images carried aphorisms, proverbs, symbols and metaphors expressed through visual form. As carriers of abstract or tangible information *adinkra* images were firmly rooted in the proverbial literature of the Akan. As a communicative system *adinkra* images carried Akan traditional wisdom regarding observations upon God and man, the human condition, upon things spiritual as well as the common-place and upon the unavoidability of death. *Adinkra* stamps [symbols] are therefore an example of the penchant and skill of the Akan to set proverb or verbal statement into visual form (Mato, 1986, pp. 228-229).

Mato notes that the *adinkra* cloth is an important form of funerary clothing, as well as clothing for other festive occasions. In connection with funerary rituals, he discusses some aspects of Akan cosmology. Mato, however, fails to elaborate on what he refers to as "symbolic literacy" (p. 223) as he does not go beyond the limited discussion of Akan cosmology to address other concepts and beliefs of the Akan (e.g., political beliefs, attitudes about money, social values) and the Akan social organization that the *adinkra* cloth and its symbols, as "symbolic literacy," write about.

On the other hand, the 1997 exhibition at the Smithsonian National Museum of African Art made the attempt to use the *adinkra* cloth believed to have belonged to Asantehene Prempeh I to demonstrate how the Asante express complex cultural, spiritual, and philosophical concepts through their art (National Museum of African Art, 1997). This exhibition goes beyond Mato's (1986) discussion of Akan cosmology to recognize that the multilayered and complex meanings of the *adinkra* symbols express clear messages of the power and authority of the Asantehene (p.13). Because the exhibition was based on only one cloth which was designed with a limited number of symbols – twenty-two symbols to be exact – other aspects of Akan beliefs, attitudes, and relationships encoded in scores of *adinkra* symbols were not discussed in the exhibition's accompanying catalogue.

Willis (1998, p. 28) recognizes that "the symbols on the cloth constitute a language that is multi-layered." He also affirms the view that "the adinkra symbols reflect cultural mores, communal values, philosophical concepts, or the codes of conduct and the social standards of the Akan people" (ibid). Willis further claims that

> *Adinkra* symbols have a historical "core" or group of original symbols. Over the years, new symbols have been periodically introduced, while "core" symbols have been stylized and fused. Others have been created with words being into the designs, and others depicting man-made objects, for example, a Coke bottle a Mercedes-Benz logo. Today there are over five hundred documented and identifiable symbols, but the total number of all symbols has not been accurately documented to date (Willis, 1998, p.28).

Willis makes a significant contribution in recognizing that the symbols in *adinkra* cloth constitute a language that is multi-layered. By providing us with a visual primer, he is recognizing that the symbols constitute a set of visual markers – a writing system. He, however, makes the mistake by asserting that there is a historical "core" or group of original symbols. He does not provide the historical evidence to support this assertion. Apparently, he, as well as other writers, takes Rattray's fifty-three symbols (see Appendix D) as the "core" symbols. It must be noted that Rattray failed to include several symbols that were in use at the time of his stay in Asante. For example, Rattray did not mention some of the symbols to be found in sample cloth that Bowdich collected in 1817 (see Appendix A). If "the total number of all *adinkra* symbols has not been accurately documented to date," as Willis claims, how does he know what constitutes the "core" symbols? He indicates the symbols are also to be found in media other than cloth, for example, in architecture and woodcarvings. Architectural and woodcarvings are media that tend to use three-dimensional representation of symbols. The *adinkra* cloth tends to make use of two-dimensional representation of symbols. There are, therefore, symbols to be found in woodcarvings and architectural designs that cannot be found in the *adinkra* cloth. Similarly, there are some symbols to be found in the cloth and not in woodcarvings or architectural designs. That the *adinkra* symbols include contemporary symbols such as the Mercedes Benz logo (#741) reflects the dynamic nature of the language of the Akan as well as the creativity of the cloth designers in adapting symbols to express the new ideas and concepts that have become part of the Akan experience. A dynamic language is not limited to few concepts and ideas that are depicted by some core words or symbols. It is, therefore, puzzling for Willis to make the assertion that there is a historical "core" or group of symbols.

The collection of *adinkra* symbols in this book represents an attempt to open up the neglected realm of these "pictograms" and "ideograms" to the world of the reader's imagination in an organized manner. The book views *adinkra* symbols as a system of visual marks — a system of writing — with which the Akan communicate. These visual marks serve to record, store and communicate certain information about the Akan. The book elaborates on the communicative aspects of Akan textiles by interpreting the encoded meanings of the *adinkra* symbols and signs, and also argues that the set of pictograms and ideograms of the Akan, as a way of writing, has been in daily use as an aid to thought, a means of comprehension, and a method of bearing witness or authentication. *Adinkra* symbols draw extensively upon traditional expressive genres that include folk songs, riddles and quizzes (*abrɔme ne ɛbisaa*), poetry (*awensɛm*), stories (*anansesɛm*), drum poetry (*kyene kasa*), libation and prayer (*apaeyie*), oral history (*abakɔsɛm* or *mpaninsɛm*), funeral dirges (*nsubaa* or *sudwom*), and proverbs (*mmɛ* or *mmɛbusɛm*). The *adinkra* symbols are utilized in this book as a multi-vocal metaphor to interpret the contextual meanings and functional uses of the symbols and signs developed by the Akan in their textile production, and in other visual media[10]. This book links the narratives associated with the symbols in order to discuss some aspects of Akan viewpoints on a variety of issues.

The names and the interpretations of these symbols may also be useful for framing hypotheses for sustained research which looks at Akan cosmology, myths, histories, rituals, early public taxation and accounting systems, religion, folktale, political organizations, the role of the military in society, and daily customs. For the Akan in particular, as Cole and Ross (1977, p. 9) have noted,

---

[10] Other visual media that utilize some of the proverbs, aphorisms and stories encoded in the *adinkra* symbols include the gold weights and other metal works (see Appiah, 1979); wood carvings (e.g., stools - see Sarpong, 1971; and Patton, 1979, 1980); combs (see Antiri – 1978); and linguist's staff (see Yankah, 1995 and Ross, 1982); and state swords (*akofena* - see Ross, 1977).

the relationship between the visual and the verbal is one of the cornerstones of their aesthetics. The identification of symbols and patterns embodied in Akan textiles in this book is just a first step in understanding the complexities of symbolism in Akan visual arts. As Ross (1977, p. 25) further points out, the highly conventionalized verbal component in Akan iconography demands a greater exploration of language, patterns of nomenclature, etymology, and the use of euphemisms, similes, and metaphors to fully appreciate nuances of meaning the Akan attach to their visual markers.

Analysis of the textile symbols and patterns of the *adinkra* cloth provided in this book will facilitate the understanding of how the Akan use the motifs in the cloth as a writing system to record and store their beliefs, history, knowledge, and accomplishments. Such an understanding may help explain some of the changes and continuities in, for example, the bureaucratization of chieftaincy and new sources of wealth that have occurred and continue to occur in the Akan society. This book contributes to the view that a language includes the full spectrum of color, symbol, and word; that textile art and language are inextricably bound together; and that drawing, printing or weaving a symbol in cloth can make a legitimate and exciting involvement with literature and indigenous knowledge systems. Understanding such indigenous knowledge systems may help adult literacy program planners, for example, to utilize a people's symbols and signs to facilitate reading and writing of phonetic system among adults. The study of *adinkra* cloth symbols can also illuminate and help in the analysis of social and political organization of the Akan as well as of the greater Ghanaian society. Such an analysis may have value more generally for anyone involved in symbolic analyses within particular societies or cross-culturally.

Data collection for this study included (1) inquiries to museums, galleries and private collections of Ghanaian textiles, particularly the *adinkra*, and observations and interviews of *adinkra* manufacturers and distributors[11] and other crafts people in Accra and in the Kumasi areas, (2) correspondence with and interviews of persons knowledgeable about African textiles in general and *adinkra* cloth in particular, (3) library research, and (4) procurement, classification and photographing of a collection of samples of *adinkra* symbols and cloths from Ntonso and Asokwa in the Kumase area, the main centers of *adinkra* cloth production in Ghana.

I have benefitted from the works of Rattray (1927), Antubam (1963), Kyerematen (1964), Sarpong (1971; 1972; 1974; & 1990), Mato (1986), and Menzel (1972) in identifying many *adinkra* symbols and the everyday expressions, proverbs, and aphorisms that have been associated with these symbols. Charts and monographs by Glover (1971), Kayper-Mensah (1976), Quarcoo (1972, 1994), Ofori Ansah

---

[11] Cloth designers, stamp carvers and cloth distributors and some of the knowledgeable people interviewed included the following:

Auntie Afia, wife of Nana Baffour Gyimah who owns the cloth production and distribution company, Baffour Gyimah Enterprise, at Tewobabi near Ntonso and several of the employees of the enterprise, particularly Agya Yaw Yamaa, cloth stamper, Kwaku, cloth stamper and Wofa Yaw, stamp carver and cloth designer. Interviewed on May 23-24, 1993 and May 23-26, 1994. Nana Baffour Gyimah now utilizes the computer is his kente and adinkra cloth designs (personal interview 2008).

Teacher John Nsiah, stamp carver, Ntonso. Interviewed May 23-24, 1993; May 23, 1994.

Nana Antwi Buasiako, Asantehene Kyeame. Interviewed at Ayigya, Kumasi May 23-25, 1994; May 29-30, 1996.

Stephen Appiah, stamp carver and cloth stamper, Asokwa. Interviewed May 24-25, 1994; May 29-30, 1996.

Kusi Boadum, cloth stamper and member of the Kumasi Metropolitan Assembly. Interviewed at Asokwa, May 24-25, 1994.

Nana J. V. Owusuh-Ansah, Research Fellow and artist, University of Science and Technology, Kumasi. Interviewed May 26, 1994.

(1978, 1993), and Owusu-Ansah (1992), and museum collections, catalogs and photographs have also been very helpful.

In the foregoing discussion I have attempted to provide a framework for viewing the *adinkra* textile symbols as a writing system. The remaining chapters in this book are developed as follows. Chapter 2 discusses the *adinkra* cloth history and *adinkra* production processes, origins of the *adinkra* symbols, and Akan color symbolism. Chapter 3 illustrates some of the aspects of pictographic, ideographic and phonographic writing systems incorporated in the *adinkra* cloth symbols. The chapter also discusses stylization and how the *adinkra* symbols were (are) derived.

In Chapters 4 through 10 the narratives associated with the *adinkra* symbols are grouped into thematic areas in order to discuss some of the various ideas, events, and beliefs of the Akan that the symbols encode. Each of the Chapters groups several *adinkra* symbols into related thematic areas and discusses Akan views about these thematic areas. These discussions draw extensively on Akan oral literature that comprises proverbs, aphorisms, stories, songs, funeral dirges, riddles and quizzes, as well as everyday expressions. In Chapter 4, the thematic areas of Akan beliefs and views about the universe, God, self, and spirituality are discussed. Chapters 5 and 6 discuss Akan political beliefs and governmental organization. Chapter 7 discusses some aspects of Akan views about beauty, love, marriage and family relations. Chapter 8 groups several *adinkra* symbols to discuss some aspects of Akan social values and ethics. Chapter 9 decodes several *adinkra* symbols in order to address some aspects of the social and economic arrangements that the symbols encode while Chapter 10 focuses on symbols that relate to knowledge and education. Chapter 11 provides a summary of my contention that the *adinkra* symbols constitute a writing system, discusses the implications of such a contention, and makes suggestions for further research on Akan art from similar perspective, particularly with regards to the symbols of the gold weights, wood carvings, and other textiles (*kente, akunintam* and *asafo* flags). The thematic area of Akan history is not set apart and discussed separately. However, some historical events encoded by *adinkra* symbols are discussed where and when they occur throughout the book.

Even though the discussions in the various Chapters center on the bigger Akan society in general, specific examples are drawn from the Asante. The proverbs, aphorisms, and everyday expressions associated with these symbols are provided in italics in the Akan (Asante Twi) language with their meanings in English.

CHAPTER 2

Tete ka asom no na ɛfiri kakyerɛ.
Nimpa a wonnim wɔn abakɔsɛm te sɛ dua a onni ntini
Preservation of a people's culture has its basis in oral tradition
People without knowledge of their history are like a tree without roots

THE ADINKRA CLOTH

INTRODUCTION

Cloth use is almost a universal experience. Historically, cloth has been venerated by people of the most varied cultural backgrounds, and it has furthered the organization of social and political life. Davis (1992, p. 4) claims "that through clothing people communicate some things about their persons, and at the collective level this results typically in locating them symbolically in some structured universe of status claims and life-style attachments." Schneider and Weiner (1989, p. 1) write:

> Malleable and soft, cloth can take many shapes, especially if pieces are cut for architectural assembly. Cloth also lends itself to an extraordinary range of decorative variation, whether through the embroidery, staining, painting, or dyeing of the whole. These broad possibilities of construction, color, and patterning give cloth an almost limitless potential for communication. Worn or displayed in an emblematic way, cloth can denote variations in age, sex, rank, status, and group affiliation.... Cloth can also communicate the wearer's or user's ideological values and claims. Complex moral and ethical issues of dominance and autonomy, opulence and poverty, continence and sexuality, find ready expression through cloth.

The Akan have used cloth not only for personal adornment but also as a medium of communication. The communicative aspects of cloth among the Akan have been discussed in a limited way as "proverb cloths" by Aronson (1992) and Domowitz (1992) and as "textile rhetoric" by Yankah (1995), and, in the case of *adinkra*, as a funerary item by Mato (1986). Domowitz (p. 85), for example, notes that "proverb cloths offer an accessible public voice to those who are constrained to silence." Yankah (1995, p. 81) on the other hand, notes that the cloth design, along with the mode of wearing it may be used "not just to praise political heroes, to commemorate historical events, and to assert social identities, but also as a form of rhetoric - a channel for the silent projection of argument."

Davis (1992, p. 5) suggests, "clothing styles and the fashions that influence them over time constitute something approximating a code. It is a code, however, dissimilar from those used in cryptography; neither can it be more generally equated with the language rules that govern speech and writing." The code contained in cloths is heavily context-dependent, has considerable variability in how its constituent symbols are understood by different social strata and taste groupings; and it is much more given to "undercoding" than to precision and explicitness (Davis, 1992, p. 7). Undercoding occurs when in the absence of reliable interpretative rules, persons presume or infer, often unwittingly, on the basis of such hard-to-specify areas as gesture, inflection, pace, facial expression, context, and setting, certain molar meanings in a text, score, performance, or other communication (p. 11). At the same time, it would be a mistake to assume that the undercoding of clothing and fashion is necessarily inadvertent or the product of an inherent incapacity of the unit elements constituting the code (fabric, color, cut, texture) to signify clearly as do words or icons (Davis, 1992, p. 11).

The *adinkra* cloth is one important art object that constitutes a code in which the Akan have deposited some aspects of the sum of their knowledge, fundamental beliefs, aspects of their history, attitudes and behaviors towards the sacred, and how their society has been organized. *Adinkra* cloth has played a significant part in furthering the organization of social and political life in the Akan society.

Figure 2: A chief wearing black *adinkra* cloth as he waits his turn to swear before theAsantehene at Manhyia Palace. Members of his entourage are wearing black, red and white adinkra cloths

Mato (1986) has described the *adinkra* cloth as one of the significant items used in Akan funerary rites. The *adinkra* is more than an item for funerary rites. It is also an important item utilized in the rituals associated with the installation of the king. For example, *adinkra* cloth features prominently in the oath swearing ceremony (*ɔhene nsuae*) for the king and queenmother (Fig 2). On May 30, 1996 at the Manhyia Palace in Kumasi, I witnessed the oath swearing ceremony for four chiefs who had been elevated by the Asantehene from sub-chief status to that of *ɔmanhene* (paramount chief). These four chiefs swore the oath of allegiance to the Asantehene. The Asantehene, the other paramount chiefs, and the four newly elevated paramount chiefs as well as their courtiers all wore *adinkra tuntum* (e.g., *kuntunkuni*) for the ceremony. The swearing ceremony marked for each chief a transition from a status of lower responsibilities to a status of higher responsibilities. Nana Antwi Buasiako, one of the twelve Asantehene *akyeamefoɔ*[12], explained to me that the *ɔhene nsuae* ceremony is a sacred and solemn occasion and that is why the *adinkra tuntum* is worn[13]. The *adinkra* cloth also features prominently in the political and religious rituals associated with the blackening of the king's stool.

Another significant function of the *adinkra* cloth is evident from an analysis of the color background as well as the constituent symbols that are incorporated in the design of the cloth. The colors and the constituent symbols of the *adinkra* cloth evoke concepts that relate to social and political organization, beliefs and attitudes, complex moral and ethical issues about the self and one's responsibilities, and knowledge and education. The *adinkra* cloth symbols are but one example of a textile tradition that demonstrates how the Akan express complex cultural, spiritual, and philosophical concepts through their art.

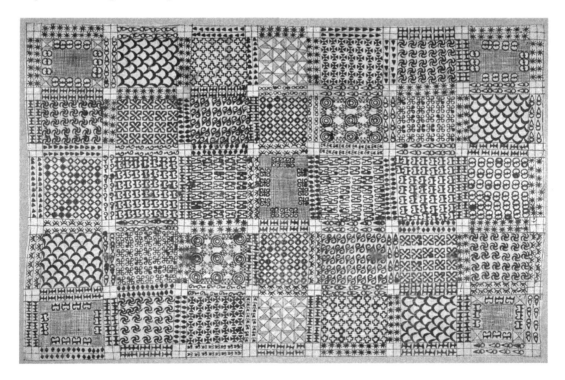

---

[12] *Ɔkyeame*, singular (*akyeamefoɔ*, plural) has been interpreted as a linguist or spokesman for the chief. He is more of a counselor, diplomat, and confidant to the king.

[13] Nana Antwi Buasiako, personal interview at Ayigya, Kumasi, May 30, 1996.

**Figure 3: 1896 *Adinkra* cloth (on top) is at the Smithsonian and 1825
adinkra cloth (bottom) is at the Museum of Ethnology in Leiden**

The catalogue that accompanied the 1997 exhibition, *Adinkra: The cloth that speaks*, that was held at the Smithsonian National Museum of African Art in Washington, DC indicates that "the multi-layered, ideogrammatic language of the symbols on this cloth reveals culturally specific yet universal concepts of leadership, diplomacy, philosophy, and government." The exhibition was about the cloth the Asantehene, Prempeh I was believed to have worn during his capture by the British in 1896. The catalogue, therefore, only explains this one cloth with about 20 symbols as "a unique historical document that reveals some of the complexity of the late nineteenth century Asante political climate" (National Museum of African Art, 1997, p. 1). There are also the 1817 cloth with about 20 *adinkra* symbols at the British Museum in London and the 1825 cloth with about 18 *adinkra* symbols at the National Museum of Ethnology in Leiden, Holland (see Fig 3).

The *adinkra* cloth is pregnant with text. For the Akan the *adinkra* text encodes some of the people's significant historical events and describes their institutions and their fundamental beliefs that have been preserved in the collective memory of the people. The text encoded in the *adinkra* cloth forms the subject of discussion in the rest of the book from Chapter 3 thereon. The color symbolism of the Akan is discussed later on in this chapter. To provide context for these discussions, we first examine the history of the *adinkra* cloth and the origins of the *adinkra* symbols.

HISTORY OF ADINKRA CLOTH

The country known today as Ghana has been inhabited almost continuously since the early Stone Age, some 500,000 years ago, with succeeding populations leaving traces of their respective cultures in the form of various tools, artifacts, and sites. The Iron Age came to Ghana about 5000 BC, and most of the ethnic groups now inhabiting the country had developed their modern civilization by 1200 AD (Boahen, 1977)[14]. The first direct European contact with Ghana from the coast dates back to the mid-15th century (Dickson, 1971). Prior to that, the Akan states and empires had engaged in the trans-Saharan international trade and trade on the coast of the Gulf of Guinea.

The Akan have, over the years, developed very complex and highly symbolic forms of weaving and printing textiles[15]. The Asante, for example, not only developed the art of weaving (*nwentoma*) of which the *kente* is a special and well known one, they also developed the art of printing the *adinkra* cloth. The Asante, as well as other Akan, also developed the *kyɛnkyɛn* cloth from the bark of a tree (*Antiaris africana*); cloth from raffia material (*doso*)[16]; and *okunitam* (appliqued cloth).

Trade in Cloth

Before the arrival of Europeans on the coast[17], the Asante traded with people outside the forest belt to the north, particularly Mande and Hausa merchants who acted as middlemen between the forests and coastal people on one side, and the caravans from across the Sahara Desert and the Mediterranean coasts on the other (Boahen, 1977). In addition to the trans-Saharan trade, there existed an extensive trade among the peoples of what later came to be known as the Gold, Ivory, and Slave Coasts in the Gulf of Guinea. The main articles of trade on the coast before the arrival of the Europeans were cloths, kola nuts and beads (Boahen, 1977; Lovejoy, 1980). Astley (1745, p. 231) points out that the Ivory Coast cloth, known as *quaqua* cloth, was "a sort of cotton stuff" sold on the Gold Coast and used "for clothing the common people." A Dutch map of the Gold Coast dated December 25, 1629 shows a region where clothes were woven like carpets and worn among the Acanists [Akans], and that people in this region made use of horses but had no firearms (Fynn, 1971, p. 3).

In addition to the *quaqua* cloth, "there were also cloths from Whyddah, Ardra and Benin to the east." The Whyddah cloth was a strip about two yards long and about a quarter of a yard broad. Several of the strips were commonly joined together to make a bigger band of cloth. The Ardra cloths were said to be small and narrow bands whereas the Benin cloths consisted of either three

---

[14] The origins of the Akan as a group of people has been heatedly debated. In 1965 this debate was joined by a series of seminars at the University of Ghana. Papers presented in the series have been published in the journal *Ghana Notes and Queries* and elsewhere. A. Norman Klein (1996) has tried to reconstruct the origins of the Akan and their ancestral practices. He cites very important prehistoric stone axe, Nyame Akuma, found by archaeologists and originally identified by Rattray (1954 pp. 294-301). In his attempt to reconstruct Akan origins, Klein (1996) dismisses Rattray and Ivor Wilks (1993 pp, 64-66) for relying on the oral tradition account of 'the hole in the ground from which our ancestors sprang' to look for the history of the Akan (ibid: 254). Instead, he tries to reconstruct the origins based on radiocarbon evidence and sickle cell traits found in the Akan area. To me, Klein's evidence does not help in any way. For, he succeeds in showing that the Akan have a long history of residence in their present abode, the forest areas of Ghana, but fails to show the origins of their ancestral practices.

[15] In addition to weaving and printing, embroidery and appliqué techniques for utilizing textile are also well known to the Akan.

[16] Raffia was in time replaced by cotton yarns spun from locally grown cotton. It was soon discovered that cloth could be woven from the silk material out of the long silky yarns produced by a species of spider, *ɔkɔmantan* (Kyerematen, 1964). Later the Akan weavers would unravel the colored silk cloths obtained through trade with the Europeans and use the threads for weaving. This enabled the Akan weaver to increase the number of colors available to him.

[17] Portuguese travelers to the West African coast reported that Africans wore loin cloths and wrapping cloths. Linguistic, archeological, and documentary evidence suggests that cotton spinning and weaving existed widely if unevenly in West Africa (Schaedler, 1987; Brooks, 1992).

or four bands. "The color of the Benin cloths was blue, or blue with white stripes" (Fynn, 1971, p. 11). It is therefore possible that the Asante learned textile production from either their neighbors to the west or the east through the coastal trade, as well as from the north as a result of the trans-Saharan trade.

The first European traders on the Guinea Coast played the role of middlemen who carried commodities between such places as the Cape Verde Islands in the west and Benin and Angola to the east. As Alpern (1995, p. 10) points out, most of the cloths European ships carried to the Gold Coast "came from elsewhere in Kwaland, notably Yorubaland (Ijebu), Benin, the western Niger River delta and the southern Ivory Coast. But Senegal, Sierra Leone, and Cameroon also furnished cloth. So did the Portuguese island colonies of São Tomé and Cape Verdes."

ADINKRA SYMBOL ORIGINS

The first recorded account of the existence of *adinkra* symbols is from a drawing of an Akan celebration in Thomas E. Bowdich's book *Mission from Cape Coast to Ashantee*, published in 1819. The British government sent Bowdich to Ghana in 1817, and his book that came out of his expedition was the first European account of the Ashanti people. The drawing from the book does not explain the origins of the *adinkra* symbols, but it does illustrate that the *adinkra* symbols and their adornment on clothing was already an established practice of the Ashanti people by the early 19th century, if not much earlier.

Although various hypotheses have been developed to explain the origin of the symbols, the exact origin of the symbols used in the textiles of the Akan people is yet to be specifically determined. One hypothesis is that they are derived from talismans and scripts believed to have Muslim associations from North Africa as a result of the trans-Saharan trade (Rattray, 1927; McLeod, 1981; Mato, 1986). This hypothesis has been premised on three factors: (a) some of the symbols and their names are alleged to have Islamic origins; (b) *adinkra* symbols are mostly of geometric and abstract shapes, something that conforms to Islamic art; and, (c) there exists an *adinkra* cloth as claimed by Bravmann (1974) and believed to have been seen by Roy Sieber that has Islamic or Arabic writings. Mato contends, for example, in an elaborate examination of historical sources (principal source being Rattray's work) that "islamic writing, amuletic symbols or kufic 'script' have been given as probable source for *adinkra* symbols" (Mato, 1986, p. 64). He further illustrates the Islamic sources thus: "A number of *adinkra* symbols have Islamic links either through their form: Mohammedan Lock [that is, *mmra krado* #433], Wise man's knot [that is, *nyansapɔ* - #794], or *Nsaa* - the Northern cloth [that is, *nsaa* - #803]; or through related Asante proverbs" (pp. 64-65).

From the production technique perspective, it has been suggested that the *adinkra* symbols have Islamic origin. This line of argument is advanced with the "empirical evidence" that Sieber saw an *adinkra* cloth with Arabic or Islamic writing (Mato, 1986, p. 67). I raised this line of argument with Sieber in a personal interview on July 22, 1996 at Bloomington, Indiana. He told me that what he saw was a sick man wearing a cloth with Islamic inscription[18]. This was to ward off any evil spirits so that he would recover from the sickness. Sieber said this was not to suggest that *adinkra* symbols had Islamic origin. He further pointed out that the issue should not be whether the Asante created

---

[18] There is a factory-made cloth called *Kramo nte Hausa* (the Muslim does not speak Hausa) that has Arabic (Islamic) inscription. There is a hand-made imitation of this cloth in the Berlin Museum fur Volkerkunde that I have seen personally. This Berlin sample does not resemble in either shape or form an *adinkra* cloth.

the symbols or adopted them from other people. Assuming the Asante borrowed or adopted symbols from others at all, the issue as Sieber pointed out to me, should be what the Asante did with what they adopted or borrowed.

Danquah (1964) effusively dismisses the Arabic or Islamic influence thus:

> It may be curious that the Mohammedans themselves do not seem to know many of these symbols and the names and uses for them among the Akan are entirely un-Mohammedan. At any rate no cloths stamped with the Adinkra symbols are met with among the Mohammedans, and the Adinkra system of mourning is unknown to them. We may safely conclude that there is something intensely native in these symbols interperative (sic) of Akan faith and tradition (Danquah, 1964, p. xxxvii).

Whether or not Bravmann or Sieber once saw an *adinkra* cloth, that line of argument does not hold water when one examines that claim more closely in relation to the *adinkra* production technique as used in the Asokwa and Ntonso areas near Kumase. The *adinkra* cloth producers use the block-print technique in which they use carved blocks called a*dwini nnua* (design blocks), a broad stick called *daban*, and a comb-like tool called *nsensan nnua*. This technique has not changed much from what Bowdich observed in 1817 nor from what Rattray observed in the 1920s. To make Islamic or Arabic inscriptions would require the use of a writing brush or stick. The cloth stamper does not use a writing brush nor a stick. Even when they stamp phonetically-based inscription (e.g., *owuo sɛɛ fie*), the letters are carved onto the *adwini nnua*. If the production technique has not changed much over the years, then there is no evidence from that angle to support the contention that the *adinkra* symbols have an Islamic origin.

The fact that some symbols look Islamic in form or have related names or proverbs does not provide a convincing evidence of Islamic influence, and for that matter, Islamic origins for the *adinkra* symbols. Wilks' articles (1962, 1993) may be used here to show that Rattray and subsequent scholars like Mato are wrong in claiming that words like *nsaa* and *kramo*, and symbols like *nyansapɔ* and *mmra krado* are of Islamic origin. Wilks points out that these words and others like *pɔnko* (horse), *adaka* (box), *krataa* (paper), *kotoku* (sack), and *tawa* (tobacco) are Mande and not Arabic in origin. One of the fifty-three odd symbols that Rattray identified from the *adinkra* cloth is the *nkotimsefoɔ pua* (hairstyle of the queenmother's attendants) which is likened to the swastika symbol (Rattray, 1927, p. 267). Should one construe some of the contemporary symbols that include the logos for Mercedes Benz and VW cars as German influence? The verbal form of the Akan language is full of words borrowed from other languages. For example, words like *bokiti* (bucket) and *kɔpoo* (cup) are borrowed from English, and *asopatere* (shoes) and *paano* (bread) are borrowed from the Portuguese (Wilks, 1993). The Akan are not unique in adopting and borrowing words and symbols from other languages. Why should scholars attempt to diminish the creativity of the Asante (and Akan people in general) to adopt and borrow from other cultures? As Gilfoy (1987, p. 26) points out, the trans-Saharan trade that might have been the source of Islamic influence was "by no means one-way." It is possible, therefore, that the Moslems might have copied some of the Akan symbols.

The Akan have had close contacts with numerous other ethnic groups (from within and outside the continent of Africa) for many years and they have demonstrated a readiness to appropriate and utilize items produced by these other groups. In a culture as highly organized in pre-colonial times as the Akan had developed, it is foolhardy to engage in a futile discussion that seems to attribute originality and creativity to outsiders other than the people themselves. In this light, one will ask with Picton (1992, p. 28): "Why is it always assumed, however, that it was North Africa [or for that matter, outsiders] that influenced the sub-Saharan region rather than the other way around?" According to Delaquis (2013) there is no direct linkage between *Adinkra* and Islamic writing as some scholars have proposed. She explains that *Adinkra* bears ideographic (characters that represent an idea or concept) nature and employs the stamping (and screen) technique of printing while Islamic writing is calligraphic and syllabic in nature.

There are other more plausible hypotheses to explain the origins of the *adinkra* cloth symbols. Darkwah (1999, p. 59) points out that "[w]hile the Asante role," in the cultural development of the Akan, "is generally known it is not always remembered that other Akan sub-groups, less successful militarily than the Asante, also made important contributions to the development of what is often described as 'Asante culture'" (ibid.). Some of these Akan sub-groups[19] such as Bono, Akwamu, Denkyera, and Adanse had state systems that preceded the Asante state system (Daaku, 1966; Kumah, 1966; Bravmann, 1968). Indeed, the pre-colonial state, Asante for example, successively removed skilled artisans from defeated states and resettled them closer to the Asante capital of Kumasi. With the defeat of the Denkyira, Johnson (1979, p. 61) writes, "Not only the Denkyira regalia but also the craftsmen and specialists responsible for its manufacture, upkeep and manipulation fell into the hands of the victors; indeed, the oral traditions preserved in many Ashanti villages state that some of the craftsmen, including the chief goldsmith, defected before the final victory (Agyeman-Duah, n. d.: no. 13)." A neighborhood in Bonwire, the seat of Asante *kente* weaving is called Denkyira. This was where some war captives were settled from the Denkyira war. In the following sections three pre-Asante Akan states – Gyaman, Denkyira and Bron – are examined for possible clues regarding the origin of the *adinkra* cloth symbols.

The Denkyira Hypothesis

Another view, however, suggests that the art of weaving cloth and printing the *adinkra* cloth was known in Denkyira and other Akan areas even before the "*Osa-nti*" war which occurred around 1700. This war ended the rule of the Denkyira over the Asante, and also gave rise to the Asante kingdom. The Asante, according to this explanation, learned the art of weaving and printing cloth from the Denkyira craftsmen and specialists who either defected or were captured during the war (Agyeman-Duah, n.d. no. 13). Wilks (1975, p. 456) writes: "The first and second Asokwahenes, Nuamoa and his full brother Akwadan, were among the many Denkyira who voluntarily transferred their allegiance to Osei Tutu in the late seventeenth century." When Akwadan defected he was said to have carried a trumpet that was made of gold. This must refer to a gilded *abɛntia* - gilded state horn (called *nkrawobɛn*).[20] These Denkyira people are said to have introduced several innovations

---

[19] The term Akan has been used to cover a wide variety of ethnic groups who occupy a greater part of southern Ghana and the south-eastern Cote d'Ivoire (Ivory Coast). The groups constituting the culturally and linguistically homogenous Akan ethnicity include the Adanse, Agona, Ahanta, Akuapem, Akwamu, Akyem, Aowin, Asante, Assin, Baoule, Bono, Denkyira, Fantse, Nzema, Sefwi, and Wassa. Together these groups constitute over 40 percent of the country's population (Dolphyne and Kropp-Dakubu, 1988; Bodomo, 1996); and they dominate about two-thirds of the country's land area as Ashanti, Brong-Ahafo, Central, Eastern and Western Regions, and the northern part of the Volta Region (see map).

[20] In relating the history associated with the *nkrawobɛn*, Appiah told me in a personal interview on May 24, 1994 at Asokwa that his ancestors, one of whom was Nana Gyetua, brought this horn from Denkyira to serve the Asantehene. When I checked with the record by Wilks (1975, p. 458), Nana Gyetua (Gyetoa) was the ninth Asokwahene. One should note that Wilks' record is derived from oral history.

not only in textile and other crafts but also in government and military organization. The Denkyira hypothesis is buttressed by the fact that a section of the Bonwire township is named Denkyira for the Denkyira people who either defected or were captured during the "*Osa-nti*" war. Oral history as told to me by several informants from Bonwire pointed out that the Denkyira crafts people were settled there and other parts of Kwabere to ply their trade.

If one accepted this hypothesis, then the 1818 Gyaman war must have resulted in bringing to Asokwa Gyaman war captives[21] who might have introduced additional technological improvements (e.g., the use of carved *apakyiwa* in stamping as compared to the use of feathers in the painting technique that Bowdich mentions in the quote below) in the textile industry. In the *adinkra* production process, Asokwa informants maintained that it was Nana Adinkra's son, Apau (or Apaa) who introduced innovations such as the use of calabash for carving out the stamps[22]. He is also believed to have introduced the very first symbol (*adwini kane*), *adinkrahene* (king of the *adinkra* symbols). He is remembered and honored with the symbol *Adinkraba Apau* (Apau, Son of Adinkra-#316-317). Other symbols are believed to have been copied from the carved column (*sekyedua*) of the stool and other regalia of Nana Adinkra of Gyaman (Kyerematen, 1964). This hypothesis is problematic because the Bowdich collection of 1817 has the *adinkrahene* symbol that is believed to have been introduced by Nana Adinkra's son following the 1818 Asante-Gyaman War.

The Gyaman Hypothesis

Another hypothesis is that the name *adinkra* is associated with Nana Kwadwo Adinkra, King of Gyaman, who replicated and dared to claim that he too, like the Asante King, had a Golden Stool.[23] In 1818, the Asantehene Nana Osei Bonsu declared a punitive war against Nana Adinkra as his claim was considered an act of insolence that violated the Asante assertion that the likeness of the Golden Stool should never be said to have existed before or after the historic descent of the Asante Golden Stool. Nana Kofi Adinkra was attacked and defeated for making such a claim. Among the war booties captured from Gyaman were the *adinkra* cloth and stool symbols, some craftsmen, and the technical know-how for making the *adinkra* cloth. This explanation for the origin of the *adinkra* cloth and its symbols, however, appears to be anachronistic when viewed in the light of Bodwich's written account. Bodwich (1819) witnessed the production of *adinkra* and *kente* cloths during his visit to Kumasi in 1817, that is, one year before the punitive war against Nana Adinkra of Gyaman.

There is claim in recent times that the first *adinkra* symbol made by Nana Kwadwo Adinkra was the *bi nka bi* – bite not one another (#420) symbol. He engraved this on a gourd (*dua toa*) at a village called Mina (now in ruins) which was located a few miles west of Suma Ahenkro, the capital of Suma Traditional area in the Brong Ahafo Region. The *bi nka bi* symbol was used to ward off a potential civil war. Nana Adinkra is believed to have created and named other symbols. He explained their meanings and significance to his chiefs who in turn taught their people about these symbols. Nana

---

[21] The Asante had a population policy of settling skilled war captives in craft towns (see Chapter 9).

[22] Appiah and Boadum, personal interviews at Asokwa, May 24, 1994.

[23] The Asante nation had been formed following the *nkabom* (unity) meeting of various chiefs called together by Osei Tutu and Okɔmfo Anɔkye. Okɔmfo Anɔkye conjured from the sky a Golden Stool for the Asante king and decreed that no other king should have a golden stool or the likeness of it (see the discussion of stools in Chapter 5 and the discussion of the *nkabom* meeting in Chapter 6).

Adinkra caused these symbols to be engraved on a golden stool he had made for himself. It was this golden stool that was immediate cause of the 1818 war between the Gyaman and Asante.[24]

One informant from Asokwa related to me that when the Gyamans were defeated, the body of King Adinkra was found in a pile of other dead people. When his body was retrieved from the pile, it was found to be covered with the *ntiamu ntoma* (stamped cloth). Thereafter, the *ntiamu ntoma* became known as *adinkra ntoma*.[25] People in the Asokwa and Ntonso areas continue to differentiate *adinkra* cloth from *kente* by referring to *adinkra* as *ntiamu ntoma* (stamped cloth) and *kente* as *nwentoma* (woven cloth).[26] The *adinkra* cloth is further distinguished as being *ntiamu* or *nhwemu* (stamped or whisked painting) and *nwɔmu* (embroidered). Three stages are employed in the making of the *adinkra* cloths: (1) dyeing (*hyɛ ntoma aduro*), (2) printing or stamping (*ntiamu*) and whisked painting (*nhwemu*), and (3) embroidering (*nwɔmu*) or simple sewing of the pieces together. The *ntiamu* and screen printing techniques are shown in the following pictures (Fig 4).

**Figure 4: Adinkra cloth producers using the block print (left)
and the screen print (right) techniques**

The Bron Hypothesis

The Bron (Abrɔn, Bono or Brong) is believed to be the first Akan state. Warren (1975, p. 3) writes, "historically, the Bono claim – and this is substantiated by oral histories from other Akan states – to have originated the Akan crafts of gold-smithing and kente cloth weaving." Poasnansky (1987) provides some archaeological evidence from Begho to substantiate the Bron hypothesis that cloth weaving and other Akan crafts must have first occurred in the Bron state. The Bron state

---

[24] Personal interview of Nana Odeneho Dr Affram Brempong III, paramount chief of Suma Traditional Area in the Jaman North District, Brong Ahafo. Accra, August 13, 2016.

[25] Kusi Boadum, personal interview at Asokwa, May 23, 1994.

[26] Teacher Nsiah and Agya Yaw Nyamaa, personal interviews at Ntonso, May 22, 1994; Appiah and Agya Ampɔfo, personal interview at Asokwa, May 23, 1994.

was in a strategic economic location as it traversed the transition zone of the forest and savannah belts between the Sudanic nations on the edge of the Sahara. Bron towns such as Techiman were important early market towns on the Djenne trade route.

Long before the decisive war of 1699-1701 against Denkyira, the Asante under Osei Tutu defeated the Dormaa state to the north. The defeat of the Dormaa gave rise to Gyaman. A reluctant group of subjects under Bofu Bini refused to accept Asante rule. This group moved further north to establish what became known as "*Gya man – they have left their nation*" (Terray 1987). Subsequent Asante-Gyaman wars were either to strengthen Asante domination and control over the resources (especially gold) of the area and the northern trade routes, or they reflected the resistance of the Gyaman to Asante domination.

The Asante invasion of Bron ensured access to the crafts and resources and control of trade routes. The power of Kumase manifested itself through the interactions of people known as the *ahenkwaa* (royal court servants), *abofoɔ* (hunters) and *batadifoɔ* (royal court traders) of the Asantehene. It was through these interactions that possibly cloth weaving and printing and other crafts were transferred to Asante. Or the Asante invasions of Bron resulted in the transfer of innovations in weaving and printing that might have improved on existing local weaving and printing. There still thrives cloth printing at Techiman, an important market center in Bron.

Etymological Explanations

Yet another view presented by Danquah (1944) is that the word *adinkra* derives from the Akan word *nkra* or *nkara* which means message or intelligence. This message or intelligence is what the soul takes with it from God upon obtaining leave to depart to earth, that is, enter the human being upon birth. The Akan call the soul of the person *ɔkera* or *ɔkra*, and the soul is the spiritual aspect of God that enters the human being upon birth and leaves the person at death. *Adinkra* is the parting or send-off message or intelligence that the soul carries to and from God. Perhaps the association of *adinkra* with *okra* (soul) as parting message provided the basis for the view that the *adinkra* cloth was a cloth for mourning.

One informant[27] also explained that the name *adinkra* became associated with the *ntiamu toma* (stamped cloth) that was given to Prempeh I to take with him into exile. He was given *ntiamu ntoma* as *adi nkra* (parting cloth) to mark his taking leave of his people. He was given *adinkra* cloth in which was stamped the *ɔsrane* (moon). This was to symbolize that the king may come and go, but the people as nation will forever be there. From then on *ntiamu ntoma* became known as *adinkra*. This hypothesis seems to be based on the etymological hypothesis because at Ntonso and Asokwa, the cloth producers continue to refer to *adinkra* as *ntiamu ntoma*. The problem with this explanation is that Prempeh carried not only *adinkra* cloth; he also took several *kente* (or *nwentoma*) cloths with him. If the cloth (*ntiamu ntoma*) he took with him into exile was to mark his taking leave of his people, then one will surmise the *nwentoma* (*kente*) should also mark the occasion of his taking leave of his people as he was taken into exile by the British.

Another etymological explanation offers that the term *adinkra* is a corruption of the word *adwini kane* (first design or first symbol). Each of the designs or symbols in the *adinkra* cloth is called *adwini*

---

[27] A reader of a draft of the manuscript, who asked to remain anonymous, offered this explanation. This explanation may be based on the etymological hypothesis and does not seem to register with other informants. One informant intimated that it was a *kente* cloth that was later created and named *ɔhene aforo hyɛn* (the king travels in a boat to mark his exile from Ghana.

(design) and the cloth is referred to as *adwini ntoma* (designed cloth) or *ntiamu ntoma* (stamped cloth). Bowdich (1819, p. 310) wrote:

> The white cloths, which are principally manufactured in Inla and Dagwumba, they paint for mourning with a mixture of blood and red dye wood. The patterns are various and not inelegant, and painted with so much regularity with a fowl's feather, that they have all the appearance of a coarse print at a distance[28].

The debate should not be about where *adinkra* symbols originated but, more importantly, that linguists do not regard *adinkra* as true writing. *Adinkra* symbols are ideographs because they represent ideas and not just things. *Adinkra* symbols have specific names and meanings, which have a specific phonetic and/or semantic value. As Gelb notes: There are no pure systems of writing just as there are no pure races in anthropology and no pure languages in linguistics (Gelb, 1963, p. 199).

Whatever the source of the name and the symbols, the *adinkra* is more than a mourning cloth. In one sense, it can be viewed in terms of the Akan symbolism of color encoded in the background of the *adinkra* cloth; in another sense, the symbols and the patterns of stamping them in the cloth constitute text that needs to be examined for what it encodes. The discussion below focuses on the Akan color symbolism encoded in the *adinkra* cloth.

AKAN COLOR SYMBOLISM

Among the Asante as well as all Akan, color classification is basically tripartite. These colors exist as complementary parts of triadic series. The three basic colors or ranges of color are *tuntum*, *fufuo* and *kɔkɔɔ*. *Tuntum* designates all very dark shades which approach absolute blackness. *Fufuo* covers pale, white, grey and cream colors; and *kɔkɔɔ* all red, brown and yellow shades (Antubam, 1963).

All shades of white (*fufuo*), for example, ivory, white glass, egg shell, white clay (*hyire*), are generally associated with coolness, innocence, peace, purity, virtue, virginity, victory, virtuosity, and rejoicing and happiness (Antubam, 1963). Spiritual entities such as God and deified spirits of ancestors that live in the spiritual world are associated with white; the lower world, abode of chthonic creatures and demons, is associated with black. Hagan (1970, p. 8) points out that *fufuo*

> is the ritually auspicious color and it has immediate association with victory and spiritual purity. It is associated with the sacred, and it is considered the color of gods and kings; the symbol of the purity and sacredness of their persons and estate. *Fufuo* also expresses joy and hope and well-being. That aspect of the human person which bears a man's destiny and directs his fortunes (*kra*) is associated with *fufuo*,....

Rattray (1927, p. 175) points out a contrast: "The corpse of a dead priest is draped in white and sprinkled with white clay (*hyire*) or powder, symbolizing the antithesis of ordinary funerary customs, which possibly mark out the wearers as being in a state of sorrow or defilement."

All shades of red (*kɔkɔɔ*, for example, *memene* and *kɔbene*) are associated with heat, anger, crisis,

---

[28] Even though Bowdich claims that the *adinkra* cloth was painted with fowl's feather, the sample he collected (now at the British Museum) was definitely produced with the block-print technique.

grief, blood, danger, witchcraft, and warfare (Antubam, 1963; Hagan, 1970). Hagan (1970, p. 9) notes that "Akans generally point to blood as the paradigm of the red color cluster and much of the ambiguity in the symbolic meaning of the color derives from the mixed associations of blood. Blood stands for life and vitality... Akans believe that blood is the means by which a *kra* [soul or spirit - #42-43] might be given human form. But as blood stands for life, so does any blood which does not give life, or is spilled wastefully, stand for death."

The broad connotations of black (*tuntum*) are less precise, but are usually associated with night, death, loss, and ancestors (Antubam, 1963; Hagan, 1970). Black "does not," as Hagan (1970, p. 9) points out, "necessarily connote defilement or profanation. The Stool of kings or elders who die in battle or of old age while in office are consecrated and held sacred to their memory, and they are black." Antubam (1963, p. 79) suggests that black symbolizes spirituality and age as "all objects which are dedicated to the spirits of the dead are purposely treated to appear black; and objects of war booty, except gold and silver, are blackened."

All shades of yellow, for example, the color of juice of the ripe pineapple, symbolize prosperity, royalty, glory, the prime of life, and maturity. Yellow also signifies the presence and influence of God in the society and the rule of a king (Antubam, 1963). On a spatial and temporal plane, the Akan envision life as a circular continuum of colors. Life starts with white and runs clockwise towards youth and adolescence with yellow. During *abadinto* (child naming ceremony) the child is dressed in white and is given *pokuaa* (gold nugget) as *kera sika* (gold for the child's soul) symbolizing continuous life and prosperity for the child. Adult life is reached with brown (*dansinkran*), and ends with black for death. At the intermediary points, the main colors combine and gradually change shades; the center of the Akan life cycle, being the sum of all parts, is conceived as multi-colored.

During funerals brown, black and red (for example, *kuntunkuni*, *birisi*, and *kɔbene*) *adinkra* clothes are usually worn. When *adinkra* is used as a mourning cloth, three types of color backgrounds, *kɔkɔɔ* (all shades of red) and *tuntum* (all shades of black) on one hand, and *fufuo* (all shades of white) on the other hand are used. *Tuntum* and *fufuo*, when used together for funerary purposes, symbolize the Akan concept of dualism such as life and death, beginning and end, and crisis and normalcy, victory/peace and crisis/chaos, sacred/profane, and mourning and rejoicing. Red (*kɔkɔɔ*, for example, *kɔbene*) and black (*tuntum*, for example, *kuntunkuni* and *birisi*) *adinkra* cloths are worn together by the immediate relatives of the deceased person, while only black (*tuntum*) *adinkra* is worn by the other mourners (see Fig 5 and 6 below). As Hagan (1970, p. 10) explains, "at this level black and red refer to opposite categories and relationships": family and non-family members. Akan Christians have incorporated their color symbolism into their Christian religious rituals. Good Friday (*Yesu wuo* - #111) is marked by the wearing of *tuntum* and *kɔkɔɔ* mourning clothes, and Easter (*Yesu wusɔre* - #115) is marked by the wearing of white to symbolize the triumph of Jesus over death and his ascension to heaven.

Bright background colors of white and all shades of yellow are worn for all diverse occasions. White *adinkra* is usually worn when a very old person dies. This signifies the attainment of victory over death and the earning of glory and rest which is the lot of good ancestors. White *adinkra* is also worn to indicate a return to normalcy after mourning or to give thanks (*aseda*) for recovery from illness, and to mark victory or innocence during trial (Antubam, 1963; Sarpong, 1974).

As a signal for the end of the Odwira[29] festival, the king wears white *adinkra* to mark the return

---

[29] Odwira is an annual festival that signifies regeneration and renewal of life. The ancestors are remembered in statewide ceremonies during which the sub-chiefs renew their oath of allegiance to the king.

to normalcy. White *adinkra* is also worn by the Asantehene-elect for some stages in the ritual of enstoolment at Pampaso and also in the Bampanase Courtyard (Agyeman-Duah, 1962).

Blue is the color for love and feminine tenderness. According to Antubam (1963, p. 82), blue "is likened to the serene appearance of the crescent moon in the heavens. It is also often used to symbolize the role of a queen mother." *Adinkra* cloth with indigo blue dye (*birisi*) is considered as *ntoma tuntum* ('black cloth') for funeral purposes (e.g, *kunayɛ* - widowhood).

Figure 5: A bereaved family member wearing red and Black *adinkra* cloths at a funeral

Figure 6: A sympathizer wearing black *adinkra* cloth at a funeral

Adinkra Cloth Patterns

Another way in which *adinkra* cloth may be understood is to examine the name given to each cloth pattern (e.g. *Kwasiada adinkra* - Sunday *adinkra*), and the constituent symbols in each cloth. In other words, the type of symbols predominantly stamped into the cloth together with the background colors carries messages and also determines the occasion for which the cloth is to be used.

In general, the printing of the symbols does follow particular patterns which give specific names to the finished cloth. Examples of the names for the finished cloth are: (1) variations of *adwinasa* such as *Kwasiada adinkra*, *adinkra akyi adinkra*, *mmaa man*; and *ɔhene kɔ hia* (the king is gone to the women's quarters [harem]) – Figure 7; (2) *m'akoma mu tɔfe* (my sweetheart); (3) *abeteɛ ntema*; (4) *ɔsrane ne nsoroma ntoma* (moon and stars cloth); and, (5) *kontonkurowi* (rainbow) – Figure 6. Also on demand, a particular symbol or set of symbols will be used to meet customers' requests (for example, *koroyɛ* - #187, *owuo sɛe fie* - #127, and *mercedes benz* - #738). The cloths may be named after individuals, events, and social messages, including proverbs (Rattray, 1927, pp. 236-268), as well as tell stories.

When used by officials of the king's court, for instance, the *adinkra* cloth may present a message in lieu of the spoken word. In such usage the wearer of the cloth can rely entirely on the rhetoric of his visual icon to state, in very general terms, the official policy he represents[30]. For example, in connection with the grand funeral rite (*ayikɛseɛ*) for his immediate predecessor, Nana Agyeman Prempeh I, Otumfuo Sir Osei Agyeman Prempeh II wore *adinkra fufuo* with the *dɛnkyɛm* motif. The white background color signified the installation of a new king as return to normalcy vis-a-vis the crisis situation the state had been thrown into by the death of the predecessor. The *dɛnkyɛm* motif signified adaptation to the changing circumstances following the colonization of Asante by the British[31]. Nana Opoku Ware II, the successor to Prempeh II, on the other hand, wore *adinkra fufuo* with the *mframa dan* (wind resistant house) motif. Polakoff (1982, pp. 98, 100) notes: "The choice made by Opuku [sic] Ware II was especially appropriate for the stormy political mood of African countries." The use of *mframa dan* motif in this instance might have signified chieftaincy and the indigenous political system it represented as being more stable and secure than the Westminster parliamentary system colonialism had imposed on the country. When Nana Opoku Ware II was installed as Asantehene, Ghana had just returned to civilian rule under the Progress Party led by Dr. K. A. Busia after a three-year military rule. Before he became the Asantehene, Nana Opoku Ware II, as J. Matthew Poku, had served as a Commissioner (Minister) for Transport and Communications in the 1966-1969 military government and also as Ghana's ambassador to Italy.

---

[30] Nana Antwi Buasiako, an Asantehene Kyeame, explained to me in a personal interview (May 24, 1994) that the wearing of an *adinkra* cloth by the Asantehene to make a policy statement, is a deliberate decision made by the king in consultation with his counsellors. The *Manwerɛhene*, the chief public servant in charge of the king's clothing and personal effects, then charges the Asokwahene to commission the production of the cloth to suit the occasion.

[31] The British captured Kumase in 1896 and exiled Prempeh I to the Seychelles Island in the Indian Ocean. The Asantehene was reduced to the status of Kumasehene and the Asanteman Nhyiamu was abolished. When Prempeh I was returned from exile in 1924 the British would only allow him to rule as Kumasehene. He died in 1931 and was succeeded by Prempeh II under whose reign the *Asanteman Nhyiamu* was restored in 1935 and he, thence, ruled as *Asantehene*.

Figure 7: Bloc-printed *Adinkra* cloths named *ɔhene kɔ Hia* (the King is gone to the harem) on the left, and *Kontokurowi* (Rainbow) on the right

Figure 8: Screen-printed *Adinkra* cloths named *adwinasa* on the left and*Kwasiada Adinkra Adwinasa* on the right

I witnessed similar use of the cloth to make oblique statements at a funeral ceremony that I observed in Kumasi on May 28, 1994. Some immediate family members of the deceased wore factory-made and hand-printed *adinkra* cloth with the symbol *owuo sɛɛ fie* (death destroys the home – # 125-127). When I asked why the use of that particular symbol, one of the people wearing that cloth responded that it was their father who had passed away and they wanted to convey their feelings about how poorly they had been treated by the dead man's *abusua* (matriclan) members. Upon further inquiry, I learned that the dead man's *abusua* members had thrown out the man's children from his house as he had died intestate.

PRODUCTION PROCESSES

Adinkra is a printed cloth that utilizes the block-print technique. The technique used by the Asante is indigenous. The original fabrics onto which the symbols were printed were locally woven cloth produced from locally grown and hand-spun cotton. The cloth serves as the 'canvas' on which the symbols are printed. The background color, in the past, was usually either plain white, indigo, rustic red, or brown. Sources of natural dyes included barks of trees and roots, leaves and flowers, and fruits. For example, green dye could be extracted from papaya (pawpaw) leaves, and brown could be obtained from cola nuts. The most common background dye is *kuntunkuni* produced from the bark of the roots of the *kuntunkuni* tree, imported from the savannah regions to the north. The bark is soaked first and then pounded, and water is added and strained. The liquid is then boiled, strained again, and cooled after which the dye-stuff is ready for use. After dyeing and drying, the cloth is stretched out on a printing table or the ground padded with foam or old sacks for the stamping. Contemporary *adinkra* cloths have varied background colors and the fabrics that serve as the canvas for printing are usually factory-made.

The pigment which is used as ink for the block print is prepared from the bark of the *badeɛ* tree (*bridelia micranta* of the natural order *euphorbiaceae*). The epidermis is first removed and the rest of the bark is pounded. After soaking in a barrel for three days, it is then pounded and strained, and lumps of iron slag (*etia*) are added to the solution to hasten evaporation as it is boiled till it is gluey thick, yielding a black fabric paint which the craftsmen call *adinkra aduro*.[32]

The stamps (*adwini* or *adwini nnua*) used for the block printing are made from pieces of old calabash or gourd (*apakyiwa* or *koraa - lagenaria vulgaris*) on which are carved the different symbols (see Fig. 9).[33] A small handle is made from sticks (*praeɛ*) which are tied into a knot and pegged into the back of the calabash pieces. To apply the stamps, the cloth is laid out on a dry flat clean piece of ground padded with foam, old sacks, or board, and it is held taut with pins or wooden pegs. The cloth[34] is divided into rectangles, squares or parallelograms (panels) by using either a wooden comb (*dua afe* - #460-466), *daban* (iron bar or a measure - #830), or *nsensan nnua* (line-making sticks - #854). The *dua afe* or the *nsensan nnua* is dipped into the *adinkra aduro* and applied free hand to draw the line patterns.[35]

---

[32] Some *adinkra* cloth printers at both Asokwa and Ntonso said they had experimented with factory-made fabric paint but abandoned its use because it does not have the shining appearance as *adinkra aduro*. One will also imagine that the fabric paint is more expensive, and to minimize costs, the printer is better off using the local product. There is also the attachment to "tradition" and the printer does not want to take risks regarding customer taste.

[33] In comparison to the prints on old cloths, the prints on recent cloths seem much bigger. This suggests that the printer is able to accomplish more now than in the old days. Such blocks as the *dweninmɛn ntoaso* (#342), *abeteɛ ntema* (#755) and *adinkrahene ntoaso* (#314) are examples of the bigger sized prints. The screen-print technique also allows the use of bigger symbols.

[34] There are two types of cloth sizes, one for the man and one for the woman. The man's cloth varies from a young man's (that is, small) size of 90" X 216" (usually called half piece - *ɔpofa*) to a full grown man's size that varies from a medium size of 90" X 288" (what is usually called the 8 yard-size) to a large size of 135" X 432" (what is usually called the 12 yard-size or full piece - *ɛpoɔ*), and the woman's may be three pieces of 45" X 72" each or two pieces, of which one is 45" X 72" and the other is 45" X 144" (called the *dansinkran* and worn in toga-style similar to the man's). The man-size cloth is divided into six horizontal fields (rows) by eight vertical fields (columns) forming forty-eight panels. One symbol is usually printed in each panel and the symbols in each panel may be repeated in some order to form a pattern for each cloth. It is in the system of patterning and the creative use of symbols and colors that the variety of *adinkra* cloths arises.

[35] The *dua afe* (wooden comb) or *nsensan nnua* has two, four, six, eight, or ten "teeth." The numbers of lines made by the *dua afe* and *nsensan nnua* have symbolic meanings themselves. One symbolizes the indivisible, the *kra* (soul) of *Nyame*. *Nsatea koro* means the same as *Gye Nyame* (except God). Two symbolizes *Nyame* as a duality, divisible by birth. *Nsateanu* means *Memma mo mmo ne yɔ me man* (I congratulate you people of my state). Three symbolizes *Nyame* as the creator and ruler of the universe that is a continuum of the sky (*ewimu*), earth (*ewiase*), and the underworld (*asamando*). Three is also considered a lucky number. Four symbolizes *Nyame* as the creator and ruler of the four cardinal points of the compass and the revolving heaven. Five symbolizes *Nyame* as a Supreme Being. Six symbolizes the dialectical processes of life, death and resurrection or rebirth. It is the symbol of strength, vitality and rejuvenation. Seven is the symbol for the universe and the state. It represents the seven planets each of which presides over the seven days of the week, and the seven *abusua* that form the state. Eight symbolizes procreation, fertility and fecundity. Nine (i.e., 3+3+3) symbolizes the

Figure 9: Teacher Kofi Nsiah of Ntonso carving *adinkra* block-printing stamps

**Figure 10: Adinkra cloth producer using *nsesan nnua* to
draw lines as he uses the block-print technique**

triad comprising *Nyame*, *Nyankopɔn*, and *Ɔdomankoma* that rules the universe (Meyerowitz, 1950; Antubam, 1963).

These initial line designs are known as *nsɛnsan* (lines -# 855-858), *kɛtɛwa* or *kɛtɛpa* (good bed - # 510), *ɔwɔ aforo adobɛ* (snake climbs the raffia palm tree -# 215-217), *nhwemu, nkyɛmu* (divisions- # 823-824), or *daban* (a measure - #830)[36]. The other *adinkra* symbols are then printed in each of the rectangles on the cloth. Some of the symbols are designed by using the *dua afe* (for example, *asambo*), *nsɛnsan dua* (e.g., *mframadan*), the heads of different sizes of nails (e.g., *sumpie*), and the *praɛ* handle of the carved *adinkra* stamp (for example, *tuo aboba*). Sometimes no lines are drawn and the stamps are applied in freehand style to the cloth. In this method, one or two symbols (usually *donno*, *nsoroma*, and *donno ntoaso* or *donno nta*) are used to serve as boundary lines within which the other symbols are printed. Or the *nwɔmu* (embroidery) design is utilized as lines to divide the cloth into sections for printing.

Instead of using the block-print technique, some *adinkra* cloths are screen-printed in Ntonso with images adapted from traditional *adinkra* stamps. The screen-printed technique employs the use of work benches raised well above the ground to enable the cloth producer to work comfortably while standing. The screens are developed outside of the town by individuals engaged in screen-printing of t-shirts. A flat piece of wood is used as squeegee to draw the acrylic paste across the design area thus transferring the design onto the cloth. This development has greatly impacted on the production of *adinkra* cloths, reducing the production time, enhancing the designing and incorporation of more symbols, and augmenting the accuracy of design registration.

The *nwɔmu* (embroidery) technique is being substituted with strips that are woven and sewn together (see Figs. 11 and 12). Also whole cloths are now woven with the *ahwepan* (plain weave) technique before being screen printed. *Kente* cloths are also being embossed with *adinkra* symbols by using the appliqué technique.

The *adinkra* cloth production process is differentiated by sex and age. Young and middle-aged women usually prepare the dye-stuff and the *adinkra aduro* and they also dye the cloth prior to it being block-printed. Men tend to prepare the *adinkra aduro* and do the weaving, embroidery and the block and screen printing. While young boys are often given the embroidery (*nwɔmu*) part to do, older men and women tend to carve symbols onto the calabash pieces. Even though the production of the cloth tends to be carried out with family members as the production unit, hired labor on a piece rate basis is also utilized to carry out some of the major stages of the cloth production (dyeing, printing, sewing, and embroidery) for bulk sales to retailers. Asokwa producers tend to make cloth to order, while Ntonso producers tend to produce on a commercial scale for the market. Producers at Asokwa tend to be full time workers producing *adinkra* cloths, whereas some of the producers at Ntonso tend to split their time between producing *adinkra* cloths and farming.

Adinkra symbols continue to change as new influences impact on the Akan and Ghanaian culture as some of the symbols now record specific technological developments such as the use computer assisted design (CAD) techniques. There are also machine-printed *adinkra* cloths being produced in Ghanaian, British, Dutch, Japanese, and French textile factories (see Fig 13). The factory-made prints are color fast, whereas *adinkra* cloth produced by the indigenous block-print process is not color fast. On the other hand, the indigenous cloth producers cannot match the factory producers with respect to pricing as the factory lends itself to the utilization of the economies of scale. Some of the indigenous cloth producers at Ntonso and Asokwa are stamping on commercial wax print cloth, resulting in what has been termed as "fancy" *adinkra* cloth. The Ntonso and Asokwa producers are also being more creative with the applique and embroidery techniques (see Fig. 12).

---

[36] Sometimes a brush-like tool is used to make these lines and the whisked painting effect of the brush work gives rise to the type of *adinkra* cloth called *nhwemu* (whisked design).

The factory printed cloths that incorporate *adinkra* symbols do not seem to have specific names for the constituent symbols. Rather a name is given to the cloth as a whole (see for example Fig. 13). The criteria for choosing names for the wax prints are based on popular culture, issues trending at the time, or momentous socio-political events. Sometimes, names are quite banal, simply reflecting the design on the cloth than any deeper meaning. For instance, there is one design of fans – for fanning oneself when the weather is hot.

**Figure 11: Asantehene Otumfoɔ Osei Tutu II (seated) wearing *adinkra*
cloth called *KwasiadaAdinkra Adwinasa*. The symbols are screen-
printed and colored *nwɔmu* embroidery is employed.**

Some people name wax prints simply by just looking at the dominant object in the design – such as *Dua kor* (One tree), and *Akyekyedeɛ akyi* (shell of a tortoise). Others rely on names printed on them at the selvedge edge from the factory (see Fig. 13). As Willard (2004, p. 182) notes: "Factory-printed cloth has different levels of usage. Producers may not foresee the various meanings the cloth may acquire once it leaves the factory. Consumers and users apply their own meanings according to market trends and use the cloth to communicate within their own societies, while also viewing the cloth as an investment." The indigenous *adinkra* cloth producers are concerned about the massive appropriation of their symbols and designs by the factory producers as it appears Ghana's copyright right laws do not seem to protect their intellectual property rights.

Figure 12: A woman wearing *adinkra* cloth with appliqué and embroidery techniques

Figure 13: Factory wax-printed white *adinkra* cloth produced by Printex
in Ghana. The cloth is called *Me dunsini abu ɔsoafoɔ ne hwan*

CHAPTER 3

Ɔbɔadeɛ te sɛ obi a ɔretwa puru; ɔno na onim n'ahyase ne n'awieeɛ
Only the Creator of the universe, like the creator of the circle, knows its beginning and its end

ADINKRA SYMBOLS

STYLIZATION

The *adinkra* symbols are based on various observations of and associations between humans and the objects they make and use, floral and fauna scenes, the human body and its parts, and elements of nature and abstract ideas. There is an increased use of phonological script in recent years. Examples of the use of phonological script are to be found in such symbols as *asɛm pa asa* (the truth is gone - #820), *owuo bɛgya hwan* (who will be spared by death? - #110), and *onipa bɛwu na sika te ase* (one will die and leave one's wealth behind - #124).

Adinkra symbols have been classified in the past on the basis of the sources of their derivation - fauna, flora, geometric and so forth. Ofori-Ansah's chart (1978, 1993), for example, classifies the *adinkra* symbols from these sources of derivation. "But symbols," Cohen (1979, p. 90) explains, "are highly complex socio-cultural phenomena and can therefore be classified according to a variety of criteria, depending on the purpose of the classification, which in turn depends on the theoretical problem that is being investigated and the variables that are considered in the study."

In this book the *adinkra* symbols are viewed as a form of writing made up of ideograms and pictograms and, increasingly in recent times, phonograms. This classificatory system is illustrated in Table 2. In rows 1-4 are examples of symbols that are pictograms based on parts of the human body; flora and fauna; celestial bodies; and human-made objects. Rows 5-7 contain ideograms that are in part combination of pictograms that suggest action. For example, the symbol in the quadrant 5a represents a bird holding a snake by the neck (*anommaa ne ɔwɔ* - bird and snake - #218), and 5b represents a mythical bird that flies with the head turned backwards (*sankɔfa* - go back and retrieve - #781). On the other hand, the symbols in Columns 7b-7h are modifications of the symbol in Column 7a. Each modification is based on an addition of another symbol to the *Gye Nyame* (except God - #3) symbol. The symbol in quadrant 7g, for example, is a combination of the *sepɔ* (dagger - #447) with what is essentially the *Gye Nyame* symbol. In Row 8 are examples of phonograms that are based on alphabets in the English and Twi languages. The rise of alphabetic writing dates to contact with Europeans in the 15th century (Gerrard, 1981).

The symbols in Table 3 show some of what Frutiger (1991) sees as the main stages of stylization or degrees of iconization. These stages include the first level of schematization in which the drawing is a recognizable drawing, e.g., *dɛnkyɛmfunafu* (siamese twins crocodiles - #171), *nsakorɔ* (one hand - #238), *sankɔfa* (go back and retrieve - #781), *adwa* (stool - #291), *akofena* (state swords - #261), *ɔhene tuo* (king's gun - #403), and *ɔsrane* (crescent moon - #615). The second stage is a cross-cut representation of the object, e.g., *dɛnkyɛmfunafu* (siamese twins crocodiles - #171), *nsakorɔ* (one hand - #240), *sankɔfa* (go back and retrieve - #784), *adwa* (stool - #281), *bese saka* (bunch of kola nuts - #704), *akokɔ nan* (hen's feet - #518), *ɔhene kyiniiɛ* (king's umbrella - #275), and *mframadan* (wind-resistant house - #532). The other level of schematization is one in which the outward form of the object completely disappears and only a part of the function of the object is explained, e.g., *dɛnkyɛmfunafu* (siamese twins crocodiles - #177), *nsakorɔ* (one hand - #239), *sankɔfa* (go back and retrieve - #783), *adwa* (stool - #284), *aban* (castle, #248), *gye Nyame* (except God - #10), and *owuo mpɛ sika* (death accepts no money - #109). As Frutiger points, out "in the progressive course of schematization, verbal explanation becomes essential. The stronger the degree of iconization, the more dependent it becomes upon explanatory language" (Frutiger, 1991, p. 230).

Table 2: Writing Systems Encoded in the Akan Adinkra Cloth Symbols

Writing System		EXAMPLES								EXPLANATION
		a	b	c	d	e	f	g	h	
Pictograms	1	Hand	One Finger	Heart	Love Each Other	Eye	Eye	Tear Drops	teeth and Tongue	Parts of the Human Body
	2	Crocodile	Butterfly	Fish Skeleton	Tortoise	Bird	Palm Tree	Leaves	Birds in a Tree	Flora and Fauna
	3	Sun	Crescent Moon	Moon and Star	Star	Water	Lightning	Sky and Earth	Totality of the Universe	Celestial Objects
	4	Stool	State Swords	Gun	Building	Comb	Mrcedes Benz	Cutlass and Hoe	Flag	Human-made Objects
	5	Bird and Snake	A Mythical Bird	Scale	Axe	Opened Container	Berries	Fish and Crocodile	Siamese Twin Crocodiles	Combination of Pictogram Suggesting Action
	6	Circle	Concentric Circles	Circles	Bar or Line	Lines	Hand	Measuring Rod	Partitioning	Ideograms based on Lines and Circle
Ideograms	7	Except God	Predatory Animal	God Loves You	Thy Kingdom Come	God is King	God Unite Us	Death Killed God	Thy Will be Done	Combination of symbols to represent ideas
Phonograms	8	The Alphabets								Combination of pictogram and alphabetic representation
		a	b	c	d	e	f	g	h	

39

AKAN ADINKRA WRITING AND SPIRITUALITY

Abraham (1962, p. 111) indicates that the Akan "expressed their philosophico-religious ideas through art." The philosophico-religious themes in the Akan art tend to be associated with the origins and structure of the universe, life, and social organization. As art, the well-known *adinkra* symbols embody manifold religious, political, philosophical, ideological, and historical associations. They make reference to personal grandeur, political solidarity, prosperity, the peace of the nation, and economic constraint, among other ideas and concepts. The *adinkra* symbols together with other Akan symbols such as those found in gold weights and wood carvings incorporate a considerable amount of material from the various oral genres that include maxims, proverbs, songs, funeral dirges, folktale, anecdotes, and everyday expressions. These genres reflect many important aspects of Akan society such as the aesthetic, religious, ethical, and social values. They record everyday events and social interactions.

The *adinkra* symbols, as well as the other Akan visual symbols and images, were used as a store of information, and were also used for communication. "An Asante," writes McLeod (1976, p. 89), "on being shown a particular image, will attempt to recall or discover the verbal formula to which the image corresponds." The *adinkra* symbols were used to communicate not only among human beings but also between human and spiritual beings. The latter use was probably even more important in the early development of Akan writing. For example, from Rattray's (1927) pioneering study in which he identified about fifty-three symbols (see Appendix #A), as well as from the samples of the *adinkra* cloth collected by Bowdich in 1817 (now in the British Museum – Appendix B), Prempeh I's cloth (now in the National Museum of African Art, Washington, D. C. – Appendix C) and the cloth sent to King Willem l of Holland in 1825 (now in Rijksmuseum voor Volkenkunde, Leiden – Appendix D), one can see that several of these symbols were used for communication between human and spiritual beings.

Table 3: Degrees of Schematization

Level 1: Recognizable Object	Level 2: Cross-cut representation of object	Level 3: Abstract representation of object
Sankɔfa bird	Sankɔfa bird	Sankɔfa bird
Nsakorɔ	Nsakorɔ	Nsakorɔ
Adwa	Adwa	Adwa
Dɛnkyɛmreku Funtumireku Funtumfurafu	Dɛnkyɛmreku Funtumireku Funtumfurafu	Dɛnkyɛmreku Funtumireku Funtumfurafu
Recognizable Object	**Cross-cut representation of object**	**Abstract representation of object**

Table 4 below illustrates some of the early symbols for spirituality that are incorporated in the *adinkra* cloth. *Nyame dua* (God's altar - #67), for example, symbolized the presence of God, God's protection and spirituality. This altar was placed in front of houses to serve as a medium for communicating with God and the spirits of one's ancestors. The *mmusuyideɛ* (sanctity or good fortune - #73) symbol was woven into place-mats that were placed beside the king's bed so that he would step on three times each night before going to sleep (Rattray, 1927, p. 266). This was to wish himself good luck and God's protection as he slept. In the morning, before the king stepped out to undertake his routine for the day, he would touch three times the *biribi wɔ soro* (there is something in the heavens - #134) symbol that hung from the lentil of the bedroom door. Each time he touched the symbol he would repeat: *Nyame, biribi wɔ soro na ma ɛmmɛka me nsa* (God, there is something in the heavens, let it reach me). The king did this to wish himself good luck, high hopes and high expectation for the day (Rattray, 1927, p. 266).

Writing systems are similar to organized religions in some respects of their function and significance. The two have often been closely connected. Sacred scriptures are often written in scripts that are regarded as being sacred as their contents. Language and orthography may be carefully preserved as an essential manifestation of the sanctity of a religion, making its holiness tangible. Antique Arabic script is retained untouched for the Qur'an, ancient Hebrew for the Jewish Scriptures, roman script for Catholic Croats and Cyrillic for Orthodox Serbs. Latin has been critically important in Catholic history, and the language of the King James Bible for English Protestants. The name hieroglyphics means sacred writing. In many cultures, from ancient Egypt to medieval times, the writing system has been seen as so sacred, and has been so complex, that it could be read only by the priestly caste and pious scholars, who supported and were supported by an illiterate aristocracy.

Table 4: Examples of Adinkra Cloth Symbols for Spiritual Communication

Symbol	Narrative
Gye Nyame	The symbol reflects the Akan belief of a SUPREME BEING, the CREATOR who they refer to by various names - e.g., *Ɔbɔadeɛ, Nyame, Onyankopɔn, Twedeampɔn*.
Hye anhye	This represents the idea that GOD, the SPIRIT, never dies, or GOD lives forever. The Akan belief is that the human soul, an image of God, the Spirit, lives in perpetuity. Thus, there is life after the death of the physical part of the human being.
Nyame dua	The symbol represents God's presence everywhere and every time. The Akan used to place the God's altar in front of the house as a sign of God's presence and protection.
Mmusuyideɛ	Every year, a cleaning ritual (***mmusuyideɛ***) was performed in the past. During the ceremony all streets of the townships were swept clean each morning and evening to remove mystical danger and to prevent disease or death from entering the township.
Nyame nwu na m'awu	This symbolizes that there is something in a human being that is immortal and eternal, indestructible and imperishable, and that it continues to exist in the world of spirits. The Akan belief is that the human soul is in the image of God, the Creator who does not die. Thus human soul does not die, or the human soul dies only when God dies.
Biribi wɔ soro	This symbol was hung above the lintel of a door for the king to touch three times repeating the words of the aphorism for good luck, high hope and good expectations as he went out to carry out his duties each morning.
Adwa - Stool	The stool is believed to inhabit the soul of the nation. As a symbol of state power it embodies the past, present, and the future of the nation, that is, it marks continuities across generations and groups and close solidarities between the living and the dead. Through the stool, the king serves as a link between the living and the dead as well as the yet-to-be-born members of the society.

A recent development in the use of *adinkra* symbols for communication between human and spiritual beings has been the incorporation of some of the symbols into the liturgical arts of the Christian Church in Ghana. Crakye Denteh, Quarcoo and others of the Institute of African Studies, University of Ghana consulted with the Labadi Emmanuel Methodist Church as it incorporated five adinkra symbols to convey the Christian theology that the Star Son (*ɔba nyakonsoroma - #136*) of God (*gye Nyame - #3*) became the sacrificial (*musuyideɛ - #71*) lamb (*dweninimmɛn - #333*) for the household (*Fihankra - #530*). Quarcoo (1968, pp. 55-56) illustrates this incorporation of *adinkra* symbols into the liturgical arts of the Emmanuel Church (Methodist) at Labadi, a suburb of Accra thus:

> Worked actually into the walls are motifs usually referred to as Adinkra designs. All along the walls of two long sides of the building are the patterns; namely, the 'Gye Nyame' - God is the answer - or except <u>God</u> [#3]; the eight-ray sun or star [#136]; the 'Mmusuyide' [#71] - sacrifice; the '<u>Dwennimmen</u> [#333],' the sign of a lamb, humility and divinity; and the 'Fihankra [#530],' the household. For the first time, at least in recent times, the attempt has been made to use signs in such sequence as to run as a 'sentence'. God; son of the sky, sacrifice, ram and household. When verbs are supplied, we get something like this — 'God's son became a sacrificial lamb for the household [shown in Figure # 1 below].' This is the core of the Christian message. There is, of course, the cardinal point of the Resurrection on which faith stands.[37]

Figure 1: God's Son Became the Sacrificial Lamb for the Household

Table 5: God's Son Became the Sacrificial Lamb for the Household

God's son became the sacrificial lamb for the household

Other *adinkra* symbols that Quarcoo identifies as having been incorporated in the liturgical arts of the Emmanuel Church are *Nyamedua* (God's altar - #63-71), *akofena* (state swords - #260-264), *mmeramubere* (female cross - #25-28), *mmeramutene* (male cross - #22-24), and *adwa* (stool - #278-292). He writes the following about the *adwa* (stool - #278-292):

> it is a symbol of solidarity, and love; at the same time an artifact whose association with government and politics, magic and ritual, the world of the living and the ancestors, is very significant. It is meaningful to the Ghanaian and it could be made meaningful to the Ghanaian who already know of the black stools, both as altars of the ancestors and the mundane things which help to remind them of their history, unity, solidarity, continuity and link with the dead, the living and the yet-to-be born. This is why it may be a useful visual art to help people to comprehend the teaching of the church about the nature of the Christian Spirit world (Quarcoo, 1968, pp 60-61).

---

[37] Quarcoo's reference to a sequential arrangement of the *adinkra* symbols into a sentence is obviously based on the assumption that all writing systems are of a linear form.

Similarly, the Our Lady of Mercy Catholic Church at Community One, Tema has a front wall with several *adinkra* symbols in relief form (see Fig. 1). The symbols on the wall include *Gye Nyame* (except God - #3-11), *Nyame dua* (God's altar - #63-71) and *Mmusuyidεε* or *Kerapa* (Sanctity or good fortune - #72-80). In Kumasi, The Asante Diocese of the Catholic Church under Archbishop Sarpong has translated liturgical rites and the Bible into Asante Twi; uses Asante symbols in liturgical celebrations; has composed and employs liturgical songs based on local tunes and idioms; and makes use of local musical instruments such as drums, flutes, shakers, and xylophones (see Appendix E). In addition, the diocese has decorated some walls of their congregations with Asante religious art forms, as well as employing locally woven *kente* cloths and vestments for their priests (Obeng, 2000).

Figure 14: Our Lady of Mercy Catholic Church in Tema, Ghana

Also, the Ghana Christian Council of Churches has incorporated the *dεnkyεmmireku funtumireku* (Siamese-twin crocodiles - #172) symbol in its corporate logo in order to emphasize the view that the denominations may differ but they can work together to achieve the common goal of bringing the salvation of Christ to all human beings. Concurrent with the Churches incorporating Akan symbols into their liturgical arts, *adinkra* cloth makers are increasingly utilizing Church icons as new symbols for the cloth. Examples of Church icons that have been incorporated in the *adinkra* cloth include *Yesu asεnnua* (Cross of Jesus - #113-14), *Yesu wuo* (Jesus' death - #111), *bonefafiri* (atonement or forgiveness #886), and *Yesu wusɔre* (the Resurrection of Jesus - #115).

COMPANY LOGOS AND BRANDING

Another recent development in the use of the *adinkra* symbols is their utilization by the Ghana Publishing Corporation and other publishing companies as book cover designs. Also, the symbols have been incorporated in the logos of institutions like the universities, secondary schools and public and private corporations such as the banks (see Table 6). The Ghana Standard Board, for example uses the *hwεhwεmu dua* (measuring rod or standard of measure - #800-801) symbol obviously to depict the nature of the mission of the Board — to set and verify high standards of product quality for the locally produced manufactured products.

Upon taking office as Prime Minister in 1951, Nkrumah was faced with the challenge of uniting the myriad ethnic groups within Ghana's borders to form a single unified nation. This was made even more difficult by the presence of multiple foreign influences, including the lasting presence of British culture, from outside the continent. Nkrumah's solution for dealing with these competing cultural forces was to construct a homogeneous Ghanaian identity based on an idealized African past. As a major component of this plan he sponsored artwork that blended elements of Ghanaian visual culture with symbols from all over Africa. The Nkrumah administration (1951-1966) utilized several *adinkra* and other indigenous symbols on stamps (Fig. 15), coins, and public buildings as part of deliberate effort to promote national identity and to foster national integration and African Personality. These national symbols were designed not only for domestic consumption, but also as a form of branding to project a normative image of the nation to the rest of the world in order to gain legitimacy.

Table 6: Adinkra Symbols as Logos of Some Institutions

Hess (2001) points to Nkrumah's selective use of the Asante *kente*, stool, and royal appellations in developing a national aesthetic. What in the literature has been referred to as Asante art/craft should be properly designated as Akan art. What Kumasi did was to appropriate Akan art in a deliberate policy of using art to build an Asante identity. What Nkrumah did was the intensification of the use of art for national integration and national identity, as well as the use of art to promote the African Personality. In that regard Nkrumah did not only use Akan (Asante) art, but he also used art from the other ethnic groups, particularly Ewe, Ga and the northern ethnic groups.

The Ewe *kente* and drums carved by Ewe woodcarvers featured prominently in some of the arts commissioned by the state. Various new designs were introduced during the Nkrumah era as *adinkra* symbols. These included *yɛ hwɛ yɛn anim* (we face forward- #246), *mmɔfra bɛnin* (#517), *Akosombo nkanea* (#681), *ɔbaa na ɔman wɔ no* (#297), and *komfoaku* (#772).

"The iconic and symbolic photograph of Ghana's declaration of independence from Great Britain on 6 March 1957 shows an emotional and gesturing Prime Minister Nkrumah, along with some of his senior ministers who were all dressed in the 'traditional' smock [*batakari*] typically worn by men in the Northern Territories. Such a symbolic gesture of dress put on by the new leaders of Ghana was meant to emphasize the need for national unity to the far corners of Ghana – from the Northern-most capital of Tamale to the southernmost and national capital of Accra - that all tribal and regional groups in the country were an integral part of the new Ghana. The message of the importance of national solidarity as symbolically expressed in dress was also meant for the powerful Asantes, but also for ideological partners external to Ghana." (Fuller, 2010).

It is quite interesting to note that the northern *batakari* has now become the "t-shirt" of all the major political parties in Ghana. The *batakari* signified national integration, not just a garb for the northerner. The prison garb worn by those CPP leaders who were imprisoned for their role in the 1950 Positive Action became the garb of pride, honor, national integration and national identity. The *kente* would become the cloth for the honorable, not only the royal – as the first all Ghanaian cabinet ministers and members of the national legislature were seen wearing *kente*. Ghana under Nkrumah gave a gift of *kente* cloth, *ɔbaakofoɔ mmu man* (one person does not rule a nation), to the UN to mark the rise of the non-aligned movement in global geo-politics. Ewe and Asante *kente* would eventually be "wrapped in pride" by African Americans and Ghanaians in the diaspora (Ross, 1998). The new Embassy of Ghana building in Washington, DC would appropriate several *adinkra* cloth symbols in branding Ghana in the United States (see Fig. 16).

Figure 15: Postage stamps with *adinkra* symbols issued in 1959 (on the left) and 1961 (on the right) in "branding" Ghana to the world

It needs to be stressed that "the numerous gifts of carved Asante stools, *kente* and so on presented to foreign dignitaries were not the handiwork of state artists." The woodcarvings were in most cases the work of Bambir Brothers who originated from Ajumako Asaasan in the Central Region. The Bambir Brothers were brought to Achimota to work with Antubam on a number of national cultural symbols and branding projects that included the Accra Community Centre, the old Parliament House, the state chair and state stool, the speaker's mace and the presidential sword (*akofenata* - #270).

Other *adinkra* symbols reflect some social interactions. One of my informants at Asokwa explained the story behind the symbol *Onyame adom nti* (by the grace of God - #141) to me thus: Opanin Kwasi Dwoben was commissioned to print *adinkra* cloths for the wife of a prominent national political leader in the early 1960s. After the work had been completed, the woman refused to pay the previously agreed upon price. Opanin Dwoben politely asked the woman to take the cloths for no fee at all. As the woman left, he remarked *Onyame nti me nwe ahahan* (by the grace of God, I will not eat leaves - #141)[38]. Eating leaves among the Akan is associated with sheep and goats in the house and animals living in the wild. He then later came up with the design, *Onyame adom nti* (by the grace of God - #141) to remind himself and tell the world about his encounter with the woman.

Figure 16: Adinkra **cloth symbols on the fence wall in front of the Ghana Embassy, Washington, DC**

Adinkra Symbols and Anansesɛm

There are several of the *adinkra* symbols that encode *anansesɛm* - folk stories. Some of these stories were told to me by some of the cloth producers or bystanders as I interviewed the cloth producers at Ntonso and Asokwa. I will illustrate with three of the many stories that are linked to some of the *adinkra* symbols: *ma w'ani nsɔ dea wowɔ* (be content with your lot - #570), *dadeɛ bi twa dadeɛ bi mu* (some iron can break others - #679) and *seantie yɛ mmusuo* (disobedience may have disastrous consequence - #868).

The symbol *ma w'ani nsɔ dea wowɔ* (be content with your lot - #570) is linked to the story in which

---

[38] Appiah, personal interview at Asokwa, May 24, 1994.

a man decides to commit suicide rather than live in poverty. The man looks for the tallest tree in the forest to hang himself so that no one will find him out. He decides to leave his clothes under the tree for he came to this world naked and he would leave it naked. As soon as he gets to the top of the tree and he makes the noose to put around his neck, he noticed someone running away with his clothes which made him realize that there is someone else poorer than he is. The man quickly climbs down the tree to chase after the other person to get his clothes back. When he catches up with the other person, the other person gives back the clothes and tells the man: *ma w'ani nsɔ dea wowɔ na nea ahia no ne nea wɔawu* - "be content with your lot for the poor person is the dead person. While one has life, one has to make the best of it for life is an opportunity the Creator has given us to do something that is worthwhile."

The story linked to the symbol *dadeɛ bi twa dadeɛ bi mu* (some iron can break others - #679) is a metaphor the Akan use to express the idea that no one is unconquerable. This image derives from the use of chisel or hacksaw (metal) to cut another metal. The story is told of how the leopard taught its cubs to cry: "There is nothing in this world that can overcome us." One day when the mother leopard left to go hunting to feed her cubs, a deer stopped by the leopard's den. He taught the cubs to cry: "There is something in this world that can overcome us." When the mother leopard returned and heard her cubs cry the way the deer had taught them, she was very angry. She decided to teach the deer a lesson in minding his own business. The next day as mother leopard left to go hunting, she encountered the deer. Mother leopard demanded an explanation from the deer why he would teach her cubs to cry: "There is something in this world that can overcome us." Before the deer could utter a word of explanation, the mother leopard jumped to attack him. The deer, being nimble-footed, was able to jump to the side, making the leopard miss him. The mother leopard fell into a thicket of thorns and was fatally injured as she was impaled by a big thorn. As she lay bleeding to death, the deer went to call the cubs to come and see what had happened to their mother. When the cubs came to the scene, they realized that their mother had died. The deer then told the cubs: "If there is nothing in this world that can overcome everyone, your mother would not have died. There is something in this world that can overcome everyone." The story teaches the lesson that no one in this world is unconquerable.

The *seantie yɛ mmusuo* (disobedience may have disastrous consequence - #686) symbol incorporates lessons of respect for the elderly and social control as contained in the *anansesɛm* (folk story) of the same title. In this story a beautiful young woman refused the suggestion of her parents to marry a young man of their choice. This young woman then set some very stiff requirements to be fulfilled by any man who wanted to marry her. One such requirement was that the man should be able to shoot an arrow through a fresh egg without cracking the egg-shell. Many a young man who courted her failed to meet these stiff requirements. One day, a monster turned itself into a handsome looking young man and went to court this young woman. He was able to meet the requirements set by the woman so he married her. A week after the marriage rites had been performed the young man decided to take his wife to his 'town.' When the newly-wed couple reached the groom's 'town,' – in the middle of nowhere in the thick forest - he turned himself back into the monster that he really was. The night that the monster was going to eat up the young woman, there came to her rescue none other than the young man who her parents had chosen for her and she had rejected. He rescued her from the monster and took her back to her home where they got married. Her parents admonished her with the proverb: *obi nware ne kuromanni nnu ne ho na seantie yɛ musuo* - no one does regret from marrying from one's own town, and disobedience may have deleterious consequence. In essence, the devil (that is, one's townsfolk) you know is better than the angel - that is, the stranger - you do not know - #868.

There are numerous accounts of how some of these symbols were developed, particularly in recent years. There is the story of the man who could not afford to buy a Mercedes Benz. He asked for a cloth that is made up of the internationally known logo of the giant automobile manufacturer. If he could not afford to ride in the prestigious car, he could afford to wear its logo in his cloth, hence the Mercedes Benz symbol (#741).[39] Mato (1986) catalogues several of these accounts of historical and everyday events.

Sometimes, two or more symbols are placed together to express an idea or a proverb. An example of this is given by the symbol *ɔdɔ bata akoma ho* (love is in the heart - #484) in which the *akoma* (heart - #470) and *nkotimsefoɔ pua* (hairstyle of the queenmother's attendants - #370) are combined. Other examples include *owuo kum Nyame* (death killed God - #105) and *aboa ɔbɛyɛ nnam no* (predatory animal - #152). Owusu-Ansah (1992), son of Asantehene Prempeh II and a research fellow at the College of Art, University of Science and Technology at Kumase, has developed over one hundred new symbols. Many of his symbols are modifications or adaptations of some of the old symbols, such as *gye Nyame* (except God - #3). In the symbol *Onyankopɔn dɔ wo* (God loves you - #92), for example, the *gye Nyame* symbol is modified to incorporate the heart symbol. He also developed completely new symbols such as *meso nanka mentumi* - #787; *gyina pintinn* - #824; *boa me na me mmoa wo* - #200; and *pagya wo ti* - #634. In the case of symbols such as *owuo sɛe fie* (death destroys the household - #125-127), *asɛm pa asa* (the truth is gone - #822), and *ɛkaa nsee nkoa* (the weaver bird wishes - #595-597) pictorial signs are combined with alphabetical symbols.

The question of authorship of the old *adinkra* symbols is a very difficult one. Though they might have originated from individuals, no helpful information regarding the authorship of old symbols could be gathered from the cloth producers or from other people who know about the symbols. The authorship of contemporary symbols is, of course, easier to determine. The cloth producers generally come up with the symbols and several of these have been catalogued by Mato (1986). Occasionally, individuals may bring their own symbols to be carved and stamped. Examples of symbols that were brought by some individuals to the cloth producers include the *koroyɛ* (unity - #187) and the *benz* (#740-741) symbols[40]. When the Asantehene, Otumfoɔ Opoku Ware II departed for the village in 1999, Teacher Kofi Nsiah of Ntonso created a new symbol which he named *otumfoɔ wuo yɛ ya* – the passing away of the king is a sorrowful occasion (#128). Ɔpanin Teacher Kofi Nsiah himself passed away in 2001, a painful loss as his death marked the closing of a library of indigenous knowledge he stored in his head. Owusu-Ansah's (1992) work, as well as that of Agbo (2006) and Kquofi, et al (2013), is an example of the ingenuity of contemporary artists to "tinker" with and add to the time-honored *adinkra* motifs. The increased use of screen printing techniques and CAD has made it possible for new symbols that encode more ideas and meanings of the society.

Some of these *adinkra* symbols show direct relationship between the objects they represent, and show less abstraction. Other symbols represent something else other than themselves. For example, *nkuruma kɛse* (big okra - #323-331) is used to symbolize the benevolence associated with the practice within the Akan extended family system in which adults raise not only their own biological children, but also the children of others. Children are highly treasured, and being able to bear and raise several children successfully gives one status and prestige in the Akan society. In this sense, the *adinkra* symbols as ideograms and pictograms are to be read in a cultural context.

---

[39] Boadum, personal interview at Asokwa, May 24, 1996.
[40] Appiah, personal interview at Asokwa, May 24, 1994.

Some of the meanings of the symbols as given by their sources of derivation are described in the following sections in this chapter.

SOURCES OF DERIVATION:

Flora and Fauna

The *adinkra* symbols include examples of diverse varieties of flora and fauna. By using plants as symbols, the Akan recognized the sense of beauty in the realm of vegetal life. They also used these examples not so much as ornaments or decoration but much more as drawings with a symbolic content to express life, growth, fertility, procreation, development, and so on. The indigenous flora is mainly represented by fruits (e.g., *nkuruma kɛse* - #323-331, *asaawa* - #763, *bese saka* - #706-712), leaves (e.g., *ahahan* - #854, *Nyame adom nti* - #141, and *adwerɛ* - #119), and seeds (e.g., *wawa aba* - #607-612, and *fofoo aba* - #587-589, peanuts - #710), and plants such as cocoa (#703), *kwadu hono* -#866, plantain (#764), *babadua* (#226), and palm tree (#705).

The symbols based on fauna show how animals have played a very important role as the essential archetypes of all that is instinctive, and as symbols of the principles of material, spiritual, and even cosmic powers. The *Ananse ntontan* (spider's web - #38-41), for instance, symbolizes orderliness, architectural creativity, the structure of dwellings and settlement, and the structure of life and society. This symbol also stands for the sun and its rays and the vitality and creative powers of God. In some Akan stories, God is referred to as **Ananse Kokuroko** (the Great Spider or the Great Creator). The *ɔkɔdeɛ mmɔwerɛ* (eagle's talons - #410-411) and *akoo mmɔwerɛ* (parrot's talons - #408-409) also symbolize the snatching abilities and the strength in the claws of the eagle and the parrot.

For earth-bound human beings, birds with their ability to fly were seen as more than an embodiment of earthly faculties. Domestic birds like the chicken must have been an exception. But even the chicken was seen as an archetype of all that is instinctive. The *akokɔ nan* (hen's feet - #517-523) symbol, for example, depicts the motherhood instincts: tender care, firmness, protection, love and discipline. In her efforts to protect her chicks from the preying hawk, the mother hen may step on her chicks. She does so in order to protect but not to harm them. *Akokɔ* (fowl or rooster - #846-848), on the other hand, depicts gender division of labor (*akokɔbedeɛ nim adekyeɛ nso otie onini ano* - a hen could herself discern the break of the day yet she relies on the cock to announce it)[41], or matrilineage (*akokɔbedeɛ na ne mma di n'akyi* - the chicken follows the hen rather than the rooster). The chicken egg (*tumi te sɛ kosua* - power is like the egg - #197-198) is likened to power as a precious yet delicate thing; it is also a source of life that must be handled delicately and firmly. Too much firmness or careless handling may crush the egg. Other human characteristics are still projected onto animals today, in a manner that finds expression in commonly used similes and metaphors. Thus, the Akan speak of someone being as "humble as a dog" (*kraman ahobrɛaseɛ*), "dumb as sheep" (*woagyimi te sɛ odwan*), and "as eloquent as a parrot" (*n'ano ate sɛ akoo*).

---

[41] Yankah (1995, p. 70) writes, "the same [symbol] now stands for the proverb: *Akokɔbere nso nim adekyeɛ* (The hen also knows the dawn of day), conveying a sense of equality [of woman] with man."

The Human Form and its Parts

The heart, eye, hand, mouth, and the head are some of the parts of the human body that are used as *adinkra* symbols. The head is reflected in the symbol *tikɔrɔ nkɔ agyina* or *tikɔrɔ mmpam* (one head does not constitute a council - #192-193). This means one person cannot rule a nation by oneself. The eye is used to symbolize love (*ɔdɔ aniwa* - #454), sleepiness and the fragility of the physical self (*anikom nnim awerɛhow* - #120-121), self-discipline or being in a state of agitation (*ani bere a, ɛnsɔ gya* - #571-581), agreement (*ani ne ani hyia* - #664), and vigilance (*ɔhene aniwa* - #318-320). The heart is used to express love and devotion (*ɔdɔ firi akoma mu* - #475-478) and patience (*nya aboterɛ* - #470-474). The teeth and tongue symbol (*se ne tɛkerɛma* - #189-191) depicts, in one sense, the interdependence of members of a society in working together to achieve a common goal. In another sense, the symbol represents the reconciling and adjudicating role played by the tongue between the two sets of teeth (Yankah, 1995, p. 49). The hand symbol (*nsakɔrɔ* - #238-240) represents cooperation or power, and the inadequacy of human beings vis-a-vis God. One hand is not big enough to be used to cover the sky. Yet several hands working together in united action may serve to benefit the entire society.

Hairstyles (*pua*) for both men and women served as symbols of status. Women wore varied coiffures to express their social status in terms of age and marital status. Old women wore closely shaven hairstyles (*dansinkran*). The queenmother's attendants wore various kinds of hairstyles (*mmodwewafoɔ pua* - #376-377, and *nkotimsefoɔ pua* - #370-375). Men wore various hairstyles to identify themselves as members of special groups, for instance executioners (*adumfo*), key bearers (*nkwantanan* - #363), and court heralds (*nseniefoɔ*). Before major festivals and ceremonies men would grow their hair long so that status coiffures and special hairstyles would be made for the occasion. Some of the courtiers had coiffures such as *mpuaansa* (three tufts - #364-366), *mpuaanum* (five tufts - #357-362; #892), and *mpuankrɔn* (nine tufts - #195). The *adinkra* symbol, *gyawuatikɔ* (Gyawu's hairstyle of bravery - #389-396), is one such coiffure that was first worn by the war hero, Bantamahene Gyawu.

Human-Made Objects

The *adinkra* symbols include a number of human-made objects such as motor vehicles such as (benz - #740-741, Toyota - #742-743, VW -#738-739), house and buildings (*asɔredan* - #109, *fie* – #544-546), communication devices such as tv - #747-751, and foon - #744-746, and household items such as *kɛtɛ* - #513, *kyiniiɛ* - #271-275, *nsaa* - #806-810, *mpaboa* - #224, *kɛntɛn* - #765, *toa* - #730, *apaso* - #684, and *duafe* - #463-469. The *etuo* (gun - #404-407), for example, has been incorporated in funeral and political rituals as discussed below. Motor vehicles of all sizes have helped open up the country for development. The motor vehicles and their usage have introduced new social problems as encoded by the symbol *sitia bɛkum dorɔba* (the steering wheel may kill the driver - #715-717). While some meanings attached to these symbols of human-made objects are derived from the prestige and status linked with some of these objects, other meanings are linked to the functional uses of some these objects. The *akuma*, (axe - #695-697), for example, is used for felling trees, but the *adinkra* symbol is metaphorically used as peace symbol as encoded in the following maxim: *Dua biara nni hɔ a ɛyɛ den sɛ akuma ntumi ntwa, nanso asɛm biara yɛ den a, yɛmfa akuma na ɛtwa, na yɛde yɛn ano na ɛka ma no twa* - There is no tree that is so hard that it cannot be felled with an axe; however, no matter how intractable a case may be, it must be settled by counseling and negotiations, not with an axe. The symbol is used to connote the view that there is no issue or problem so difficult that it cannot be resolved by peaceful means.

Geometric and Abstract Figures

Geometric figures were obviously drawn from observations of nature. For example, the full moon representing circle (*bosom* or *ɔsrane abɔ puru* - #17) and the crescent moon (*ɔsranefa* - #618-621) representing the semi-circle presented themselves constantly to the Akan's observation. But in nature itself it was difficult for the eyes to meet really straight lines, with precise triangles or squares, and it seems clear that the chief reason why the Akan gradually worked out conceptions of these figures is that their observation of nature was an active one. To meet their practical needs, they manufactured objects that were more and more regular in shape. They built dwellings, stretched bowstrings in their bows, modeled their clay pottery, brought them to perfection and correspondingly formed the notion that a pot is curved, but a stretched bowstring is straight. In short, they first gave form to their material goods and only then recognized form as that which is impressed on material goods and can therefore be considered by itself as an abstraction from the material goods. In similar ways notions of geometric magnitudes of length, area and volume as well as fractional parts (e.g., *abunu* - half and *abusa* - third) and numbers arose from practical activities and observation of nature.

Antubam (1963) explains the symbolic significance of the circle, semi-circle, oval, triangle, squares and rectangles, and other geometric and abstract figures. The circle (*puru* - #17) symbolizes "the presence and power of God, and sanctity in the male aspect of society" (p. 105). Sarpong (1974, p. 101) writes that "the circle is the symbol of the presence and power of God." It also "stands for the life-stream which, as it were, flows continuously." The notion of a circle is embodied in such symbols as *nyame dua* (God's altar - #63-71), *ananse ntontan* (spider's web - #38-41), *mate masie* (I have heard and kept it - #802-805), *mpua anum* (five tufts - #357-362; #892), *adinkrahene* (king of the *adinkra* symbols - #303-310), and *sunsum* (spirit or soul - #42-43). The concentric circles signify the universe and its creator. Only the Creator of the universe, like the creator of the circle, knows its beginning and its end (#17). The Creator is also at the center of the circle.

The square and the rectangles stand for "sanctity in the male aspect of both God and man" (Antubam, 1963, p. 106). They depict such qualities attributed to the nature of God as perfection in wisdom, honesty, justice, courage, fairness, mercy, perpetual growth, or incarnation. The square or rectangular notion (*anannan* or *ahinanan*) is embodied in such symbols as *kerapa* (#72-80), *nsaa* (#806-810), *aban* (#247-256), *fihankra* (#528-533), *mframadan* (#534-536), *nkyɛmu* (#826-827), *kurontire ne akwamu* (#194), *funtumfurafu* (#168-177), *damedame* (#820-821) and *blɔk* (#537-543).

The semi-circle as represented by the crescent moon (*ɔsrane* or *ɔsranefa* - #618-621) symbolizes the female aspect of society. It is a symbol of fertility. "It bears with it all the bounty of the female, tender kindness, grace, and sereneness" (Antubam, 1963, p. 108). Sarpong (1974, p. 102) says the crescent moon shape "bears with it all the beauty and female qualities of the woman - tender kindness, gracefulness and serenity." The *adinkra* symbols *ɔsrane* (or *ɔsranefã*) and *ɔsrane ne nsoromma* depict this notion of the semi-circle.

The straight or upright cross (*mmeramutene* - #22-24 or *asɛnnua* - #113-114) appears in several *adinkra* symbols such as *mmeramutene* (male cross - #22-24), *aban* (castle - #247-256), *kerapa* (sanctity - #72-80), *Nyame nwu na mawu* (I die only when God dies - #55-59), *akomantoaso* (joined hearts - #490-491), *Yesu asɛnnua* (cross of Jesus - #113-114), and *donnontoaso* (doubled drum - #501-509). It symbolizes "the rightful or pious interference of a male parent on earth" (Sarpong, 1974, p. 102). The female cross (*mmeramubere* - #25-28) in the form of X represents "ill-will, negative attitude or evil intention." From this basis "it is a taboo to cross legs; it is bad manners and regarded as contempt of court if one is in an Akan traditional court," and if one is caught sitting with the legs crossed in the Akan traditional court, one may be charged with contempt of the court (Sarpong, 1974, p. 102).

It is used to illustrate the idea of cross roads: the point of intersection called *nkwantanan* (#363) that depicts a central point from which radiate four major roads. The central point stands for the seat of government, while the directions of the roads represent the four major divisional wings of the state. Among the Akan, each traditional area has four divisions, called wings and administered by wing leaders (otherwise known as sub-chiefs, referred to in the Akan language as *Mpakamfoɔ).* Thus, in effect, the right-angled cross is used to signal the power of the head of state. The divisional wings of each traditional area, which are founded on the basis of defensive and warring strategies, include: 1) the vanguard, Adɔnten, led by *Adɔntenhene;* 2) the rearguard, *Kyidɔm,* led by *Kyidɔmhene;* 3) the Right Wing, *Nifa* led by *Nifahene;* and 4) the Left Wing, *Benkum,* led by *Benkumhene.*

The two crosses (*mmeramutene* - #22-24 and *mmeramubere* - #25-28) also symbolize the various attributes of the two sexes which form the very core of Akan gender beliefs and sexual behaviors in the society. These beliefs affect almost all aspects of Akan behavior, from marital relations, care of menstruation and pregnancy, adultery beliefs, and ideas about kinship relations, to details concerning the nature of ancestral propitiation, inheritance, and funerary rites.

The triangle (*ahinansa* - #871-872), as incorporated in the medallion called *adaeboɔ,* symbolizes Nyame (God) as the ruler of the universe which is a continuum of the sky (*ewimu*), the earth (*asaase*) and under the earth (*asamando*). The triangle also symbolizes the pride of state. The triangle is depicted by such other symbols as *ɔdomankoma* (creator - #14-15), *Nyame aniwa* (God's eyes - #19), *and Onyankopɔn bɛkyerɛ* (God will provide - #148).

Other geometric and abstract figures include the chevron or inverted V, which represents growing anew or the vitality of fresh growth (Antubam, 1963). The chevron shape is incorporated in symbols like the *mmodwewafoɔ pua* (hairstyle of the queen's attendants - #376-377), *asambo* (chest feathers of the guinea fowl - #459-461), and *ɔwɔ aforo adobɛ* (snake climbs the raffia palm tree - #215-217).

SOCIAL CHANGE

Hunter and Whitten (1976, p. 409) point out that "writing systems are rich sources of information about language change in general, about the history of specific languages, and about the structures of past languages." Changes occurring in the society serve as sources for new ideas and new symbols. As language, the *adinkra* system of writing has built on tradition and incorporated new ideas, symbols, and words. There is the increased use of the phonological scripts. This is evidenced, for example, by the use of symbols such as ABCD (#853), *asɛmpa asa* (the truth is gone - #823), and *ɛkaa obi nkoa* (someone wishes - #594).

As a record of history, the *adinkra* symbols show evolutionary developments in the cultural, historical, and social relationships that have occurred and continue to occur in the society. With time, the *adinkra* cloth has absorbed most of the existing symbols from other Akan arts and created new ones; it has tended to add and accumulate and appropriate symbols from other cultures to reflect the dynamic nature of the language of the Akan. As a reflection of the changes society is experiencing, the *adinkra* symbols themselves have undergone changes in size and design.

The Akan believe that society is dynamic. This belief is implied by the expression associated with the symbol *mmere dane* (time changes - #837). The dynamic forces that impinge on society result in changes in the society. These changes may be due to fundamental laws of nature and demographic and technological developments, among other factors. The fundamental laws of nature that are encoded in the *adinkra* symbols include development and self-preservation. Development is indicated by symbols such as *mmɔfra bɛnyini* (the young shall grow - #517) and *woyɛ abɔfra a* (while you are young - #566). Self-preservation is encoded in several symbols such as *nni awu* (thou shall not kill - #584) and *ɔbra yɛ bɔ na* (life is a struggle - #661). One is also urged to adapt one's self to suit the changing times and conditions as indicated by the expression *mmere dane a, dane wo ho* (when times change, adapt yourself - #844).

Several of the symbols in the *adinkra* cloths record social changes that have been brought about by both external and internal factors. For example, the *aban* (castle, fortress - #247-256), *kurontire ne akwamu* (council of state - #194), *ɔhene tuo* (king's gun - #404-407), *UAC nkanea* (chandilliers - #760), *benz* - #740-741, *television* - #747-751, *foon* - #744-745, *nsɛnee* (scale - #828), VW - #738-739, Toyota - #742-743, benz - #740-741, *sititia bɛkum dorɔba* - #715-717, and *sedeɛ or serewa* (cowrie shell - #723-728) symbols record specific technological developments and historical events that led to particular changes and factors that influenced the direction of such changes in the Asante (Akan) and Ghanaian society. On one hand, for example, the *nsɛseɛ* (scale - #828) and the *sedeɛ* (cowrie shall - #723-728) symbols point to the monetization of the Akan economy long before direct contact with Europeans. On the other hand, some symbols point to selective borrowing of ideas from other societies. *Etuo* (gun - #404-407), for example, came with the Europeans. It has been incorporated not only in the language, but also into important political as well as funeral rituals of the Akan. When the king-elect takes the oath of office he is given the *ɔhene tuo* (king's gun - #404-407) which he fires to demonstrate his ability to honor his responsibility as the military commander-in-chief to ensure protection, security, and peace in the society. During funerals the gun is fired in the morning to signal the beginning of the funeral, and is fired again in the evening to mark the end of the funeral for the day. The gun salute also serves "as an important means of announcing the event of death and the journey of the deceased to both the living and the dead, near and far" (Nketia, 1969, p. 144, fn 2). This use of the gun is being replaced by the loud booming music from "sound system" that blast out mournful as well as joyous music.

The symbol, *kurontire ne akwamu* (council of state - #194), for example, records the military and governmental structural changes introduced by Osei Tutu in the 17th century. Osei Tutu participated in *ahemfie adesua*[42] (palace training) in statecraft and governance in Denkyira and Akwamu prior to becoming the Asantehene. During his reign he applied some of the knowledge and skills he had acquired from his "schooling" in Denkyira and Akwamu. He was superbly supported in this venture by the legendary Ɔkɔmfo Anɔkye. These changes not only resulted in the strengthening of the Asante military capacity, but also in laying the foundation for increased bureaucratization of the indigenous governmental system (Wilks, 1975, 1993).

The *aban* or *abansoro*[43] (fortress, palace, castle or two-story building - #247-256) symbolizes, in the words of McCaskie (1983, p. 28) "an iconic representation of Culture as an idea." It also records the special relationship between Asante and Elmina. As Yarak (1986) suggests, "wealthy *Edena* [i.e.,

---

[42] Akan *ahemfie adesua* is the subject of discussion in the classic, <u>Forosie</u> by Efa (1968, 1944).

[43] This symbol is said to record the construction of a stone castle in Kumase that was completed in 1822. Variants of this symbol pre-date the construction of this castle. For example, the cloth collected by Bowdich in 1817 has one of these variants of the *aban* symbol. The word *aban* refers to the king's palace and the word *abansinase* refers to the area of the ruined palace or the old place of settlement.

Elmina], *vrijburgher* [free citizens][44] and Dutch merchants placed skilled artisans at the disposal of the Asantehene to aid in the construction of the king's 'stone house' at Kumase during 1819-21." This castle was made of carved stone and was completed in 1822 during the reign of the Asantehene Osei Bonsu (1804-1824). It was roofed with brass laid over an ivory framework, and the windows and doors were cased in gold, and the door posts and pillars were made of ivory (McLeod, 1981). Wilks (1975) referred to the *aban* as "The Palace of Culture." The 'stone house' or two-story building (*abansoro* or *abrɔsan*)[45] represented an adaptation of the structural form of the European castles and forts and architectural designs on the coast.[46] This castle was ransacked and destroyed by the British during the 1874 British-Asante War.

The social changes that the *adinkra* symbols record are not limited to the changes of the past; contemporary changes taking place in the larger Ghanaian society have been and continue to be captured by the *adinkra* symbols. The *adinkra* symbols for Mercedes Benz (#740-741), VW, Toyota, television (#747-751), *Akosombo nkanea* (#681), *foon* (#744-746), and Senchi/Adomi bridge (#768-771), for example, show some of the new technological changes and the new vocabulary that have been introduced into the country. They serve as new status symbols and indicators of economic development in the society. Even though the television[47] was introduced into Ghana only in 1965, it has had a tremendous impact on the entire nation. Another recent symbol that has been added to the *adinkra* symbols is the *foon* - #744-746. The symbol represents the freeing up of the telephone communication system in the late 1990s in Ghana. Mobitel was one of the first private companies that introduced mobile (cell) telephony to break the monopoly of the state-owned telephone company[48]. The mobile (cell) telephony has facilitated improved communication and financial transactions (for example, mobile money services and banking) in the country. Within the last 23 years, Ghana's mobile phone industry has done a fantastic job in providing affordable telecommunications services to the public. This has resulted in a phenomenal mobile penetration rate of over 80 percent. The industry has played a vital role in driving wider economic growth across the country and contributing significantly to the government finances.

In the health sector, for example, Teleconsultation is an innovation to quicken surveillance response and provide prompt health care to people in remote areas and other places cut off by the effects of climate change such as extreme flooding. It takes advantage of mobile telephony where coverage is available, to provide medical consultation services on mobile phones to patients and health facilities at referral levels. It is an initiative of the Climate Change and Health project,

---

[44] The *vrijburgher* were mulatto children descended from African mothers and Dutch fathers. They were considered free citizens as they were subject to Dutch law and not to the traditional law of the Elminas (Feinberg, 1969).

[45] The King's personal residence in the Manhyia Palace is known as *Abrɔnsanase*. The word *abrɔnsan* is derived from the word *abrɔnsan* (European-styled house). *San* is another word in Akan for dan (building or house) as explained to me by Rev. Joseph Yedu Bannerman in a personal interview at Winneba, May 13, 1993. For example, *aburosan* (corn barn), is a raised structure or granary for storing corn.

[46] Dantzig (1980, p. vii) refers to the castles and forts along the coast as "a collective historical monument unique in the world: the ancient 'shopping street' of West Africa." In having a castle built in Kumasi, the Asantehene, apparently wanted to redirect the geography of trade once more through Kumasi rather the coastal area.

[47] The radio was introduced in Ghana in 1935 as part of the colonial government's effort to control the media in the country.

[48] One telephone ccompany uses a collage of adinkra symbols to decorate walls and glass window panes in its stores. The employees wear on Friday factory-made clothes designed with adinkra symbols.

supported by the United Nations Development Programme (UNDP) and Global Environmental Facility (GEF). The project aims to develop systems and response mechanisms to better integrate climate change risks into the health sector. It involves training health sector workers, and it sensitizes decision-making bodies at local and national health policy levels. Health nurses share their telephone numbers with health volunteers, opinion leaders and other community members for timely updates on health situations for prompt medical advice, especially during flooding and other weather related emergencies.

The mobile telephone has also been used in monitoring national presidential and legislative elections to help enhance free and fair elections. In the 2000 elections, for example, the mobile phone was used around polling stations to thwart any potential vote rigging. Through the use of mobile phone people call in to radio and television stations to air their views on various issues. The mobile phone has also become a new status symbol for some people.

Again in the health sector, new symbols like *bɔ wo ho ban* (#896) and *sankɔfo wo rɔba* (#897) are being used to educate the people that condom use is an important measure of protection against HIV (Bennett, 2010). The logo of the Toronto Black Coalition for Aids Prevention (Black CAP) features four *adinkra* symbols that encode "unity, strength, hope and that we are linked together in life and death" (– www.blckcap.org). An HIV/STD intervention program supported by the National Institute of Mental Health of the National Institutes of Health that was tailored for heterosexual African American couples of differing HIV status (serodiscordant) resulted in a significant increase in safer sex behaviors among those couples in a study by Emory University in Atlanta. The intervention programs were culturally based and modeled after the African concept encoded by the *adinkra* symbol, Eban (#527), which symbolizes safety, security, and love within one's family and relationship space. The research finding was published in the July 12, 2010, online issue of *Archives of Internal Medicine*[49]. The Afiya Center in Dallas, Texas addresses the unique needs of women by providing public health education, policy advocacy, community organizing, and leadership development. In addition, they place a special emphasis on the experiences of marginalized women affected by HIV/AIDS and poverty. While many may not be familiar with the term reproductive justice, The Afiya Center, since its inception, swiftly identified the sexual health and reproductive justice framework as effective means to challenge structural power inequalities. The word Afiya is of African-Swahili origin meaning *"health and wellness."* Afiya Center's logo, *Sesa Wo Suban* (#600-603) is an *adinkra* symbol, which means *"life transformation."* The *Sesa Wo Suban* symbol is synonymous with the message the Center purveys as it relates to women's lives. The Center strives to create positive changes in the lives of women by way of education, awareness, and advocacy.[50]

Another recent use of the *adinkra* symbols is to be found in the *Akobɛn* (#397-403) initiative of the Environmental Protection Agency of Ghana. AKOBEN program is an environmental performance rating and disclosure initiative of the Environmental Protection Agency (EPA), Government of Ghana. Under the AKOBEN initiative, the environmental performance of mining and manufacturing operations is assessed using a five-color rating scheme. The name of the environmental rating program—AKOBEN—has its roots in Ghana's tradition of *adinkra* symbols (#397-403), and it stands for vigilance and wariness—a set of behavior that is pertinent for environmental conservation. AKOBEN also signifies alertness and readiness to serve a good cause.

On the other hand, the *UAC nkanea* symbol (UAC lights - #760) does not merely depict the

---

[49] See http://shared.web.emory.edu/whsc/news/releases/2010/07/hiv-std-intervention-program-boosts-safe-sex-behaviors-among-african-american-couples.html

[50] See www.theafiyacenter.org

introduction of street electric lights.[51] It also points to the ubiquitous presence and dominant influence of the UAC (Unilever) Group of Companies and other foreign companies in Ghana as a result of the incorporation of the Ghanaian economy into the world capitalist system.[52]

The Akosombo *nkanea* – Akosombo lights (#681) symbolizes the effort of the Nkrumah administration to transform the Ghanaian economy by undertaking the Volta River Project. The project was to be the catalyst to industrialize Ghana through the development of an integrated aluminum industry and the provision of cheap hydro-electric power. Even though the project has resulted in the extension of electricity to rural areas, it also serves as a powerful reminder of the neo-colonial and dependency nature of the Ghanaian economy.

Kookoo dua (cocoa tree - #703), *bese saka* (bunch of cola nuts - #706-712), and *abedua* (palm tree - #705) are examples of symbols that record about crops that have played important roles in the economy of the society at different times over the years. *Bese* (cola nut) was very important in the trans-Saharan trade long before Europeans had direct contact with the Akan. *Abe dua* became a very important source of vegetable oil for making soap and greasing machines in the industrialization of Europe. Cocoa became important only after the 1880s. Since then it has played a very significant role in the incorporation of the Ghanaian economy into the global system. It symbolizes new sources of wealth and the enterprise of the Ghanaian farmer. In the late 1950s and early 1960s, Ghana supplied about 25 - 50 percent of the world's cocoa. No one seems to question the entrepreneurial and market responsiveness of the peasant cultivators of Ghana with regards to cocoa production. Yet those characteristics alone have been insufficient to lift Ghana from economic backwardness. Cocoa has brought tremendous changes in land ownership and tenure systems, inheritance rights, and some disastrous family relations as well as changes in political developments in the country. Between 1903 and 1930, cocoa production brought both land and labor into the market, and radically transformed the relations of production (Kay, 1972; Austin, 2012). Busia (1951, p. 127) stated as a measure of what the Asante considered to be the disastrous effects of cocoa on family relations that "*cocoa see abusua, paepae mogya mu* - cocoa ruins the family, divides blood relations." Cocoa production carried with it a massive structural change in rural landholdings in the Akan areas. Cocoa production gave rise to very destructive land disputes that wrecked families and villages. Chiefs became willing accomplices in the new scramble for land for cocoa cultivation that disrupted the unity and integrity of traditional society. Ninsin (1991, p. 24) writes:

---

[51] UAC stands for United Africa Company. The Company is a subsidiary of the giant multinational corporation Unilever. One of the first street lights in Kumasi was placed in front of the UAC Store in the Adum section of the city and became an important landmark in the commercial center of the city, hence the name UAC lights (Kusi Boadum, personal interview at Asokwa, May 24, 1994).

[52] UAC and other European companies that operated in West Africa formed the Association of West African Merchants (AWAM), through which the companies operated rings and pools to control the West African market to the chagrin of the Africans. "Awam" has come to mean collusion and trade malpractices in the Akan language in Ghana. Webster and Boahen (1967, p. 267) indicate that so widespread was the influence of the UAC in the AWAM group of companies that Ghanaians made this remark about the UAC: "The earth is Lord Leverhulme's [head of Unilever, the parent company of UAC] and the fullness thereof." In 1947, Nii Kwabena Bonney, the Osu Alata Mantse, formed the Anti-Inflation Campaign Committee in Accra in response to high prices of goods imported into the Gold Coast by the AWAM foreign firms. The boycott had the slogan "We cannot buy; your prices are too high. If you don't cut down your prices, then close down your stores; and take away your goods to your own country." The boycott, energised the campaign for self-rule and Ghana's ultimate independence but the 1948 crossroads shooting was the catalyst.

In the wake of this new scramble, the value of land as a commodity soared. Chiefs responded by, once more, turning communal lands into a source of private wealth: they alienated communal lands to prospective cocoa farmers under various forms of tenancy arrangements.

By the 1920s, these developments had seriously disturbed social peace. For example, the extensive involvement of chiefs in land disputes and destoolments had severely breached the authority of chiefs as well as the stability of the institution of chieftancy itself.

Furthermore, the devastating effect of the cocoa diseases that afflicted acres of farms during the peak period of the 1940s and the 1950s gave rise to the expression: *Sε wo yε kookoo na anyε yie a, san konu wo abε* – when your cocoa farm fails you, go back and tend your oil palm tree (#704).

The *sankonu w'abε* (go back and tend your palm tree -#704) symbol is associated with the devastating effect of a plant diseases that afflicted cocoa farms from as far back as 1910. The three major biological problems that affected cocoa productivity in Ghana were Cocoa Swollen Shoot Virus Disease (CSSVD), Black Pod fungus disease and capsid insects (Hemiptera, Miridae, Padi *et. al.,* 2002; Chapter 2). The diseases proved to be an economic disaster for farmers as their cocoa farms were destroyed. Some farmers abandoned their farms rather than cut out diseased trees. The Cocoa Swollen Shoot Virus Disease (CSSVD) which is spread by the mealy bug, has over the years caused a significant reduction in cocoa production in Ghana. The most effective method of checking the spread of CSSVD is to eradicate diseased cocoa trees and other symptomless trees within and up to a distance of about 15 meters. Though several approaches have been used in implementing the control of the CSSVD through the cutting out and the spraying of diseased trees over the years, all these approaches have been met with fierce resistance from farmers[53].

The diseases also led to the establishment of the Cocoa Research Institute by the government. The colonial government's involvement in the cocoa industry dates back to 1866, when a nursery, which later became the Botanical Garden, was established at Aburi to supply cocoa seedlings to farmers. This led to the rapid development of the cocoa industry in the country. Later in 1947, the colonial government established the Cocoa Marketing Board (CMB) ostensibly to protect the cocoa farmers from fluctuating international prices for cocoa and unfair trade practices of foreign companies such as the Association of West African Merchants (AWAM) group led by UAC in the country. The CMB and other agricultural produce marketing boards, however, became key instruments through which Britain accumulated and siphoned financial surplus from the colonies to rebuild its war-shattered economy after WW II. From 1990 onwards three noticeable changes have taken place in the technology of cocoa production: increased use of fertilizers; the adoption of hybrid cocoa varieties, and greater control of pests and diseased trees (Bohaene, 1999; Edwin, et al, 2003; Gockowski and Sonwa 2007; Teal et al., 2006; Vigneri et al., 2004; Vigneri, 2008).

The artisanal methods used by the Ghanaian cocoa farmer to prepare cocoa beans for further processing by chocolate and cocoa processing manufacturers make the Ghana cocoa a high quality product. Product quality of cocoa from Ghana is world renowned, and it regularly exceeds the most stringent international standards. Exports are handled professionally and efficiently. International loans are repaid reliably. Internal marketing is relatively uncorrupt and effective. This

---

[53] Legg and Owusu (1976.) provide evidence that farmers since the colonial era have resisted the move to cut down the diseased trees with some reported cases of open clashes.

is a home-grown success story, under the stewardship of a state-run marketing board – the Cocobod (i.e., Cocoa Marketing Board – CMB) – which manages almost all aspects of the internal cocoa marketing process and maintains a monopoly on cocoa exports. Given the dismal history of African commodity marketing boards in general, and of Ghana's cocoa marketing board in particular, this success demands explanation. It was not the result of radical transformation but of relatively subtle changes in the system that maintained the undoubted benefits of a centralized monopoly while minimizing its damaging consequences. Success resulted from (1) building on the underlying strength of certain elements in the system, notably quality control and export management, (2) an episode of well-directed reform, and (3) effective policies and organizational structures that protected the farmers' share of the cocoa revenues over time and inhibited the Cocobod return to the politicization it suffered in the past. The case accords with the much-touted but oft-neglected lesson that both context and institutions matter for organizational performance (Williams, 2009).

However, for Ghana, cocoa has accentuated the country's fragile economy as the vicious cocoa price fluctuations on the world commodity market have had devastating effects on the country's balance of payments position particularly in the 1960s and 1970s.

In religion, *Asɔredan*[54](place of worship - #100), *Yesu asɛnnua* (cross of Jesus - #113-114), *Yesu wuo* (Jesus's death - #111), *bɔnefafir* (atonement - #886), and other symbols about Christianity also point to the pervasive influence of Christianity in the country. The Akan who in the past did not build temples in order to worship the Creator have no problem now going to the *asɔredan* (place of worship - #100) on Fridays, Saturdays, or Sundays to worship the Creator. Indigenous religious festivals such as Odwira and Yam Festival have been overshadowed by new religious festivals such as Christmas (*Abibirem Buronya* - #118) and Easter, symbolized by *Yesu wusɔre* (Jesus's resurrection - #115). On the other hand, there has been similar influence of Akan symbols on Christianity in Ghana. I have already mentioned in the early sections of this Chapter how the Christian Church has adopted some of the *adinkra* symbols into its liturgical arts (See Fig. 4). Obeng (1991, 1995) also shows how the Catholic Church, at least the Kumase diocese, as part of an *inculturation* agenda, has incorporated some of the *adinkra* symbols and their ceremonial usage into the annual Corpus Christi celebrations of the Church. Some religious priests of various denominations have incorporated *adinkra* and *kente* symbols in their clothing and vestments.

Figure 17: Seats incorporating *adinkra* symbols, St. John's Catholic Church, Saltpond, Ghana

---

[54] The *asɔredan* was modeled after one of the church buildings at Asokwa according to Appiah in a personal interview at Asokwa, May 24, 1994.

Some symbols have been utilized to reflect and comment on contemporary political developments in the greater Ghanaian society. Even though some of these symbols might have been designed and used long before they became associated with new political developments in the country, such political developments made these symbols more popular or notorious. The *akofena* (state sword - #260-269), *aban* (castle - #247-256) and *kookoo dua* (cocoa tree - #703) symbols have been incorporated into the Ghana national coat-of-arms, which is itself carved as an *adinkra* symbol (*oman asɛnkyeredeɛ* - #242)[55]. Other examples of the *adinkra* symbols that have been associated with contemporary political developments include the use of *akokɔnini* (rooster or cockerel - #846-848), *ɛsono* (elephant - #351-354), *kookoo dua* (cocoa tree - #703), *abɛdua* (palm tree - #705), *owia* or *ɛwia* (sun - #32-397), and *ɔhene kyiniiɛ* (king's umbrella - #271-275) as emblems and signs for various political parties from about the 1940s. *Ebite yie* (some people are better seated, or better placed - #733-735) gained popularity in Ghanaian political discourse during the interregnum of the National Liberation Council (NLC) military junta from early 1966 to late 1969.

Some of my informants at Asokwa, Ntonso and Bonwire explained how the *akokɔnini* (rooster or cockerel - #846-848) symbol was popularized and identified with the Convention People's Party's (CPP) red cockerel symbol in the late 1950s and early 1960s; the *kookoo dua* (cocoa tree - #703) together with *kotɔkɔ* (porcupine - #412-413) was identified with the National Liberation Movement (NLM) in the 1950s; *owia* (sun - #32-37) with the Progress Party (PP) in 1969-1972; and *abɛdua* (palm tree - #705) with the People's National Party (PNP) in 1979-1981.[56]

On the other hand some of these informants[57] were quick to deny any relation between *ɔhene kyiniiɛ* (king's umbrella - #271-275) and the ruling National Democratic Congress's *akatamanso* umbrella symbol. The informants pointed out that what was in the *adinkra* cloth was the chief's umbrella, hence the name *ɔhene kyiniiɛ*. When asked why one of the Asantehene's umbrella had the name *akatamanso*, one of the informants quickly explained that in the *adinkra* cloth he made sure that he deliberately turned the umbrella symbol upside down to show his indignation at the ruling party for appropriating "sacred" chieftaincy symbolism in order to gain legitimacy. If these *adinkra* symbols truly reflect and comment on the contemporary political developments in the country, then one wonders about the deafening silence the *adinkra* producers have maintained in their comments (or the lack thereof) about the military regimes that have dominated the Ghanaian political developments in recent years.

---

[55] The Dutch coat-of-arms (#243) that is found on the cloth that was given as a gift to King Willem I seems to have been drawn not stamped with a carving.

[56] Teacher Nsiah and Agya Yaw Yamaa, personal interview at Ntonso, May 26, 1993; Appiah and Kusi Boadum, personal interviews at Asokwa, May 24, 1994; and Mr. Afranie Duodu and Nana Osei Kwadwo, personal interview at Bonwire, May 24, 1994.

[57] In an interview on May 25, 1994 of five cloth producers at Asokwa who wanted to remain anonymous. The National Democratic Congress (NDC) led by Flt. Lt. J. J. Rawlings came to power in a political party-based election 1992 after nearly eleven years of PNDC military rule under Rawlings. Apparently, their request to remain anonymous lest they may be intimidated explains the seeming silence for *adinkra* producers to create new symbols that address the rule of the military in Ghana for the greater part of the country's existence as an independent nation.

MULTIPLE MEANINGS

As indicated earlier in Chapter 1 semiotics point out that symbols are sometimes ambiguous and therefore open to several interpretations. This characteristic of symbols gives rise to fluidity of meanings. That is, a symbol does not have fixed and, therefore, static meaning. A symbol takes on meaning in some context. This characteristic of symbols may be illustrated by the word "school." There are several views and assumptions held about this word by different people. Some people view it as a place of learning, a process of learning (e.g., formal vis-a-vis informal learning), place of work, place of domination, an authority system, a group of fish, or a group of persons who hold a common doctrine or follow the same teacher. Another example is the word mouse. In everyday usage, a mouse is some type of rodent. In computer usage, mouse is an input device.[58]

Screen-printed adinkra cloth incorporating *adinkra* and *kente* and embroideredsymbols

Table 7: Screen printing and embroidery symbols

A symbol needs not have a single agreed upon meaning. However, though the meanings individuals attribute to symbols will vary, interpretations are not entirely random or personal. "One characteristic of the symbol, as Saussure (1966, p. 68) points out, "is that it is never wholly

---

[58] Compare the meaning of the word "eye" in each of these shifty sentences:
She has a good **eye** for judging distances.
He poked the thread through the **eye** of the needle.
Winds whirled around the **eye** of the hurricane.
An **eye** for an **eye** and a tooth for a tooth.

arbitrary; it is not empty, for there is a rudiment of a natural bond between the signifier and the signified. The symbol of justice, a pair of scales, could not be replaced by just any other symbol, such as a chariot."

As Edelman (1964) writes:

> Every symbol stands for something other than itself, and it evokes an attitude, a set of impressions, or a pattern of events associated through time, through space, through logic, or through imagination with symbol (p.6)...But the meanings, however are not just in the symbols, they are in society and therefore in [people] (p.11)...One understands symbols by looking for people's differing reactions [and in] their meanings and emotions... there is nothing about any symbol that requires that it stand for only one thing, [thus] to define a symbol system [multiple] perspectives must be taken into account (p.21).

Cultural symbols evoke different meanings and feelings for different groups of people in any given society. For example, the Statue of Liberty in the U. S. means different things for various groups of immigrants in the country. For American Indians and African Americans, this cultural symbol evokes mainly negative feelings or lack of reverence. The use of the statue to portray female and maternal images in depicting human ideals: liberty and justice exposes some irony in French and American politics - women had no vote in either France or America in 1886 when the statue was unveiled.

Within a society there is a range of associations and meanings that are attached to most symbols. As participants in a common social order, each member interacts with other members of that order. Through these interactions the members of the society encounter ideas and phenomena, and the members learn from each other definitions for such ideas and phenomena. Meanings and interpretations peculiar to each member become part of the social meanings and interpretations. Through social interaction a society ensures general agreement on how symbols will be interpreted. Within that broad agreement, each individual member may develop specialized refinements of meanings. The result is that there is enough general agreement to communicate with each other, yet there is enough individual variation to make the meaning of any symbol ambiguous. This is because "it is the very essence and potency of symbols," as Cohen (1979, p. 87) puts it, "that they are ambiguous, referring to different meanings, and are not given to precise definitions."

Adinkra symbols, as cultural symbols, are no exception to this characteristic of symbols. Some *adinkra* symbols have precise and unambiguous meanings. Other *adinkra* symbols have multiple meanings. In this respect, the *adinkra* cloths function in a way that is similar to certain aspects of language as described by such linguists as Ferdinand de Saussure. He identifies what he calls the quality of "mutability," by which he means that the linguistic sign, being dependent on a rational principle, is arbitrary and can be organized at will (Saussure, 1966). This suggests that linguistic signs change their meaning over space and time. Similarly, one sees that the messages communicated by the symbols shift in meaning depending on the context in which they operate.

The meanings of *adinkra* symbols are heavily context dependent and there is considerable variability in how the symbols are understood by different social strata and taste groupings. The meaning of some of the symbols slightly changes from place to place, while some symbols represent more than one proverb or maxim in the same locality. This characteristic of ambiguity is sometimes exploited to strategic advantage. For example, the *dɛnkyɛm* (crocodile - #345-350) symbol is used to express "adaptability," a view that is based on an observation of the fact that the crocodile lives in water, yet it does not behave like fish; it breathes oxygen directly through its nostrils unlike the fish that absorbs oxygen from water through its gills. From this observation the symbol means adaptability of one to changing circumstances in life. The same symbol expresses "greatness of power," a view that is based on another observation of the way the crocodile carries its eggs in its mouth. This behavior of the crocodile is taken to symbolize the idea that the crocodile is powerful to the extent that it can swallow a stone. A king wearing an *adinkra* cloth with the symbol will be communicating to his subjects how powerful he is.

The symbol *nkyinkyimiiɛ* (zigzag - #605-609) is interpreted as zigzag in one sense or change and adaptability in another sense. Cowrie shells (*serewa* or *sedeɛ* - #723-728) were once used as currency and, therefore, symbolize wealth and affluence. They are also used by priests for religious purposes, and they, therefore, symbolize sanctity. On the other hand, *bese saka* (#706-712) expresses wealth when *bese* is used as currency or seen as an important cash crop. *Bese*, when used to welcome visitors, symbolizes hospitality. In another context *bese* is used as a symbol of wisdom and knowledge as in the aphorism *Bese pa ne kɔnini ahahan yɛtase no ɔbanyansafoɔ* (It takes the knowledgeable and wise person to distinguish between the very similar looking leaves of the red and white kola tree - #854).

Also, the meaning of a symbol is often obscure because it involves time and space, cultural, and historical relationships which are not always clearly understood. Since the symbolic meaning is obscure and subject to various interpretations, a few particular symbols have more than one name and meaning in different localities. For example, some people call the *blɔk* (cement or cinder block - #537-543) *dame dame* (checkers - #820-821) and vice versa. *Ahahan* (leaves - #854) has been associated with different interpretations in different areas and/or at different times such as *wodu nkwanta a, gu me ahahan* (leave me a sign at the intersection), *yɛnkɔte aduro a, ene ahahan* (go fetch medicine does mean mere leaves), or *bese pa ne kɔnini ahahan, yɛtase no ɔbanyansafoɔ* (it requires skill and experience to distinguish between the similar looking leaves of the red kola and white kola leaves).

In this chapter, I have given examples of how the *adinkra* cloth producer used signs and symbols to translate and store concrete information into abstract markings. Such usage served to remove the data from their context. For example, the sighting of the moon as *ɔsranefã* (crescent moon - #618-621) or *ɔbosom abɔ puru* (full moon - #17) was abstracted from any simultaneous events such as atmospheric or or social conditions (e.g., partly cloudy night). These signs and symbols also separated the knowledge from the person presenting data. For example, the *Onyame adom nti* (by the grace of God - #141) symbol presented the encounter between the cloth producer and his customer in a "cold" and static form, rather than the "hot" and flexible oral medium which involved voice modulation and body language.

In the rest of this book the *adinkra* symbols are classified on the basis of the concepts deduced from the narratives that are associated with the symbols. In order to discuss what the *adinkra* cloth producer wrote about Akan political beliefs, political and social organization, social values and family relation several *adinkra* symbols are grouped together into these broad thematic areas. The discussion of these themes is constrained by the number of *adinkra* symbols I have been able to identify. This deficiency is not limited to the *adinkra* system of writing. Hunter and Whitten (1976, p. 409) note that

> Writing systems which depend heavily or exclusively on any one of these three
> principles - pictograph, ideograph, logograph - are subject to "overloading": unless

the range of information to be represented is narrowly limited, a tremendously large number of signs is required.

Adinkra symbols as either a pictographic or ideographic system require a wide number of symbols to represent the wide range of ideas and thoughts of the Akan. This poses an "overloading" problem. The constraints of "overload" and not being able to identify all the *adinkra* symbols that have ever been used pose problems for a fuller examination of Akan thinking on the various themes discussed in the following chapters. Cloth, as a main medium in which several of the *adinkra* symbols have been encoded, is a perishable product. Besides, more new symbols are being created as part of the dynamics of a living language. In Ghana, traditional cloths like *kente*, *adinkra*, and *akunintam* that are hand-made are predominantly the preserve of the nobility and the royalty. As such, all important and sizeable collections are owned by royal courts, and are kept very confidential and very private with their own protocols and attendants. To gain access to the various collections has proved very daunting. Historic collections such as those at Akwamufie, Denkyira, the Akyem states, the Bono states, Manhyia and other paramount chiefs' collections have been difficult to be accessed, assessed and documented. Time and resources available to me have been limited and constraining. This creates the possibility that other *adinkra* symbols exist somewhere that I have not been able to identify. Or, perhaps I have not been able to draw on the extensive Akan oral literature to provide a more elaborate synthesis of what *adinkra* cloth and its symbols store and communicate. Therefore, the discussions that follow in the subsequent chapters should not be construed as limitations of Akan thinking.

CHAPTER 4

Nyame nwu na mawu
If human beings cease to exist, God ceases to exist

CONCEPTS OF THE UNIVERSE, GOD, SELF, AND SPIRITUALITY

THE UNIVERSE AND GOD

An essential basis of a people's cultural heritage is found in their views of the nature and structure of reality with regard to what is the meaning of existence, what is the nature and structure of the universe (does order exist out there in the world or do humans invent it?), and freedom or the lack thereof to make choices. Two main sources of information about the Akan view of the universe are oral sources including myths, proverbs, names, songs, prayers, vows, curses and blessings; and visual symbols and images to be found in vehicles like art, architecture and symbolic gestures of rites and rituals. These diverse manifestations have much to tell us about Akan perceptions of the universe, the nature and structure of reality, and the role of the human being in the universe. The Akan view the universe as a creation of a Supreme Being, whom they refer to variously as *Ɔboadeɛ*,[59] *Nyame, Nyankopɔn, Ɔdomankoma, Ananse Kokuroko, Ɔmaowia, Nana, Ɔmansuo, Toturobonsuo,* and *Twedeampɔn Kwame.*[60] This creator was viewed as being androgynous, that is, the creator was

---

[59] This Creator is envisaged as fire. The life-giving spirit or power that animated the fire and caused the birth of the universe is the vital force (*kra* or *ɔkra*) which enters the human being at birth.

[60] Akan give the following names and appellations to God:

Onyankopɔn	Alone; the Great One; the Supreme Being
Bɔrebɔre	Creator; Excavator; Hewer; Carver; Architect; Originator; Inventor
Ɔboadeɛ	Creator
Ɔdomankoma	Infinite; Boundless; Absolute; Eternal; Prometheus; Inventor
Obiannyɛwo	The Uncreated One
Tetekwaframua	He who endures from time immemorial and forever; One whose beginning and end are unknown; Alpha and Omega
Twedeampɔn	The Dependable One
Brɛakyirihunuade	All-knowing; All-seeing; Omniscient

simultaneously man and woman, possessing both the male and female qualities. Yet God is beyond both male and female.

The creator first created the Heavens (*ɛsoro; wimu*), Earth (*wiase; asaase*) and, the underworld or the spiritual realm (*Asamando*). The creator then populated the heavens with the sun (*owia - #32-37*), moon (*ɔsrane or ɔsranefa - #618-621*) and stars (*nsoromma - #130-138*), and populated the earth with human beings, plants, rocks, the sea, rivers, and animals. In time (*mmere*), the creator made day and night (*hann ne sum - #20-21*).

The Akan concept of the totality of the universe is depicted by the symbol *abɔdeɛ santaan* (totality of the universe - #1-2). This symbol incorporates the eye, the rays of the sun, the double crescent moon all of which are part of nature, and the stool which is human made. The universe, according to the Akan's worldview, is a natural as well as a social creation.[61] The natural aspect of the universe includes the celestial bodies[62] like the sun (*owia or ɛwia #32-37*), the moon (*ɔsrane - #618-621*), the stars (*nsoromma - #130-138*), and elements like wind,[63] lightning and thunder (*anyinam ne aprannaa - #45-46*) and water (i.e., rain - *nsuo - #47-50*), as well as human beings and plant and animal lives.

One of the expressions the Akan use to express this totality of the universe is: *Ɔdomankoma Ɔbɔade, ɔbɔɔ ɛwia, ɔbɔɔ ɔsrane ne nsoromma, ɔtɔɔ nsuo, ɔbɔɔ nkwa, ɔbɔɔ nipa, ɔbɔɔ owuo, na ɔte ase daa.* This means God the Creator, He created the cosmos - the sun, the moon and the stars and rain; He created life, the human being, and death; the Creator is immortal. The Akan, therefore, believe in a God they regard as the Great Ancestor, the true high God. He is the Creator who has always existed, and will always exist as symbolized by *hye anhye* (unburnable - #51-54) and Nyame *nwu na mawu* (I die only when God dies - #55-59). The Creator is also represented by other symbols such as *Ɔdomankoma* (Creator - #14-15), *puru* (circle - #17), and *Ananse Kokuroko* (spider - #38-41). The circle (*puru - #17*) represents the universe and its creator. Only the creator of the universe, like the creator of a circle, knows its beginning and its end. The creator is at the center of the creation. The *ananse ntontan* (spider's web - #38-41) represents the orderly structure and organization - the architectural design - of the universe.

Otumfoɔ	The Powerful One; Omnipotent
Atoapem	Ultimate; Final; Unsurpassable
Ɔmaowia	Giver of Sunshine; Source of Warmth and Vitality
Nana	Grand Ancestor
Toturobonsu,	
Ɔmansuo	Giver of Rain; Rainmaker
Ananse Kokuroko	The Great Spider; The Wise One; The G reat Designer
Amaɔmee	The Provider; Giver of Sufficiency

[61] The Akan have various stories to explain the beginning of the universe. Each story attributes the universe to a spiritual creator. The drummer, for example, believes God created the word and the drummer first. The drummer, in turn, created the drum with which the drummer spread the word.

[62] The Akan knew of other celestial bodies (*okyin nsoromma - planets*) like Mars, Venus, Jupiter, Mercury and Saturn in addition to the moon, stars and the sun (Meyerowitz, 1951). *Wi* or *ewi* is the space encompassing the earth (*asaase*). *Ɛwia* or *awia* is the sun, and *ewiase* or *wiase* is the visible world under the vault of heaven. Dunn (1960) also indicates that the *kyɛkyɛ* star is the planet Venus and that Fantse fishermen knew about the Milky Way.

[63] The wind is believed to be the messenger of God; hence the expression: *Wopɛ asɛm aka akyerɛ Nyame a, na wo ka kyerɛ mframa* (when you want to send a message to God, you tell it to the wind).

Attributes of God

The *Gye Nyame* (Except God - #3-11) symbol means that no one lived who saw the beginning of the universe and no one will live to see its end except God. He is further seen as the Creator par excellence, the Great Beginner or infinitely manifold God (Danquah, 1944). He is also personalized as *Onyankopɔn Kwame Atoapem*, the Great one who appeared on Saturday (Busia, 1954).

In Akan belief, the Creator is the source of all things (*Ɔdomankoma* - #14-15) and there is nothing beyond Him (*Onyankopɔn bɛtumi ayɛ* - #107). No one knows what the day will bring forth except God the Creator (*obi nnim adekyeɛ mu asɛm* - #60). *Nyame yɛ ɔdɔ* (God is love - #92). He has great love for His creatures and He shows His care and compassion for them by providing for their needs (Opoku, 1978, p. 28). It is by the grace of God that we live as depicted by symbols such as (#88;141;150-151). God provides us with sustenance (*Onyankopɔn ma yɛn aduane daa* - God, feed us always - #90). He sees all things (*Brɛakyihunadeɛ, Nyame yɛ huntahunuiɛ* - #18-19), and protects us (*Onyankopɔn bɔ yɛn ho ban* - #87). And He fills the pot of the poor with water (*Nyame na ogu ahina hunu mu nsuo* - #47-50).

Land - Mother Earth

To the Akan what is real is of a dual nature with corporeal-spiritual[64] and male-female components. The Akan see reality as "unity in duality comprising two conflicting elements" (Dzobo, 1992, p. 130). *Nyame* is the Spiritual component - the creator and giver of life. Mother Earth (*Asaase Efua*) is the physical component of the duality - the sustainer of life. The Akan have an image of a masculine God and feminine Earth (hence the female name *Asaase Yaa* or *Asaase Efua* for Earth and *Onyankopɔn Kwame* or *Kwame Atoapem* for God).[65] The Akan regard Nyame as the Elder vis a vis Earth, hence the expression: *Asaase trɛ, na Onyame ne panin* (Of all the vastness of earth, God is the Elder). The Akan believe that no one created God, thus God is referred to as *Obiannyɛwo* (The Uncreated One). On the other hand, the Akan wonder about what God created first in the universe and they ask questions like: *akokɔbedeɛ ne kosua, hwan ne panin?* (hen and the egg, which came first? - #118).

The symbol *asaase yɛ duru* (the Earth is mighty, #29-31) signifies the importance of land. The expression *tumi nyinaa wɔ asaase so* (all power is in land) underscores the importance of land to the Akan. *Asaase* (land) is not only the sustainer of life, it is also considered as the source of power. It has the power of fertility and it is her spirit that makes plants grow.[66] Mother Earth receives the newly born, sustains the living, and receives the dead back into her womb on internment. Before a grave is dug, a prayer is offered to ask permission of Mother Earth for her child to be buried in her womb (Opoku, 1978).

Akan custom teaches that the way God's gift of land is utilized reflects the spiritual and social

---

[64] There is no corresponding Akan word for 'matter' in the abstract sense. The missionaries invented the word *famadeɛ* (*famu adeɛ* - literally thing of the ground) to translate matter in the Bible. The Akan words for body or form cannot be generalized to mean matter as the opposite of spirit.

[65] Akan give first names to their children according to the day of the week on which the child is born and the sex of the child. There are seven first names for girls and seven for boys. *Yaa* is the name for a girl born on Thursday and *Efua* (or *Afia*) is the name of a girl born on Friday. Kwame is the first name for a boy born on Saturday. The name is said to be the soul name (*kradin*) indicating the day of the week the soul (*sunsum* or *kera*) entered the child at birth or the day of the week on which the spiritual being entered the physical world (see the section on Time in Chapter 10).

[66] Akan do not regard *Asaase* (Earth) as a deity to be worshipped as indicated by the maxim: *Asaase nyɛ bosom, ɔnkyerɛ mmusuo* - The earth is not god, she does not divine.

fabric of society. For example, the Akan consider it a crime to have sexual intercourse in the fields. People are advised to refrain from polluting the land and its rivers, streams, lakes and the sea or contaminating nature in any way that can be deemed adverse to human life. Proper land use is evidence of faithfulness to God and Mother Earth and is reflected in the health or prosperity of the society. Unjust and destructive land use, on the other hand, is believed to spell social, economic or spiritual disaster, crop failure, and epidemics. The logic here is simply that one cannot expect to do harm and violence to nature and Mother Earth, the bearers of life and existence, without precipitating crises in a society's economic, social, spiritual, animal, plant and human life. The contemporary practices of individual appropriation of land for illegal mining of minerals (gold and diamond) and/or for winning sand for building construction have led to environmental destruction and pollution of water bodies. These practices have also led to health problems such as the spread of malaria in the rural areas as ponds left by these illegal activities serve as breeding grounds for mosquitoes and other water-bourne diseases in the rural areas. Such illegal activites are inconsistent with Akan beliefs about land utilization.

The Akan believe that land as sustainer of life, ought to be owned communally.[67] Membership in the matriclan family entitles one to usufruct right in land. This belief has been punctuated and undermined by recent developments in land ownership and tenure that have resulted in individual appropriation and ownership of land. For example, the development of farms on which are planted perennial crops such as cocoa, citrus, and oil palm trees has resulted in individual ownership of land. Urbanization and development of housing for rent have also affected the traditional land ownership.

Self

The Akan belief is that the human being is made up of a physical part - a system of tissues and bones (*honam* or *nipadua*). The human being is also made up of a system of traits, habits, and attributes; that is, a personality. The Akan believe that while one is a system of tissues and bones and a personality, one is more importantly an enduring unity of experiences, a self.

In the Akan thought, anything which exists in its natural state has *sunsum* (spirit or soul - #42-43). *Sunsum* is the essence of the being or object; its intrinsic activating principle. *Sunsum* is derived ultimately from the Supreme Being, the Creator and source of all existence. The symbol *Onyankopɔn adom nti yɛte ase* (By God's grace we live - #88) conveys the Akan belief that without the life-giving force from God, the human being ceases to exist. Another symbol that captures this idea is the one that alludes to the essential nothingness of human beings (*woyɛ hwan?* - who do you think you are? - #123). Without the spiritual essence, the physical aspect of the human being is fragile and mortal as indicated by the symbols *owuo bɛgya hwan* (who will be spared by death? - #110), *owuo de dɔm bɛkɔ* (death will claim the multitude - #106), *owuo atwedeɛ* (death's ladder - #101-104), and *anikum nim awerɛhoɔ* (sleep does not know sadness - #120-121). The *anikum nim awerɛhoɔ* symbol conveys the idea that the spirit may be willing, but the body may be weak.

The Akan believe that the human being is created in the image of God and the birth of a child marks the infusion of the spiritual and the physical aspects of life into the human being. The human being as an image of the Supreme Being is born sacred and free of sin (Antubam, 1963). The human

---

[67] The Akan society is a continuum that comprises the dead, the living, and the yet-to-be-born. Land is used by the living members in such a way that it will be preserved for use by the yet-to-be-born members of the society.

being has both a physical body and spiritual part - the soul (*Ɔkra, kra* or *Sunsum*)[68] - which enters the body with the child's first breath at birth. The spiritual part is indestructible (*Nyame nwu na mawu* - #55-59) and imperishable (*hye anhye* - #51-54), hence the belief in life after death and reincarnation.

The concept *sunsum* has often been translated from the psychological perspective as personality, ego or character (Busia, 1954; Meyerowitz, 1951). Danquah (1944, p. 22) describes *sunsum* as "the power that sustains a person's character or individuality." Busia (1954, p. 197) writes: "*Sunsum* is that which you [the man] take with you to go to the side of the woman and lie with her; and then the Onyankopɔn, the Great One, will take his *kra* and bless your union." The Akan view the human being as a trinity (*agya, ɔba ne sunsum krɔnkrɔn* - #85) or triadic composite of *mogya* (blood) which is received from the mother; *sunsum* (spirit, personality) which is received from the father; and *kera* or *kra* (soul, spirituality) which is received from God, the life-giving force. This trinity[69] gives rise to the following relationships:

Mother	Father	God
Mogya	*Sunsum*	*Kra (Ɔkra)*
Abusua	*Ntorɔ (or Asafo)*	Spirit (Soul, Spirituality)

Kwame Appiah (2004), perhaps, gives a clearer summary of the Akan concept of a person in his tripartite analysis of such in the Asante tradition when he says:

> ... a person consists of a body (*nipadua*) made from the blood of the mother (the *mogya*); an individual spirit, the *sunsum,* which is the main bearer of one's personality; and a third entity, the *okra*. The *sunsum* derives from the father at conception. The *okra*, a sort of life force that departs from the body only at the person's last breath; is sometimes as with the Greeks and the Hebrews, identified with breath; and is often said to be sent to a person at birth, as the bearer of ones *nkrabea*, or destiny, from Nyame. The *sunsum*, unlike the *okra*, may leave the body during life and does so, for example, in sleep, dreams being thought to be the perceptions of a person's *sunsum* on its nightly peregrinations... (Appiah, 2004, p. 28).

The Akan view of personhood has, like many other metaphysical and moral conceptions, far-reaching effects on social practices and institutions. Using facts about these practices and institutions to reconstruct a conception of personhood underscores another important general theme in African philosophy: the practical implications of philosophical principles on everyday life. For the Akan, judgments about personhood are not matter of merely academic interest, but play an important role in shaping and supporting their highly communal social structure. To the extent that the Akan notion accommodates a common humanity as an innate source of value, it supports moral equality. At the same time, its emphasis on the social bases of personhood helps firmly to embed trust, cooperation, and responsibility to the community in cultural practices. The Akan philosophy of persons thus represents an attempt to resolve questions of identity, freedom,

---

[68] *Sunsum* and *Ɔkra* are often used interchangeably and may appear to be synonymous. Another aspect of one's spirituality is the concept of *ntorɔ*. *Ntorɔ* is traced patrilineally, and the following is a list of some of the *ntorɔ* groups: *Bosompra, Bosomtwe, Bosommuru, Bosomafram, Bosomayensu,* and *Bosompo.*

[69] The Akan view of trinity is also to be seen in the *ahinansa* (triangle - #) symbol.

and morality in favor of a communalistic way of life that has evolved as a rational adaptation to the exigencies of survival under harsh conditions (Wingo, 2008).

Nkɔnsa, woyɛ hwan? Ahemfo koraa yɛwo wɔn (Nkɔnsa, who are you? Even kings are born - #123) symbolizes the Akan idea that without God's grace and the life giving force of God, the human being is essentially nothing. And, what God has ordained no human being can change (*nea Onyankopɔn aka abɔ mu no - #99*, or *asɛm a Onyankopɔn adi asie no - #83*).

Destiny and Determinism

God is believed to give also to each individual, *nkrabea* (destiny, fate - #86). *Nkrabea* (destiny) is believed to determine the uniqueness and individuality of a person. The unique characteristics of individuals reflect the differences in individuals' destiny. This view is expressed thus: *ɛsono onipa biara ne ne nkrabea* – each person and/her unique destiny, and is indicated by the symbol *nkrabea* (destiny - #86). This view is also indicated by the aphorism: '*Nyame amma akyemfra hwee no, na ɛnyɛ ne ntware ho a*' - if God did not give anything at all to the swallow, it is not its swiftness and turning ability; this is associated with the swallow (*akyemfra* - #157-158) symbol. That is, God gave each individual some ability, talent or potential. No one can change the destiny God gives to one (*asɛm a Onyankopɔn adi asie no - #83*). Does the *nkrabea* then pre-determine what one can be? The Akan tend to believe that determinism exists. That is why they say: *kurotwa mansa tɔ nsuo mu a, ne ho na ɛfɔ, ne ho nsesan no deɛ wɔ hɔ daa* – the leopard may get wet, but that may not wash away its stripes (#691-692). Also, the Akan believe that when God was giving destiny to one no one else was there - *obi rekra ne Nyame na obi foforɔɔ ngyina hɔ bi* (Gyekye, 1987).

SPIRITUALITY

Even though the Supreme Being is the ultimate Spirit and the human being has been created in the image of God, the Akan believe that there are lesser spirits (*abosom ne asaman*), some good and some evil. The good ancestors serve as the good spirits that protect the living from the misdeeds of the evil spirits. The Akan believe in the abiding presence and protection of God, the Supreme Being who is always available as an ultimate recourse for those in difficulty. The Akan religious thought is essentially theocentric and theistic, with God at the center of it all. In this respect God is referred to as *Adinkrahene* (king of the *adinkra* symbols - #303-310; #314-315) and God is king (*Nyame yɛ Ɔhene - #13*).

The Akan believe that God interacts with humans by using vehicles like the sun (*ewia*), rain (*nyankonsuo*), wind (*mframa*) and the rainbow (*nyankontɔn*). Humans, in turn, interact with the Creator through prayers. The wind becomes a very important vehicle in humans' interaction with God as indicated by the expression: *Wopɛ asɛm aka akyerɛ nyame a na woka kyerɛ mframa* - if you wish to say something to God, you tell it to the wind. When prayer is offered to God, He is approached without priests or intermediaries. The Akan believe that everyone has direct access to God, and one's relationship with God is personal and does not require an intermediary or temple. Prayer may be offered at any place for God is Almighty, All-seeing (*Onyankopɔn aniwa hu asumasɛm biara* or *Nyame yɛ huntahunni*, also *Breakyihunadeɛ Nyame, ohu asumasɛm biara - #18-19*), and Omnipresent. He is believed to hear the slightest voice and the humblest cry (Sarpong, 1974). God is invisible, but He is believed to be everywhere just as the air we breathe is everywhere and is invisible.

Akan sacred praises or praise poems are acts of worship and offering to the Supreme Being.

The sacred praises of God offer the Akan the opportunity to share in God's strength and glory, His beneficence and beauty and in His creation and His active care of it. The Akan praise God as King (*Onyame yɛ Ɔhene* - #13). God rescues the humble and helps the needy. The Akan in this respect say: *Ankonam boafoɔ ne Onyankopɔn* (God is the helper of the lonely - #418) and *Aboa a onni dua no, Nyame na ɔpra ne ho* (God cares for the destitute). Also, God fills the pot of the lonely (*Nyame na ogu ahina hunu mu nsuo* - #731). The Akan also praise God as the physician that has the cure for all diseases. God is believed to look out for the interest of the disadvantaged. An example of this attribute of God is depicted by the symbol *wobu kɔtɔ kwasea* (if you fool the crab - #762) which is associated with the maxim: *wobu kɔtɔ kwasea a, Nyame hunu wo to* (If you fool the crab God sees your rear end). In this sense, the Akan believe in a just God.

To say that the Akan did not establish temples for worship of God nor did they have a hierarchy of priests is not to suggest that God was not regularly mentioned in prayer. Almost every Akan prayer begins with the mention of God. The Akan also see the need to make periodic and occasional supplication and sacrificial offers (*Mmusuyideɛ* - #72-80, *Nyame Dua* - #63-71) not only to invoke the good spirits to protect them from the machinations of the evil, but also to atone for any misdeeds and evil intentions of one or the community. *Nyame dua* (#63-70) is the altar from which *Nyankonsuo* (God's water) was used to bless members of a household when purification and propitiation ceremonies were performed. On such occasions, the head of the household (if it is a household ritual) or the *abusuapanin* or his deputy (head of the family, if it is a family ritual) serves as the "religious leader" or master of ceremony.

When the Akan people pray, as reflected by the symbols (*mesrɛ nkwa tenten ne nkɔsoɔ ma wo* - #62, and *momma yɛmmɔ mpaeɛ* - #81), they invoke the powers of *Nyame* and *Asaase Yaa*.[70] Life, fertility, abundance, prosperous and long life, peace, God's grace and protection - these basic virtues form the recurrent theme of most Akan prayers. These prayers show that the Akan value human life above all material things. The Akan also through their prayers ask for signs of God's nearness – that is, they ask for rain, food, prosperity, long life and peace. These recurrent ideas expressed in Akan prayer are best captured by the following prayer:

> *Yɛsrɛ wo nkwa,*
> *Yɛsrɛ wo adom;*
> *Ɛmma yɛnwu awia wuo,*
> *Ɛmma yɛnwu anadwo wuo;*
> *Yɛkɔ nnae a, yɛnwo ba;*
> *Yɛdua aduadeɛ a, ɛnso aba pa;*
> *Ma asomdwoeɛ mmra wiase;*
> *Ma nkɔsoɔ mmra ɔman yi mu,*
> *Ma ɔman yi nyɛ porɔmporɔm.*

Translation:
> We pray for life and pray for grace
> Let not death be with us by day or by night;
> May we be blessed with children,

---

[70] Asante refer to Earth as *Asaase Yaa* and Fantse refer to her as *Asaase Efua* (*Afua*). In Asante Thursday is the "rest day" while Friday is the "rest day" among Fantse for Mother Earth. On these days it is forbidden to go the farm.

And may what we plant bear good fruit.
Let there be peace in the world,
And may there be prosperity
In this land abundantly.

In the past a ritual, *Mmusuyideɛ*[71] (a purification as well as a protective ceremony), was performed for the township or village. As part of the ritual all streets of townships were swept clean each morning and evening to remove mystical danger and to prevent disease or death from entering the townships. Even though the Akan pray to God, they did not institutionalize a public practice of building temples and a lineage of priests to worship Him. The Christian and Islamic ways of worship have become prevalent and these days there are places of worship (*asɔredan* - #100). According to Sarpong (1974, p. 13), it needs to "be pointed out that the contention of a few nineteenth century writers who raised doubts about the originality of the Ghanaian conception of God is completely inadmissible." Christian teaching has, for example, confirmed the Akan conception of the soul. The Christians teach that God made the human being in his own image and the Akan belief is that the Creator gives a bit of His spirit to everyone whom God sends to the earth.

There are some religious rituals associated with the *kra* (soul) - one's spiritual being. *Akradware* (soul washing) ceremony is celebrated on a *kra da* (soul day) - the day of the week on which one was born. It is a cleansing ceremony and is celebrated on one's birth day because that is when one's soul (*kra*) can be communed with. There is also another ceremony, *ntorɔ adware* which the father and his children used to observe. *Adwera adware*, on the other hand is a cleansing ceremony one celebrates to mark the escape from misfortunes such as a long bout of illness. *Adwera* (watery shrub - #108) leaves may be used in both *akradware* and *ntorɔ adware*.

HOPE AND GOD'S GRACE

Nyame dua (God's altar - #63-71) symbolizes the dependence of human beings on God as God is the source of life and hope. Opoku (1978, p. 33) has observed that: "Among the regalia of the Asantehene is an *Onyamedua* stump covered with leopard skin, which is often carried by an attendant following closely behind him in procession. This symbolizes the dependence of not only the Asantehene but also the entire Asante nation on God."

The Akan believe that the human being is like the star that is dependent on God (*Ɔba nyankonsoromma te Nyame so na ɔnte ne ho so* - #130-138). There is the hope that one's star will shine one day (*da bi me nsoroma bɛpue* - #139-140). This serves as a motivating factor for one to keep on in life with the expectation that there is light at the end of the tunnel. Other expressions of hope and expectation captured by *adinkra* symbols include *ade pa bɛba* (something good will be forthcoming - #142), *Onyankopɔn bɛkyerɛ* (God will provide - #148), *Onyankopɔn adom nti biribiara bɛyɛ yie* (by God's grace all will be well - #150-151), *Onyankopɔn bɛyɛ me kɛse* (God will make me great - #149), and *biribi wɔ soro* (there is something in the heavens - #143-147). In the past the *biribi wɔ soro* symbol was hung above the lintel of a chamber door in the king's palace for the king to touch three times repeating each time the expression: *Nyame biribi wɔ soro na ma ɛmmɛka me nsa* (God there is something in the heavens, let it reach me). This was to wish the king God's blessing, good luck, high hope and good

---

[71] Among the Fantse similar rituals (e.g., *ahobaa* and *akwambɔ*) were celebrated annually to purify the community and ward off bad spirits and bad omens.

expectation as he went out to carry out his duties each morning. On the other hand, the symbol *kerapa* (sanctity or good luck - #72-80) was woven into a bedside mat on which the king would step three times for God's protection and good luck before going to bed at night (Rattray, 1927). Another symbol used to depict hope and expectation is *anidasoɔ nsoromma* (star of hope - #139-140) which is associated with the expression: *anidasoɔ wɔ wiem* (there is hope in the heavens above).

DUALISM AND DIALECTICS

Spiritual and Physical

In the everyday life of the Akan, he/she endeavors to understand himself/herself and his/her environment and he/she tries to come to terms with duality: life and death, here and hereafter, good and bad, male and female, day and night, and the physical and the spiritual. The Akan belief is that the universe, as well as the human being, is both spiritual and corporeal (that is, physical), and that while the corporeal aspect may perish and die, the spiritual aspect is immortal and imperishable. The Akan also believe in a physical world (the earth - *asaase*) and spiritual world (*soro* - sky) that form part of a continuum: heaven and earth (*soro ne asaase* - #16). These beliefs of dualism and the imperishability of the spiritual part of the human being are marked by such symbols as *sunsum* (spirit or soul - #42-43), *hye anhye* (unburnable - #51-54), *Nyame nwu na mawu* (I die only when God dies - #55-59).

A significant aspect of the Akan dualism is reflected in the relationship between the physical and the spiritual. The spiritual component is the life force in the human being. While the spiritual part of the human being is indestructible (e.g. *Nyame nwu na mawu* - #55-59), the physical part is capable of being destroyed if proper care is not taken or when death occurs. The physical part decays or goes back to the womb of Mother Earth and the spiritual part goes to *Asamando*. The spiritual part is later reincarnated in another child. In this sense, the Akan believe in life after death and reincarnation.

Male and Female

Another significant aspect of the Akan dualism is reflected in the relationship between the male and female. Male is associated with the right, spirit of conception (*ntorɔ*), auspicious omens, normalcy and coolness, strength, superiority, and the center. The female is associated with blood of conception (*mogya*), red, warmth and heat, inferiority, weakness, inauspicious omens, and witchcraft. The right hand, associated with the male, is used in greeting[72], eating, and in giving gifts. The left hand is associated with the female. It is the hand that is used for cleaning oneself after defecating and for unpleasant tasks. It is considered an improper manner for one to point with one's left fingers. While the male is associated with the center, the female is associated with the hearth (*bukyia* - #244-245). There is ambivalence in the concept of femininity as it is associated with fertility, life, and continuity as well as danger, destruction, evil spirits, and death.

The two crosses (*mmeramutene* - male cross - #22-24, and *mmeramubere* - female cross - #25-28)

---

[72] When there is a seated gathering of people, one is supposed to shake hands in the proper way, from right to left. The Akan is supposed to know this proper way of greeting. The one who does not know and greets from left to right is said to be greeting in the female way (*okyia mmaa mu* - he greets like a woman).

symbolize the various attributes of the two sexes which form the very core of Akan beliefs about their society. These beliefs affect almost all aspects of Akan behavior, from marital relations, care of menstruation and pregnancy, adultery, and ideas about kinship relations, to details concerning the nature of ancestral propitiation, inheritance, funerals, and categorization of death.

Death and Life

The Akan view of reality as "unity in duality comprising two conflicting elements" is further illustrated by how they view death. Sarpong (1974, p. 20) sums it up thus:

> Any given existence may be defined as a dedication to, an immersion in death, not simply because it is on its way to meet death, but more essentially because it constantly realizes in itself the "situation" of death. The presence of death is so fundamental to existence that not one of its stirrings can be understood otherwise than in the light of the constitutive and systematic ordering towards death.

Death provokes dualistic "thoughts of darkness and light, weakness and strength, evil and good, sorrow and joy, non-existence and life, war and peace, defeat and victory, vice and virtue, ignorance and knowledge, in short, confusion (Sarpong, 1974, p. 21).

Death is inevitable for all as symbolized by *owuo atwedeɛ* (death's ladder - #101-104) and *owuo de dɔm bɛkɔ* (death will claim the multitude - #106). It does not discriminate between the rich and the poor (*owuo mpɛ sika* - death accepts no money - #109); *yɛbɛdane agya* (we shall leave everything behind - #732), or the old and the young. This inevitability of death is conveyed by the following stanzas in the drum poetry cited in full below:

> We have, since we arose from ancient times,
> Been exposed to incessant suffering.
> The *Ogyapam* tree and its ants are from antiquity (Nketia, 1969, p. 125).

The ants not only harass the *ogyapam* tree, they kill it; yet the ants and the tree were created together from the beginning. That is to say, the tree was destined to die; it is the law of the Creator. The Creator made man to die; and when the destined time comes, nothing can stop death because what God has ordained, no human being can change (*asɛm a Onyankopɔn adi asie no, onipa ntumi nnane no* - #85).

Death, by natural circumstances, is not a curse or the loss of a dear one, but is considered as going home to God - a victory. Death is a transition in life - a passage from the visible world of the living physical beings into the invisible world of spirits of ancestors and God. That is, the Akan view death as a phase in the biography of persons, after which the dead resume existence as spirits which interact with the living and affect the lives of the living in a variety of ways. In this sense, some of the dead are feared and venerated, and extensive recurring rituals (e.g., *fundahɔ, nnawɔtwe nsã, adaduanan ayie, afenhyia ayie, ahobaa*) are (or were) performed for them. These rituals of veneration were erroneously termed ancestor worship by European writers.

When a very, very old person dies the body is laid in state in white before being buried. The white signifies victory over death and/or peaceful transition to the spiritual world. The power of death is so irresistible that even Jesus Christ, who Christians believe as the Son of God and therefore has the antidote to death's venom, could not avoid it (*Yesu wuo* - #111).

The manipulation of dead bodies served as dominant political symbols. For example, *Asɔneɛ*, *banmu*, and *nananompɔ* served to associate the dead with supreme state power. The royal mausoleums (*asieeɛ* or *banmu* - #112) at Banpanase (*Asɔneɛ*) and Bantama (*Banmu*) serve to illustrate the manipulation of dead corpses as dominant political symbols. Kyerematen (n.d., p. 11) writes:

> it [*Asɔneɛ*] is the Ashanti equivalent for the process of embalming dead monarchs. A chamber, of a hall and bedroom, is kept for each of the successive Kings, furnished and equipped as for a living monarch. There is the bed, constantly made with a regular change of the bedding; supply of variety of cloth for different occasions; food and drink are provided and palace officials and a wife are detailed for service. After a year the skeleton is removed to the Bantama Mausoleum... Every year at a special ceremony at this Mausoleum, called the Annual Service (*Afenhyiasom*) the reigning King goes to inspect the skeletons to make sure that the gold joints are in place and to order replacements for those damaged or missing.

It is believed that the spirits of the ancestors come back to life everyday a child is born. The Akan, therefore, have no difficulty with the Christian view of life after death and resurrection. In the symbol (*Yesu wusɔre* - #115), the Akan believe the resurrection of Christ is a demonstration of God's power to overcome the venom of death - *Nyame na ɔte nanka aduro*. The naming ceremony for a baby, a week after birth, is to mark the transition from the spiritual world to the physical world of the living. It is believed that during the first week after birth the child is a spirit in transition. If it is an inauspicious spirit, it may return to where it came from before it is a week old. Such an inauspicious spirit that returns as a child may be given a funny or unusual name (*kɔ-san-bra-din* — go-and-come-back-name) to make it stay in the physical world.

The Akan's dialectical understanding of life and death as polar opposites complementing each other is best illustrated by the following Akan prayer to God:

> *Ɛmma mennwu awia wuo,*
> *Ɛmma mennwu anadwo wuo;*
> *Ɛmma mennwu koraa;*
> *Na ma me nwu.*

Translation:
> Don't let me die in the day,
> Don't let me die at night,
> Don't let me die at all,
> But let me die.

In this dialectic, as Dzobo (1992) explains, one expresses one's desire to see and appreciate the beauty of life and nature (line 1) and to be sexually active (line 2) in order to fulfill one's creative and reproductive being and have many children who may perpetuate one's name, beliefs, traditions, and philosophy of life (line 3). After one has fulfilled one's destiny one would be happy to die and join one's ancestors (line 4).

Furthermore, the Akan say that *Ɔdomankoma bɔɔ owuo na owuo kum no* (God created death and death killed Him - #105). Yet God knows the antidote for the serpent's venom (death) as indicated by the following quality of God: *Nyame na ɔte nanka aduro* - God has the antidote for the venom of death. The following drum poetry taken from Nketia (1969, p. 125) is pregnant with Akan dialectical views on the Creator, life and death:

Noble Ruler,
Condolences!
Condolences!
Condolences!
Noble ruler, we share your grief.
We sympathize with you in your bereavement.
We have, since we arose from ancient times,
Been exposed to incessant suffering.
The *Ogyapam* tree and its ants are from antiquity.
The Creator created death and death killed Him.
Thou Deceased,
Condolences!
Condolences!
Condolences!

The Akan believe that the Creator *Ɔdomankoma*, is one who is infinite, eternal, having no beginning and no end. Yet the drummer says "The Creator created death, and death killed Him." This statement must be juxtaposed with another statement: *Nyame nwu na mawu* (could God die, I will die or when a man dies he is not really dead - #55-59) for one to understand the cryptic message of the drummer. The drummer is saying in effect that as long as God is not dead, death is not an end, but a new beginning. The Akan belief is that the human soul is in the image of God, the Creator, the Eternal One. Thus the human soul does not die, or the human soul dies only when God dies. That is, if human beings cease to exist, God ceases to exist. It is the drummer's way of conveying the Akan belief that there is life after death. That is why the drummer ends his message with an address to the deceased. The deceased is offered condolences, for he is able to hear it in the other life just begun.

CHAPTER 5

Pempamsie se: Bebirebe ahooden ne koroyɛ
The strength of the many lies in unity

AKAN POLITICAL BELIEFS

Unity

The Akan have a set of beliefs about the proper order of society and how that might be achieved. These beliefs constitute the Akan political culture. Although the Akan society is diverse, it is united under a common set of beliefs and attitudes about government and politics. Several *adinkra* cloth symbols point to Akan people's views about political concepts such as unity, diversity, peace, freedom of speech and expression, human rights, war, diplomacy, pluralism and democracy. This chapter will decode some of the *adinkra* symbols in order to shed some light on Akan people's views about some of these concepts. The Akan state is made up of loosely knit matriclan families (*abusua,* singular, *mmusua,* plural) that comprise individual households. The diversity in the society is obvious in many respects other than the plural matriclans: political views, sex, age, occupation, and differences in individual as well as group ability. The need for social cohesion, cooperation, unity, and national integration in the pluralistic society is paramount.

The Akan belief indicates that the cohesive force of the family (*abusua*) is spiritual. The cohesive force of the family is expressed by the belief in the descent from a common ancestress and the belief in a community of the living, the spirits of the dead, and the yet-to-be-born members of the family. This idea of the cohesive force of the family is also symbolized by the *nkɔnsɔnkɔnsɔn* (chain - #162-167) and expressed thus: *Yɛtoatoa mu sɛ nkɔnsɔnkɔnsɔn; nkwa mu a, yɛtoa mu, owuo mu a, yɛtoa mu; abusua mu nte da.* This translates thus: We are linked together like a chain; in life we are linked, in death we are linked. Family ties are never broken. Or, people who share common blood relations never break away from one another. Membership in a family is permanent. The individual members of the family form something similar to the links in a chain. This symbol emphasizes the view that each link in a chain is important and that each one must be strong and ready to play his/her role effectively. No one in a society is a "left-over" and so everyone should be ready to fill that "space" which he/she alone, but no one else, can occupy.

Similarly, the cohesive force of an alliance of families forming the *ɔman* (nation-state, country or empire) is believed to be a spiritual one. The cohesive force holding the state together has been

76

achieved through the institutionalization of the king's stool (*ɔhene adwa* - #278-292). In Asante, this alliance of nation-states to form the Asanteman under one king, Asantehene, was achieved by the institutionalization of the Golden Stool (*Sika Dwa*) as will be discussed below.

Unity within the family (*abusua*) and national integration are based on the continual reconciling of diverse individual and group interests. Reconciling individual and group interests within the family is encoded in the symbol *abusua panyin kyerε wo dɔ* (family head assert your affection - #556). The *abusua panyin* serves as the family's delegate to the council of elders or council of state (*kuronti ne akwamu* - #194). The *abusua panyin* is also the chief arbiter in household disputes and quarrels in order to ensure peace and harmony in the family.

Reconciling national interest vis-a-vis family and individual interests is also emphasized by such *adinkra* symbols as *koroyε* (unity - 187, *pempamsie* (preparedness in unity - #178-179), and *nkabom ma yεtumi gyina hɔ* (united we stand - #186). The *pempamsie* symbol is associated with the expression: *Pempamsie se: Bebirebe ahoɔden ne koroyε; ɔman si mpoma dua dadebo a, εkɔ akɔterenee* (Antubam, 1963). This literally means that the strength of the many lies in unity; once people are resolved in unity, nothing can stop them from reaching their goal. Or, in unity lies strength. Another expression that best summarizes the emphasis on unity is embodied in the *nkabom* (unity - #187) symbol: *Nkabɔmu ma yεtumi gyina hɔ, mpaapaemu ma yεhwe ase* (United we stand, divided we fall). The symbol emphasizes the need for united action, unity in diversity, and national unity among the Akan.

The mythical Siamese twin crocodile symbol (*funtumfunafu dεnkyεmfunafu* - #168-177) also stresses the problems of trying to reconcile individual and group interests and places emphasis on cooperation and unity of purpose. The symbol encodes the idea of two-headed crocodiles that are joined at the stomach, yet they fight over food that goes to the common stomach no matter which one of them eats the food. They fight over the food because each relishes the food in its mouth and throat. The two heads signify individuality while the common stomach symbolizes the common good of all the individual members of the society. This symbol stresses the oneness of humanity in spite of cultural diversity. It also emphasizes the need for unity in the family or state. Members should not quarrel or fight for selfish interests, for what each gains is for the benefit of all. But reconciling individual and common interests is a contested terrain.

Even though people are born into a social setting, communal membership does not diminish the reality of individuality. In this sense, the individual has character and a will of his/her own. The *funtumfunafu* symbol (Siamese twin crocodiles - #168-177) depicts how the desires, interests, and passions of individual members of a society differ and may conflict with that of the common good. The two heads of the crocodiles with a common stomach symbolize the inherent conflicts in reconciling individual interests with the common good of the society. The social good must not, and cannot, be achieved at the expense of individual rights, responsibilities, interests, and desires. Gyekye (1987, p. 160) says the following about this symbol:

> (1) at least the basic interests of all members of the community are identical, and (2) the community of interests forms the basis for the maximization of their interests and welfare.
>
> While it suggests the rational underpinnings of the concept of communalism, it does not do so to the detriment of individuality. The concept of communalism, as it is understood in Akan thought, therefore does not overlook individual rights, interests, desires, and responsibilities, nor does it imply the absorption

of the individual will into the "communal will," or seek to eliminate individual responsibility and accountability.

Individuality may give rise to social conflicts. Since the nation is made up not only of individuals, but also of diverse groups of matriclans, there is the need for national unity and integration. The Siamese twin crocodile symbol also gives rise to the expression: ɔdɛnkyɛmmɛmu nhwere papam korɔ also, ɔdɛnkyɛmmɛmu wuo ama dua mono so awu or ofuruntum wuo sane mmatatwene - the death of the Siamese twin crocodile affects the tree and the creeping plant. When the crocodile is killed by hunters it is carried by being tied to a pole. The creeper is used as rope to tie up the dead animal. The death of the crocodile spells death not only for the tree that serves as the pole but also the creeper that is used as rope in tying the crocodile to the pole. In this analogy it is clear that the well-being of one depends on the well-being of others. The notion that something is "for me" is meaningless unless it is linked with the total idea that it is "for us" - this is the cardinal principle of Akan communal life.

National Integration and Cooperation

National integration is also emphasized by the use of such symbols as ese ne tɛkrɛma (teeth and tongue - #189-191) and koroyɛ (unity - #187). The teeth and tongue not only live together; they also work and complement each other. As they work together the teeth bite the tongue sometimes, yet they continue to live in harmony. The symbol depicts the complementary nature of human beings as well as nations.

The koroyɛ symbol is based on a story of three baby birds that had lost their mother. Their joint wailing from a tree near a farm developed a beautiful harmonious piece of music that attracted the attention of a farmer. The farmer decided to nurse the birds. The farmer became a mother to the birds. Very soon, the birds fought among themselves because each wanted the nest all to itself. Eventually two of them left to be on their own. The next day as the farmer came to feed them he could only hear a forlorn melodic piece of music. As he got closer to the nest he found out that the birds had broken up, he urged the remaining bird to go and look for its siblings before he, the farmer would feed them together. The bird flew away and very soon returned with the other two. The farmer fed all three birds together, and they lived together in unity happily ever after.

Unity is a source of strength as suggested by the symbol of nkabomu (unity - #188) and the saying that is associated with it: united we stand; divided, we fall (nkabomu ma yɛtumi gyina ho, mpaapaemu ma yɛhwe ase - #188). The Akan illustrate this view with the strands of the broom. When taken individually, the strands of the broom can be broken easily. But when all the strands are tied together to form the broom it is nearly impossible to break the broom. The symbol nsa korɔ (one hand - #238-240) encodes this view of united action. The Akan say: Ɔbaakofoɔ nsa nso Nyame ani hata - one man's hands cannot cover the sky. Even though the individual's hands may not be big enough to cover the sky, when all join hands together, there is the possibility of covering the sky.

Freedom, Human Rights and Freedom of Speech

Humans universally have magnificent brains that give them the ability to think, create, invent, imagine, manipulate abstract symbols, anticipate the future, and learn from the past. They have a complex vocal apparatus that enables the brain to express itself orally in the complex, highly developed communication systems we call language. Our bodies are, in part, self-regulating survival machines. Our nervous system tells us when we need nourishment, water, heat or cooling, rest or exercise. Our bodies naturally recoil from pain. We are naturally social beings who love others, bond with others, and develop mentally and emotionally through interaction with others. Because of these natural endowments, humans naturally want and value the freedom to think, to express their thoughts, to bond with others, to be free from torture, to have an adequate diet, shelter and clothing. We value and want to be free to learn and develop our mental abilities (Magnarella, 2001).

The Akan believe humans are free and responsible for their actions – for enacting "the good" through behaviors that are truthful, just, compassionate, generous, and peaceable – which create harmony in human relations and lead to the well-being of the community (Gyekye, 1987). Freedom (*fawohodie* - #206-210), to the Akan, stems from his/her desire to escape from unpleasant and painful situations. The Akan believe in the right of all people to freedom of thought and expression in all matters political, religious and metaphysical. Freedom of religion is of primary importance as the Akan say, *obi nkyerɛ akɔdaa Nyame* – God is not taught to a child (#60). God and His creation are so obvious to everyone, the Akan, therefore, did not develop institutionalized religion.

Like wisdom, speech is accessible to all people even though freedom of speech of non-adults was rigorously circumscribed and dissent on the part of a minor in the face of adult pronouncements was almost equated with disrespect or obstinacy. All the same, the Akan valued freedom of speech and expression on the part of a minor as they say: *Abɔfra hunu ne nsa ho hohoro a, ɔne mpanimfoɔ na edidi* - If a child keeps his hands clean, he eats with his elders (#566). The Akan believe in freedom of speech and expression as they say, *tɛkrɛma da mano mu, nti wɔma me nka bi* – there is tongue in my mouth, let me express my view (#189-191). As Yankah (1995) points out, "one significant aspect of the child naming ceremony involves engaging the child's most important organ of speech, the tongue." He further points out that the child naming ritual "initiates the child into the essence of truthful and discreet speech, the need for care, truth, firmness, and social responsibility in the exercise of the spoken word.

Even though there is no one word in the Akan language for the term "human rights," Akan thought recognizes:

> The right of a newborn to be nursed and educated
> The right of an adult to a plot of land from ancestral holdings
> The right of a person to remain at any locality or to leave
> The right to self-government
> The right of all to have a say in the enstoolment and the destoolment of their chiefs
> The right of everybody to trial before punishment (*obi mmua n'ano nni fɔ* - one should not remain silent to be pronounced guilty)
> The right of all to freedom of thought and expression (*wankasa wo tiri ho a, yeyi wo eyi bɔne* – if one does not speak out to one's barber, one is given a bad haircut -#684).

Despite the recognition of these rights listed above, Akan tradition also embodied some embarrassing features from a human rights perspective. One is its hierarchical structure, in which rights or privileges depended on status, descent, gender and age. Another is cultural exclusiveness, meaning that the protection of human dignity is only valid inside one's own cultural group. That is, the protection of human rights was based on ascribed status. Besides, there were practices such as slavery, human sacrifice, and the great respect for authority that sometimes led to a high level tolerance of abuse of it. Widows were not only subjected to inhuman treatment in the past, but also to indignities if the spouse died intestate as suggested by the *owuo sɛe fie* – death destroys the household symbol - #125-127.

Power

The Akan believe political power emanates from the people (both the living and the spirits of the dead ancestors). This source of political power is depicted by the *adwa* (stool - #278-292) symbol in the political organization of the Akan society. In Asante, there developed, as part of deliberate political reforms to devolve power, a hierarchy of stools: *abusua dwa* (matriclan stool); *ɔhene* or *ɔhemmaa dwa* (king's or queen's stool - i.e., stool of the royalty) - based on ascription; and *ɛsom dwa* and *mmamma dwa* (service stools, i.e., stools for public servants, administrative officers, or stools of sons and grandsons of chiefs) - based on achievement criteria.

Power is also believed by the Akan to emanate from land ownership as indicated by the expression associated with the *asaase yɛ duru* or *asaase trɛ* (mighty earth - #29-31) symbol which says: *tumi nyina ara ne asaase* (all power emanates from land). Even though land is communally owned by the *abusua* with the *abusua panin* as the trustee, land ownership by groups or individuals is an important source of power. At higher levels of the Akan political organization, the king as custodian and grantor of land, can alienate land for sale or as a gift to citizens and non-citizens.

Power, to the Akan, must be exercised judiciously and carefully by the king and his counselors and administrators. The king must rule by consensus to ensure democracy. This view of exercising political power is depicted by the *kokuromotie* (thumb - #184-185) and *nea ɔretwa sa* (the path-maker - #237) symbols. The thumb represents the king; and the other fingers on the hand represent the individual members of society, who are free, unique and independent. But they are all firmly rooted in the whole, which is the hand, and derive their being and importance from their relatedness in the whole, individually, and collectively.

The community, for example, is likened to the whole hand, that derives its functioanlity from the interrelatedness of its fingers. Without the fingers there will be no hand, without the hand there will be no fingers. The king is like the thumb of the hand and without subjects – that is, the other fingers of the hand – there is no king, and there are no subjects without a king. One cannot tie a knot without the concerted action and functional interdependence of all the fingers of the hand, big and small. On the other hand, when a leader tries to misuse or abuse his power, the masses will rise against him. This is implied in the maxim: *wode kokuromotie kɔ ayie a, wɔde sotorɔ gya wo kwan* (when one throws one's weight about at a funeral, one is bound to get slapped in the face - #184-185).

In the *nea ɔretwa sa* (#237) symbol, the leader is urged to involve his followers in decision-making and consult with his elders in governing, for the followers are better placed to realize the mistakes of the leader. The king, as a path-maker, does not know whether his actions and behaviors may be right or wrong. It is the people as followers who see the mistakes of the king. This may be illustrated by a situation in which a prominent king misspoke in public. He publicly said: *"me wɔfa wuiɛ nti na mebedi n'ade* – upon the death of my uncle, I have been made his successor." The ɔkyeame quickly interrupted the king with the correct public expression: *"Nana kyerɛ sɛ ne wɔfa kɔ n'ekura nti na yɛde no asi nan mu* – the king has gone to his ancestral village, that is why his nephew is his successor." The king made the mistake of not speaking metaphorically. He was corrected because the Akan believe that the king – as path maker - in making the public statement did not realize his mistake and the *ɔkyeame* – as the follower - in recognizing the king's mistake, had to correct him.

Another symbol that encodes the Akan belief that power emanates from the people is the *nsoromma ne ɔsrane* (stars and moon - #492-497). *Nyankonsoromma na ɔman wɔ no na nnyε ɔsrane a* - the state belongs to the stars not the moon. The stars represent the people and are contrasted with the moon, representing the king. The people, like the stars, are permanent and always there; the king, on the other hand, may come and go just as the moon waxes and wanes.

Yet another symbol that chronicles the Akan belief about power is the *εsono* (elephant - #351-354). In the expression: *wodi εsono akyi a, hasuo nka wo* (when you follow the elephant, you do not get wet from the dew on bushes), the symbol uses the analogy of the elephant to stress, in one sense, the might of and the protection offered by the king. In the expression: *εsono kokuroko, adoa na ɔman wɔ no* (the elephant may be big and mighty, the nation does not belong to the elephant but to the deer), the symbol uses the analogy of the elephant, in another sense, to portray the view that power derives not from the king but the people. Also, in the expression: *ɔbaakofo na okum εsono ma amansan* (when the individual hunter kills the elephant, it benefits the entire community), the elephant symbol is used to suggest the interdependence of the individual members of the community. Despite the size and might of the elephant it can be brought down by an individual. The success of the individual in bringing down the elephant benefits the entire community of people.

Power-sharing is an important aspect of the Akan political beliefs. The king and queenmother are co-rulers. Even though the female ruler has been conspicuously absent from local administration under the various colonial and post-independence laws and ordinances that does not mean that the female ruler has not carried out her constitutional responsibilities. Oduyoye (1979) suggests that it is due to the tenacity of the queenmother in administering protective regulations for women that matrilineal inheritance has survived in Asante and other Akan communities and has been guaranteed in national laws.

Power is not only shared between the king and the queenmother. It is also shared among the rulers and their councilors. The power-sharing guarantees that the ruler does not become despotic and dictatorial. In Chapter 6 we will see how the queenmother is the only person who can publicly rebuke the king. *Adinkra* symbols that encode the Akan belief of power-sharing include *tikorɔ nkɔ agyina* (one head does not constitute a council - #192-193), *kontire ne akwamu* (council of state - #194), and *nam porɔ a* (when the fish rots - #235-236). In the *nam porɔ a* (when the fish rots - #235-236) symbol, for example, the Akan believe that corruption in society starts from the leadership — *nam porɔ a, efiri ne ti* (when fish rots, it first rots from the head). This implies not only power-sharing, but also indicates that the head is still held responsible for the problems of the society.

Democracy and Akan democratic practices

The views discussed in the preceding section about power and authority underpin Akan people's belief in democracy and the practice of democracy. The Akan hold the view that democratic rule must be based on consultation, discussion, consensus building, and coalition formation. Democratic practices are found in family relations as well as in the higher forms of governmental organization at the state and national levels. *Tikorɔ mpam* (One head does not constitute a council - #192-193), *Tikorɔ mu nni nyansa,* or *ɔbaakofoɔ mmu man* (wisdom abounds not only in one head, or one person does not rule a nation - #194), and *wo nsa da mu a* (if your hands are in the dish - #196) are some of the *adinkra* symbols that depict Akan views on democratic rule in the family as well as the *kuro* (town) and *ɔman* (nation-state). These symbols depict the value of consultation and discussion in arriving at decisions, especially at the court of the king.

Underpinning the democratic practices is the view that power is fragile as symbolized by *tumi* tesɛ kosua (power is like an egg - #197-198). This symbol depicts the fragility of power. As a symbol of democracy it suggests the virtue of sharing political power, for it is not safe to hold power in one hand. Power-sharing is symbolized by the *kuronti ne akwamu* (Council of State - #194). At the *abusua* (family), *kuro* (town) and *ɔman* (nation-state or empire) levels of government, use is made of variations of the Council of State to devolve and share political power through the following structures: *abusua mpanimfoɔ*, *kuro mpanimfoɔ* (made up of *abusua mpanimfoɔ*, *ɔdekuro*, *asafohenefoɔ*, *akyeamefoɔ*, and the queenmother), and *ɔman mpanimfoɔ* or *aberɛmpɔn* (made up of various chiefs, elders, and military leaders). The Council of State notion of governance is incorporated in the symbol called *kontire ne akwamu* (council of state - #194).

The Akan believe in participatory democracy. Participatory democracy in the Akan political system is, for example, evidenced by the process for the selection (election) of the king. The prospective candidate to occupy the king's stool (*ɔhene adwa* - #278-292) is nominated by the queenmother subject to the approval by the council of state (*kurontire ne akwamu* - #194), and the masses of the people (*nkwankwaa* or *asafo* - symbolized by *asaase aban* - #227). This participatory system of government has an inherent defect. It has a monarchical basis which opens up opportunity for only royal members from the matrilineage to become kings. This problem is compounded by the fact that, within any given royal family, succession to stools is ill-defined and eligibility is broad (Henige, 1975).

Resolving the constitutional problem posed by this defect in the indigenous Akan political system is very difficult, and has occasionally resulted in constitutional crises and civil unrest. This may be illustrated by the political crises that resulted in a civil war and interregnum of what Wilks (1975) describes as "republican form of government: *kwasafoman*" in Kumasi in the mid-1880s. Wilks (1975, p. 540) writes: "The *nkwankwaa*... remained unconvinced of the virtues of a monarchical system, and for a brief period of time Kumasi existed under a republican form of government: *kwasafoman*." The commoners group made of *nkwankwa* - sometimes referred to as *mmerante* (commoners, masses or youngmen), some *asikafo* (a nascent class of rich traders), and some chiefs established *kwasafonhyiamu* (council of commoners and chiefs). Ironically, their claim to legitimacy was the *ohene adwa* (the king's stool - #278-292) - the Golden Stool. This period is marked by a *kente* cloth that is called *Ɔyokoman na gya dam* (crisis in the Ɔyoko nation). The recent constitutional crises in several places such as Kumawu and Wenchi paramountcies are partly attributable to the ill-defined rules of succession in the monarchical system.

The belief in participatory democracy is depicted by the symbol *wo nsa da mu a, wɔnni nnya wo* (if your hands are in the dish, people do not eat everything and leave you with nothing - #196). This implies participatory democracy and ensures a sense of ownership in the decision reached in the political process. Participatory democracy is also exemplified by civic responsibility and service to the community. This is implied in the expression attributed to the monitor lizard that his is to help build, but not to destroy his state (*ɔmampam se: me deɛ ne sɛ merepam me man, ɛnyɛ mammɔeɛ* - # 462).

Another set of symbols that depicts the Akan belief in participatory democracy is the state sword (*akofena* - #260-269, and the *nsuaeafona* - #257-258) and their use in the swearing of oath during the installation of the chief-elect. The installation process is done in public before his councilors and the masses of the people. Rattray (1927, p. 82) records twelve injunctions embodied in the oath swearing process, and acknowledged by the chief-elect. These injunctions are as follows:

1) Do not be a womanizer
2) Do not become a drunkard

3) Heed our advice
4) Do not gamble
5) We do not want you to disclose the origin of your subjects
6) Do not abuse us
7) We do not want you to be miserly
8) We do not want one who disregards advice
9) We do not want you to treat us as fools
10) We do not want autocratic ways
11) We do not want bullying
12) We do not want beating

These injunctions are, in one sense, an unambiguous assertion of the people's right to participate in the running of the affairs of their community or state. They are, in another sense, an indication of the confidence of the people have in insisting on the exercise of political power that will reflect their wishes (Ajei, 2001).

The requirements of these injunctions, as Ajei (2001) elaborates, could be reduced to the following prescriptions that highlight the ideals, values and aspirations of the people thus:

- 1 and 2 assert respectively, profligacy offends our values and a leader whose reflective ability is dulled by intoxicants does not meet our ideals of leadership
- 4 says that we do not want a leader who will dissipate the wealth of the state
- 3, 8, 9 and 10 are restatements of the principle of the sovereign will of the people. They all say that the chief cannot act without the concurrence of his councilors who are representatives of the people, and that any such act is liable to be set aside
- 6, 8 and again 9 and 10 state that government is expected to distribute equitably the wealth of the community, and to create an environment conducive to individual enterprise
- 5 prohibits action that would create discord among the citizenry.

All the above prescriptions would seem to suggest that the chief does not acquire an indefeasible right to office once installed. It is the right of his electors to unseat him for any reasonable cause, and the injunctions and the prescriptions of the oath constitute, variously, this cause (Ajei, 2001, p. 14). Some of the *adinkra* symbols that encode these injunctions and prescriptions include, but not limited to, *tikorɔ nkɔ agyina* (#192-193); *nea ɔretwa sa* (#237); *mmɔ adwaman* (#586); *nni awu* (#584); *seantie* (#686); *brɛ wo ho ase* (#671); *mpɔmpɔnsuo* (#259); *nea ɔpɛsɛ ɔbedi hene* (#302); and *ɔhene papa* (#300).

Cooperation and unity of purpose are not only important at the communal level, they are also important at the individual level. When one undertakes a good cause, one is given all the support one would need. This is captured by the expression *woforo dua pa a, na yɛpia wo* (when you climb a good tree, you are given a push - #680). Also, just as one hand cannot wash itself, so it is difficult for an individual to provide for himself/herself. Similar view is implied in the maxim: *nipa nyɛ abɛ dua na ne ho ahyia ne ho so* (the human being is not like the palm tree that s\he should be self-sufficient - #705). Other symbols that depict this notion of interdependence is *boa me na memmoa wo* - #200 and *boafo yɛ na* - #201-202). As one tree does not constitute a forest, and one tree cannot withstand a storm, it is necessary for one to join with others to work to achieve what is good for the individual as well as the community of individuals. People and countries depend on one another for much that they require in order to survive. The world would be a difficult place to live in, if people did not agree to cooperate with one another.

Another symbol that depicts this notion of interdependence is *boa w'awofoɔ* (help your parents - #564). In this regard, the Akan say: *sɛ w'awofoɔ hwɛ wo ma wo se fifiri a, ɛwɔ sɛ wo nso wohwɛ wɔn mmere wɔn se retutu* - if your parents take care of you as you grow your teeth, you should take care of them as their teeth fall out. This is the system of interdependence between parents and their children. Yet another symbol for interdependence and fellowship is *nnamfo pa baanu* (two good friends - #205). The proverb associated with this symbol is: *hu m'ani so ma me nti na atwe mmienu nam daa no* (the deer is always seen in pairs so that one will help the other out in case of any emergency).

Nationalistic and Patriotic symbols

The Akan are enjoined to be patriotic. Crisis situations such as war and natural disaster offered opportunities for the Akan to display his/her patriotic responsibilities. One symbol that encodes this sense of patriotic responsibility is *boa w'aban* (help your government - #203). Another symbol implies that the one who is bringing success in the form of wealth to his/her society should not be stopped. This is conveyed in the following maxim: *Yɛrepere adeɛ a, yɛpere ba fie; na obi a ɔrepere adeɛ akɔ kotɔko no, yɛnsi no kwan* (When we strive for wealth, we bring it home; and we don't stop the one who strives for wealth for the land of the porcupine - #214). Also, the Akan is urged by his or her community to be patriotic in the saying that *apɛsɛ yɛ kɛse a, ɔyɛ ma dufokyeɛ* (when the hedgehog grows fat, it benefits the wet log - #241). In contemporary times the *adinkra* cloth makers have incorporated the flag (*frankaa* - #836) and the Ghana coat-of-arms (*ɔman asɛnkyerɛdeɛ* - #242) in order to promote nationalistic and patriotic feelings among the citizenry.

Unity in Diversity in Asante

The founding of the Asanteman (Confederacy) required the highly complex system of integrating individual and group interests at various levels of the political structure. *Asanteman Nkabom* was achieved by various means of integration including spiritual, military, political and economic means, and inter-marriages. Spiritually, the Golden Stool (*Sika Adwa*) represents the soul (*sunsum* - #42-43) of the Asante nation. This reliance on the soul is in consonance with the Akan belief system in which the soul (*sunsum* - #42-43) is the medium through which one's affiliation to one's relationship group is achieved and validated. Through the Golden Stool, the *ɔman adwa* (state stool of the Asante), the Asante forged national integration and group unity. The following story is one version of how the Golden Stool was institutionalized.

In Asante mythology, Osei Tutu and Ɔkɔmfo Anɔkye are said to have called all the chiefs of the other paramountcies to an assembly (*nhyiamu*) in Kumasi on a Friday. Anɔkye is said to have given an inspirational speech on the principles and advantages of unity by drawing an analogy of the broom. The individual strands of the broom are easily broken, yet when the strands are put together to form a broom, the broom is unbreakable. Based on this analogy he pointed out that in unity is strength and disunity spells fall and oppression. He then pointed out the dangers inherent in the subsidiary position of the Kumasiman and the other *aman* (states) at the meeting vis-a-vis Denkyira.

The mythology goes on to illustrate how Anɔkye is believed to have conjured down from the skies a supernatural stool of solid gold. He ordered the surrender of nail-parings and hair clippings of the kings and queenmothers gathered at the meeting and set some of the clippings afire together with the surrender of the regalia (state swords, ancestral stools, etc). In the midst of the smoke,

Anɔkye is believed to have conjured a Golden Stool (*Sika Dwa Kofi*) from the heavens. He then smeared on the stool some of the concoction he had made from the remaining nail-parings and hair clippings and mixed the remaining part of the concoction in palm wine and gave the mixture to the kings and the people in the gathering to drink. Anɔkye then told the kings and queenmothers at the meeting that their spirits (*sunsum* - #42-43) had entered the Golden Stool. The Golden Stool enshrined the essence of the nation, and its destruction would mean the destruction of them all as a people. He decreed that the custodian of the Golden Stool, the Kumasihene, would become the Asantehene. The institution of the Golden Stool also required the *amanhene* to swear allegiance, that is, surrender part of their sovereignty to the Asantehene and observe a code of moral laws (*mmara ahoroɔ aduosuon-nsɔn:* seventy-seven laws) said to have been decreed by Anɔkye.

When the reigning Denkyirahene at that time, Boamponsem heard about this meeting, Wilks (1992, p. 111) writes, he "mocked the attempts of Kumaseman to build up its strength thus: '*ɔsa nti na eyinom aka wɔn ho abɔm yi;*' hence the name *ɔsa nti fo* or Asantefo - the because of war people."

The Kumaseman (rather the Oyoko family) needed to forge unity and integration of the various matriclan groups. Rattray (1927, p. 273) says of the mythology of the founding of Asanteman thus:

> What Komfo Anotche now achieved was the amalgamation of the other clans - Beretuo, Asona (Offinsu and Ejisu), and Asenie (Amaku) - under Osai Tutu, to fight the Dominas, whose chief was an Aduana. So remarkable did this achievement seem to the Ashanti, who were accustomed to the isolation and strict independence of the numerous petty chiefs, that they ascribed the feat to Anotche's magical powers.

If the unity (*nkabom* - #188) ritual performed by Osei Tutu and Ɔkɔmfo Anɔkye resulted in a military coalition to bring together the matriclans or the separate *amantoɔ* in order to fight the Denkyira, then after the Denkyira War the military coalition was transformed into a political union. In this union the Golden Stool became the single most important unifying symbol of the people. It is believed if the *sunsum* (soul - #42-43) of the nation is enshrined in the Golden Stool, then it must be more important than any one person or group of persons, even the king. It is believed to be the shrine of the Asante nation.

The symbolic importance of the Golden Stool is described by Fraser (1972, p. 141-2) thus:

> The honors accorded the Golden Stool are, broadly speaking, those rendered to an individual of the highest rank. The Stool must never touch the bare ground, and, when it is exhibited on state occasions, it rests on its own special throne, the silver-plated *Hwedomtea*, an elaborate chair.... Not only does the Golden Stool have its own throne, it also has its own set of regalia, including state umbrellas, elephant-skin shield and rug (*Banwoma*), a gold-plated drum, a lute, and its own bodyguard and attendants. Indeed its name, *Sikadwa* (or *Adwa*) Kofi, "The Golden Stool That Was Born on Friday," conforms to the Akan custom of naming people, in part, according to the day of the week on which they are born. The Stool is viewed as a living person, a sacrosanct being that houses the soul and spirit of the Ashanti people.

Other significant symbols that became politically manipulated to foster national unity and integration included the various uses of the *akofena* (state sword - #260-269) as discussed in Chapter 6. The various *amanhene* forming the Asanteman have to use the Asantehene's state swords, for example, the *mpɔmpɔnsu* (#259), to swear allegiance to him. Every year the *amanhene* have to attend the Asantehene's *Odwira* in Kumase where the corpses and stools of past Asantehene are manipulated as political symbols. See Chapter 4 for a brief discussion on the political symbolisms associated with the corpses and stools of past Asantehene.

Diplomacy, Conflict Resolution, War and Peace in Asante

The Asante people have been portrayed in the past as "war-like people." This description was based on the view that the Asante Empire rose from the desire of the people to merge together for the purpose of fighting the Denkyiras. The war against the Denkyiras was to assert the Asante people's right to self-determination, independence and freedom (*fawohodie* - #206-210). War was not only directed at an external enemy. The enemy could come from within as indicated by the symbol *fie abosea* (household pebbles - #229-231). And the enemy from within is more dangerous and destructive than the enemy from without.

Furthermore, the Asante symbol *kɔtɔkɔ* (porcupine - #412-413) and the war cry: *kum apem a, apem bɛba* (when you kill a thousand, a thousand more will come) have been said to describe the warlike nature of the Asante people. No animal dare meet the porcupine in a struggle is the apparent motto of the Asante. Other symbols that are suggestive of war as an instrument for attaining political ends include *tuo aboba* (gun bullets - #223), *tuo koraa* (even the gun - #228), *ohene tuo* (the king's gun - #404-407), *akofena ne tuo* (sword and gun - #416), *ɛkyɛm* (shield - #417), *pagya* (strikes fire - #414-415), *ɔkɔdeɛ mmɔwerɛ* (eagle's talons - #410-411), *aprɛmmoɔ* (canon - #225), and *mpaboa* (sandals - #224). Declaration of war would be signaled, for example, by sending gunpowder and bullets (*tuo aboba* - #223) and sandals with the statement: *wonni mpaboa a, pɛ bi; wonni atuduru a, pɛ bi na me wo wɔ bi ka wɔ ɛseramu* (prepare for war and meet me on the battlefield).

If the Asante were militaristic at all, they used their military genius and strategy to stand up against external aggression, oppression and suppression and to fight for their freedom and independence (*fawohodie* - #206-210). The Asante also saw war as the natural extension of diplomatic activity and the army as the chief instrument in the conduct of foreign policy.

The Asante were peace-loving people in the past as they are now. The Asante valued the use of diplomacy and peaceful conflict resolution as a valid instrument of political action. The symbol - *ɔwɔ aforo adobɛ* (the snake climbs the raffia palm tree - #215-217) - which was incorporated into almost every piece of regalia of the king, provided a basis for the development of a negotiating principle: tactfulness and patience. The snake does not possess limbs yet it is able to climb trees. It does so through tact and patience even though it recognizes it has to go through twists and turns in the process of climbing. The symbol extols the importance of diplomacy and prudence as the necessary ingredients of real valor.

The symbol *ɛse ne tɛkrɛma* (#189-191) connotes the Akan notions about conflict and conflict resolution. The symbol is associated with expressions such as *ɛse ne tɛkrɛma mpo ko na wɔwie a, wɔn ara asan asiesie wɔn ntam* – even the teeth and tongue do fight and later settle their differences; *ɛse ka tɛkrɛma nso wote bɔm* – the teeth bite the tongue sometimes, yet they continue to live in harmony; *tɛkrɛma wɔ hɔ a, ɛse mmɔ nkuro* – in the presence of the tongue the teeth do not litigate or narrate the arbitration proceedings; and the tongue lying between the two sets of teeth, literally staves off any potential tension between the two. The symbol connotes the Akan notion that conflict is inevitable in any social setting and that when conflict arises it is important it is resolved peacefully to ensure harmony in the society (Agyekum, 2006).

Another basis for the development of a negotiating principle is incorporated in the maxim: *Dua biara nni hɔ a ɛyɛ den sɛ akuma ntum ntwa nanso asɛm biara yɛ den a yɛmfa akuma na ɛtwa, na yɛde yɛn ano na ɛkã ma no twa* - there is no tree so hard that it cannot be felled with an axe; yet, however difficult or intractable an issue may be it must be settled by counsel and negotiation not with an axe. As Dupuis (1824) indicated, it was "a maxim associated with the religion" of the Asantehene, "never to appeal to the sword while a path lay open for negotiation." This maxim is encoded in the *adinkra* symbol *akuma* (axe - #695-697).

The elaborate protocol associated with diplomacy was accepted and practiced by the Asante government and its envoys. "Thus, notification of the dispatch of embassies, requests for audiences, the holding of the audience itself, and the message delivery all followed prevailing conventions and accepted formats" in diplomacy and the conduct of foreign affairs. "To a society that was used to formality even in private receptions and greetings, and to members of a profession that was drawn largely from a group that was well acquainted with the art of court ceremony, diplomatic protocol must have seemed a normal and familiar practice" (Adjaye, 1984, p. 235). Asante diplomats and emissaries performed various functions as ambassadors-at-large, roving ambassadors, and resident ambassadors. Their functions were both covert and overt.

The Asante government did not set up an office for Foreign Service as a distinct branch of government. However, there developed with time the specialization of certain individuals and *afekuo* (bureaus) in diplomatic appointments, the standardization of procedures regulating appointments and conduct regarding diplomatic and Foreign Service, and individual experts and territorial specialization for the conduct of foreign affairs.

There developed four distinct bureaus (English, Dutch, Danish, and Arabic) for formulating and carrying out foreign policy. The Butuakwa Stool, for example, specialized in Fante affairs[73], and the Boakye Yam Kuma Stool specialized in Elmina and Dutch affairs. At the individual level notable experts included Akyeame Boakye Tenten and Kofi Bene (peace negotiators) and Bosommuru Dwira and Kofi Afrifa (British affairs) and the Owusu Ansas. Yaa Akyaa (also known as Akyaawa), daughter of Asantehene Osei Kwadwo, distinguished herself as a diplomat. For her pioneering role as a diplomat, she acquired the nickname *Yiakwan* (path-maker or trailblazer). She headed the Asante mission that negotiated and signed the Treaty of Peace and Free Commerce with the British on April 27, 1831 (Adjaye, 1984).

Asante diplomatic service personnel utilized a set of emblems which served as their credentials and ranking. The highly ranked *akyeame* were associated with their golden staffs (*akyeamefoɔ poma*); the "large crooked sabres with golden tilts" (*tumi afena* - #257-258 or *akofena* - #206-269) were associated with the *afenasoafoɔ*; *nseniefoɔ* were identified by their monkey skin caps; and the round, gold plates identified the *akradwarefoɔ*. These emblems were recognized as symbols of authority not only by the appointing government but also by the host governments that received them (Adjaye, 1984).

The *Sika Akuma* (Golden Axe) was carried only by the Afenasoafohene or his immediate deputy or representative. The *Sika Akuma* symbolized resolution of conflict through peaceful negotiation. It signalled that the message carried by the bearer of the Golden Axe was the final one, the last resort to conciliatory processes on the part of the government before turning over the conduct of affairs

---

[73] In his autobiography, Nana Baafour Osei Akoto (1992, p. 20) indicates that "The Butuakwa Stool serves as the liaison between the Asantehene and some paramount chiefs in the country namely, that of Juaben State, Kokofu State, Nkoranza State, Agona-Asante State, Akim Abuakwa State, New Juaben State, Yendi in the Northern Region, and the Adonten Clan of Kumasi."

to the military authorities. This occurred, for example, in 1807, when Fante militants rejected any negotiated settlement of differences and actually seized the Golden Axe. War inevitably followed.

The conduct of Foreign Service gave rise to the use of other written forms such as Arabic, Dutch, and English as means of communication with foreigners. The *ɔhene krakye* (the King's secretary), for instance, emerged as the official specializing in the English correspondence of the Asantehene. However, "written diplomacy" was not regarded as a substitute for "oral diplomacy;" the written communication was only employed as a supplement to the traditional oral medium (Adjaye, 1984).

Peace (*asomdwoeɛ-* #233; #220) is highly treasured by the Akan. The king's palace is referred to as *asomdwoeɛfie* (house of peace - #234). The Akan require their newly installed chiefs to plant a tree as a sign of peace, continuity of state authority and proper succession. During the planting ceremony, the trees planted by his predecessors were decorated with white cloth or *hyire* (white clay), and before these trees the new chief would swear an oath to rule well and guard his people and maintain peace in the state. Thus, these trees symbolized the spiritual coolness or peace (*adwo* - #220) and orderliness of the state. The trees also serve as shady areas in towns and villages (*nnyedua ase*) where people gather for festivals, games (*ɔware, ntɛ, and dame*), and for town meetings. As McLeod (1981) points out, before going to war, a chief would swear an oath that he would not permit the enemy to cut down the trees. "Being a symbol of political unity and therefore also of military strength," Platvoet (1985, p. 183) writes, "the Akan *gyedua* featured not only in the political processes of concluding peace, but also in those of waging war... Before going to war, the ruler of a town might visit the central *gyedua* of his town and swear to it that he would not take to flight nor allow the enemy to capture the town and cut down its *gyennua*."

On the other hand, "rebellion against a ruler was often proclaimed by the 'young men' [*nkwankwaa*] striking off leaves and twigs from the (central) *gyedua*, thus stating their intention to depose him, with, or at times without, the due processes of law.... Such an attack upon the *gyedua* and the king was possible only if it expressed a widespread feeling" of disaffection (Platvoet, 1985, p. 190). When the chief died, the *werɛmpefoɔ* would tear down some of the branches of the *gyedua* trees as a sign of disorder which had come upon the Asante nation following the chief's death.

The masses of the people form what may be referred to as *asaase aban* (earth fortress - # 354). When the masses rise, as they did in the Yaa Asantewaa War of 1900 and the civil war of the 1880s, they are uncontrollable. In 1896 Asantehene Prempeh I prevented his people from fighting the British in a war which, he, in his judicious foresight, felt must be avoided. Of his own volition he chose to be taken prisoner and be exiled rather than lose thousands of his people. However, in 1900 when the Governor went to Kumasi and demanded the surrender of the Golden Stool (*Sika Dwa*) so that he could sit on it as the representative of Queen Victoria, the masses could not be restrained any longer. They listened to the speech in utter silence, dispersed quietly, and prepared for war against the British. The war effort by the masses to save the Golden Stool from falling into the hands of the British was led by Yaa Asantewaa, queenmother of Edweso (Boahen, 1972).

CHAPTER 6

Sɛ ɔman mu yɛ dɛ a, yɛn nyinaa te mu bi
If there is peace, prosperity and stability in a state, we all live in it

GOVERNMENTAL ORGANIZATION

STATE AUTHORITY

The sovereignty and power of Akan rulers are expressed through many objects that constitute the royal regalia. The palace, linguist's staffs, stools, swords, crowns, umbrellas, musical instruments, military accoutrements and other items all together play a significant role in enhancing the ambience of the ruler and in calling attention to his authority. The *adinkra* cloth producers make use of some of these items of regalia to chronicle the political organization and history of the nation, and functions of individuals in the political system of the society. These *adinkra* symbols also testify to the technical excellence of the people and the highly complex bureaucratic organization the society developed in a centralized monarchical state system.

In Asante, as in other Akan societies, the most important item of the regalia of the royalty is the stool (*ɔhene adwa* or *akonnwa* - #278-292). Before discussing the symbolism of the king's stool, we need to point out that there are several types of stools used by all manner of people. Stools may be "classified according to the sex of the user," writes Sarpong (1971, p. 17). He points out that men have their stools as do women. "The social status of the persons who use stools for official purposes," Sarpong continues, "affords still another purpose of stools." Another interpretation of the existence of male and female stools is that these depict the masculine and feminine qualities of leadership. The *esenkɛse* and *forowa* stools, for example, depict the responsibility of the King to ensure provisions from the hearth (*bukyia* - #244-245), represented by the queenmother, for his people's material needs, hence the expression: *ɛsɛn kɛseɛ a ɔgye adididodoɔ* - the big pot that provides for many. There are the chief's stool (*ahennwa*), queenmother's stool (*ahemmadwa*) and the poor person's stool (*adammadwa* - literally two-penny stool). In everyday sense, the stool is also a symbol of hospitality. When one goes to another's house one is first offered a stool to sit on and then water to drink to signify that one is welcome to the house.

Ɔhene Adwa -**King's Stool**

The *ɔhene adwa* (king's stool - #278-292) encodes the Akan philosophical construct of state territoriality. As Preston (1973, p. 81) points out, the *ɔhene adwa* "exists only in relation to specific laws of custody of the earth [*asaase* - #29-31] and this custody has its origins in prime occupancy of territory which is considered a de facto sacred act." That is, the existence of *ɔhene adwa* carries a territorial concept with it. This territory may be *kuro* (town) or *ɔman* (state). In essence, where there is no stool, there is no town or state.

There are two types of stools associated with the political system: the blackened stools of the ancestors and the white stools of the reigning king.[74] The stool of the reigning king is white or the natural color of the wood from which it is carved.[75] The stools of the kings who proved to be great leaders are blackened and preserved in a special ceremony to honor them after they have passed away. The blackened stools are believed to inhabit the spirits of the ancestors, and are, therefore, believed to constitute the soul (*sunsum* - #42-43) of the nation.

These blackened stools are kept in the temple of stools (*nkonnwafieso*) as symbolic memorial and shrine of the great ancestors. As Sarpong (1971, p. 38) explains: "the stools are blackened firstly, in order that they may not appear too nasty; secondly, so that they may properly represent the dead and signify the sorrow of the living at the death of their chiefs; thirdly, so as to produce a feeling of awe in those who appear before them; and lastly, [as a method of preservation], to render the stools durable since they must be perpetually present to receive the sacrifices and offerings of the people."

The stool of the *ɔhene* is the sacred symbol of his political and religious authority as it represents the permanence and continuity of the nation (Busia, 1954). When a successful king dies in office his stool is blackened and added to the ancestral stools. In the olden days when there was a natural catastrophe, the incumbent ruler would deliberately stand on top of the stools of the ancestors as a sign of desecration in order to enrage and wake up the spirits of the ancestors to help the living deal with the catastrophe (McLeod, 1981, p. 117).

Because the stool of the king is believed to enshrine the ancestral power, it is considered sacred and religious, and its occupant is expected to be pure in heart and to hold high ethical and moral standards. As a symbol of state power it embodies the past, present, and the future of the nation, that is, it marks continuities across generations and groups and close solidarities between the living and the dead. Through the stool, the king serves as a link between the living and the dead as well as the yet-to-be-born members of the society. The king has the responsibility to preserve the stool for posterity. The stool binds all the members of the family (and thus the nation) together. These views about the Akan stool are succinctly summed up by Preston (1973, p. 81) thus:

> Stools are the symbolic axis of the leadership complex. Stools enshrine the collective spiritual essence of past, present, and future generations of the state's populace, and the collective ancestral *kra* of the royals past, present, and future. The *ɔmanhene* symbolically sits on the consecrated stool of the founder of the state, who indeed actually did sit upon the stool before its ritual elevation.

---

[74] Chiefs have added to their collection of stools adaptations of European chairs. These adapted chairs are the *asipim* and *konkromfi*.

[75] The stool is oftentimes made from white wood such as *ɔsɛsɛ* (*funtumia sp.*), *nyamedua* (Apoctnaceae Alstonia), and *tweneboa* or *kodua* (cedar). Occasionally colored wood such as mahogany may be used in carving stools.

Each king decides on the symbol to be incorporated in his stool.[76] This public policy statement associated with the stool is encoded in the *adinkra* cloth Fig.18. For example, Asantehene Nana Prempeh II chose the *nyansapɔ* (wisdom knot - #797-799) to convey the notion that he would solve the Asante nation's problems by sagacity rather than by the power of the sword. Other king's stool symbols that have been incorporated in the *adinkra* cloth include *dame dame* (checkers - #820-821), *ɛsono* (elephant - #351-354), *mmeramubere* (female cross - #25-28), *kɔtɔkɔ* (porcupine - #412-413), *dɛnkyɛm* (crocodile - #345-350) and, *ɔsrane* (crescent moon - #618-621). Sarpong (1971) provides a catalogue of several of the king's stools.

Figure 18: Screen-printed *adinkra* cloth called *Yenni hene kwa* - one does not become a king for no reason

The most important *ɔhene* stool of the Asante nation is the *Sika Dwa Kofi* (Golden Stool – Fig.19). The *Sika Dwa* is believed to be the abode of the soul (*sunsum* - #42-43) of the Asante nation. It symbolizes the power, health, and wealth of the Asante nation. It is exhibited only on the installation of the Asantehene, at durbars such as the *Adae* and *Odwira* festivals, and on special occasions for the formal presentation of the Asantehene to his people. Such occasions present assurances of the stool's safekeeping and an opportunity to enjoy the hospitality and munificence of the leader. More discussion on the *Sika Dwa* has been provided in Chapter 5.

In the Asante society, as Wilks (1975) points out, the ultimate fount of all political authority (*tumi*) has been symbolized by the Golden Stool (*Sika Dwa Kofi*), and the ultimate assignee of the

---

[76] There are three parts to the stool: the base, the middle, and the top. The middle portion usually incorporates a symbol which may be associated with a proverb, a maxim or some phenomenon (Rattray, 1969; Sarpong, 1971). The symbols incorporated in the stool served to give names to the stools. In the past the symbols served to determine social class and status, age and sex of the owner.

wealth of the nation was symbolized by the Golden Elephant's Tail (*Sika Mena*). "As a 'natural' feature of society... political-jural authority flowed downwards from the Asantehene to the people under the Golden Stool, and as an equally 'natural' feature of society... wealth flowed upwards from the people (by various forms of taxation) to the Asantehene, under the Golden Elephant's Tail (Wilks, 1975, p. 430). Thus, the custodian of the *Sika Dwa* (the powerful – *otumfoɔ*) was he who legitimately exercised *tumi* (political power). The *Sika Mena* symbolized the highest level of government at which wealth was appropriated and redistributed (*ɔgye*); thus in addition to being *otumfoɔ* the Asantehene was also *ɔgyefoɔ* - the taking one (Wilks, 1975, p. 430). The Golden Axe (*Sika Akuma*) symbolized the power of the Asantehene to resolve disputes peacefully, that is, serve as the chief judge. This is depicted by the following expression: *Dua biara nni hɔ a ɛyɛ den sɛ akuma ntumi ntwa, nanso asɛm biara yɛ den dɛn ara a, yɛmmfa akuma na ɛtwa, na yɛde yɛn ano ɛka ma no twa* - There is no tree that is so hard that it cannot be felled with an axe; however, no matter how difficult an issue may be, it must be settled by counseling and negotiations, not with an axe (#695-697).

Figure 19: The Golden Stool on public display

Ɔhemmaa adwa - Queenmother's stool

The queenmother was the co-ruler and had joint responsibility with the king for all affairs of the state (Rattray, 1923; Meyerowitz, 1951; Busia, 1951; Aidoo, 1981; Arhin, 1983; Manuh, 1988). This important constitutional role of the queenmother was illustrated by the Asante political organization in which the *ɔhemmaa adwa* (queenmother's stool) was the *akonnua panin*, the senior stool in relation to the *ɔhene adwa* (king's stool). As Aidoo (1981, p. 66) points out: "As a full member and cochairman of the governing council or assembly of the state, the queen mother's presence was required whenever important matters of state were to be decided." This is incorporated in the *sumpie* (pyramid - #294-296) symbol. The queenmother sitting side by side with king on the *sumpie* is one of the significant occasions for the public display of the constitutional role of the queenmother. The queenmother who successfully carried out her constitutional and other responsibilities was honored as *ɔhemmaa papa* (good queenmother - #301). See the previous chapter for more discussion about this power-sharing arrangement between the king and the queenmother.

Ɔkyeame Poma - Linguist's Staff

Next in importance to the stools are the staffs of the linguists (*akyeame poma* - #182-183). At public functions, the *ɔkyeame* carries a staff (or mace) of authority. The *ɔkyeame* position is an appointive one, and it is not inherited. The appointment is often based on achievement characteristics. Any linguist is a very intelligent and eloquent person. He has the ability to polish whatever is said to *ɔhene* or from *ɔhene* to his people. He can shape or change a speech in a more refined way. An *ɔkyeame* is traditionally referred to as the *ɔhene yere*, the chief's wife. The staff is usually carved from wood and may be embellished with gold leaf. Usually the top part of the staff is a symbol designed to communicate specific messages either about the status and authority of the *ɔkyeame* or the message he, as a diplomat, is authorized to convey on behalf of the king at specific public functions. Some of these staffs convey Akan beliefs, political organization, and social values (Yankah, 1995). Other staffs encode various aspects of the Akan leadership complex. The Asantehene linguists, for example, carry the following staffs among others:

1) *fɛntɛmfrɛm a ɔmene ɛsono* – the bog that swallows the elephant.
2) *apɔnkyerɛne da nsuom yɛ kɛse sɛn ara a, ɔne apitire nnsɛ da* – no matter how big the frog may grow to be, it will never become the mudfish (catfish).
3) *aboa biara nni soro a ɔwe kube* – no bird eats coconut.
4) *ɔbaako werɛ aduro a egu* – when one person scrapes the bark of a tree all by oneself it falls

Akofena - State Swords

Figure 20: Mampong State Swords

Another important set of regalia are the gold-hilted state swords as indicated by the *adinkra* symbols *akofena* (state swords - #260-269) and *tumi afena* (sword of power - #257-258) – see Fig.20. *Akofena* symbolizes state authority, power and legitimacy. *Akofena* is also known as *nsuaefena* as it is used by chiefs to swear the oath of office and by sub-chiefs to swear allegiance to a higher authority. The most significant feature of the swearing the oath of office ritual – acceptance of certain injunction and their prescriptions by the chief-elect – was discussed in Chapter 5. There are various state swords that are used for specific functions. Kyerematen (1964, p. 34, 36) distinguishes as many as six categories and sub-categories of state swords for the Asantehene. Two major categories are the *kɛtɛanofena* and *akofena*. *Kɛtɛanofena* swords are either *akrafena* or *bosomfena*, which are carried respectively on the right and left sides of the king in state processions. The division of these swords into two groups embodies and represents two distinct spiritual elements. Those carried on the Asantehene's right (*akrafena*) represent his soul or life-force (*kra*) and are washed, along with other items of regalia, as part of the annual soul-cleansing ceremony (*odwira*). The swords carried on the Asantehene's left (*bosomfena*) represent his ego, spirit or personality (*sunsum*) that he inherits from his father. This complementary division of regalia also mirrors that of the Asante court, which presents itself during public occasions in the form of an arc with distinct right and left wings. The third and somewhat more common name for the swords in the *bosomfena* category is *nsuaefena* (lit. 'oath swords'), which reflects the fact that they are used by the Asantehene to swear his oath of office during installation ceremonies and by the lesser chiefs. These swords may also function as badges of office that vouch for the veracity of official messengers who are entrusted to deliver verbal communications.

Each Asantehene is required by custom, dating back to Opoku Ware I (who reigned around 1731-1742), to create their own two swords: *akrafena* and *bosomfena*. State swords known as *akrafena* (literally, soul sword) are used in the rituals for purifying the chief's soul and various blackened ancestral stools. The "*akrafena* and *bosomfena* together are representative of the spiritual and physical, masculine and feminine, individual and political dualities necessary to form a complete society in both royal and non-royal classes" (Erlich, 1981, p. 43). The four principal state swords of the Asantehene are the *Bosommuru*, *Mpomponsuo*, *Bosompra* and *Bosomtwe*. The *Bosommuru*, first made for Asantehene Osei Tutu, is the state sword with which every Asantehene dedicates himself to the service of the nation. It represents Osei Tutu's *sunsum* (soul - #42-43) and is one of the *bosomfena* or the left-hand swords. The *Mpomponsuo* (symbolizing responsibility - #259) belonged to Asantehene Opoku Ware I. This is a special *akofena* with which the Asantehene swears the oath of office. The *amanhene* in turn use this state sword to swear the oath of allegiance and loyalty to the Asantehene. "The oath system as known today in Ashanti," according to Hagan (1971, p. 49, n. 21) "perhaps dates back to Opoku Ware who instituted the use of the *Mpomponsuo* for oath taking." *Mpomponsuo* (responsibility - #259) is the foremost example of the *akrafena*, or the right-hand swords (Fraser, 1972, p. 145).

Asantehene Kwaku Dua I made the third most important state sword, *Bosompra* as his *bosomfena* and *Kraku* as his *akrafena*. *Bosompra* is one of the foremost examples of the left-hand state swords. It is used by the Asantehene to send messages to the Queenmother. The embossment (*abɔsodeɛ*) on this state sword is a treasure container (*kuduo*). It symbolizes the responsibility of the King to ensure provisions from the hearth (*bukyia* - #244-245), represented by the queenmother, for his people's material needs, hence the expression: *ɛsɛn kɛseɛ a ɔgye adididodoɔ* - the big pot that provides for many.

The fourth most important Asante state sword in the *kɛtɛanofena* group of swords is the *Bosomtwe*, which is linked with a deity that resides in Lake Bosomtwe. The embossment on this sword is the *dɛnkyɛm* (crocodile - #345-350) which symbolizes power, greatness and adaptability. There are a variety of state swords with symbols embossed on the blade for use by the state functionaries according to their rank or status in the governmental structure (Ross, 1977; Fraser, 1972; Kyerematen, 1964). Examples of symbols that are encoded in the *adinkra* cloth that may be found as *abɔsodeɛ* (embossment) on state swords include *kɔtɔkɔ* (porcupine - #412-413), *bese saka* (bunch of kola nuts - #706-712), *nkatehono* (groundnut shell - #713), *akuma* (axe - #695-697), and *nsoromma* (star - #130-138).

State swords known as *asomfena* (service or courier swords) are carried by state traders, royal messengers and ambassadors as tokens of credibility and credentials on diplomatic and other state missions. The *ahoprafoɔafena* (fly whisk bearers sword) is an example of service sword. Other specialized swords included the *abrafoɔafena*, *sepɔ* (dagger - #450-452) and *afenatene*. The *abrafoɔafena* looked more like a bayonet than a sword and was used by the constabulary, *abrafoɔ*. The *sepɔ* was a small knife "used in the past by executioners for thrusting through the cheeks of their victims to prevent them [from] uttering a curse [on the king]" (Kyerematen, 1964, p. 36).

The "*afenatene*, literally the long sword, is differently shaped and is not carried about but planted in the ground. It has a triple blade, much shorter than that of the other swords in proportion to the rest of the sword, and between it and the hilt is a long shaft of various decorative forms such as plaits and spirals" (Kyerematen, 1964, p. 34).

Chiefs maintain a group of sword-bearers, each of whom carries one of the various state swords on public occasions. While swords were an important military weapon in the past, their use these days is ceremonial as they have unsharpened blades. An example of such swords is the *dɔmfonsan* which was "used on the battlefield for swearing the oath of fidelity and for leading the army" (Kyerematen, 1964, p. 36).

Figure 21: Factory printed *adinkra* cloth with *akofena* and *adinkrahene* symbols

Other State Regalia

Other important symbols of state authority that have been encoded in the *adinkra* cloth include the umbrella (*ɔhene kyiniiɛ* - #271-275), king's gun (*ɔhene tuo* - #404-407), king's crown or head band (*ɔhene kyɛ* or *ɔhene abotire* - #298-299), horns (*mmɛntia* or *ntahera* - #276-277)[77], iron bells

---

[77] Sarpong (1990) explains that the horns are of great variety and serve several purposes. The Amoakwa has been detailed by the Asantehene for the Asantehemaa, and together with *dawuro* (bells - #386-389) and

(*dawuru* - #386-388; #384-385), drums (e.g. *donno* - #500, *donno nta* #501-509, *atumpan* - #883, *kete*), and palanquins. The king's gun (*ɔhene tuo* - #404-407) symbolizes the military responsibility of the king to guard and ensure the security and defense of the nation. The symbolic importance of the gun is to be inferred from the following text used in the swearing of the king-elect to become the Asantehene:

> I am the descendant of Osei and Opoku
> of Bonsu and Agyeman
> I am direct nephew of Prempeh.
> Today the soul of Agyeman Prempeh has gone whence it came and his gun lies idle.
> By your grace and the grace of Kumase people
> You have presented the gun to me
> If I do not protect and govern you well
> as did my forbearers
> I swear the Great Oath (Kyerematen, n.d., p. 18).

The Asantehene-elect later fires the *ɔhene tuo* (the king's gun - #404-407) to demonstrate his capability of commanding the state's military forces on the battlefield. Soon after being formally sworn into office, he holds the *Mpomponsuo* (responsibility - #259) sword in his right hand and the *ɔhene tuo* (king's gun - #404-407) in the left, and steps out to dance to the *atoprɛtea* rhythms of the *fontomfrɔm* ensemble (Kyerematen, n.d.). This ceremonial use of the instruments of national defense and security is also encoded by the *adinkra* symbol called *afena ne tuo* (sword and gun - #416 - see Fig.22).

The umbrella (*ɔhene kyiniiɛ* - #298-299), on the other hand, indicates who the king is among a gathering of people as reflected in the aphorism: *Nea kyiniiɛ si no so na ɔyɛ ɔhene* (He who has the umbrella over his head is the king). The umbrella is also symbol of the protection the king is believed to provide for the nation. Fraser (1972, p. 145) notes that "these huge objects are both practical sunshades and symbolic, quasi-architectural, space-defining forms that help express the chief's role as ruler." When the king dies it is metaphorically said that "Nana has removed his umbrella; we shall be scorched to death by the sun" (*Nana atu ne kyiniiɛ; owia na ɛbɛku yɛn*).

The Asantehene has no less than 23 different umbrellas each of which is used on a particular occasion (Fraser, 1972). Some of these umbrellas are the *Bɔ-aman*, *Akatamanso*, *Nsaa kyiniiɛ*, and *Akropɔnkyiniwa*. On the top of the umbrella is usually placed a carved symbol (*ntuatire*) with a specific meaning. These include symbols like *sankɔfa* (go back and retrieve - #773-793), *babadua* (bamboo specie - #226), *akobɛn* (war horn - #397-403), *akokɔbaatan ne ne mma* (the hen and her chicken - #), and *tikorɔ nkɔ agyina* (one head does not form a council - #192-193). These symbols are deliberately displayed as part of the king's regalia on festive occasions so that "all who see them may read, mark and inwardly digest what they stand for" (Kyerematen, 1964, p. 1). Even though the first published illustration of the state umbrella was by Muller in 1673, the use of state umbrellas in West Africa had been the subject of commentary by Arab chroniclers who observed them in ancient Mali (Fraser and Cole, 1972, p. 308).

---

atumpan drums - #883 it forms part of the Queenmother's ceremonial orchestra (*ɔhemaa agorɔ*). Other horns include the *nkrawobɛn* (#276 - which is believed to have been brought to Asante by some Denkyira defectors during the 'Osanti' War), *asikabɛn*, *kwakorannya*, *nkofe*, *nkontwewa*, *durugya*, and *atɛntɛbɛn*, and these are grouped into various ensembles.

**Figure 22: Factory printed *adinkra* cloth with the gye Nyame, ɔhene tuo,
akofena, adinkrahene, *kyiniiɛ* and *atumpan* drum symbols**

The drums (symbolized for example by *donno* - #500, and *atumpan* - #883) and the horns
(symbolized for example by *abɛntia* #277 and *nkrawobɛn* - #276) are the divine media that give vocal
expression to the existence of the soul of the nation and its continuity. These media are used in
providing music and to transmit ancestral history and other sacred texts. Drum texts are utilized
as (a) invocation of ancestral spirits and to recall ancestral history; (b) eulogy; (c) proverbs; and
(d) to communicate greetings, praises, congratulations, warnings, emergency calls and general
announcements. Particular drums and horns are used to extol the praises of the king. There are
several types of drums, for example, *atumpan* (talking drum - #883), *donno* (bell drum - #500), *mpintin*,
and *fontɔmfrɔm*. The drum messages, for example, may be used to refer to the king as the powerful
one, the benefactor, the people's mother (*nkuruma kɛse* - #323-331), the valiant one, and the vigilant
and all-seeing one (that is, *ɔhene aniwa twa ne ho hyia* - #318-320). The ɔhene is also referred to in
various contexts by the drummer as *nkuruma kɛse* (#33-331), *ɛsono* (#351-354) or *dɛnkyɛm* (#345-350).
The good king may be referred to as the elephant (*ɛsono* - #351-354) that provides shelter, security
and protection to his subjects so that they do not get wet, that is, they are not harmed.

Some drums (*donno* - #500 and *atumpan* - #883) are used for special purposes. For example,
asuboa drum is used to imitate the cry of the crocodile, the *etwie* drum is used to imitate the roar of
the leopard. The *etwie* drum was used in the past in military campaigns to deceive the enemy. The
aworobɛn was in the past played behind a thief to disgrace him publicly (Sarpong, 1974; Nketia, 1969).

The horns (*mmɛnson, ntahera* or *mmɛntia* - #276-277) are used by the horn-blowers of the various
horn ensembles to allude to the power of the king thus: "He is like the hawk that roams all nations,
he will come home with victory." 'It is the horns that make us know who is a king or a chief' is a well
known adage spoken in relation to the king. The horns are also used to mention very witty historical
events or to draw attention to the king in very few words. They are also used to call attention to
the skill, diligence, craftiness, and power of the king. An example of a horn message is as follows:

Woahunu mmoa nyinaa brɛboɔ, woahunu ntɛtea brɛboɔ pɛn? This literally means: You have seen the liver of all animals, but have you ever seen the liver of the ant?

Ahemfie - **Palace**

The seat of government is called *ahemfie* or *aban* (palace, castle, fortress, or stone house - #247-256). The *aban* or *ahemfie* is usually a massive and monumental piece of architecture which appears, in its relative permanence, to symbolize the enduring character of divine kingship (Fraser and Cole, 1972, p. 308). The palace tends to create an isolating spatial envelope that provides shelter for leaders.

During the reign of Asantehene Osei Bonsu, a magnificent palace (*Aban, Abrɔsan,* or *Abansoro*-#247-256) was built. This palace was made of carved stone and was completed in 1822. It was roofed with brass laid over an ivory framework, and the windows and doors were cased in gold, and the door posts and pillars were made of ivory. Wealthy merchants of Elmina are believed to have aided in the construction of the king's stone house at Kumase (Yarak, 1986). The *aban* has been referred to as the Palace of Culture. This fortress was ransacked and blown up by the British in the 1874 war (McLeod, 1981; Wilks, 1992).

Attached to the *ahemfie* would be the harem (*mma mu* also known *hia* or *hyiaa*), quarters for the women. There is an *adinkra* symbol called *ɔhene kɔ hia*, and one of the names of the *adinkra* cloths is also called *ɔhene kɔ hia* (The king is gone to the harem to visit his wives - #322). The Asantehene's palace is called *Manhyia*. The personal residence of the king within *Manhyia* is called *Abrɔsanase*.

There is a raised platform or dais (*sumpie* - #294-296) that stands in the front yard of the king's palace. This is used by the king for making public addresses. At Manhyia Palace there are two such royal daises: *Sumpie Kumaa* (also known as *Bogyawe*) and *Sumpie Kɛseɛ* (also known as *Dwaberem*).

GOVERNMENTAL STRUCTURE

In this section, I use the Asante governmental structure to discuss Akan political organization as coded by the *adinkra* symbols. The Asante people developed a highly structured state organization with systems of rules and regulations that were used to govern the society. The authority and power systems set out the statuses within the social structure indicating who must take and receive orders. The Asante political structure was based on corporate kin groups with the primary unit being the family. The head of the household, usually the man, served as the head of that political unit. The household head was mirrored in instituted officers of progressively larger political units with basic unit as the extended family (or matriclan - *abusua*), to the town (*kuro*)[78], and the highest unit being the nation-state (*ɔman* or *ɔmantoɔ*). This is depicted as follows:

Political Unit	Head of Unit
Fie (Household)	*Fie panin* (*agya* or *wɔfa*)
Abusua (Family or matriclan)	*Abusua panin*
Kuro (village or town)	*Ɔdekuro* or *Ɔhene* and *Ɔhemmaa*
Ɔman or *ɔmantoɔ* (nation-state or kingdom)	*Ɔmanhene* and *Ɔhemmaa*

---

[78] There is also the *akuraa* (hamlet or farmstead) which is considered a temporary settlement usually of members of a household on a farm. This is headed by the head of the household.

The head of each unit serves as the religious, legislative, judiciary, and administrative leader for the unit. At the *kurow* and *oman* levels of government, the leader is considered as the supreme priest of all the gods in his dominion, and he represents the priests (*nsumankwa* – medicine men and *akomfo* – religious practitioners) in the legislative council. He also has the duty to see to it that all the rituals and ceremonies connected with all the gods of the dominion are carried out so that the welfare of his people is not endangered. The *ohene* who carried out his responsibilities and ensured peace and progress in the state was considered *ohene papa* (good king - #300). The *ohene papa* (good king - #300) represents *Nyankopon* the masculine aspect of the Supreme Being on earth. The *ohemmaa papa* (good queenmother - #301) represents Nyame, *oma owia* (giver of the sun), the feminine aspect of the Supreme Being on earth. At the higher levels of the political system, the *odekuro* and *omanhene* also serve as the military leaders. Membership in the military organization (*asafo*) was patrilineally determined. At the higher levels of the political system, the *odekuro* and *omanhene* are chosen by the queenmother subject to the approval of the council of state, and the masses.

At the *kuro* level there is a village or town council (*nhyiamu*) made up of the *odekuro* and *abusua mpanyimfoo* (heads of the various matriclans in the town/village) and *ohemmaa*. The council regulates the village/town affairs such as settling disputes arising among members of different lineages. The council also carries out such welfare services as ordering the periodic cleaning of the village/town, the clearing of bushes around streams that were the main sources of water for the community, and the maintenance of paths leading to the main farm areas or to the capital (*ahenkro* or *akropon*) of the state (Busia, 1951, pp. 63-65). Such voluntary services are led by the *asafo* (the militia).

The village/town council also serves as the channel of communication between the village/town, the division, and the state. It transmits orders (a) to make contributions in cash and/or in kind for state funeral rites and toward installation expenses of the heads of the division and the state; (b) to levy fighting men for war; and, (c) to execute policies relating to divisional and national concerns.

Orders are transmitted to the general public through public announcements by the *dawuroboni* (town crier) depicted by the *adinkra* symbol *Agyin dawuro* - Agyin's iron bell (#384-385). In emergency situations such as fire or some natural disaster, the *asafo* drum or *akoben* (war horn - #397-403) would be sounded to call every able-bodied person to action. Answering such clarion calls was considered an honorable and patriotic duty. One was considered a coward who was able but would not volunteer one's services in times of national crisis. *Kosankobi, wokasa obaa ano a, Kobiri nku wo* (deserter, may *Kobiri* [a deity] kill you if you dare speak as a man to a woman – (#397-403) was a way of deriding cowards.

Governmental Structure in Asante

The Asante Constitution was such that at the head of the Asante governmental structure stood the Asantehene (Asante king) and Asantehemaa (Asante queenmother). He was considered the guardian of the temporal and spiritual unity of the kingdom. Although the Asantehene had enormous powers that clearly gave him the potential of becoming an autocrat, his exercise of those powers and his independence in decision-making were, in fact, closely circumscribed by the legal and customary norms of the polity and the Seventy-seven (77) Laws given to the state by Okomfo Anokye. Blatant violations of these laws and norms could result in public and formal charges leading to impeachment and destoolment. The queenmother had the constitutional responsibility to advice and guide the king, and she had the right to criticize and rebuke him in public (Aidoo, 1981; Manuh, 1988).

Below the Asantehene were the *amanhene* of the confederate states (*amantoɔ*), and under these were the *adekurofoɔ* - chiefs of the various towns and villages. The Asantehene – as Kumasehene - was the *primus inter pares* (first among equals) as far as the *amanhene* were concerned. The *amanhene* had their obligations to the Asantehene, but they also had compensating rights. The *amanhene* had to swear oath of allegiance and loyalty to the Asantehene promising to heed his call by day or night; they were obliged to supply him with fighting men when so required and contribute to a war tax (*apeatuo*) or a national levy imposed by the Asantehene for some specific purpose; and they recognized a right of appeal from their own courts to the Asantehene's court at Kumase.

The *amanhene* were expected to attend the Asantehene's *Odwira* festival. They also recognized certain trade regulations of the Asantehene and his conduct of foreign affairs. The *ɔmanhene* combined executive, judiciary and legislative as well as religious functions. The *ɔmanhene* also served as the commander-in-chief of the army. In assuming office, the chief would swear the oath of office using *akofena* (state swords - #260-269).

The Asante Empire comprised a Confederacy and the tributary states. The Confederacy consisted of the sovereign states (*amantoɔ*) of Mampɔn, Bekwai, Nsuta, Dwaben, Kumawu, Kokofu, Kumasi, Offinso, Asumegya and Ejisu where each one of them had its own *ɔmanhene* and a council of state. The Kumasehene is also the Asantehene, *a primus inter pares*. Each of these *amanhene* swears the oath of allegiance and loyalty to the Asantehene. In Kumasi, for example, the council of state is headed by the Kumasehene (who is also the Asantehene). The Bantamahene, who is also the Kumase Kontirehene, is the senior ranking functionary and presides over the affairs of the council in the absence of the Asantehene. The Kumasi Kontirehene is the commander-in-chief of the Kumase army. Next in command in the Kumasi army is Akwamuhene who also serves as the Asafohene.

The Asantehene presided over two important decision-making councils of state: *Asantemanhyiamu* (Assembly of the Asante Nation) and the Council of Kumasi.[79] The origin of the *Asantemanhyiamu* presumably dates from the formation of the Asante kingdom in the late seventeenth century.

Originally the *Asantemanhyiamu* was intended to function as the supreme legislative and judicial body of the *Asanteman*. However, the unwieldiness of the convocations of the *Asantemanhyiamu* and its inadequacy for the management of the complex day-to-day affairs of government became such that the Council of Kumase gradually assumed, *de facto*, the powers of the *Asantemanhyiamu*. With time, especially after the 1874 war in which the British defeated Asante, dissenting local politicians in the various *amantoɔ* reacted against Kumase's highly centralized style of governing and its dominance in nearly all phases of political life - decision-making, appointments, control over the public sector of the national economy, instruments of coercion, and foreign policy.

The hierarchy in the Akan governmental structure as exemplified by the Kumase system of government (Council of State) comprised the King, the Queen Mother, the *Kontire ne Akwamu* and *Mpanimfoɔ* (Elders), and *Gyaasehene*, and *Gyaasewahene*. The *Mpanyimfoɔ* (Elders) consisted of *Abusua Ahemfo* (Clan Chiefs), viz: *Ɔyokohene*, *Beretuohene*, and *Aduanahene*. The remaining members of *Mpanyimfoɔ* comprised the leaders of the various military divisions in the state, namely, *Benkumhene*, *Nifahene*, *Twafoɔhene*, *Adɔntenhene*, *Ankɔbeahene*, *Kyidɔmhene*, and *Akyeamehene*.

The Kumasi Council of State was presided over by the *Asantehene* and operated as the highest court of justice and chief advisory body to the *Asantehene*. By the middle of the nineteenth century the Kumase Council of State had extended its influence over Asante domestic administration, the conduct of foreign policy, and central government operations in trade, public works, guild craft,

---

[79] Each of the confederate states had its own Council of State. For example, the Dwabenhene was the head of the Dwaben Council of State. The Kumase Council served as Advisory Council to the Asantehene.

and fiscal and monetary regulations. Membership in the Council of Kumasi varied over time and according to the type of business under discussion. Senior Kumasi *ahemfo* occupied seats on the Council. Heads of the civil and military organizations and other appointive bureaucratic and princely offices were also members of the Council. Other members included the *abusua ahemfo*. The Council brought in outside expertise by making people with specialized skill and knowledge in specific areas of governmental affairs adjunct members without voting rights. The *Asante Nkramo* (Asante Muslims), who served under the administrative supervision of the *Nsumankwaahene* of Kumase as scribes (*ohene krakye*), physicians, and spiritual advisors, constituted a very important group of such experts.

PUBLIC SERVICE

Public administration (*amammuo*) was developed into specialized service in which individuals acquired training and expertise. *Ahemfie adesua* (literally court learning) was the means by which individuals acquired the training and expertise to render public service. Public administrative roles in Asante society are described by the term *ɛsomdwuma* - literally public service work. Those employed in such roles are known as *asomfoɔ* or *nhenkwaa* (the king's courtiers). In the Asante society public service was developed into a highly complex hierarchy (Wilks, 1966) that initially was based on ascriptive characteristics but later developed to include individuals who earned their positions by achievement. The hierarchy ranged from the chief at the top through a layer of advisors (*akyeamefoɔ, mpanimfoɔ, akɔmfoɔ,* etc.) to the courtiers (*nhenkwaa*). Later as the political economy of the Asante Empire expanded other public service positions were created and these included *akwanmufoɔ* (road constructors), *nkwansrafoɔ* (road guards who collected tolls), *asokwafoɔ* (drummers, hornblowers) and *nsumankwaafoɔ* (scribes, medicinemen and herbalists). A new division of chiefs was created - the *gyaasewa* division - to be responsible for palace administration, public works and public trade (*bata fekuo*). Some of these public servants distinguished themselves successfully and were promoted to the status of chiefs, military leaders, envoys, governors, and *aberɛmpɔn*.

Rattray (1969) distinguished the following offices of public servants in the Asantehene Palace in Kumasi, capital of Asante: *akyeame* (spokesmen); *akonnwasoafoɔ* (stool carriers); *asokwafo* (drummers, horn blowers); *akyiniiɛkyimfoɔ* (umbrella carriers); *banmufoɔ* (caretakers of the royal mausoleum); *adwarefoɔ* (bathroom attendants); *akradwarefoɔ* (chief's soul-washers); *ahoprafoɔ* (elephant tail switchers); *papasoafoɔ* (fan bearers - #367-369); *soodofoɔ* (cooks); *asoamfoɔ* (hammock carriers); *akokwafoɔ* (floor polishers); *sanaafoɔ; fotosanfoɔ; adabrafoɔ* (eunuchs); *nsɛniefoɔ* (heralds); *afonasoafoɔ* (sword bearers); *atumtufoɔ* (gun bearers); *akyɛmfo* (shield bearers - #417; #879-880); *kwadwumfoɔ* (minstrels); *asumankwafoɔ* (scribes, medicine men and herbalists); *abansifoɔ, akwansrafoɔ,* or *akwansifoɔ* (highway policemen or road guards) - responsible for the protection of state traders, regulation of state trade, and control of immigration; *akwammɔfoɔ* (road maintenance group) - responsible for felling trees obstructing highways, clearing the highways of weeds, building bridges across rivers; and *abrafoɔ* (executioners). These various public servants were distinguished from one another by their haircuts (e.g., *mpua anum* - #357-362;892, *nkotimsefoɔ pua* - #370-375, *nkwantanan* - #363, and *mmɔdwewafoɔ pua* - #376-377), by the state swords (*akofena* - #260-269) they carried, helmets and medallions they wore, and the keys (*nsafoa* - #378-380) they carried.

In the royal household the king is served by four senior public servants who are responsible for his well-being. These are the *Gyaasehene* - chief of the royal household; *Daberɛhene* - the chamberlain in charge of the king's bed chamber; *Manwerɛhene* - the chief in charge of the king's clothing and personal effects; and the *Soodohene* - the chief of the royal cooks and culinary matters. Under these senior public servants served various people as the *abenasefoɔ* (king's wardrobe attendants), *mmɔwerɛbufoɔ* (barbers and manicurists), *mansufoɔ* (providers of drinking water), *patamufoɔ* (caretakers of drinks), *sɔmesisifoɔ* (waist-holders), *kaneasoafoɔ* (lamp bearers), and *aburamfoɔ* (goldsmiths). From these various positions functionaries were appointed to conduct diplomatic negotiations and the resolution of possible military disputes in the conquered territories and provinces administered from Kumase. These provincial administrators were known as *nhwɛsofoɔ*.

MILITARY

The king's gun (*ɔhene tuo* - #404-407) as pointed out earlier, signifies the military leadership of the king. This military responsibility is also signified by the symbol *ɔkɔdeɛmmɔwerɛ* (eagle's talons - #410-411). Even though the Asante, like the other Akan societies, had no standing army, the *asafo*[80] - i.e., a people's militia - was a well-established social and political organization based on martial principles. Every able-bodied person belonged to an *asafo* group; every child automatically belonged to his or her father's company. Internal sub-divisions within an individual company included the main fighting body, the scouts[81], reserves, and the minstrel unit whose main job it was to sing patriotic and war songs to boost the morale of the military.

In Asante, major reforms undertaken by Asantehene Osei Tutu in the late seventeenth century included the reorganization of the military by creating the *Kontirehene* and *Akwamuhene* as the military generals. Even though they were equals, the *Kontire* was regarded as the first among equals. The original *Kontire* (also known as *atuo nson* - seven gunners) was composed of Amankwatia, Safo Pasoam, Gyedu Kumanini, Akyampon Kofi, Brefo Apaw, Firam Gyereba, and Awua Kokonini. The Soaduru division created by Obiri Yeboa was reorganized and renamed the Akwamu in commemoration of Osei Tutu's sojourn and education in Akwamu (Wilks, 1975, 1992). These military and political reforms are encoded in the symbol *kuronti ne akwamu* (council of state - #194).

The *asafo* companies forming the Asante national army[82] were organized into main fighting divisions thus: *adɔnten* (vanguard - main body), *twafoɔ* (advance guard), *kyidɔm* (rearguard - under

---

[80] Asafo companies existed in all the Akan states. The Fantes went a step further by incorporating some European customs in their Asafo companies. The typical Asafo company, in a Fante township, according to Aggrey (1978), was headed by the *Tufohene*, the military advisor to the chief of the township. Next in line was the *Asafobaatan*. *Supi* was the commanding officer, and the divisional captain within a company was called the *Safohene* (for the male) or *Asafoakyerɛ* (for the female). Other ranks in the Asafo were the *Asafokɔmfo* (the priest), *ɔkyerɛma* - head of the *akyeremafo* (the drummers), *frankaakitani* (flag bearer), *sekanbɔni* (sword maker), *ɔkyeame* (spokesperson or linguist), and *abrafo* (executioners). Datta (1972) distinguishes between formal and informal offices, the former being characterized by a specific ritual with which the assumption of the office was marked. Among these offices are the *tufohene, asafobaatan, supi, safohene, frankaakitani, sekanbɔni,* and *ɔkyeame*. These office-holders take the appropriate oath on the assumption of office at formally organized ceremonies.

[81] The Akan Asafo scouting system is what Baden Powell is believed to have used as the model for creating the Scout Movement (Tufuo and Donkor, 1989).

[82] The Manponhene served as the Kontirehene of the Asante national army, the supreme commander of which was the Asantehene.

the *kyidɔmhene*), *nifa* (right wing)[83], *benkum* (left wing), *akwansra* (scouting division), *ankɔbea* (home guard), and *gyaase* (the king's bodyguard). *Asafo* companies were also differentiated by the different colors of headgear and hairstyles worn by members, exclusive drums, horns and other musical instruments, appellations, and emblems. Other units within the main divisions included *afonasoafoɔ* (the carriers of spears and shields), *sumankwaafoɔ* (the herbalists and medicine men), and the *asokwafoɔ* (heralds).

The *adinkra* symbols that relate to the military organization of the state include *ohene tuo* (#404-407), *gyawu atikɔ* (#), *akobɛn* (war horn - #), *akoo mmɔwerɛ* (parrot's talons - #408-409), *pagya* (strikes fire - #414-415), *ɔkɔdeɛ mmɔwerɛ* (eagle's talons - #410-411), and *tuo abobaa* (gun bullets - #223). In times of war or other national crises the *akobɛn* (war horn - #397-403) or war drums would sound, and every able-bodied person was expected to respond to the call to action. Answering the clarion call was deemed an honorable and patriotic duty.

In the past Asante warriors could be summoned from all areas to Kumase by drum beat and the sound of the war horn (*akobɛn* - #397-403) with the message: *Asante kotoko monka ntoa* - Asante porcupines, seize your gun and powder-cartridge belts. The Asante military's fighting strategy was likened to the porcupine's strategy of shooting its quills in barrages and how quickly it would reproduce them for protection against its predators. The *kotoko* symbol (porcupine - #412-413) and the expression: "*Asante kotoko, kum apem a, apem bɛba* - Asante porcupine, you kill a thousand, a thousand more will come" has become synonymous with Asante bravery, military prowess and gallantry. In present times the *asafo* continues to play an important role in emergency situations and in providing welfare services (e. g., fire, floods, or search parties for someone lost in the bush or drowning) especially in the rural areas.

Military titles of honor that were conferred on individuals for their heroism and bravery included *ɔsabarima*, *baafoɔ*, *ɔsahene*, *katakyie*, *aberɛmpɔn*, *ɔsagyefo*, and *ɔgyeatuo*. The *ɛkyɛm* (shield - #417; #879-880) symbol depicts heroic deeds and bravery. Such heroic deeds were treasured long after the death of the hero as implied in the following maxim: *ɛkyɛm tete a, ɛka ne meramu* (When a shield wears out, the framework still remains - #417; #879-880). The prestigious title of *aberɛmpɔn* was conferred on individuals who not only rendered but also excelled in military service. This title was later conferred on successful *batafoɔ* (state traders). Chiefs who earned the *aberɛmpɔn* title were allowed to carry *sika mena* (gilded elephant tails). The highly prestigious title of *aberɛmpɔn* was seldom conferred for other than valor, but later it became one with which distinguished service to the state might be rewarded. Hence the expression: *ɔbarima wɔyɛ no dɔm ano, na wɔnyɛ no fie*, meaning a man is made facing the enemy [on the battlefield], not in the home.

JUSTICE, LAW, AND ORDER

The Akan did not separate in different individuals or institutions the functions of the executive and the judiciary. To understand the Akan system of justice, law and order encoded by the *adinkra* symbols the Kumase state organization will be used here for illustrative purposes. The Council of State in Kumase, for example, functioned as a court both of legislation (*amansɛm*) and of justice (*asɛnnie*). Its sessions were in the *Pramakɛseɛso* - the great courtyard of the Asantehene's palace. The

---

[83] The Asante national army differed from the *amantoɔ* (state) armies in that each of the *nifa* and *benkum* wings had two sub-divisions - *nifa* - right and *nifa nnaase* - right-half, and *benkum* (left) and *benkum nnaase* - left-half (Busia, 1951).

Council was the highest court of justice. Legal hearing or trial session was referred to as *asεnnie*, and the court of justice was known as *asεnnibea*; courtiers who gave advice during legal cases were known as *atrankonnwafoɔ*.

The court proceeds with the litigants stating their cases and calling their witnesses. They are then examined by the assessors (*akyeame*). After consultation the assessors advise the chief as to his decision. The decision of the lower courts could be appealed to the higher courts. In the capital of the *ɔman* the *akyeame* could hold supernumerary courts of their own to relieve the pressure of work upon the regular courts. The decisions of the Council of State were publicized by the *nseniefoɔ* (heralds) and *dawurofoɔ* (gong-beaters, as in *Agyin dawuro* - #384-385; #386-388). State executioners (*adumfoɔ*) carried out public executions when one was sentenced to death. Condemned prisoners were held with handcuffs (*εpa* - #446-449) and executions were carried out with *sepɔ* (executioner's knife or dagger - #) during annual public ceremonies. *Abrafoɔ* (police) maintained public order and patrolled the streets at night and enforced curfew allowing no one to leave the town after nightfall. The *abrafoɔ* and *adumfoɔ* effectively enforced the *mmara* (law) promulgated by the *Asantemanhyiamu* and/or the Council of State.

A dispute within a household was regarded as *afisεm* or *abusuasεm* (e.g., slander, insults and other abuses, assault, and cases regarding personal property), and such disputes fell to the jurisdiction of the *ɔhemaa* (queenmother), *abusuahene* or *abusua panin* and his council of elders (*badwafoɔ*). If the dispute involved acts hateful to the state or the gods (such as invocation of the *Asanteman Ntam* also known as the *Ntam Kεse* - Great Oath and *ɔman akyiwadeε* - state taboos - like treason, invocation of a curse on a chief, incest and adultery) the case would fall to the jurisdiction of the Asantehene's court or a court of officeholders (e.g., *akyeame*) delegated by the Asantehene to sit on such a case.

The *ɔhemmaa* had her own *ntam* (oath) which was the formula for invoking the judicial process. She had her own court with female counselors and *akyeame* who acted as prosecutors and judge. The *ɔhemmaa* court served as a refuge for a fugitive from the *ɔhene's* court. The fugitive could successfully seek the *ɔhemmaa's* intervention (*dwantoa*) in cases carrying the death penalty. While the king's court dealt with *amansεm* (matters of state), *εfisεm* (domestic matters) were dealt with by the *ɔhemaa*. In certain cases, however, male litigants could apply to have their civil cases transferred from the king's court to the queenmother's court where fees and fines were generally lower (Aidoo, 1981; Arhin, 1983b; Manuh, 1988).

It is an absolute principle of Akan justice that no human being could be punished without trial. In Akan legal practice, one was presumed innocent until proven otherwise as symbolized by *dwantire* (ram's head - #427-433). Every person had the right to defend himself/herself as indicated by the maxim: *Obi mmua n'ano nni fɔ* - One should not remain silent to be pronounced guilty, Fairness was also presumed to prevail in the society, and no one should provoke another without just cause (*obi nka obi* - #420-426). The symbol (*ankonam boafoɔ ne Onyankopɔn* - #418) points out the Akan belief that God ensures that there is justice and fairness for all, irrespective of their social class, status, or condition in life. Even though God ensures fairness and justice, the individual is required to do unto others what s/he would want others do unto him/her (*nea wopε sε* - #419). Litigants were also urged to be conciliatory to each other for in the Akan belief, *obi nkyε obi kwan mu si* (to err is human - #453).

CHAPTER 7

Akɔkɔ nan tia ne ba so a, ɛnku no
Parental admonition is not intended to harm the child

AKAN FAMILY SYSTEM

FAMILY (ABUSUA)

The human being, to the Akan, is a communal being. The expression, *Onipa firi soro besi a, obesi onipa kuro mu* (When a person descends from heaven, i.e., when one is born, s/he descends into a human society) suggests an Akan conception of the person as a communitarian being by nature. This also presupposes the priority of the cultural community in which one finds oneself. The Akan also say: *Nipa nyɛ abɛdua na watena ne ho so* – A person is not like a palm tree that he/she should be self-sufficient in his/her existence. By such expression, the Akan hold the view that life is essentially and vitally communal and involves a contractual sense of obligation of the individual members of an *abusua* to the group or collective. A series of events in the *abusua*, such as marriage, births, illnesses and deaths, gives rise to urgent obligations. The communitarian nature of the human being is also expressed in the Akan belief that one is a member of an indivisible continuum of ancestors, the living, and the yet-to-be-born. As noted earlier, this is depicted by the *nkɔnsɔnkɔnsɔn* (chain - #162-167) symbol. Even though the Akan believe a person is by nature a social (communal) being, they also believe one is, by nature, other things (e.g., an individual) as well (Gyekye, 1992).

The center of the Akan social system is the family. The family is an extended one which may comprise the head of the household, usually a male (*agya* - father, or sometimes *wɔfa* - uncle); the wife (*yere* - or *yerenom* - wives) of the head; their unmarried children; married sons and their wives; and possibly nephews and nieces of the head. The head of the household wields both political and spiritual (religious) power. He acts as the intermediary among his household members, as well as between his household and other households, the larger society, and the spirits of the ancestors. The head of the household is the administrator of all family property, and the arbitrator of household disputes.

The households form the basic unit of the *abusua*. Membership in the *abusua* is matrilineal. Within the *abusua* the mother-child (*mogya* - blood) relationship is of paramount importance, hence the expression: *Woni wu a na w'abusua asa* (when your mother dies that is the end of your lineage). The *abusua* is said to be analogous to the bunch of palm nuts which has clusters (*mmɛtema*, pl.; *abɛtema*, sing.). One's *bɛtemasofoɔ* implies a unit of one's closest relatives, the cluster that forms a segment of the lineage as a whole. Each female member and her children constitute one cluster. Thus, Akan say that *abusua mu wɔ mpaeɛ* - the lineage has branches or segments based on the *abusuafoɔ mmaa* - the female members of the lineage. Another analogy for the segments within a family is implied in the symbol *abusua hwedeɛ* (#552) in which a grass field is depicted as clusters of grass. *Hwedeɛ* is a species of grass that grows scattered in little tufts or clusters. In this symbol the *abusua* is seen like this grass, and like grass it burns in the typical wildfire manner when set ablaze by family disputes. Sibling rivalry, family disputes, and petty jealousies can set sisters apart as if they are enemies, not family members – hence the expression, *abusua hwedeɛ gu nkuruwa, menko medeɛ na egya da mu* – every family has its internal crisis or dispute that may be simmering, mine has set the family ablaze (#552).

The *abusua* is the basic social group for most aspects of institutionalized social interactions, including success to high state offices (e.g., queenmother and king), inheritance of property (especially of land and other immovable properties), one's status as a citizen (commoner or royal), and one's links with the spiritual world, especially where one's body is interred after death (Busia, 1954; Fortes, 1950).

Family Totem

Each *abusua* is identified both by its own proper name and its common emblem (*nsɛnkyereneɛ* - totem or symbol, see Table 8 below and Fig.23). The Akan *abusua* groups are: (1) *aduana* (also known as *atwea, ntwaa, aowin, aborade* or *adwinade*); (2) *asakyire*; (3) *asinie* (also known as *aseneɛ*); (4) *asona* (also known as *nsona, odum, odum-na, dwum,* or *dwumina*); (5) *berɛtuo* (also known as *twidan* or *tena*); (6) *ɛkoɔna* (also known as *asɔkɔre, ebirade, kɔna,* or *adɔnten*); and, (7) *oyoko* (also known as *daku, yogo, yɔkɔ, ɔwɛko, agona* or *anɔna*)[84]. All persons bearing a common clan name (that is, belonging to the same *abusua or abusuakuo*), resident however widely apart, are considered to be related by blood. In this regard, the *abusua* or *abusuakuo* functions "as a kinship charter for any Akan outside his [her] natal home or state - a visa, so to speak, for temporary or permanent residence" (Chukwukere, 1978, p. 136). All *abusua* members are expected to observe mourning rituals on funeral occasions.

TABLE 8: AKAN MATRICLANS, THEIR TOTEMS AND GREETINGS

	Abusua name	Totem	Greeting Response
1.	*Aduana (Atwea, Ntwaa, Aowin, Aborade, Adaa, Amoakere* or *Adwinade)*	Dog or Frog	*Yaa saa na*
2.	*Oyoko (Daku, Yogo, Yɔkɔ, Eguana, Ɔwɛkɔ, Agona* or *Anɔna)*	Hawk/Parrot	*Yaa buru/Yaa ago na*
3.	*Asakyirie*	Vulture	*Yaa akorɔntɔn*
4.	*Asinie (Aseneɛ)*	Bat	*Yaa adu na*
5.	*Asona (Dwum,* or *Dwumina)*	Crow/Fox	*Yaa asɔ na; Yaa doku na; Yaa (Nsona, odum, odum-na, Ofori na)*
6.	*Koɔna (Asɔ kɔre, Dehyena, Ɛkoɔna, Ebirade* or *Adɔnten)*	Water buffalo	*Yaa adeɛ na; Yaa ahwene*

---

[84] The Asante claim there are eight *abusua* groups as they consider Oyoko to be separate abusua. All the other Akan groups recognize seven *abusua* groups as shown in Table 1.

| 7. | *Berɛtuo (Twidan, Tena)* | Leopard | *Yaa twi na; Yaa piafo* |

Totems are sacred emblems symbolizing common identities. Totems which are visual symbols that represent plants, animals and sometimes natural items may be carved or sculptured on a monument as a representative of a particular image of told stories about ancestors, animals and spirits. These totems encode some of the Akan mythology. These are also associated with ceremonies. In totemic rites, people gather together to honor their totem. In so doing they use rituals to maintain the social oneness that the totem symbolizes. Various interpretations are given for what the totems mean and how they were derived. As can be determined from some of the interpretations below much of the origins of the Akan family are shrouded in Akan mythology.

The *Ɛkoɔna* family is said to be the first family (*ebusua piesie*) out of which the other families emerged. The totem for *Ɛkoɔna* clan is Buffalo (*ɛkoɔ*). It simply means massiveness. It is said in Akan mythology that it was a hunter who discovered a herd of buffalo (*ɛkoɔ*) which turned themselves into human beings by peeling off their hides. The hunter became interested in one of the female buffalos and took its hide. When they were about to turn themselves back into buffalos, one of the females could not find her hide and she remained a human being. The hunter finally came out from his hide-out when the other animals left, and took the animal turned into woman for a wife.

The descendants therefore called themselves *Ɛkoɔnafo*. They are also referred to as *Ekuo ne Asipim. Ahwenie a ɛda yaawa mu. Ɛsono nni hɔ ɛkoɔ ne Piesie*. The family is also sometimes referred to as *Asɔkɔrefoɔ*. It is believed that most of the Akan families originally belonged to this family and this makes them the mother of all the families. They were the first settlers in Adanse and thus the royal family of Adanse was *Ɛkoɔna*. The *Ɛkoɔna* family members are believed to be the first among the Akan who built houses hence the name "*Adan-sifoɔ*" (house builders). It is traditionally believed that it was the *Ɛkoɔna* family that gave birth to the *Ɔyɔkoɔ*. This started when some portion of the family broke their taboo and ate the meat of a buffalo (the *akyiwade* – the forbidden or taboo meat of the *Ɛkoɔnafoɔ*). The people were then referred to as *Ɔwe ɛkoɔfo* - those who eat buffalo meat.

Figure 23: Seven Akan Abusua Totems

The totem for the *Aduana* clan is a dog, with firebrand in its mouth or a dog emitting fire from its mouth. It was this animal (dog) which led the *Aduanafoɔ* to their new settlement. They highly regard the dog, and anything that they say often comes to pass. It is believed that their mouth is supposed to carry fire (*wɔn ano yɛ gya*). Another interpretation of the *aduana* totem is that at one time floods made the *aduana* family move to a new settlement on a higher ground. In their haste to escape the raging floods they forgot to take fire with them to the new settlement. A dog was instructed to swim across the waters to the old settlement to bring back firebrand. The dog did just as it was instructed. That made life more pleasant in the new settlement and dog was adored and made the totem of the *aduana* family. Hence the name *ɔtwea* (dog) for the *aduana* family.

The totem for *Asona* is the crow (*kwaakwaadabi, akonkoran* or *anene*) or the fox (*ɔsɔ*). In Akan mythology, it is told that a gong gong was beaten to announce the death of *Nana Onyankopɔn* (God) and they needed someone or a clan to go and wake him up. The crow went to where *Nana Onyankopɔn* was and started shouting Kwame, Kwame! (God's name). Another clan said to the crow, let our ears rest (*momma yɛn aso nna*) which was corrupted to *Asona*.

Another explanation for the use of the crow and a beautifully colored snake as the totem of the *Asona* family is derived from a story that purports that an old woman who was travelling with her siblings chanced upon a pot of gold. Around the pot was a snake with yellow and red colors. As the siblings tarried and pondered what the pot of gold and the snake signified, the old woman rushed and retrieved the pot of gold. The snake fatally struck the old woman, and a crow swooped down and struck the snake. Even though the old woman could not be saved, she did not die in vain; she secured the pot of gold for her people. The siblings of the old woman were able to carry away the pot of gold. Hence the expression: *asonafo wompre kwa* – *asona* people do not hustle in vain.

An explanation for the fox as a totem for *Asona abusua* is that a hunter who lived alone met an older hunter who wondered why the young man lived alone. The young hunter indicated he is yet to meet a woman who he would marry. The old hunter gave the young man a charm with which the young man could turn an animal into a woman he could marry. The young man thanked the old hunter and went off hunting. The young hunter encountered the deer, duiker, and the bear in succession, but the charm failed to work on any of these animals. At the point of exasperation, he encountered a vixen. He quickly tried the charm on her and to his surprise, instantly there appeared before him a beautiful woman. He took her home for his wife. The descendants of the woman became known as as *asonafo* – the fox (*ɔsɔ*) people. Hence the use of the fox as a family totem for the *Asona*.

The symbolic quality of the *Asona* clan is statesmanship and patriotism and this is even portrayed by *Asona* women of today. The *Asona* clan is among the few families where the women were given the privilege to rule as Kings or Chiefs, and three examples could be given here. Nana Abena Boaa who ruled Offinso (1610-1640), Nana Afia Dokuaa who ruled Akyem Abuakwa (1817-1835), and Nana Yaa Asantewaa who ruled Edweso (1896-1900). One of the accolades of the *Asona* family is that they look so beautiful and pretty. The saying goes this way: "*Asonafoɔ a, ahoɔfɛ adware wɔn, wɔn atikɔ tesɛ obi anim.*" Literal meaning is - the people of the *Asona* family are so pretty that the back side of the head is as beautiful as someone's face. *Nananom asonafoɔ a yɛnnkɔ nsuo ngu obi ahinam* – *Asonafoɔ* do not fetch water to be put in the pot of another person. That is, *Asonafoɔ* venture to gain.

The vulture (*ɔpetɛ*) is the totem for the *Asakyiri*. It is claimed that *Asakyiri* and *Asona* were brothers and sisters (siblings) and were known as *Asona ne Akyiri* which was corrupted to *Asakyiri*. *Asakyiri* followed *Asona* and settled at Bono Manso. The women adopted the vulture as their totem and the males (men) also adopted the vulture as their totem as they were calm, peace-loving. Later they accepted the vulture as a symbol for the whole clan. The vulture feeds exclusively on carrion and performs a very useful function by disposing of potential sources of disease. It is the symbol of purification and of transformation. As old decayed flesh is removed, new life emerges. That is the vital role this amazing bird plays for the health and well being of mankind and all other life forms.

Many people do not like vultures because of an impression that, since they feed off carrion, they must be unclean birds. The truth is that vultures are actually quite clean, and they perform the valuable service of eliminating the remains of decaying animals. This is one of the gifts the vulture holds for us; the cleaning up of messes. Many times we create physical and psychic messes that we do not want to deal with. The vulture can guide us to the efficient and joyful resolution of such problems.

The totem with which the *Agona* clan is associated is the parrot (*Ako*) which is noted for its fluency. Probably that might be the reason why *Agonafoɔ* are fluent in their speech. The *Oyɔkoɔ* family is said to have come out of the *Ekuona* family. The *Oyɔkoɔ* clan was forbidden to eat Buffalo (*ɛkoɔ*) but in the past, during a severe famine, they were compelled to eat it. They were been laughed at for eating buffalo, which they were not supposed to eat. The people used to say *Awe-ɛkoɔfo* which has been corrupted to *Ayɔkɔfoɔ*. The totem that is associated with the *Ayɔkoɔ* clan is the Hawk (*osansa*) which is noted for its rapacity. There is an adage which says that *Osansa fa adeɛ a ɔde kyerɛ amansan*. It tries to exhibit its braveness by showing whatever it picks to the public by lifting it high.

The leopard is a visual symbol that is used to represent the *Bretuo* (or *Twidan*) clan. It is believed that a leopard once turned into a man and got married to a woman. The leopard did not settle permanently with the woman. The woman then complained of frequent movements (*mabrɛ ne otuo*). This was corrupted to *Bretuo*. Another myth was that, the name originated as a result of people who were fond of picking mushrooms (*mire*) which became *mire tufuo* which was corrupted to *Bretuo*. This family is often referred to as *etene ne bretuo* because *etene* or *tana* is said to be a younger sister of the big *Bretuo* family. *Bretuo* is also said to be the sister of the *Agona Abusua*. According to Rattray, the *Bretuos* are said to have descended from the skies to settle at Ahensan in Adanse. It is believed that it was a turkey buzzard that directed them from the skies to settle at Behenase from Adanse.

Another explanation offered is that a hunter observed a leopard laying in a lair by a field of pineapples. The leopard would pounce on animals that stopped by to feed on the pineapples. One day the leopard succeeded on preying on two animals. The leopard then dragged one prey aside to feed on it. The hunter then sneaked to grab the other animal. The leopard became friends with the hunter in appreciation of the fact that the hunter did not shoot to kill the leopard. The leopard promised to kill for the hunter, hence the hunter became dependent on the leopard for his meat. The way the leopard stopped the hunter from using his gun to hunt game led to the saying *ɔbrɛ tuo* - stopped the gun, which became corrupted as *bretuo* for the hunter's family. The hunter was said to rely on the leopard for his meat – thus the expression *me dan etwie* (I rely on the leopard), which became corrupted as *twidan*. There is also the expression said of the *twidanfoɔ*: "*Kurotwamansa a ɔnam ne sika aborɔbɛ nti ɛkɔm nne no da* – the leopard that knows of no hunger because his golden pineapples."

Ntorɔ/Egyabosom

A patrilineal lineage grouping known as *ntorɔ*[85] also exists among the Akan. Among the Asante the *ntorɔ* is what determines one's characteristics like personality and disposition, and the spiritual bond between father and child. It is the father's *ntorɔ* and the mother's *mogya* (blood) together with *kra* (soul) from God that forms the human being. While the father-child (*ntorɔ* - spirit) relationship is considered spiritually-based, the mother-child relationship is considered biologically (or physically) based. The patrilineage determines one's membership in *asafo* companies and societal responsibilities (civic and military). Among the Asante and other Akan groups the *ntorɔ* lineage gives rise to the use of particular surnames. Thus, one could to some extent tell a person's *ntorɔ* by the surname one uses. Examples of some of the names which are commonly but not exclusively found among people of the same *ntorɔ* group are:

> Bosommuru: Osei, Owusu, Poku, Saakodie, Amankwaa, Safo, Nti, Anim.
> Bosompra: Dua, Boakye, Boaten, Akyeampon, Agyeman, Ofori, Bediako.
> Bosompo: Ayim, Dakwa, Boadu, Antwi, Poakwa, Bonsu, Osei, Otutu, Apea, Kusi
> Duko, Bafi, Adom.
> Bosomtwe: Ofosu, Boafo, Gyadu, Kwatia, Boate, Atakora Osafo
> Bosomafram: Afram, Peasa, Dame, Amponsa, Awua, Anokye
> (Mensah, 1992).

FAMILY HEAD

The head of the *abusua* is known as *abusua panin*. The *abusua panin* has certain responsibilities and obligations as implied by the symbol *abusua panin kyerɛ wo dɔ* (family head assert your affection - #556). He sees to it that enmity and strife, quarrels and dissensions do not occur among relatives in the *abusua*. Such incidents of strife are inevitable as the Akan recognize that the *abusua* is like a forest (*abusua te sɛ kwaeɛ* - the family is like forest - #553-555) made up of a variety of individual trees. From a distance the trees seem clustered together. When one gets closer to the family or one enters the forest, one finds individual trees or individual persons. Dissensions and quarrels may bring disunity and create factions within the *abusua*. The *abusua panin* is responsible for managing these social conflicts from exploding into open disputes and quarrels. The *abusua panin* watches over the welfare of the whole group. He has the power and the duty to settle private disputes between any of his fellow members so that peace and solidarity can prevail in the group. As the following expression implies the *abusua panin* is expected to be fair and firm, protective of all members, and to be benevolent, kind and sympathetic: *Woyɛ damprane a ase yɛ nwunu; abusua panin kyerɛ wo dɔ* (You are

---

[85] Fantse people call the patrilineage *egyabosom*. Members of the *ntorɔ* or *egyabosom* are believed to have the same spirit as the father is believed to transmit his *ntorɔ* to his child. The *ntorɔ* groups vary from seven (Busia, 1954) to twelve (Danquah, 1951). The Asantehene's Kyeame, Nana Antwi Boasiako indicated to me that there are ten (others indicate 12) *ntorɔ* groups in Asante. These were listed by Nana Buasiako in a personal interview at Ayigya, Kumasi on May 24, 1994 as *Bosomtwe, Bosompra, Bosomuru, Adomakodeɛ, Aboadeɛ, Anineɛ, Asafodeɛ, Akandadeɛ, Anyaadeɛ,* and *Atweneɛ*. Opoku (1976) lists them as *Bosomuru, Bosompra, Bosomtwe, Bosomafram, Bosompo, Bosomakon, Bosomkonsi, Bosomayensu, Bosomafi, Bosomsika,* and *Bosomkrete*. Other names include *Bosomnketsia*.

like the giant shade tree in the desert; family head assert your affection - #556). Also the benevolent *abusua panin* may be referred to as *abasatea a adɔeɛ wɔ mu* (the slender arm full of benevolence).

The *abusua panin* is the chief representative of the *abusua* in its political and legal relations with other *abusua* and the greater society. He is the custodian of the ancestral stools of the lineage and he takes the lead in organizing corporate obligations, such as the funeral of a deceased member of the *abusua*.

Family and Funeral

Funeral is an occasion on which the unity and solidarity of the lineage receive public expression, as funeral expenses are shared among adult members of the lineage. This public display of *abusua* unity and solidarity is depicted by the symbol *abusua dɔ fun* (the family loves the corpse - #558-562). Decent, elaborate and expensive funerals constitute a strongly marked goal for the Akan (*ayieɛ fɛ ne ka - #563*). *Abusua panin* is the chief mourner. If the deceased person is a husband and father, his *abusua panin* formally presents two sets of *nkaansã* (notification drink) to the family of his wife and children on the one hand and to the head of his *ntorɔ* or *asafo* group on the other hand. The *nkaansã* to the *asafo* group requires the group to provide services in the form of grave digging, bearing the coffin to the cemetery, and performing other mortuary rites to honor the deceased member. The *nkaansã* to the wife and children requires their matriclan to present *esiedeɛ* for the burial of the deceased husband and father. The *esiedeɛ* usually consists of material things which include the coffin, clothing,[86] toiletries, and drinks, and cash to be used to defray other expenses incurred because of the funeral.

Funeral has become an event for conspicuous consumption (*ayieɛ fɛ ne ka - #553*). All funeral rites today have similar features that also constitute items of expenditure. These include announcements on the radio and in the press, detailing all the deceased's relations and, in certain cases, friends concerned in the rites. The details emphasize their "station in life" and their places of sojourn, including - indeed, emphasizing - the major foreign cities, such as Berlin, Bonn, Hamburg, London, Paris, New York and Washington. It matters not whether those mentioned can attend the funeral or not. The details serve a dual purpose. They emphasize the social status of the deceased, as demonstrated in the number, occupations and locations of his maternal relations and his children, and they inform the sundry friends of the relatives of the deceased of the program of the funeral rites. The compounds and grounds where the funeral is held must be lighted up. A well-to-do family in a village which lacks electricity may hire a generator. The seats for the funeral are hired from local entrepreneurs or others in the nearby towns, as also are the canopies and catering services and sound system and video recording and photography, from people who specialize in those lines of business.

Funeral rites have thus been transformed into an institution of economic and social, rather than, religious significance in response to changes in the economy, society and material culture of the Akan people over the last century. Banks and other financial institutions have jumped into the fray by offering funeral coverage accounts and loans. The increasing trend in the commercialization of funerals has incited a hot public debate in Ghana about the disproportionate cost of current funeral practices. Making money out of death evokes negative sentiments. "Much of contemporary Akan popular culture that has crept into funeral ceremonies can be viewed as commercial exploitation...

---

[86] In Asante, when a married man dies his wife's family gives three pieces of clothing: *ntoma kɔkɔɔ, ntoma tuntum* and *ntoma fufuo* - to the maternal family of the deceased man as part of the *asiedeɛ*.

The creeping commercialization is transforming bereavement into a largely monetized venture" (Aborampah, 1999: 268). Some of the Christian churches have introduced some constraints to contain the burgeoning funeral expenses.

Family Dissension

An *abusua* that is rife with open disputes and dissensions is depicted by symbols like *abusua bɔne* (malevolent family - #551) and *abusua hwedeɛ* (family dispute - #552). The inherent sibling rivalry within the clusters of sisters and their children (*abɛtemasefoɔ*) is one major source of disputes within the Akan family. Other sources of dissensions within the family include, but not limited to, chieftaincy disputes; individual interests versus the common good; new sets of economic incentives that have forced the youth to migrate to urban areas in search of jobs, thus reducing the number of family members in the rural areas to shoulder the family's obligations; Akan inheritance laws that result in conflict between a man's wife and his children on one side and his *abusua* on the other, and property rights over real estate (developed and undeveloped land).

Akan inheritance law requires that unless there is a deed of gift by a man to his wife and children of which the lineage (*abusua*) approves, the property of a man who dies intestate goes to his matrilineal heir and not to his own children and wife. Conflicts about the Akan inheritance law have done more to bring into the open the rival claims of matrilineal kinship and paternal responsibility. A popular expression that decries the Akan inheritance law is: *wɔfa wɔ hɔ nti merenyɛ adwuma* (the maternal uncle is there for me to inherit so I won't work).

If the family is the royal or ruling family, chieftaincy disputes may center on competition by potential candidates to occupy the stool of the ruling family. There is no well-defined succession line to the chiefship in a given royal family. A number of eligible candidates may have "parties" formed around them to contest for the position. Such a contest may rift the family into hostile camps. One famous situation centered on who should become the next Asantehene after the death of Kwaku Dua II in 1883. The conflict resulted in a civil war in the royal Oyoko Family. This civil war became known as *Ɔyokoman na gya dam* (Crisis in the Oyoko nation) for which a *kente* cloth has been named.

HOUSING

The Akan's nature as beings-in-relation results in a societal system in which none is left in want of basic human needs for shelter, clothing and food. Housing and architectural styles reinforce social organization and emphasize family unity. The compound (*fihankra* - #528-533) in Akan societies consists of a central courtyard (*adiwo* in Twi, *paado* in Fantse) which serves as the center of household activities, surrounded by multi-room rectangular building. This courtyard is the living area of the house; it is there that arbitrations occur, cooking is done, children play, stories are told and family celebrations and funerals are held. Thus, though one can identify a biological family living within the house there can be no real privacy for its daily activities. Children do things together and, having ample opportunity to hear and watch adults, become fluent in speech and custom at an early age. They are expected to pick up good manners, care for one another and give due respect to adults.

The *dampan* (literally, empty room) is semi-private and has multiple uses: from receiving guests, and holding court to laying the dead in state during funerals. Then, there are the private rooms:

living room, bed rooms, bathrooms, etc. There is also the kitchen, which very often extends into the open courtyard. In a big Akan house, there is the women's quarters (*mmaa mu*) which will have its own open courtyard and a number of private rooms. The kitchen and the bathrooms will usually be in these quarters. In the Asantehene's Palace the women's quarters is called *Hia* or *Hyia*. The concept of *fihankra* reinforces the idea of close family ties and unity.

Another interesting feature in the Akan house is the *pato* (*dampan* in Fantse), a covered space walled on three sides and opening onto the courtyard. It is the living space used for dining, receiving guests, holding arbitrations and for laying bodies in state at funerals. Like the *pato* it is covered, but is enclosed on two sides leaving the entrance and courtyard ends open. The *fihankra* symbolizes protection, security and spirituality. In front of the house is placed a stump called the *Nyame dua* – God's altar (#63-71) which represents God's presence and protection. When one enters the house, the open courtyard (*adiwo* in Twi; Fantse call it *paado*) represents the public space within the house (see Fig.24). This open courtyard has multiple uses. It is usually surrounded by a verandah where guests may be received. A bigger group of guests will usually be received in the *dampan*. The *dampan* (literally, empty room) is semi-private and has multiple uses: from receiving guests, and holding court to laying the dead in state during funerals.

The concept of **fihankra** reinforces the idea of close family ties and unity. The Akan house is not only well ventilated, it is resilient and can withstand the hazards of storms, rainfall and the tropical hot weather. This is encoded in the symbol *mframadan* - well ventilated or breezy house (#534-536). The incorporation of symbols in Akan architecture was traditionally limited to public buildings such as the king's palace (*ahemfie*) and shrine building (*abosom dan*), and, in some cases, the homes of high ranking community leaders. In contemporary times the symbols are incorporated in both private and public buildings in order to emphasize Akan aesthetics as well as the social significance of the buildings.

The uncompleted *fihankra* will have a fence (*ɛban* - #527) built to complete the unfinished sides. These days the *ɛban* is built around completed houses, especially in the urban areas for decorative purposes as well as for additional security and as a status symbol. The traditional wattle and daub houses have been replaced by cement or cinder block houses (*blɔk dan* - #537-543). To build a house is seen as a measure of accomplishment more valuable and enduring than money. This may be inferred from the Akan expression: *Yɛbisa wo fie a woasi, na nyɛ wo sika dodoɔ a woanya* - we ask to be shown the house you have built, not how much money you have accumulated. The block house is not only a symbol of protection, security and shelter as all houses are so regarded, the block house has also become a new status symbol (see Fig. 25). This is indicated by the expression: *wonni sika a, wonsi blɔk dan* (if one does not have money one cannot build a cement or cinder block house - #537-543).

This display of affluence as suggested by the preceding expression is further seen in the extensiveness of the cement or cinder block wall that people build as a fence (*ɛban* - #527) around their houses. The wall, as a decoration and communication device, tends to incorporate some of the *adinkra* and other symbols. Interestingly, the wattle and daub houses were very cool and therefore suited to the tropical climate of Ghana. The cement or cinder block houses, on the other hand tend to be very warm and humid. Whether one builds a wattle and daub or a block house, a well-built, reinforced and well-ventilated house symbolized in the *adinkra* cloth as *mframadan* (well ventilated or breezy house - #534-536) is highly regarded by the Akan. The *mframmadan* symbolizes stability and security.

Figure 24: Courtyard in Akan Traditional House

The home as the first agency of socialization is very crucial in the instruction of children in selecting and adjusting their relations from their age-set playmates to their mother's food circle, the kinship group. The child who strays into a playmate's house and eats there is admonished to stay at home (*tena fie* -#549) as indicated by the following expression: *Wonam nam a ohyia na wohyia; aboa antena fie a, ɔgye abaa* (when one does not stay at home one gets into trouble; the animal that roams is often beaten). The same idea is expressed also by the proverb: *Akokɔba a ɔbɛn ne ni na ɔnya sonsono serɛ di* - The chicken which keeps close to mother-hen gets the benefit of the best part of the worm.

BEAUTY AND LOVE

Beauty (*ahoɔfɛ*) is seen in terms of physical characteristics as well as certain social and moral qualities such as humility, etiquette, elegance, and gracefulness. A round face, a smile, and white, clean set of teeth, and well groomed or coiffured hair are some of the physical characteristics considered beautiful. A well-mannered person is also considered beautiful. In fact, good character, to the Akan, is more valued in a person than mere physical beauty as encoded by the symbol *ahoɔfɛ ntua ka* - (beauty does not pay - #656-657). The symbols such as *afafrantɔ* (butterfly- #455-458), *mampam se* (alligator teeth - #462), *asambo* (chest feathers of the guinea fowl - #459-461), and *dua afe* (wooden comb - #463-469) also depict the Akan view of a beautiful person. A man may, for example, express his love and admiration of a beautiful woman thus: *Ne se nwɔtwe a ɛsisi nyaaanyaa sɛ mampam se; ɔbaa ahoɔfɛ, amampamma, mepɛ wo nkɔnse* (Her teeth have gaps between them like the young alligator lizard; beautiful woman with spirals around your neck, I love you - #462).

Figure 25: The Golden Tulip Hotel building in Kumasi, Ghana showing some *adinkra* ymbols

Love (ɔdɔ) emanates from the heart not from the head as encoded by the symbols *ɔdɔ firi akoma mu* (love is from the heart - #475-478) and *ɔdɔ bata akoma ho* (love is close to the heart - #484). First love is like madness; it is illogical (*ɔdɔ foforɔ* - #454). Love will make one cry tears of joy or sorrow as suggested by the symbol *ɔdɔ nisuo* (love tears - #481-483). In Akan love relationships, the man takes the initiative in courting a woman. Courtship is very discreet. Courtship romance is illustrated by the following expression associated with the *ɔdɔ aniwa* (Love eye - #454) symbol: *ɔdɔ, mehu wo a, mebɔ m'ani asu; mefa wo a, mefa siadeɛ*- my love, when I look at you, my eyes are sanctified; I bound in good luck when I touch you. The following poem by Aquah Laluah (1960) called *The Serving Girl* further illustrates the meaning attached to the *ɔdɔ aniwa* (love eye - #454) symbol:

The calabash wherein she served my food
Was polished and smooth as sandalwood.
Fish, white as the foam of the sea,
Peppered and golden-fried for me.
She brought palm wine that carelessly slips
From the sleeping palm tree's honeyed lips.
But who can guess, or even surmise
The countless things she served with her eyes?

During the courtship the woman will urge the man not to deceive her (*nnaadaa me* - #487) and will encourage him to go forward to her people and ask for her hand in marriage. A man in love may give gifts to the woman he admires. Gifts that were developed into symbolism of their own were the *dua afe* (wooden comb - #463-469) and *akuaba* (wooden dolls). Young men in love would present wooden combs to their girlfriends. On the handle of the comb would be carved symbols with such names as *kae me* (remember me - #486), *megye wo awodɔm* (I wish you to be a mother of several children), and *ɔdɔ yɛ wu* (love survives till death or love-unto-death, or love is everlasting). Women would also give gifts and use their musical groups to sing the praises of their lovers. The *donno* (bell

115

drum - #500) is prominently played by women in these musical groups. The women composed their love songs to praise or make references to loved ones, brothers or some outstanding men in the community. In the past, any man who was thus honored was supposed to give the women presents. An example of such love songs sung by a women's musical group as translated by Sarpong (1977, p. 24) is

> Osee yei, yee yei!
> Ɛtwɛ Adwoa ei!
> Obi di wo na
> Wamma wo ade a
> Ku no oo!
> Ose yei, yee yei!
> Ata Kwasi Adwoa ei!
> Otoo too to.
> Yɛrepɛ kɔte atɔ oo!
> Sɛ mmarima nni kuro yi mu?

Translation:
> Rejoice, rejoice!
> Vagina of Adwoa
> If someone 'eats' you (has intercourse with you)
> And fails to reward you,
> Slay him!
> Rejoice, rejoice!
> Ata Kwasi Adwoa!
> Good for nothing!
> We are in search of penis to buy!
> Little realizing that this village is devoid of men.

Success in courtship depends to a very great extent on winning the girl's mother's favor. Winning the mother's favor may be done through giving gifts such ɔtwe serɛ (deer's thigh) and nkyene (salt) or by rendering services such as clearing the farm of the girl's mother. Yet, without the father's approval the match will not be allowed. The father has to make sure that the suitor of his daughter will be able to support her. Parents must satisfy themselves that their future relations-in-law are agreeable with respect to certain characteristics that include the following:

wɔnyɛ ntɔkwakofoɔ - they are not quarrelsome
wɔnyɛ masotwefoɔ - they are not litigious
wɔnyɛ bonniayɛfoɔ - they are not ungrateful
wɔnyɛ odifudepɛfoɔ - they are not greedy
wɔnyare yarebɔneɛ - they are not suffering from diseases such as leprosy, epilepsy and
cushion's syndrome

The woman should be
ɔdeyɛfoɔ - industrious
obu nipa - respectful

ɔte kasa - obedient
ɔte ne ho ase - sexually faithful
ahoɔfɛ - beautiful (beauty is not by any means a decisive factor).

The man should be
Osifoɔ - industrious
ɔyɛ ɔbarima paa - manly and potent
ne ho nni asɛm - character is without blemish.

MARRIAGE

Marriage (*aware* or *awadeɛ*) to the Akan is a configuration of beliefs and practices about the place of children, endogamy and exogamy, and the significance of the family in the society. For two people to get married to each other, they must fall outside the ring of prohibited marriages. One such prohibition is that the spouses should not be of the same lineage (*abusua*). The Akan considers it an abomination (*musuo*) for one to marry from one's *abusua*. This is viewed as incestuous relationship as implied by the following maxim: *wo nuabaa aserɛ so a, wonna so* (if your sister has big and beautiful thighs, that is not where you sleep - #514-515). The husband and the wife must belong to separate clans or kindred groups (*mmusua*). The man proposes to the woman – *mɛware wo* (I shall marry you - #488). Upon favorable responses from the woman's parents, his people will arrange for a marriage ceremony.

Marriage is a union not only between the two people in love, but also of the two families (*mmusua*) of the lovers that is why future relations-in-law must be found to be agreeable as indicated above. Marriage as a contract is not like the bond of blood in *abusua* relations. This view of marriage is associated with the symbol *aware yɛ ayɔnkoyɛ, ɛnyɛ abusuabɔ* (the contract of marriage is a contract of friendship that can be broken; it is not like the bond of blood in family relationships - #489). Implied in this view is the possibility of divorce. However, this is not to suggest that divorce is a common practice among the Akan. To this Akan say *aware nyɛ aware na, na ne gyaeɛ* - getting married is not as difficult as getting out of it.

For a marriage to be considered legal it is required that the woman's father or *wɔfa* (maternal uncle) should accept *tiri nsã*[87] (head drink) from the prospective suitor and hand it to the head of her *abusua*. In return, the bride's father gives *aseda nsã* (thank-you-drink) to the groom and his people. The *tiri nsã* and the *aseda nsã* together make the marriage legally binding on both families as these drinks are drunk by relatives of both the bride and the groom as witnesses to the union. *Tiri nsã* ensures marriage stability as it is refundable by the woman's family if she is blameworthy for the dissolution of the marriage. On the other hand, if the man is blameworthy for the dissolution of the marriage he loses both the woman and the *tiri nsã*. *Tiri nsã* gives the husband (1) exclusive sexual

---

[87] *Tiri nsã* is offered as thanks to the bride's family in allowing the suitor to marry her. It is not a head price (a bounty) paid to her parents as has been wrongly interpreted by some people. Neither is it a marriage license fee paid to some state official who grants a license for the marriage. The process of offering the *tiri nsã* is variously referred to as *wayɛ ɔbaa no ho adeɛ, wada ne tiri ase* or *wasi ne tiri nsã* (ie., to give thanks to the bride's family in offering her hand in marriage). This "thank you" drink is reciprocated in the form of the *aseda nsã* that is offered by the bride's family to the groom and his family members present and acting as witnesses to the union.

rights over his wife and the legal paternity of all children born to her while the marriage lasts; and (2) the right to essential domestic and economic services from the wife. The *tiri nsã* obliges the man to (1) provide the wife and her children with food, clothing and housing; (2) give her sexual satisfaction and care for her when she is ill, and be responsible for debts she contracts in the course of the marriage (*mmaa pɛ dɛ kyiri ka* - #547); and, (3) obtain the wife's consent if he wishes to take an additional wife (*yerenom bebree awareɛ* - #512). The woman would claim she has been picked easily like a snail (*w'afa me nwa* - #907), if the prospective husband neglects to seek her consent before he takes on additional wife or wives.

The responsibility of the man for the wife's debt incurred during the marriage is enshrined in the time-honored Asante marital pledge: *Wode ɔbaa yi rekɔ yi, sɛ ɔkɔbɔ ka a, wo dea; sɛ ɛnso ɔkɔfa sadeɛ a, ɔde kɔ n'abusua mu. Wo pene so?* (As you take away this woman with you, should she incur any debt it will be your liability; but if she comes by a treasure she takes it all to her lineage. Do you agree?). If the husband wants to take a second wife, he has to give *mpata nsã* (pacificatory drink) to the first wife. This is in effect to ask the wife to share her sexual rights over the man with another woman. The first wife has the right to refuse the *mpata nsã* and thus stop the man from taking on an additional wife. If the first wife refuses to accept the *mpata nsã* and the man goes on to marry a second woman, the first wife can seek divorce for that reason.

Some Akan Views on Marital Problems

Marriage is viewed as a long journey (love survives till death or love is everlasting - #463-469), problematic (*aware yɛ ya* - #499), and not to be rushed into (*obi ntutu mmirika nkɔdɔn aware-dan dɔteɛ* - #488). The promise to marry someone carries such responsibility that one is urged not to rush into it as it is a commitment for life. One cannot sample it first to determine whether one likes it or not before one plunges into marriage (*aware nyɛ nsafufuo na yɛasɔ ahwɛ* - #498). It, therefore, requires patience (*nya akoma* - #470-474); truthfulness (*kyɛkyɛ pɛ aware* - #492-497); commitment (*fa w'akoma ma me* - #485); devotion and persistence (*ɔdɔfo nyera fie kwan* - #479-480); and cooperation, understanding and respect (*akoma ntoaso* - #490-491). Akan marriages are either monogamous or polygynous, but polyandry is not practiced (Sarpong, 1974). Sarpong claims that polygyny accorded social status and economic advantage to the men.

A woman who has a good marriage is believed to benefit herself as well as her family (*abusua*) as indicated by the *aware papa* symbol (*Ɔbaa nya aware pa a, ɛyɛ animuonyam ma ɔno ne n'abusuafoɔ* - Good or a very successful marriage is beneficial for the woman as well as her family - #510). The woman who has a good and successful marriage is said to sleep on a good bed (*ɔbaa kɔ aware pa a na yɛde no to kɛtɛ pa so* - #513).

Some of the characteristics of good marriage include being able to produce children, an indication that she sleeps on a good bed. A fruitful woman may be compared with the fruit of okra plant containing many seeds as symbolized by *nkuruma kɛse* (big okra - #323-331). The lack of children in a marital relationship may be grounds for divorce.

On the other hand, a bad marriage is said to destroy or corrupt a good woman (*aware bone sɛe ɔbaa pa* - #511). The Akan also says that *aware bone tete ntoma* - bad marriage leaves one in tatters. A bad marriage may be characterized by infidelity, adultery, spousal abuse, laziness, incessant interference by the spouse's relatives (especially by the man's sisters and mother), and impotence and infertility (*saadwe*). A married woman may commit adultery despite the fact the husband is good to her (#511).

Divorce (Hyireguo or Awaregyaeɛ)

Divorce, to the Akan, is neither anti-social nor religious sacrilege. Marriage is dissolvable only after relevant complaints have been stated and heard by arbitrators. Such complaints may stem from many factors including economic (e.g., incapability of maintaining wife), friction between the couple (e.g., owing to disrespect, disobedience, quarrels) or friction with spouse's kin (e.g., interference from in-laws), and sexual deficiencies (e.g., infidelity on the part of the husband, adultery or suspected adultery on the part of the wife, impotence of wife or sterility of husband). Either the man or the woman can seek divorce. A married woman can seek divorce from a husband who neglects her sexually or who can be proved to be impotent or sterile (*kɔte krawa*), or who neglects her and the children, or an abusive spouse. It is considered shameful and disgraceful for a man to physically assault a woman (*barima mfa n'ahoɔden nware* - #499); on the other hand, a woman is not supposed to say to a man that he is a fool and therefore, abuse (physical, psychological or otherwise) by the man or by the woman can be basis for divorce. Adultery was naturally a ground for seeking divorce. There were certain forms of adultery by the woman that were permissible in the past. The husband could only be in adulterous relation with another married woman, because he could have more than one wife. In polygamous relationships, sometimes the rivalry among the wives is communicated indirectly with such rhetoric and ecpressive language as *ahwene pa nkasa* (precious beads do not jingle -#902), *afa me nwa* (you have picked me easily like a snail - #907), and *mede nkwan pa regye* (my tasty soup – that is, my cooking will take control of him).

A person can earn a bad reputation of being "unmarriagable" when it is proved against a man that he is inept in the art of marriage, *onnim awareɛ* (literary, he does not know how to marry), that is, he

- - might ill-treat his wife
- - does not maintain and support his wife adequately
- - does not concentrate on marrying a wife; *ɔsosɔ mmaa so* (literary, he pecks at women)
- - boasts around about the adultery fees he collects on his wife (wives) - *ɔde ayefare sika twampoa* (#683),
- - or against a woman that she is
- - notoriously quarrelsome
- - sexually unfaithful
- - incurably lazy, an ineffective housekeeper and a bad cook
- - a pilferer of the husband's money.

Cruelty and neglect were also grounds for separation and divorce. Desertion by the man for a period of three years conferred on the wife the right to marry another man. Incessant interference by relatives (especially by those of the man) may be basis for divorce. The symbol *meso kɛntɛn hunu a na worehwehwɛ mu* (even when I carry an empty basket you search through it - #765) expresses the spouse's displeasure at the interference by the marital partner's relatives. The man's relatives, especially his mother and sisters may interfere in his marriage on the pretext that he is neglecting his *abusua* responsibilities towards his nephews and nieces, that is, his sisters' children.

Sometimes no definite reason may be given as the basis for divorce. When no definite reason or a vague one is given it is always to be understood that the man or the woman finds it embarrassing or degrading to reveal the actual cause for divorce. It may also be that a partner may not want to injure the reputation or cause harm to the other partner.

PARENTAL AND CHILDREN'S RESPONSIBILITIES

Parents are expected to be responsible for all their children – handicapped or not, as the woman's womb is a passage for all manner of children (*yafun yɛ akwanten* - #516). Paternity is acknowledged by the man's acceptance of responsibility of maintaining his wife during her pregnancy period, and by giving her and her child a number of customary gifts (e.g., *funumatam* - cloth to cover the navel) immediately after the child is born. The child's naming ceremony (*aba dintoɔ*) is the critical assertion of fatherhood by the man. The naming of the child gives the father the opportunity to honor his relatives, particularly his parents by naming his children after them. The pregnant woman who could not name the man responsible for her pregnancy was derided as *wanhwɛ asukorɔ so ansa nsuo* (she slept around with several men, that is, a woman with loose sexual morals), consequently no one man could be held responsible for her pregnancy. In the past it was regarded a disgrace to the child and the mother if the child was not named by its father. The child without a known father is derided as "*onni seɛ kyiri botire*" (a child without a known father does not eat the head of a slaughtered animal).

The norms and practices of socialization make differential demands and expectations on the parents. Parental admonition of their children is not intended to harm the children as symbolized by the way the hen may step on her chicks to protect them (*akokɔ nan tia ne ba so a, ɛnku no* - #520-526). It is regarded as the duty and the pride of fatherhood for the husband to raise his children and to set them up in life. The father is dominant in the upbringing of the sons, while the mother plays a dominant and crucial role in the upbringing of the daughters. In the past the father took his son to farm and taught him how to farm, or taught him his craft if the father was a craftsman. These days the father is responsible for the schooling (and/or apprenticeship training) of his children. Even though the father is responsible for the upbringing of his children, Akan say that *ɔba nyin ɔse fie na ɔnka hɔ* (a child grows up in its father's house but never becomes a member of the father's lineage).

The mother is expected to teach her daughter feminine manners and skills for how successful or otherwise she is in socializing her daughter becomes evident when the daughter marries. This is expressed by the saying: *ɔbaa kɔ aware a, ɔde ne ni na ɛkɔ* - when a woman goes into marriage she goes with her mother. The daughter is socialized to be serviceable and submissive to her father, her sibling brothers, and older persons. The mother is expected to transmit her craft and occupational skills to her daughter. Among the crafts and industries in which women engage are pottery, manufacture of beads, soap-making, sewing, baking, and cooking.

A good mother is referred to as *ɔbaatan* (motherliness - #514-515). She is benevolent as she is considered a mother to all children. Sarpong (1974, p. 69) describes the Akan view of motherliness thus:

> Motherliness requires a woman to provide, by way of preparation, adequate food and shelter for her own children and when necessary, for those of others and for strangers. In some places in Ghana, a deceased woman who is known to have been benevolent is bewailed as: "The woman who gives to both mother and child." "Grandmother, the cooking pot that entertains strangers." "The mighty tree with

big branches laden with fruits. When children come to you, they find something
to eat."

Such praises may also be heaped on a man who is viewed as good father. Such a good father may be praised as "*agya a woyɛ mmɔfra ni* - the father who's a mother to children" or the "*abasatea a adɔyɛ wɔ mu* - slender arms that always take care of the needy and the vulnerable."

Children are taught to respect, support and protect the elderly. The respect for the elderly is indicated by the symbol: *woyɛ abɔfra a* (while you are young - #566). Children are responsible for the upkeep of their parents when the latter get old. The responsibility children have for their parents is indicated by the symbols - *Boa w'awofoɔ* (help your parents - #564) and *boa mpanimfoɔ* (help the elderly - #565). The bond between the father and his children is given tangible expression in funeral rites. The children are required by custom to provide the coffin for his burial. The following statement is said of children when they provide a coffin for their father's burial: *wosi dan ma wɔn akoraa* - they put up a house/room for their father. This expresses the children's final filial obligation to their father. It is considered a serious failing on the part of a man if he dies with no child born to him to give him this last respect. It is derisively said of such childless (and often regarded irresponsible) man: *n'adaka ayɛ no ka* - the cost of his coffin has become his own obligation, meaning he was left with no one with the obligation to pay for his coffin.

CHAPTER 8

Ahoɔfɛ ntua ka; suban pa na ahia
Beauty does not pay; it is good character that counts

SOCIAL VALUES

The ethics of a society is embedded in the ideas and beliefs about what is right or wrong, what is a good or bad character; it is also embedded in the conceptions of satisfactory social relations and attitudes held by the members of the society; it is embedded, furthermore, in the forms or patterns of behavior that are considered by the members of the society to bring about social harmony and cooperative living, justice, and fairness. The norms, mores, and values of the Akan people are derived in part from the Akan view of the nature of the universe. The Akan view the nature of the universe as a duality: spiritual and physical; the dead and the living; masculine and feminine; good and evil; the heavens and the earth; and natural and social. While the individual is a creation of a Supreme Being, the individual is also a social being. The Akan is a citizen of an undivided community of the dead, the living, and the yet to be born. Thus, to the Akan, morality and values have a spiritual source. God and the ancestors are believed to have keen interest in the moral order of the society. Ancestors are believed to be constantly watching over their living relatives, punishing those who break the customs or fail to fulfill their social obligations, and blessing and helping those who obey the laws and customs and fulfill their social obligations. God is believed to be all-seeing and has keen interest in the moral order of society. This belief is why the Akan say: *wobu kɔtɔ kwasea a, Nyankopɔn hunu w'akyi* (when you fool the crab, God sees your rear end - #762).

One symbol, *ɔbra te sɛ ahwehwɛ* (life is like a mirror - #604), seems to provide a summary of the Akan basic ethical standard. One sees himself/herself reflected in a mirror. From this mirror image one is able to appraise one's self as being a unique person, different from all others. This mirror image enables one to imagine how one appears to other people. It also enables one to imagine how others judge one's appearance, and thereby enables one to experience feelings of pride or shame. In life, one's feeling of self is reflected in the mirrors of faces, words, and gestures of those around one. From this perspective, the Akan is taught early in childhood to do nothing that will bring disgrace to himself/herself as a member of the community as conveyed by the maxim: *animguaseɛ mfata ɔkanniba* (disgrace does not befit the Akan). The Akan is always aware that his/her well-being lies in the welfare of his/her society.

The salient features of the Akan value system include the value of life, the value of human being, and the value of the communal social organization.[88] Among the most important social values of the Akan are diligence and hard work, virtue, truthfulness, obedience, honor, selflessness, excellence, and respect. A child is taught very early to work hard and readily in the house, on the farm, or in following a particular trade or profession. *Adwuma adwuma o; adwuma yie or adwuma da wo ase* (Work, work; work is good or work is grateful to you) is a popular greeting the Akan exchange at the work-site.

There are certain norms and mores that are accepted by the Akan as moral standards to which everyone is expected to conform in their everyday behavior. These forms of accepted behavior become the minimum morality that characterizes the behavior of the average citizen who endeavors not to violate the customs or social values or laws of his/her society. The basic ethical standard requires one to behave, in one's relations with all persons, in such a way that nothing one does may bring discredit on one's family. Whatever one does - good or bad - is a pointer to what sort of family one comes from. Several *adinkra* symbols such as *nni awu* (do not kill - #584), *di mmara so* (observe rules - #585), *sesa wo suban* (change your character - #600-603), and *yɛ papa* (do good - #568) encode some of these moral standards of the Akan people.

Gyekye (1987, p. 147) notes: "The concept of character, *suban*, is so crucial and is given such a central place in Akan moral language and thought that it may be considered as summing up the whole of morality." He further points out that "moral virtues arise through habituation, which is consonant with the empirical orientation of the Akan philosophy" (p. 150). The Akan say: *ahoofɛ ntua ka, suban pa na ɛhia* (beauty does not pay; it is good character that counts - #656-657). In other words, good character is more valuable than physical beauty.

In Akan moral thought a person is not born with a settled tendency to be good or to be bad. Antubam (1963) indicates that the Akan does not believe one is born with an original sin. One's character is determined by one's deeds or actions which are learned. Since one can desist from certain actions, then one can certainly change one's character. This view is captured by the symbol, *sesa wo suban* (change your character - #600-603). Also from the expression *woyɛ papa a, woyɛ ma wo ho; woyɛ bone nso a, woyɛ ma wo ho* (when you do good you do it onto yourself; what you do that is bad, you do onto yourself - #568) implies that one lives with the consequences of one's actions. Therefore, one has the freedom to choose to be good or bad. It is on this basis that society has standards for punishing wrong-doers.

Among the Asante, Ɔkɔmfo Anɔkye is believed to have handed down to the society a code of seventy-seven laws to govern legal and moral judgement. The code covered such areas as sexual behavior, respect for old age and authority, honor, discipline and the value of life. Honor is a value treasured by the Akan either as an individual or as a community. The importance of this moral value is expressed by the following: *Fɛdeɛ ne owuo, fanyinam owuo* (between death and dishonor, death is preferable - #599).

---

[88] Other aspects of Akan value system are discussed in the other chapters. For example, under the section on Akan attitudes toward money in Chapter 9, symbols that depict the virtues of kind-heartedness and commitment to the poor and the vulnerable in society are discussed.

RESPECT FOR HUMAN LIFE AND HUMANITY

The Akan belief that life is the most valuable thing in the whole world is expressed by the symbol *nni awu* (do not kill - #584). The aphorism associated with this symbol is: *nni awu na nkwa yɛntɔn* - do not kill for life is priceless. This symbol depicts the high value the Akan place on human life. Human life, to the Akan, is too precious to be wasted by senseless killing. The Akan also say that *nipa yɛ fɛ sen sika* (the human being is more beautiful and more valuable than wealth or treasures). The Akan belief is that human life has within itself the power of change, growth and development. This dynamic, creative power in the human must work towards building up instead of destroying as indicated by the aphorism: *ɔmampam na ɔse, me dee ne sɛ merepam me man, ɛnye amammɔeɛ* (The monitor lizard says, mine is to help build up, but not to destroy my state - #462).

The Akan believe that all human beings are children of God as indicated in the maxim: *nnipa nyinaa yɛ Onyankopɔn mma.* From this perspective, the Akan believe in the basic equality of human beings. The symbol, *woyɛ hwan* (who do you think you are? - #123), questions the very personhood of one. The Akan is deeply hurt when s/he is given cause to say, 's/he behaved toward me as though I were not a human being.'

Exchanging greetings is not only a mark of showing respect but is also considered part of decency and decorum. The starting point of harmonious social relations is to the Akan, the exchange of greetings. Greeting is more than showing courtesy; it is considered an acknowledgement - a sign of recognition of the other person as a fellow human being. It is to confirm your very existence as a human being. To greet someone, that is, to recognize the existence of one whom you pass in the street as a fellow human is, to the Akan, an obligation. Greeting also means the greeter is polite and cultured. People exchange greetings verbally and/or with gestures like a handshake. There are several types of greetings depending on the occasion, time and place, and gender and status of the people interacting in the greeting process. *Mekyia wo* (I salute you - #644), *nante yie* (goodbye - #655), *yɛbɛhyia bio* (we'll meet again - #652-653), *akwaaba* (welcome - #646), and *abusuafoɔ ho te sɛn?* (how is the family - #548), and *wo ho te sɛn?* (how are you? - #647) are adinkra symbols that depict some of the common Akan greetings and expressions of friendliness, hospitality, and forms of acknowledgement of the basic equality of human beings. *Mema wo hyɛden* (accept my condolences - #116) is the common way for one to express one's condolences and sympathy to a grieving family or individual.

RESPECT

Respect (*obuo*) is a central concept in Akan moral thoughts. The Akan is expected to respect one's self and also to show respect for the elderly and people in authority. The Akan say: *Wo bu wo ho a, na yɛ bu wo* - when you respect yourself, you are respected in return. Self-respect is depicted by the symbol *bu wo ho* (respect yourself - #569). Not being arrogant (*nyɛ ahantan* - #583; *nyɛ konkron* - #891), not being boastful (*ntwitwa wo ho nkyerɛ me* - #638), being humble (*brɛ wo ho ase* - #671), and having patience (*nya aboterɛ* - #582) are examples of symbols that depict acts of self-respect in the Akan society. The self-respecting person is one who knows how to control one's anger. It is said to such a person: *ani bere a, ɛnsɔ gya* (no matter how flaming red one's eyes may be, flames are not sparked in one's eyes - #571-581). By this expression one is urged not to succumb to one's emotions, but to exercise restraint in trying and difficult moments.

RESPECT FOR OLD AGE AND AUTHORITY

The one who has self-respect is also respectful of others, especially the elderly. The elderly are to be respected as they serve as the intermediary between the dead and the living. The chief as a person in authority, as well as the elderly, is considered to be sacred as he/she is thought to be in closer proximity to the ancestors (Sarpong, 1974). The elderly and the person in authority are regarded as the moral exemplar and are thus a standard which descendants should emulate. Respect for the elderly is depicted by *adinkra* symbols such as *boa mpanimfoɔ* (help the elderly - #565). Another symbol of respect for the elderly is *woyɛ abɔfra a* (while you are young - #566). One who is disrespectful is said to be arrogant. To such a person is said *ɛhuru a, ɛbɛdwo* (it will cool down after boiling - #658). Respect for the elderly and the person in authority is reciprocal as the elderly and the person in authority are expected to show respect to their subjects and the young, The Akan say: *Ɔpanin hu sɛ deɛ mmɔfra nante a, wɔsoa n'adwa* (when the elder learns to walk with the young, they carry his stool - #911). Also, *Sɛ ahennwa wɔ animuonyam a, na ɛnkyerɛ sɛ ɔhene a ɔte so anim yɛ nyam* (even if the stool is respected it does not mean that the chief is worthy of respect - #278-292). Being an elder or a person in authority does not automatically confer privileges on such a person, for the elderly and the person in authority must behave in responsible ways in order to earn the respect, authority and the service due the elder and person in authority.

SELFISHNESS AND JEALOUSY

The Akan also places emphasis on social conduct and carrying out one's social obligations as part of good character. Volunteering your time, that is, making yourself available in giving personal help, rather than donating money, in other words, generosity that consists of personal service and hard work is more honorable and has wider application and can be useful to more people. This is captured by the symbol: *yɛ papa* (do good - #568) and the associated expression: *Woyɛ papa a, woyɛ ma wo ho* - When you do good you do it unto yourself. The Akan is taught to eschew selfishness (*pɛsɛmenkomenya* - #878) and jealousy (*ahooyaa* - #587-589). Selfishness destroys a nation as encoded in the *pɛsɛmenkomenya* (#878) symbol. The selfish person is also considered to be a hypocrite. Hypocrisy is eschewed by the Akan as encoded by the symbol *nku me fie* (do not kill me in the private and then mourn me in public (#129). The jealous person is said to be like the *mfofoɔ aba* (seed of the *mfofoɔ* plant - #587-589). This symbol is associated with the maxim: *sɛdeɛ mfofoɔ pɛ ne sɛ gyinantwi abɔ bidie* (what the *mfofoɔ* plant always wishes is that the *gyinantwi* seeds should turn black and die). The Akan must eschew jealousy and covetousness as the *mfofoɔ aba* symbol indicates. Other symbols that convey to the Akan the need not to be jealous and covetous include *ɛkaa obi nko a* (someone wishes - #594) and *ɛkaa nsee nko a* (the weaver bird wishes - #595-597). The Akan is rather urged to be circumspect (*hwɛ w'akwan mu yie* - #670) in order not to fall into the machinations of enemies to be treated like how the cockroach is treated when it falls into a flock of fowls – *tɛfrɛ tɔ nkokɔ mu a, sosɔ ne wɔsosɔ no* (#682).

Envy and hatred are bad conducts that the Akan should steer his/her life away from. The envious person suffers shame and disgrace. *Atamfoɔ ani awu* (adversaries are ashamed - #660) and *atamfoɔ rebrɛ* (adversaries are suffering - #592-593) are examples of symbols used to indicate the sufferings the envious persons go through. The gossip is said to expose the shortcomings of others except his own (*kata wo deɛ so* – #590-591. The gossip is an envious person, so the Akan is urged not to gossip (*nni nsekuo* - #598). Rather than engaging in idle talk or gossip, the Akan is urged to think about herself/himself (*dwen wo ho* - #675-676) and also to put herself/himself to productive work (*gyae me ho nkontabuo na pɛ wo deɛ* - #590-591).

KINDNESS

There are several symbols that depict the virtues of kind-heartedness and commitment to the poor and the vulnerable. The symbol *momma yɛnnodɔ yɛn ho* (let us love one another - #567) conveys the Akan ethic that what is of value at the personal level is inseparable from that at the social level. This means that the practice of basic values is inseparable at the personal and social levels. Being a friend to the poor, providing shelter for the widow and the orphan, honoring one's parents and showing respect for the elderly and for the human personality are virtues that stem from knowing that *nipa nyinaa yɛ Onyankopɔn mma* (all human beings are the children of God). The *nkuruma kɛse* (big okra - #323-331) symbol also portrays the virtue of kind-heartedness as implied in the maxim: *Amoawisi, nkuruma kɛse a ɔwo mma aduasa nso ɔgye abayɛn* (Amoawisi, the benevolent one who bore thirty children of her own yet raised other people's children - #323-331). The good family head (*abusua panin*) who provides for the orphan and the widow in the family is also said to portray these virtues of kind-heartedness and commitment to the poor and vulnerable (*abusua panin kyerɛ wo dɔ* - #556).

GRATITUDE AND CONTENTMENT

Ackah (1988, p. 34) writes: "The Akan is always particular about the behavior towards him of someone to whom he has made himself useful." This embodies the Akan concept of reciprocity, a central idea in Akan value system. There are essentially three forms of reciprocity: compensatory, obligatory, and initiatory reciprocity. The compensatory type of reciprocity is indicated by the symbol *pagya wo ti na gye aseda* (raise your head and accept thanksgiving - #634). The symbol *woyɛ papa a, woyɛ ma wo ho* (when you do good, you do it unto yourself - #568) expresses the view that a good deed returns to those who do it. This also suggests the compensatory type of reciprocity. The obligatory type of reciprocity is based on the demands of justice. This is conveyed by the symbols *nea wopɛ sɛ* (do unto others - #419) and *pagya wo ti na gye aseda* (raise your head and accept thanksgiving - #634). The Akan says *onipa yɛ yie a, ɔyɛ gye ayɛyie* (a good deed deserves praise). Also, when an Akan makes a present he accepts thanks (*ɔkanni kyɛ adeɛ a ɔgye aseda* - #634). These expressions convey the view that one must offer thanks in anticipation of a favor or service that will be rendered. The ungrateful person is likened to a stranger who returns a good favor with ingratitude (*woyɛ ɔhɔhoɔ papa ɔde wo ti bɔ dua mu* - #635-636). Of the ungrateful person it may be said: '*kae da bi' yɛde se boniayɛ* ('remember the past' is said to the ungrateful person). Also, to the ungrateful person may be said *anyi me ayɛ a, ɛnsɛe me din* (if you will not praise me, do not tarnish my good name - #678).

When young people take care of their elderly parents, they are expressing their gratitude to their parents for taking care of them in their childhood days. The gratitude children show to their elderly parents is depicted by the symbols *boa w'awofo* (help your parents - #564) and *boa mpanimfoɔ* (help the elderly - #565). These acts of service to one's parents and the elderly encompass the three aspects of reciprocity in the Akan value system.

The Akan are urged to be content with their lot as we saw in Chapter 3 of the story of the man who wanted to commit suicide rather than live in poverty. This is expressed by the following: *ma w'ani nsɔ nea wowɔ* (be content with your lot - #570). The following analogy is also given to illustrate the need to exercise contentment: if you have a small head and you try to increase the size by adding layers of mud onto your head, when it rains such layers will fall off. The Akan have to make do with the little they have. They have to capitalize on any least opportunity, for if a quantity of water does not suffice for a bath it will at least be sufficient for drinking (*nsuo anso adwareɛ a, ɛso nom* - #570).

GOOD HEALTH

Good health as an important social value to the Akan is indicated by the recurring theme of health and long life evidenced in Akan prayers. The *adinkra* symbol, *mesrɛ nkwa tenten ne nkɔsoɔ ma wo* (I pray for long life and prosperity for you - #62), conveys the Akan's value for good health. When the Akan exchange greetings with each other the first thing enquired is the health of each other (*wo ho te sɛn?* - #647) and the health of family members (*abusuafoɔ ho te sɛn?* - #548). Good health is also signified by the symbol *mmɔ adwaman* (do not fornicate - #586). In this symbol the idea is conveyed that promiscuous lifestyle is not only immoral but also carries the risk of incurring sexually transmitted diseases. The Akan believe in a sound mind and a sound body. One must not suffer from any "unclean" diseases like sexually transmitted diseases, leprosy, epilepsy, madness, sleeping sickness, smallpox and blindness. Such diseases were believed to be used by the gods to punish evil-doers and communities that failed to honor ancestral taboos. Another symbol that relates to the Akan concern about good health is encoded in the symbol *tɔntɔnte ne tetɔnte* (#876) that infers that as one drinks one should be mindful of the effects of drinks on one's health.

WORK ETHICS

The Akan believe that when God created the universe He created work as part and parcel of human beings, as indicated in the following: *ɔdomankoma bɔɔ adeɛ, ɔde adwuma bataa nipa ho* (God created work as part and parcel of human beings). Work ethics of tenacity, diligence, industry and frugality are encoded in symbols such as *tabono* (paddle - #616-617), *ɔkɔtɔ* (crab - #720-722) *okuafo pa* (good farmer - #698), *aya* (fern - #622-627), *afa* (bellows - #699-702), *sapɔ* (sponge - #877), *wo nsa akyi* (the back of your hand - #666), *komfoaku* (#772), and *nsɛneɛ* (scales - #828). The symbol *tabono*, for example, suggests that hard work, like steady paddling, inspires confidence and industry. The *asɔ ne afena* (the hoe and the machete - #694) symbol encodes the Akan view that *woansɔ w'asɔtia ne afena mu anyɛ adwuma a, ɔkɔm bɛde wo* - one must work to live. The *sapɔ* (sponge - #877) symbol encodes the maxim that one must be diligent in soaking one's sponge with water to undertake and accomplish something worthwhile. Even the discarded sponge has its usefulness when the need arises (*sapɔfo yɛfa no da hia da* - #877).

The ethic of hard work is of prime importance among the Akan. It is a disgrace for an Akan to be regarded as lazy (*akwadworɔ*). *Akwadworɔ* means sloth, laziness, or tardiness. Akan popular maxim teaches that there is nothing in laziness except tattered clothes (*akwadworɔ mu nni biribi no, na nyɛ ntomago*). The *komfoaku* – pride of labor (#7720) symbol encodes the Akan view that hard work and pride of labor are necessary for one's, as well as society's development. Parents are very particular about training their children to grow to be productive adults. Mothers are particularly burdened to cultivate proper work ethics in their daughters lest the daughters would grow up and turn out to be lazy wives. Laziness on the part of the wife would be grounds for divorcing her. Laziness as the grounds for the divorce of a woman is considered a disgrace to her and her mother.

The Akan is taught to believe that life is dynamic and problematic; one has to struggle all the time to make life meaningful. This is conveyed by the symbol *ɔbra yɛ bɔna* (life is a struggle - #661; #605-609). This is because the life course is not straight (*ɔbra ne kwan yɛ nkyinkyimiiɛ*) as indicated by the symbol *nkyinkyimiiɛ* (zigzag - #605-609). To follow a meandering path one needs to critically assess one's bearing and direction from time to time. The meandering path represents life's course as strewn with obstacles. One must stop at each obstacle, one must think and reorient one's steps in order to attain one's goal in life. There are many encounters in a person's life. One may encounter ups and downs, joyous and sad moments (*ani hunu yaa* - #639-642), and pleasantly wonderful and ordinary events. The Akan believe it is the duty of the virtuous person to bear the vicissitudes of life patiently by enjoying the happy and wonderful moments as well as having the perseverance and hardiness of the *wawa aba* (seed of the *wawa* tree - #610-615) to withstand the adversities of life. The Akan stress that failure in life is more painful than the pain one might feel when being cut with a saw. This is encoded by the symbol *ɔbra twa wo a. esene sekan* (life's agonies - #674). The Akan is reminded that life struggles are not pleasant all the time. This is because like the sweetness induced by the *asaawa* berry, pleasant situation in life does not last forever - *ɔdɛ nka anomu* (#763). Also, the Akan is reminded that *ɔbrakwan atwedeɛ, obi reforo kɔ sor no, na obi so resane, na obi so deɛ, ogyina na ogyina* (the social ladder is such that some people move up, some people move down, and other people stay in the same position - #890). In society, some individuals and families experience drastic changes in social status and lifestyle. Vertical social mobility in the Akan society refers to moving up or down the so-called social ladder.

The foregoing discussion suggests there is the possibility of making mistakes in the decisions one will make in life's choices. Akan say *nea oretwa sa nnim sɛ n'akyi akyea* (the path-maker or the trailblazer does not know that the path is crooked or curved behind him - #237). For that reason, one should not only be self-critical, but one should be able to listen to criticism, advice and suggestions from others. The Akan say *wo nsa akyi bɛyɛ wo dɛ a, ɛnte sɛ wo nsa yamu* (the back of your hand does not taste as good as the palm - #666). For one to be able to tolerate criticism and take other people's advice, one needs to be humble (*brɛ wo ho ase* - #671).

The symbol *gye w'ani* (enjoy yourself - #650) suggests that life must be enjoyed to make it worthwhile. The symbol urges one to make the best out of life. The symbol *nya aboterɛ* (be patient - #582) conveys the idea that with patience one can move mountains of difficulties. Another symbol that portrays the need for patience and persistence in life is the *ɔsrane* (crescent moon - #618-621) which suggests that the moon does not form a circle hastily.

There has been institutionalized a system of rewards and punishments to encourage individuals to avoid vices and to pursue certain virtues. One virtue cherished by the Akan is success in life. Success in life has its own reward. The Akan say that *ɔbrane twa apɔ a, yɛma no mo* (recognition and praise come with good deed - #633). Some of the rewards may come after one is dead as the Akan say *aponkyerɛne wu a, na yɛhunu ne tenten* (it is when the frog dies that we see its full length - #659). Similarly, Akan say *ɛkyɛm tete a, ɛka ne meramu* (when a shield wears out, the framework still remains - #417; #879-880).

CHAPTER 9

Mmirikisie a yɛantumi annɔ na yɛfrɛ no nsamampɔ
The farm that is not tended is referred to as a sacred burial ground

ECONOMICS, ACCOUNTABILITY, AND SOCIAL INEQUALITY

INTRODUCTION

The pre-colonial Akan economy had passed the stage of subsistence economy as the development of centralized government, the local and long distance trade, and the use of money had led to the intensification of production. The principal sectors of the economy were agriculture, hunting, fishing, mining, crafts and trading. Nonetheless, production for domestic consumption was the dominant feature of the economy. Economic organization was largely based on the household whose productive activities were mainly oriented towards own use rather than for exchange. There was some limited government involvement in the economy. The centralized Asante government, for example, greatly influenced at least road (foot path – *akwantempɔn*) construction, trade and gold production.

I briefly discussed in Chapter 3 *kookoo dua* (cocoa tree - #703), *bese saka* (bunch of kola nuts - #706-712) and *abɛ dua* (palm tree - #705) as examples of symbols that encode crops that have had significant impact on the Akan as well as the greater Ghanaian economy. The *adinkra* cloth also encodes several other symbols that relate to the nature of the pre-colonial Akan and contemporary Ghanaian economy as well as some of the economic activities of the people. Symbols such as *ɔbohemaa* (diamond - #718-719) and *okuafoɔ pa* (good farmer - #698) and *afena ne asɔ* (cutlass and hoe - #694) suggest mining and farming as forms of economic activities. Other symbols such as *sitia bɛkum dorɔba* (the driver may die at the steering-wheel - #715-717), Senchi/Adomi bridge (#768-771), *benz* (#740-741), *foon* (#744-746) and VW (#738-739) also point to economic activities of more recent times; and the *ɔpaani apaadie* (laborer -#686-687) symbol encodes the intensification of labor market formation in the Akan and the Ghanaian society.

AGRICULTURE

Land, one of the important inputs for agriculture, was believed by the Akan to be the sustainer of life. On the basis of this belief, every Akan was entitled to usufructuary rights to land for the purposes of raising food crops. Agriculture was undertaken on small plots of land over which the effective or usufructuary rights of cultivation were vested in the *abusua* as a corporate body. Cultivation was carried out by the nuclear family on relatively small plots. The Asante make a definite distinction between land (*asaase*) ownership and the usufruct right to land (*didi asaase so* - right to eat from the land). This distinction is embodied in the Asante maxim: *afuo yɛ me dea, asaase yɛ ɔhene dea* - the farm, that is, the usufruct right to the land is mine, but the land belongs to the king). Thus Ollennu (1962) describes usufructuary title to land as the right of the individual citizen to the enjoyment of cultivation rights and even to the right of transmitting his individual enjoyment either by gift, will or inheritance to others.

The Akan believe that land (*asaase* - #29-31) is the sustainer of life and, therefore, it ought to be owned by the *abusua* as a corporate body so that every member of the *abusua* would have access to the use of land for raising crops for one's subsistence. Members of the *abusua* acquired portions of the *abusua* land through enterprise, effective occupation, and grants from the *abusua panin* or the king (McCaskie, 1980). The cultivator had exclusive rights to such naturally propogated economic trees as the kola and rubber. The cultivator did not pay dues, levies, or rents for the usufruct rights to the land.

The state could not alienate land effectively held by the *abusua* lineages and individuals (Busia, 1951, pp. 42-50). Even though the state cannot alienate land already occupied by a subject, the king as custodian and grantor of land can assume the right of alienating, by sale or gift or otherwise, unoccupied lands to foreigners and companies for economic exploitation. In certain instances, some chiefs have unilaterally assumed the right to alienate land in order to promote national development. "This action by chiefs has been regarded as a breach of the traditional principles governing tenure" (Kyerematen, 1971, p. 37).

Cultivation was based on the use of such principal farm tools as cutlass or machete and hoe (*afena ne asɔ* - #694), axe (*akuma* - #695-697) and digging tool (*sɔsɔ*). These farming tools were manufactured by the local blacksmith (*ɔtomfoɔ*). The blacksmith shaped these tools from *daban* or *dade bena* (iron bar or measuring rod - #833) with the aid of *afa* (bellows - #699-702) and other tools. In general, localities were able to grow enough food for their own consumption, and in some areas, for example, around Kumase surplus food was produced for the market.

Food crops cultivated included yams, cocoyam, corn (maize), groundnuts - as indicated by *nkatehono* - #713, bananas - as indicated by *kwadu hono* - #866, and vegetables (peppers - as indicated by *mako nyinaa* - #752-754, beans, okra - as indicated by *nkruma kɛse* - #323-331, egg plant/garden eggs, etc.). After contact with Europeans other food crops were introduced into the Akan (and the greater Ghanaian) society. These crops included vegetables (e.g., tomatoes), plantain and varieties of cassava (manioc). Crops like the oil palm and rubber that grew wild became increasingly important as cash crops, and new cash crops like cocoa and coffee were introduced later. From the middle of the nineteenth century the missionaries, especially of the Basel and Wesleyan Missions opened agricultural stations for experimentation and extension of agriculture.

The Akan valued the oil palm tree (*abɛ dua* - #705) for its various uses. One could make the assertion that the Akan had a nascent integrated industry based on the oil palm tree. The oil palm industry initially consisted merely of picking the fruits from wild palm groves and extracting oil from the pericarp. The oil was in the early years used principally as cooking oil and also for soap-making and was put in *kyɛmferɛ* (potsherd - #850-851) as fuel for oil lamps. The oil from the kernel (alluded to by the symbols *mmɔdwewafoɔ* - #376-377 and *mede me se abɔ adwe* - #755) was used as pomade for the skin and as cooking oil. The shell of the kernel was used as active charcoal by blacksmiths for various purposes including iron smelting and forging and the making of gunpowder. The palm branches were used as building materials and also for weaving baskets (*menso wo kɛntɛn* - #765) and making *apa* or *apata* (drying mats or storage barn - #714). Palm wine tapping was an important occupation for a number of men. As the slave trade ended, the oil palm industry expanded to satisfy growing demands in the soap and margarine factories in Europe. There entered into the oil palm industry several European companies to buy the oil palm products (particularly palm oil and kernel oil). The giant UAC (*UAC nkanea* - UAC lights #760) first entered the Ghanaian market as Lever Brothers to buy oil palm products.

KOLA PRODUCTION

Kola nuts (*bese* - #706-712) was exported from the forests of Asante to the trans-Saharan trade markets in the north. The kola nuts trade was constrained by (1) transport owners who operated donkey caravans that carried kola nuts to the north, and (2) the confinement of kola nut production, based firmly in lineage structures. The Akan in the forest belt where kola trees grew wild were exhorted to exploit the kola nuts for productive use and not to behave like the ants on the kola tree. This exhortation is encoded in the maxim: *nhohoɔ a ɔtare bese ho, ɔno a ɔnte new nso ɔnte ntɔn* – the ant on the pod of kola nuts does not pluck the kola nuts to et or sell - #706-712. This provided incentive for individuals enter the kola trade to amass wealth. As part of the northern trade, three media of exchange were utilized: (1) cowries (*sedeɛ* - #723-728) which was not accepted as a store of value by the Akan; (2) gold dust for which many traders carried their scale (*nsɛneɛ* - #828) and weights, *abrammoɔ* for measuring quantities of gold dust; and (3) kola nuts (Arhin, 1979).

COCOA

Kookoo dua yɛ sika dua (cocoa is a money tree - #703) signifies the importance of this cash crop in the Ghanaian economy. The *kookoo dua* symbol also encodes important historical, political, and economic narratives in the affairs of the greater Ghanaian society. Until the 1880s, the palm oil, rubber, and kola nuts that entered into the international trade were produced mainly through collection and gathering. As demand for these crops increased their cultivation was intensified. Cocoa and other crops were introduced and cultivated, especially after the abolition of the slave trade (Dickson, 1971; Reynolds, 1973). Ghana exported no cocoa beans in 1892, yet nineteen years later overtook Brazil (whose crop was itself a national record) as the world's largest exporter of the commodity (Clarence-Smith 2000: 238-9). That was at the level of 40,000 tons a year; Ghanaian output reached 200,000 in 1923, and passed 300,000 in 1936. This was an example of the 'cash crop revolution' of the late nineteenth and early twentieth centuries in the so-called 'peasant' colonies of tropical Africa – those colonies in which Africans retained control of the vast majority of cultivable land, rather than seeing much of it appropriated for use by European settlers or companies (Austin, 2012).

According to Austin (2012) as general phenomenon, this 'cash crop revolution' had three parts.

The first, exemplified in the forest zone of southern Ghana, was indeed the massive expansion of export agriculture, largely as an African initiative, in areas with favorable land quality and location. In coastal regions of West Africa producers, many of them small, had already begun to supply European markets with agricultural produce (palm oil, groundnuts) several decades before colonial rule, during and after the abolition of the Atlantic slave trade (Hopkins 1973: 125-35; Law 1995). But the size and geographical range of Africans' entry as producers into intercontinental agricultural markets was multiplied between colonization and the 1930s depression. The second part, qualifying the term 'revolution', was the much slower and more fitful growth of agricultural exports from less naturally favored areas (for instance, cotton from the interior of French West Africa), often prodded by the colonial administrations. The third part was the complement of the first, and a partial response to the limits of the second: the emergence, sooner or later, of a migrant-labor system (*apaadie* -#686-687) which channeled workers into the main export-crop growing areas from the drier and/or more remote parts of the same or neighboring colonies (Austin, 2012).

The success of cocoa farming as an industry bears eloquent testimony to the entrepreneurial skills of the Akan and other Ghanaian farmers. It also suggests that the pre-colonial Akan economy, contrary to the view expressed by Szereszewski (1966), was not "essentially static." The pre-colonial Akan economy did respond to market demands by being innovative. "Innovation," as La Torre (1978, p. 11) puts it, "should be understood here to include not only technological change, but rather any deliberate alteration in accustomed modes of economic activity, such as, for example, the rearrangement of social relations to acquire control over labor."

Indigenous modes of production such as *nnɔboa*[89]; labor market forms (*apaadie* #686-687) such as *awowa* (pawn labor), *atabrako* and *apaadie*[90] forms of daily wage or annual (*afenhyia apaadie*) wage, and forms of sharecropping like *abusa* (one-third of profit from sale of produce), *abunu* (half of profit from sale of produce) and *nkotokuo ano* (a fraction of the sale price of a bag load of produce); and capital accumulation methods such as *susu* and *huza*[91] were not only incorporated, but were intensified in the cocoa industry and other agricultural production. The colonial government's labor conscription laws to recruit labor from the north of Ghana for public works and mining in the south helped to intensify the use of the indigenous sharecropping system of tenure such as *afenhyia apaadie* and *abusa* (see Robertson, 1982; Aidoo, 1983). The failure of the colonial labor conscription laws in Ghana may be attributed in part to the intensified use of the traditional wage and sharecropping systems by Ghanaian farmers in the cocoa industry. Conscripted laborers from the north, and from French territories to the north and west, and German territory to the east who ran away from government labor camps or taxation schemes had alternative jobs with better wages

---

[89] *Nnɔboa* (reciprocal labor) is system of cooperation in which a group of people pull their labor together to help each member of the group in turns on each one's farm. In this system no wage is paid, the one on whose farm the group will work on during the day provides food.

[90] The one who hires his/her labor for monetary consideration is called *ɔpaani* (laborer, sing. - *apaafoɔ* - pl.). The laborer may be paid on daily basis (*atabrako* - usually by the piece rate method) or on annual basis (*afenhyia apaadie*).

[91] Huza is a Krobo system of land purchase in which land is bought in blocks by "companies" and, later, divided the land into individual strips in proportion to the company member's financial contribution, The Krobo huza had territorial ambitions and it was centrally organized by the Krobo paramount chiefs who controlled and managed the companies. It was a form a political organization with a leader - huzatse and other officials. The Krobo huza companies were marching like armies to conquer the uninhabited forest lands of the Akim (Hill, 1970).

and better working conditions on cocoa farms in the Akan areas. This led to the rise of zongos in various cocoa growing areas in the Gold Coast Colony.

The success of the cocoa industry has resulted in significant structural changes in the political economy of the Akan as well as the greater Ghanaian society. The success of the cocoa industry has also resulted in the intensification of the market economy as land and labor were transformed into commodities. Land purchase and leasing increased as a direct result of the expansion of the cocoa and the cash crop industry. The success of the industry also hastened the process of capital accumulation and stimulated labor migration and labor market (Hill, 1970). Even though cocoa has helped in significant structural changes in the national economy, the country's national economy has remained primarily dependent on the export of raw materials with very little value added.

CRAFT INDUSTRY

The Akan, for example, are known to have had a measure of technology which, while not spectacular, was still not inconsiderable. For the purposes of war they devised usable weapons, and for the purposes of peace some artifacts pleasing in themselves and others useful in a variety of ways. Abraham (1962) notes that "The Akan had iron and steel enterprises. Iron and steel implements have been discovered; and the sites of some foundries have also been unearthed... They had precious metal ornaments, and their artistry and skill in the treatment of gold and jewelry impressed the early European visitors." These accomplishments presupposed a good deal of careful observation and some experimentation. This fact is even more evident in the case of traditional medicine, which, as Abraham also notes, reached in pre-colonial times "a high degree of efficacy." Craft industry (*adwindie*) symbolized by, for example, *afa* (bellows - #699-702)[92], *adwa* (stool - #278-292), *kɛntɛn* (basket - #765) *akofena ne tuo* (sword and gun - #416), *ahina* (pot - #731) and *kyɛmferɛ* (potsherd - #850-851), covered such activities as weaving of baskets and textiles, wood-carving, pottery, metal-works (gold- and black-smithing, indicated by *afa* - #699-702), food processing and soap-making. Craft production was carried out on individual basis, as well as on family basis, and apprentices tended to be close kin.

Basket weaving, encoded in the *kɛntɛn* (basket - #765) symbol, was the work of men. Baskets were woven from palm and raffia branches, canes and creepers. One of the important products of basket weaving industry was the palanquin for carrying the royals. Cloth weaving, dyeing and printing, suggested by the *nsaa* (hand-woven blanket - #806-810) symbol, involved men as well as women.

Pottery, indicated by the *kyɛmferɛ* (potsherd - #850-851) symbol, was exclusively a woman's industry. However, men had exclusive monopoly in making the smoking pipe (*taasɛn*). Pots were made for household as well as ceremonial uses. Pots were used in the house as cooking utensils, cups and dishes. Among the Akan, pottery vessels were commonly found in burials of the past. One Akan group the Kwahu, for example, is well known for the funerary pottery (terracotta) found by archaeologists. Some of the archealogical pottery findings include ancient clay stoves, clay hearths (mukyia -#244-245), clay smoking pipes and clay vesseels for cooking or serving food, and for carrying and storing and serving water. Among the funerary rituals of the ancient Akan people are pottery sculptures dedicated to the memory of their ancestors that served as grave markers. Although these pottery sculptures are sometimes full figures, they are more often just heads. These heads are thought to commemorate the royalty.

---

[92] Bosman (1705) noted that the bellows used by the Akan were an invention of their own.

Smithing (gold-smithing, blacksmithing, and the casting of gold-weights), suggested by symbols such as *afa* (bellows - #699-702), *nsɛneɛ* (scales - #828), *aso ne afena* (hoe and cutlass - # 694), and *daban* (iron bar or measuring rod - #833), was a very important craft industry. Probably the most important products of the blacksmiths were agricultural implements of various sorts (axes, hoes, and cutlasses). Other items produced by blacksmiths included hinges, bolts, swords (*akofena* - #260-269), knives, rings, chains, and musical instruments. The blacksmiths also repaired firearms as well as manufactured small quantities of firearms, gun-powder and bullets (*etuo aboba* - #223).

Gold-smithing seems to have been under the close control of the political authorities in the Asante area. The courts of the Asantehene and certain other bureaus (*fekuo*) contained a number of offices occupied by goldsmiths (e.g., *adwumfoɔhene* and *buramfoɔhene*), who supervised the work of the smiths (*aburamufoɔ*) employed by the court. Goldsmiths worked the gold into a variety of personal ornaments (bracelets, chains, breastplates, rings, trinkets, and so on).

As part of deliberate population policies of various Asantehene, craft villages were founded around Kumase with war captives or refugees in such places as Bonwire and Anawomase (textile weaving), Asokwa and Ntonso (textile dyeing and printing), Breman, Fumesua and Adum (metalworks and goldsmithing), Pankrono and Tafo (pottery), Mamponten (soap making), Daaba (beadmaking), Sewua and Adwumakase Kese (metalworks, textile weaving and drum-making), Banko and Nsuta (umbrella-making), and Ahwia (wood carving). The craftsmen and women were apparently free to make and sell anything except for items reserved for the king's palace as part of the royal regalia.

LIVESTOCK PRODUCTION

Symbols such as *akokɔ* (rooster - #846-848), *akokɔnan* (hen's feet - #520-526), *dwenimmɛn* (ram's horns - #332-341), *dwantire* (ram's head - #427-433) and *ɛsono* (elephant - #351-354) suggest the possibility of the raising of livestock in addition to hunting. Such possibility would give rise to tanning and leatherwork. The possibility of tanning and leatherwork are also indicated by other symbols such as *ɔhene kyɛ* (king's crown - #298-299), *donno* (bell drum - #500), *atumpan* (talking drums - #883), and *mpaboa* (sandals - #224). Other products of the leather works included cushions and soldier's belts and pouches.

HUNTING AND FISHING

Hunting (*ahayɔ*) and fishing were carried out on both individual and communal basis. These economic activities are encoded by symbols such as *bomokyikyie* (the river fish - #831), *ɔkɔtɔ* (crab - #720-722), *nam porɔ* (fish rots - #235-236), *afidie* (trap - #756), and *etuo ne akyekyedeɛ* (the gun and tortoise - #221). As part of the Asante population policy, many coastal Fante war captives were settled around Lake Bosumtwe, where their skills as fishermen could be put to good use. Hunting required special skills as suggested by the expression: *gye akyekyedeɛ kɔma agya nyɛ ahayɔ* - taking a tortoise to one's father is not considered hunting. Towns such as Sunyani grew as important meat processing centers for hunters.

MINING

Adinkra symbols that incorporate ideas about mining include *ɔbohemmaa* (diamond - #718-719), *ɔkɔtɔ* (crab - #720-722) and *nsɛneɛ* (scale - #823). The principal methods of gold and diamond production were panning of alluvial streams and wetlands, and in the case of gold, quarrying or surface mining of gold-bearing ore (*mmoaboa*), and shaft mining (*amenapeaa nkoron* or *nkrontu*). "Akan miners in the eighteenth century dug slanting pits with broad steps to a depth of as much as 150 feet. The miners at the bottom dug out the ore and loaded it on trays, which were then passed to the surface by means of a human chain" (Hopkins, 1973, p. 46). The pit or shaft mining was known as *nkoron dwuma*, and the miner was known as *nkorontufoɔ*. Gold extraction by pit mining was shrouded in secrecy. The mined gold was utilized as money and jewelry (encoded by symbols such as *nsɛneɛ* (#828) *adaeboɔ*, *akrafoɔkɔmu* (#312-313), and *ɔhene kyɛ* (#298-299).

Panning of alluvial streams and wetlands is alluded to by the *adinkra* symbol *ɔkɔtɔ* (crab - #720-722). The crab in the wetland areas where there were prospects for alluvial gold, in digging its hole, would expose gold nuggets. This was one of several methods of prospecting the Akan used to identify possible sites for panning or digging along the banks of such rivers as the Ankobra, Pra and Offin. The panning method of production, now popularly known as "galamsey," is increasingly making a comeback in very environmentally destructive form in recent years. Present day "galamsey" has been a major contributing factor in creating environmental destruction in the country. Other minerals from contemporary Ghana include bauxite, manganese, and diamonds.

WASTE MANAGEMENT

Symbols such as *sapɔ* (sponge - #877) and *propobinsin* (scarab or grub - #885) allude to the concern of the Akan about waste and waste management and the usefulness of recycling. The maxim, *sapɔfo yɛfa no da hia da* – the old discarded sponge has its days of usefulness when needed (#877), is one way the Akan appreciate the need for recycling. The Akan associate the vulture (*pɛtɛ*) and *kukrubin* or *propobinsin* (scarab - #885) with waste management. The vulture and the scarab show that human waste (excrement), as well as other forms of carrion, is a reservoir of strength and energy that is capable of being recovered and recycled.

It is well recognized that the Akan and the bigger Ghanaian society has a waste management problem. Even though the country has difficulty managing its waste problem these days, yet it allows the importation electronic waste as used goods from abroad. Perhaps one could learn a lesson or two from the vulture and the scarab.

MONEY AND PUBLIC ACCOUNTING SYSTEM

In Asante, the state's involvement in the economy was manifested in the following ways:

1) intentional intervention of the state in economic processes through
   a) the protection and encouragement of trade
   b) the prosecution of warfare that brought skilled persons to be settled in craft villages
   c) the conduct of foreign relations to ensure trade stability

2) taxation and government expenditures such as tributes; taxes on trade; death duties; court fees and fines; and taxation on gold production

3) the use of gold dust as currency.

Some *adinkra* symbols such as *bese saka* (bunch of kola nuts - # 706-712), *serewa* or *sedeɛ* (cowrie shells - #723-728) and *daban* (iron bar - #833) encode the monetization of the Akan economy long before the contact with Europeans. Kola nuts, cowrie shells, beads, and gold dust were used as currencies at one time or another. European traders also introduced other currencies such as manillas, iron bars and rods (called *nnabuo* or *nnaredwoɔ* - Garrard, 1980, p. 3), and copper rods. New forms of accounting based on indigenous systems were developed as part of trade with the Europeans. These new forms of accounting included the bar, sorting, and the ounce (Hopkins, 1973, p. 111).

In Asante, as in other Akan communities, there once existed a very complicated and elaborate accounting system based on gold dust (*sika futuro*) and gold weights (*mmrammuo*) encoded by the *nsɛneɛ* (scales - #828) symbol - see Fig.26. The value of the gold dust was assessed by weight and the Gyaasehene controlled the Asantehene's treasury by keeping the weights (*mmrammuo*), spoons (*nsaawa*), scoops or shovels (*mfamfa*), scales (*nsɛneɛ*- #828), and other appliances of the accounting system. Gold dust was demonetized as currency in Ghana in 1912 as result of the establishment of the West African Currency Board.

Gold weights had equally important use as an ideographic or pictographic script in the social and political organization, and knowledge system of the Akan. The use of gold weights as ideographic or pictographic script has been largely neglected except for the brilliant work of Niangoran-Bouah (1984). The gold weights, like other Akan art, were created and used "like spoken language, to commemorate social or historical events or entities, to express philosophical or religious views, aspirations, and dreams, or simply to ask questions, or to express displeasure" (Nitecki, 1982). Leyten (1979, p. 26) calls the gold weights "tales in bronze" and characterizes them as "indelible symbol[s] of the achievements of their owners," because they revealed how each individual perceived his own life, his position in society, his ambitions, and his achievements. At the political level, for example, many of the gold weights were used to refer to the chiefs symbolically with regards "to their abuse of power, sometimes to their strength and wisdom" (Cole and Ross, 1977, p. 79). McLeod (1978, p. 307) notes that Akan art "was also used as a mnemonic for important historical or mythical events and to communicate, in the absence of [alphabetized] writing, certain verbal expressions" (Arthur and Rowe, 1998).

The gold weights were kept in a bag called *futuo* and the functionary responsible for keeping the state treasury bags was known as the *fotuosanfohene*. The most important *futuo* of the chief was called *sanaa futuo* and the weights in this bag were used on special occasions like the Adae and Odwira festivals. The functionary responsible for this bag was called *sannaahene*. The chief's weights served as the standard and were usually heavier than ordinary people's weights. By this mechanism the state was able to transfer surplus from the people to the state treasury. The weights served as denominations[93] for exchange and other monetary transactions (Bowdich, 1819; Reindorf,

---

[93] *Peredwan* was the highest denomination and was about three and one half ounces of gold dust. Other denominations included *poahuu, poa, pɛsaa* (or *pɛsewa* - which is the name given to the smallest unit of the currency in use in present-day Ghana), *daama, taku, takufa, soa, agyiratwe,* and *bɛnaa* (Garrard, 1972, 1980; Ott, 1968).

1895). Rattray (1969a, p. 117) provides the following description of how the Asantehene's Treasury operated:

> A large box, known as the *Adaka kesie*, divided by wooden partitions into three compartments of equal size, was kept in the room in the 'palace' known as *Dampan kesie*. This box was in joint charge of the Chief and Head-treasurer. The key of the chest was in the charge of three persons, the Chief, Head-treasurer, and the Chief of the Bed-chamber (the *Dabere Hene)*; it was kept underneath the chief's sleeping-mat. The three partitions of this box contained packets of gold-dust, each containing one preguan [*peredwan*] (i.e., about £8). This chest represented a kind of 'capital account'. All moneys paid into the Treasury were weighed, made up into bundles of a pereguan, and deposited in it. There were at least three witnesses to every transaction, and a fourth, if necessary, in the person of the official who first received the payments. Nothing less than a pereguan was deposited in this box, and nothing less was withdrawn; the Sana[a] Hene (Head-treasurer) accumulated receipts for lesser amounts in another box, for which his subordinates were responsible, until these sums amounted to a pereguan, which was then transferred to the *Adaka kesie* (big box).

Figure 26: The gold weight system showing a scale, spoons, containers and weights

Funds were transferred from the *Adaka kesie* to the *Apem Adaka* (the Great Chest - literally Box of thousand *peredwans*). The system was basically a simple one that required that, each time a *peredwan* was removed from the *apem adaka* (the Great Chest), it was replaced by a cowrie and a cowrie was removed each time a *peredwan* was paid in (Bowdich, 1819). Accounts were balanced at the end of each day. Major audits were carried out once in each Asante month, at the end of the Great Adae (Akwasidae), for it was at that time that the greatest volume of Treasury business was transacted (Wilks, 1975). In Kumase, the *Gyaasewahene* was responsible for keeping the state accounts[94]. *Batafoohene* (Minister of Trade), *Sanaahene* (Minister of the Treasury), and *Gyaasewahene* (Minister of Finance) were some of the appointive posts created by the Asantehene to promote and control, especially, external trade. The following chart shows the organizational structure of the Exchequer in the Asantehene palace.

Asantehene's Exchequer Court			
Gyaasewa - Exchequer	*Gyaasewahene* (Treasury Minister)		
Sanaa - Household (Treasury)	*Sanaahene* (Household Head Treasurer)		
Ahwerewamuhene: Custodian of the Golden Elephant Tail - Head of the *Ahoprafo* (Tax collectors)			
Akyeame - Counselors			
Damponkɛse – Treasury	*Fotosanfohene*	-	Treasurer
Bureau	*Ebura*	*Atogye*	*Bata Fekuo*
	Royal Mint	Revenue Collection	State Trading
Head	*Adwomfoohene*	*Kotokuokurahene*	*Asokwahene*
	Head of the Smiths		Minister of Trade
Civil Servants	*Buramfoɔ*	*Togyefoɔ*	*Batafoɔ*

Akan Attitudes about Money

Money is seen by the Akan as a resource either to be invested or consumed. This attitude towards money is best conveyed by the *bese saka* (bunch of kola nuts - # 575-581) symbol. The red ant on the pod of kola nuts; it does not pluck the kola nuts to eat or sell. The meaning of the symbol alludes to the dog in the manger attitude that some people have towards economic resources like money. Some other proverbs give further clue to how money was viewed in the society. For example, *wonni sika a, anka ɛyɛ anhwea kwa* literally meant if gold (dust) was not made use of (in an exchange), then one would simply call it sand. Also, *sika nkɔ adidi nsan mma kwa* literally translates into money is not put out to come back with no profit. Thus, gold as money was viewed and used (1) as a form of savings, and thus as a mark of secured prosperity; (2) as a form of investment in the purchase of land and labor for food production; and (3) in the promotion of trade in the form of finance capital - a mark of risk-taking entrepreneurship (Wilks, 1993).

---

[94] The Gyaasehene also had a functionary detailed to check off the months by dropping a cowrie shell into a bag each new moon. The calendar kept by this functionary was based on *adaduanan* (forty days) or six weeks. The month was known as bosome, and *adaduanan mienu* (two *adaduanan*) was the same as *abosome miensa* (three months). The first new moon after the Odwira festival marked the beginning of the new year (*afe foforo*).

The symbol *sika tu sɛ anomaa* (money flies like a bird - # 729) suggests the Akan view of money as something like a bird that can fly away from its owner if the owner does not handle it properly. This implies that investment must be made wisely so that a good return will be made on it. From this perspective individuals were provided with a capital outlay or seed money (*dwetire*) by their parents and relatives, or through borrowing (*bosea*) on which an interest (*nsiho* or *mmoho*) was charged. Traders and other business-people would extend credit (*ade firi*) in which case markers such as *nsensan* (lines - #858-861) would be used to indicate the magnitude of the credit. This gave rise to the accounting system of *san dan ho* (make lines on the wall).

The Akan also had the view that human beings were more important or more valuable than money. The Akan hold the view that money is something that can be used to buy almost everything, except one's life. Although money is important the Akan is encouraged to be benevolent towards the poor, for when one dies one leaves one's money behind (*onipa bɛwu na sika te ase* - #24). In this regard a story is told of how a spirit disguised herself and her child into human beings in tattered clothes to test a rich man. When the woman and her child approached the rich man, he made them feel very unwelcome. He refused them water to drink and sent them away from his house by screaming at them *momfiri ha nkɔ* (go away - #651). The woman called out to her child: *bɛdan agya, ma yɛnkɔ* (you'll leave everything behind you; let's go). Two days later, the rich man died of headache. His money could not save his life, and he left all his wealth behind him. To the Akan, the honest acquisition of money is not a sufficient moral claim for one to be regarded as a good person. The rich must demonstrate their goodness by being generous to their friends and family as well as the poor stranger. This social obligation on the part of the rich stems, in part, from the view that one would leave one's wealth behind when one dies (*yɛbɛdan agya* - #732).

Even though the Akan frowned on profligacy, miserly behavior was also detested. This is conveyed by the expression linked to the symbol *apaso* – scissors (#684). The Akan would say to the close-fisted person: *wotɔn apaso so wotiri afu* – you sell scissors, yet your hair is unkempt.

STATE ENTERPRISE SYSTEM

Trading

Trading was carried out by either private and individualized local enterprises and/or state and long distance enterprises. The long distance trade to the north, which had links to the trans-Saharan trade networks, was based on the exchange of kola nuts (*bese saka* - #706-732), salt and other forest products for a variety of savanna natural and craft products and items from the Mediterranean regions for example, *nsaa* (hand-woven blanket made from camel hair - #806-810).

Asante trade in gold, ivory kola nuts, slaves was very well organized. Private individuals were not encouraged to indulge in large scale trading activities because of the risks involved. The Asante trade, in general, was a state enterprise under the management of the *Gyasewahene*, who was overseer of the King's trade and was at liberty to send the traders where he pleased. *Asokwahene* (or *Batahene*) was responsible for trading on behalf of the Asantehene. At the request of the king or *Gyasewahene*, he would be sent to the coast to purchase salt, spirits, textiles, guns, gunpowder, pewter, lead, etc. *Asokwahene* was assisted by several *fekuo* (administrative departments) generally subjects of the Gyasewahene, including *akyeremodefoɔ* (drummers), *asokwafo* (hornblowers), *asoafo* (hammock carriers), and *adwarefoɔ* (bathroom attendants)

Asante officials - *akwansrafo* - road wardens - were established at many points on all main highways, for example Ejura and Atebubu points were for the control of traffic on NE road to Salaga. They detained all traders until enquiries had been made about them, when they were allowed to pass on payment of 3 to 4 shillings worth of gold dust. Their main concern was to prevent guns and powder from being sold beyond metropolitan Asante. The purpose of this embargo was to ensure continued Asante superiority in muskets over the bow and arrow wielding peoples of Northern Ghana (Fynn, 1971; Arhin, 1979). It also served to ward off plunderes.

The long distance trade to the south with Europeans from about the mid-15th century was based on the exchange of gold, ivory, war captives, and rubber, oil palm products, and much later, cocoa in exchange for a variety of products including guns and ammunition, textiles (especially silk) and liquor. While long distance trade in rubber, kola nuts and oil palm products were undertaken largely by private individual entrepreneurs (*akonkosifoɔ* and *adwadifoɔ*), long distance trade in gold, ivory and war captives was undertaken by state traders organized into various state enterprises called *bata fekuo*. Local retailing (*dwadie*) was carried out by both men and women in local periodic markets. Kumase, with its two daily markets, was the main Asante market town (Bowdich, 1819, p. 330, 334).

At least by the beginning of the 18th century the Asante economy had become highly monetized as shown in the adoption of units of gold dust (*sika futuro*)[95] as currency (Reindorf, 1895, p. 17). Bowdich (1819, p. 330) points out that in the Kumase daily markets the medium of exchange was units of gold dust as neither barter nor cowrie (*sedeε or serewa - #723-728*) was permitted.

State trade was promoted through the *bata fekuo* (state traders) using a form of public financing in which the king provided the seed capital (*dwetire*) and collected interest (*mmataho* or *nsiho*) on the capital outlay. Batahene (Minister of Trade), Sanaahene (Minister of Household Finance), and Gyaasewahene (Treasury Minister) were some of the appointive posts created by the Asantehene to promote and control, especially, external trade.

The following account in the newspaper, *The Gold Coast Aborigines* (June 30, 1900, p. 3) describes the public financing of trade:

> The chiefs of Kumasi acted as Mercantile Agents for the King, each receiving from 500 to 1000 perequines [*peredwan*] yearly which they in turn distributed to their subchiefs or captains and other subjects, who took it to the coast for goods which they took into the interior; and made thereby fabulous profits: they rendered account to the King at the end of each year. With these resources, there is no wonder that they were immensely rich and could afford to meet the exactions of the King who knew well their various wealth (cited in Wilks, 1993, p. 134).

STATE REVENUE SOURCES

The king imposed taxes, fines, fees, and tolls (*too*) to finance his administration. Even though the taxes and fines levied were not very extensive as they were mainly limited to trade, they served to appropriate and reallocate surplus from the king's subjects. In Asante the taxes, fines, and levies imposed included the following:

---

[95] Gold dust ceased to be used as currency in the Akan and the greater Ghanaian society in 1912 but it continued to be used in Asante until about 1926.

(i) Death duties - these were monies paid to the king by the successor or lineage of the deceased as the king was regarded as the heir to the personally acquired property of his subjects. In return the king contributed to the deceased's funeral expenses. The death duties included

Ayibuadeɛ (burial money),
awunnyadeɛ (applicable to the self-acquired movable property of a deceased citizen)
muhoma

(ii) court fees and fines

aseda (thank-offering, paid by the party found innocent in a suit)
atitɔdeɛ (blood-money, being a fine in lieu of the death penalty)

(iii) Levies on special occasions - these included

Ayitoɔ (levy to cover the expenses of a chief's funeral)
apeatoɔ (war tax to cover war expenditures)
fotuobɔ (a levy for the enstoolment of a new chief)
asadeɛ (war booty)
ɔmantoɔ (a national levy for some specific purpose; in recent times this levy has been used to construct roads, bridges, schools, community centers, health clinics, and market stalls in the villages).

(iv) Other tolls and fees - for example tolls and interest charges levied on traders as highway tolls – *akwamufoɔ* and *nkwansrafo* levied tolls on the highways (*akwantempɔn*) to control external trade of the *adwadifo* (private entrepreneurs) in order to promote the activities of state traders (*batafo*); traders in the Kumase daily markets were taxed by the toll collectors called *dwaberesofoɔ*

mmataho or *nsiho* (interests paid by state traders on the capital outlay from the king.

RECENT ECONOMIC DEVELOPMENT

Recent economic development in the Akan society is evidenced by several *adinkra* symbols that depict modern modes of transportation including Senchi bridge (#768-771), VW (#738-739), Mercedes (#740-741), Toyota (#742-743), and *sitia bɛkum dorɔba* (the driver may die at the steering wheel - #715-717); technological advancements in media and telecommunications indicated by such symbols as TV (#747-751) and *foon* (telephone - #744-746), rapid urbanization as indicated by *Koforidua frawase/ nhwiren* (Koforidua flowers - #766-767), and new forms of energy as indicated by *UAC nkanea* (UAC lights - #760), kanea (lamp - #888), and *Akosombo nkanea* (Akosombo lights - #681).

After slave trade was abolished the increase in trade and other economic activities such as mining, logging, and farming cocoa and other crops gave rise to the rapid development of new urban centers. Koforidua and towns like Agona Swedru rose rapidly as a result of cocoa farming and diamond mining. Newly rich people flaunted their wealth as indicated by such expressions *anya-wo-ho, asikafoɔ amma ntɛm, blɔk dan* (block house - #537-543), and Koforidua flowers (*Koforidua nhwiren* - #766-767).

To facilitate trade and governmental administration in Asante, an array of highways (*akwantempɔn*) and bridges (*atwene*), with Kumase as the center, were developed and maintained by the palace. Palace officials who built and maintained the highways were known as *akwammɔfoɔ* and *akwansrafoɔ*. The special levies that were imposed on specific occasions served as the source of capital accumulation for national development. In recent years special levy, *ɔmantoɔ*, has been used to construct roads, bridges, schools, community centers, health clinics, and market stalls in the villages. Railway and road infrastructure development was carried out by the colonial administration in the early 1900s to facilitate trade and industrialize gold mining. In 1901 the country experienced "gold rush" with estimated 3000 concessions taken up. The promise of prosperity held out by cocoa and mining underscored the need for good infrastructure of railway and roads.

Central to the issue of motor-vehicles in Ghana are the issues of status and power. To some extent motor-vehicles were incorporated as new status symbols into older pre-colonial forms and concepts relating to the expression of status and power, and to some extent motor-vehicles have led to the development of new forms of cultural expression of power. People associated with and in control of motor-vehicles were granted status in accordance with the type of vehicle concerned, accordingly wealthy car owners are known across as *me hunu wo no na waBenzi* – I saw you riding in your Benz. The motor-vehicle with its tendency to traverse language, social and cultural barriers led to new ways of seeing the world, and new relations that required new forms of cosmological understanding. There has seen a growing interest in the culture of trading, repairing and driving cars and in mobility in general. Klaeger (2009) looks at cars, buses and travelling as new loci of religious belief and practice, and talks of the 'automobilization' of religion. Busloads of the "faithful;" are bused to religious conventions and prayer camps, and "all night" vigils in both rural and urban areas. The increased mobility of people, products, exploitation of raw materials (from labor to mineral ore), information, goods and services led to the development of new economies. In the formal economy the motor-vehicle led to the development and accessing of new markets as well as the establishment of a completely new economy centered round motor-vehicles. New entrepreneurial and technical skills have been developed as petrol stations and automotive workshops and spare parts shops came to be established. New companies have been created that transported people and goods, from small single taxi companies to large-scale freight enterprises.

The increased accessibility stimulated and allowed for the development and exploitation of resources which had been hitherto neglected: mining, agriculture and service industry all received a boost. Apart from being a major pollutant motor-vehicles also contributed in no small way to extensive environmental degradation through strip-mining, logging, and forest clearance, as well as top soil loss and soil exhaustion through large scale mechanized farming practices. In addition, the economic expansion and increased mobility led to the development of, not only, the itinerant migrant laborer, but also, the daily commuter; people essential to Ghana's formal economy, but heavily dependent on the taxi and bus services of the informal economy.

The *sitia bɛkum dorɔba* (the steer will kill the driver - #715-717) symbol encodes the impact of motor vehicles in the Akan and the greater Ghanaian economy. The impact of the motor-vehicle in the informal economy has primarily been in the service industry and the health sector. African bus stations and transport depots are unthinkable without the myriad of services provided by street hawkers, food and drink sales people, guest houses, prostitution, informal restaurants and drinking bars, puncture repair men, welders, roadside mechanics and many more. Drivers maintain their concentration through the supply of stimulants, legal or otherwise, and passengers are entertained and kept occupied by everything from videos, to illegal copies of music cassettes and book and pamphlet sellers. Along the road villagers peddle handicrafts, agricultural produce, chickens, fish and more, as well as "bush meat" and charcoal for city dwellers.

New forms of corruption and taxation have developed along Ghanaian roads as many roadblocks have become an important source of income for under paid and/or coercive public servants. Associated with the informal economy is the flourishing trade in second-hand cars, which has developed in the last twenty-five years of the 20th century between Europe and West Africa. Vehicles written off in Europe and Japan are shipped to Ghana and other African countries where they continue to fulfil long and productive careers. Apart from the development of new African entrepreneurs, the second-hand car industry has also led to the establishment of a myriad of middle-men and interlopers essential to the trade. Motor-vehicles also led to the collapse of other forms of economic enterprise. Old trade routes lost their importance. Head portage and animal drawn freight came to be superseded. The service industries that had developed to cater for these now defunct routes and forms of transport ceased to exist. Similarly, during periods of extensive economic decline communities that have come to depend and rely on the motor vehicle and its roads can be struck by economic ruin.

The access of people to health care has been improved through the advent of motor-vehicles, and in recent times, the mobile phone (*foon* -#744-746). The inoculation campaigns, primary health care projects, hospital transfers, and medical extension work that characterize Ghanaian health care in the present would be unthinkable without the use of motor-vehicles. The ubiquitous taxis, for example, serve as "emergency ambulances" to convey the sick to the hospital. Yet at the same time motor-vehicles have become the main vectors for the spread of diseases in Ghana and other African countries. The rapid transfer of viruses from forest enclaves to cities, and the rapid spread of HIV/Aids and STDs (*bɔ woho ban* - #896) along the highways transecting Ghana and other countries in Africa are examples to be borne in mind.

Sitia bɛkum dorɔba (#715-71) also encodes the fears about road traffic accidents (RTA) especially during the change-over from left-hand to right-hand drive in 1974. Even though the change-over period had very low road accidents, there has been increasing concern about high rates of road accidents and accident related fatalities on Ghanaian roads. The major contributing factors to the increasing road accidents are driver behavior, poor roads, passengers and pedestrians behaviors, and non-maintenance of vehicles. In Ghana, statistics show that between 2002 and 2008, a total of 13,166 people were killed in road accidents. Of that figure, 42% were pedestrians, 23% were passengers in buses, and 12% were car occupants, while the remaining 23% consisted of riders (National Road Safety Commission, 2008). Road transport accidents have been identified to be the second cause of death in the country. With the first being malaria (Building and Road Research Institute, 2009). In 2012 alone, 2,249 Ghanaians lost their lives while 14,169 got injured through RTA and were mostly from the active labor force and predominantly those between the ages of 30-49 years (NRSC 2012).

The role of drivers, poor road networks, non-maintenance of vehicles, passengers and pedestrians are the major factors accountable for the increasing rate at which accidents occur in the country. Dankyi (2010) attributed the causes of these accidents to fatigue driving especially long distant drivers, speeding, wrongful overtaking, over loading, non-maintenance of vehicles, poor nature of road. Dankyi (2010) further found other causes for concern to be the non-use of pedestrian crossing and crossing without paying attention to traffic on the road, especially by minors. Ofosu-Ackaah (2010) in his surveillance studies in Accra, Ghana, also found over speeding, disregard to road signs and non-use of reflective triangle when vehicles break down as major factors in Ghana. Inferring from the concern identified by Dankyi (2010) and Ofosu-Ackaah (2010), a common pattern emerging is that avoidable accidents most often point to common acts of indiscipline, such as over loading, over speeding, drunk – driving and improper overtaking. The steer may certainly kill the driver (as encoded in the symbol *sitia bεkum drɔba* - #715-717), but poor handling of the steer and poor maintenance of motor vehicles and bad roads kill people and pose a health hazard in the country.

The modern bridge over the Volta River at Senchi (*Senchi bridge* - #768-771) has been incorporated into the *adinkra* symbols to depict the function of the state to direct and facilitate national development. The rapid changes in the economic activities of the people and the increased and varied sources of state revenue have resulted from the introduction of cocoa, timber, mining, service and manufacturing industries. Economic development activities have become the concern of a more centralized national government.

SOCIAL INEQUALITY

The Akan society was stratified by either social classes: *asikafoɔ, adehyeε* and *abrεmpɔn* (wealthy people and the royalty - the bourgeoisie), *nkwankwaa* (young people - the petty bourgeoisie) and the *ahiafoɔ* (the proletariat or underprivileged) according to Wilks, 1975) or by "status differentiation": *abrεmpɔn, adehyeε* and *mpanyimfoɔ* (the royalty and the elders of state), *asikafoɔ* (the wealthy), *nkwankwaa* (the free born, young people), and *ahiafoɔ, nkoafoɔ* and *nnɔnkɔfoɔ* (free born, but poor and servants and slaves) as well as by gender, according to Arhin (1983). The distribution of wealth and income based on the Akan stratification system is alluded to by the symbols *abeteε ntema* (portioning *abeteε* meal - #758-759) and *gye kɔdidi* (take this for subsistence - #736). There is also conspicuous consumption in the midst of poverty as alluded to by the symbol *asetena pa* (good living - #737).

Social inequality in the Akan society is indicated by *adinkra* symbols such as *ebi te yie* (some people are better seated, or better positioned - #733-735), *gye kɔdidi* (take this for subsistence - #736), *asetena pa* (good living - #737), *akwankyεn borɔdewa* and (roadside plantain tree - #764), *ɔbra kwan atwedeε* (life's social ladder - #890), and *mako nyinaa* (all the peppers - #752-754). *Ayɔnkogorɔ dodoɔ nti na ɔkotɔ annya tire* (too much of playing around with friends cost the crab its head - #720-722) expresses the outcome of wasteful use of one's resources in conspicuous consumption. Wasting time in playing around with friends did not only cost the crab money, but it literally cost him his head. In Akan mythology, that is why the crab does not have a distinguishable head as many other animals do.

Ohia (poverty) and *ahonyadeε* (wealth) are two words the Akan use to comment on social inequality, as well as comment on success from hard work and failure from laziness. Social inequality may stem from unequal natural endowment as implied in the expression: *mako nyinaa mpatu mmere* (all the peppers on the same tree do not ripen simultaneously - #752-754). But one's diligence and hardwork determines one's station in life as implied in the expression: *mmirikisie a yεantumi annɔ no na yεfrε no nsamampɔ* (the farm that is not tended is referred to as a sacred burial ground - #694). *Ohia ne gyimi* (poverty is foolishness) and *ohia yε adammɔ* (poverty is madness) are judgements directed "against those who had access to the rewards of business and office but nevertheless failed to achieve prosperity," according to Wilks (1993, p. 139). Social inequality was also determined by social norms and values in such instances as one's position in life based on membership in a royal family (as *ɔdehyeɛ, nkwankwaa, sikani,* or *akoa*), gender, and age. All these factors contribute to a social structure in which some people are better situated or better off than others (*ebi te yie* - #733-735).

The world capitalist economy has dominated the Akan and the greater Ghanaian economy ever since the local economy was fully integrated into the world economy after the nineteenth century. The main instrument of capitalist incorporation of modern Ghana into the emerging world economy was commercial capital. The Ghanaian economy that evolved from this incorporation was essentially a trading economy. Since its inception, this commercial economy has been incapable of transforming the technological base of the society into one that could create and sustain an industrial regime with the requisite technical and scientific capacity to create wealth and to distribute the wealth more equitably and on a sustainable basis. Right from the outset of the integration, a dualistic economy with two distinct sub-economies emerged alongside each other. The key features of the colonial economy included primary commodity production for export, investments in mining, transportation and related services, infrastructure and public works, and social development. Gold mining, lumbering, cocoa farming and agriculture continue to dominate the economy. The incorporation and domination of the Ghanaian economy is indicated by symbols such as *UAC nkanea, Benz* and *VW*. This foreign domination of the Ghanaian economy has been resisted from time to time from the beginnings of the direct contact with the Europeans through such tactics as hold-ups and boycotts. The most spectacular hold-ups of produce by Ghanaian farmers against European company-dominated price rings include the 1858-1866 oil palm boycott and the 1937-38 cocoa hold-up (Wolfson, 1953; Howard, 1978). Another spectacular resistance to foreign domination of the Ghanaian economy occurred in 1948 in a boycott led by Osu Alata Manche Nii Kwabena Bonney. This boycott turned into rioting and looting in response to the shooting death by the colonial police of three unarmed ex-servicemen who were marching towards the seat of government on February 28, 1948.

Integration into the world capitalist economy is not the only source of social inequality in the Akan and the greater Ghanaian society. Social inequality also stems from various forms of economic exploitation and oppression. One form of economic exploitation is the appropriation of the fruits of one's labor by another. This is encoded by the symbol *mede me se abɔ adwe* (I have cracked open the palm nut with my teeth - #755). The symbol portrays the exploitative situation in which one cracks the hard palm nut with one's teeth only for someone else to enjoy the kernel. It suggests that one should enjoy the fruits of one's labor.

Another form of economic oppression is alluded to by the symbol *meso nanka mentumi* (I cannot even carry the puff adder - #757). When one cannot carry the much lighter puff adder, it is oppressive to ask one to add on the much heavier python as the carrying pad. A story is told about an elephant that mounts the deer and rides him through the forest over the hills and through the swampy valleys. When the deer frantically groans about a breaking back, the elephant retorts angrily: "I wish I weighed a little less! Fancy yourself carrying the puff adder with the python for a carrying pad. A dream like this will kill your pain." Other symbols such as *akwankyen borɔdewa* (roadside plantain tree - #764), and *tɛfrɛ atɔ nkokɔ mu* (cockroach - #682) allude to forms of exploitation and economic oppression in the society. The roadside plantain tree is subjected to constant abuse and exploitation so much so that its growth is stunted.

Yet another source of inequality may be seen in the system of injustices that stems from the unequal power relations endemic in the social structure. This is encoded in the symbol *ebi te yie* (some people are better seated, or better positioned - #733-735). There is a story, popularized in the late sixties and early seventies by a song of same title (*Ebi te yie*) by the African Brothers Band, which alludes to social injustices in Ghana thus:

> There was once a meeting of all animals to discuss the problems of the animal world. All animals, including the leopard and the deer, were present at the meeting. It so happened that the leopard got seated directly behind the deer. As the meeting progressed, the leopard continually harrassed the deer. He clawed the tail of the deer to the floor and prevented the free movement of the deer and thus his active participation in the preceedings. Even when the deer attempted to raise his hand to be called to speak the leopard would pull down his hand or comment that the deer was too talkative or gibberish. It got to a point when the deer could no longer put up with the harassment he was being subjected to by the leopard. He mustered courage and yelled out above the din: "Petition please on a point of order. Chairman, secretary and honorable members of the assembly, the deliberations so far have been satisfactorily conducted, I would move for immediate adjournment; for not all of us here have good seats. Some are conveniently seated, others are not." The meeting saw beyond the words of the deer, for everybody knew the maltreatment he was being subjected to. The deer's motion was unanimously carried and the meeting was adjourned *sine die.*[96]

In the Asante social stratification system, social mobility was determined by such factors as (1) military achievement; (2) outstanding service in the Asante bureaucracy (for example, Asante Agyei who originally was a salt carrier in the *bata fekuo* rose to the rank of *ɔhene kyeame)*; (3) accumulation of wealth (for example, Yamoa Ponko and Kanin Abena (Wilks, 1975, pp. 693-4); and (4) craft skill (Arhin, 1968; LaTorre, 1978). These perspectives about social stratification in the Akan society suggest the need to critically examine the view held by several writers that the Akan society is egalitarian. Even if in the past the Akan society was said to be egalitarian, recent economic developments that have resulted in the intensification of poverty, informalization of the economy, urban squatters and slums in the country suggest a re-examination of the social structure of the Akan and the greater Ghanaian society.

---

[96] This story suggests that despite hostilities and intimidation the deer was subjected to by the leopard the deer exercised his freedom of speech and expression to table a motion for the adjournment of the meeting.

CHAPTER 10

Ɔkyena nhyehyɛɛ gyina deɛ yɛsua firi yɛn nkyiri; enti sɛ wo werɛfi na wosan kɔfa a, yɛnkyi
The past serves as a guide for the future

KNOWLEDGE AND EDUCATION

KNOWLEDGE

The Akan *ɔkyerɛma* (drummer) asks: *Ɔdomankoma bɔɔ ade, ɔbɔɔ dɛn?* – What did the Creator create? He then answers,

> He created Order
> He created Knowledge
> He created Death

Notice that order comes first. Without order, you have no cosmos, and without the cosmos, there is nothing knowable to be known and no knower to know it. With order comes knowable objects and knowing subjects (Hallen and Wiredu, 2012). The Akan, therefore, is never skeptical about one's ability to know. The Akan strongly believes one can and one does know. The symbol *nea onnim* (#876) is pregnant with the Akan's views about knowledge. The symbol is linked with the aphorism: *nea onnim sua a, ohu; nea ɔdwen sɛ onim dodo no, sɛ ogyae sua a, ketewa koraa a onim no firi ne nsa* – he who does not know can become knowledgeable from learning; he who thinks he knows and ceases to continue to learn will stagnate. To grow is to live, to stagnate is to die. Only as one continues to search for knowledge will one grow wiser. To the Akan, the continued search for knowledge, that is education (*adesua* or *ntetee*), is a life-long process.

Encoded in seveeral *adinkra* symbols is the concept of knowledge and education in the Akan society, and, thus the importance of knowledge to the Akan. This is perhaps best exemplified by the symbol *mate masie* (or *ntesie* - I have heard and kept it - #799-802) derived from the aphorism: "*Nyansa bunu mu ne mate masie*" which literally means "in the depth of wisdom abounds knowledge and thought" (Antubam, 1963, p. 159). The Akan knowledge system is based on the view that the preservation of a people's culture has its basis in oral tradition. Akan oral literary forms that serve as sources which either embody the society's knowledge or provide an insight into the people's attitude to knowledge include proverbs, riddles and quizzes, drum poetry, funeral dirges, and story-telling. The *adinkra* cloths encode several of these oral literary forms, especially the proverbs, drum poetry, and funeral dirges.

The Akan word for knowledge is *nimdeɛ*, and a knowledgeable or learned person is known as *nimdefoɔ*. The Akan word for wisdom is *nyansa*[97], and the wise person or sage is known as *nyansafoɔ*. A word that is used interchangeably with *nyansa* (wisdom) is *adwen* (thought). Thus the wise person is a thinker (*ɔdwendwemfoɔ* or *ɔbadwemma*, hence the following expression used to describe the wise person: *ɔyɛ obi a n'adwen mu dɔ* - literally, s/he has deep thoughts). The wise person is one who can analyze or critically examine problems of people and society with a view to suggesting answers (*ɔpaepae asɛm mu*, or *ɔyɛ mpɛnsɛmpɛnsɛmu*, or *ɔyɛ nhwehwɛmu*) as depicted by the *hwehwɛmu dua* symbol (searching or measuring rod - #797-798). The expression: *Nananom nyansa pɔ yɛsiane no abanyansafoɔ* (The wisdom knot of the ancestors can only be untied by the wise one), symbolized by *nyansapɔ* (wisdom knot - #794-796) also alludes to this view. *Nyansa* also means skill, dexterity, art, artfulness, learning, and knowledge. Various *adinkra* symbols (e.g., *dame dame* - #817-818, *nsaa* - #803-807, and *kyerɛ me kwan no* - #827) depict these meanings.

Knowledge is transmitted through education. Education is termed *ntetee* or *adesua*[98]. As Nketsia (2009, p. 2) puts it, "the idea of proper Akan education meant instilling The Ancient Path or treading the path of the Ancients –*ntse tsee*" (*ntetee* in Twi). He further indicates Akan education "inculcates Loyalty, Honesty, Responsibility, Obligation, Duty, Patriotism, Justice, Self-knowledge, Self-sacrifice, Frugality, Purity, Modesty, Tolerance, Honour, a sense of shame, a deep sense of and commitment to Family/Community and among other things a strong belief in an afterlife that triumphs the fear of Death. These values Akan education inculcates are embedded in such symbols as *obi nka obi* (#417-423), *yɛhwɛ yɛn anim* (#246), *mpomponsuo* (#259), *woyɛ abofra a* (#563), *nkyinkyim* (#602-606), *wo nsa akyi* (#663), *woayɛ afɛre* (#596), among others.

Ntetee or *Adesua* embraces all aspects of education: formal and informal. There are two steps involved in the knowing process: (1) sense experience of the natural world (both physical objects and social relationships) - the empirical processes, and (2) the logical organization and interpretation of sensory data into ideas - the intellectual and intuitive processes (Dzobo, 1992). To have a good ear and to retain everything heard from the master is a mark of excellence in learning as indicated by the *mate masie* (I have heard and kept it - #799-802) symbol. Knowledge or wisdom is gained through experience and this is emphasized by the proverb: *Nyansa yɛsua, na yɛntɔ* (wisdom or knowledge is something we acquire through learning; it is not something we buy). The one who does not learn a lesson or gain experience from one's mistakes is considered a fool as expressed by the proverb: *Kwasea na ne dwan te mprenu* (it is only the fool who allows his sheep to break loose twice).

The Akan believe that knowledge comes from various sources, including intuition, revelation, authority, experience, logical reasoning, and experiments. As Minkus (1980, p. 185) writes: "Extraordinary perception, divination, dreams, and possession provide means of acquiring some knowledge of spiritual reality and causality, although even then human knowledge is limited and inadequate to penetrate the mysteries of existence." The Akan view of reality as having spiritual and non-spiritual dimensions, and thus to understand and know reality requires the reliance on multiple sources of knowledge. The various sources of knowledge, as the Akan believe, are complementary and not antagonistic in one's attempts to discover and comprehend reality.

---

[97] The word *nyansa* is derived from the two words: *nya* (to gain, to find, to come by, or to experience) and *nsa* (inexhaustible). Therefore, *nyansa* is literally "that which is obtained and is never exhausted," i.e., a lesson which is learned from experience and is lasting.

[98] *Ntetee* is another term that is indicative of education. It is used more in the sense of training.

The experiences and aphorisms of the elderly form one important source of knowledge to the Akan. This is symbolized by the mythical *sankɔfa* bird (go back and retrieve - #770-790). This bird is said to fly forwards by looking backwards. In order not to reinvent the wheel, this symbol reminds the Akan of the importance of learning from the past or using the past as a guide to the future. As Nketsia (2009; p. 2) writes of the Akan. "If a people lose control of their history they lose control of the future. Without history there is no vision." The *sankɔfa* symbol requires the Akan to envision and plan for the future by using the past as a guide.

The wisdom knot (*nyansapɔ* - #794-796) is another symbol that reflects the Akan belief in the knowledge of the wise. However, authority as the sole important source of knowledge is dangerous, particularly when it leads one to surrender one's independent judgement and leads one to make no effort to search for what is true or false. This view is given credence by the expression: *Woyɛ Kwaku Ananse a, meso meyɛ Ntikuma* (If you are Kwaku Ananse, I am Ntikuma) as illustrated by the *anansesɛm*, Tar Baby Story. In this *anansesɛm* (Ananse story) Kwaku Ananse pretends to die and requests to be buried in the family farm with all cooking utensils. He then asks that nobody goes to the farm until after six weeks following his burial. After six weeks, Ntikuma and his siblings go to the farm only to realize that someone was stealing the crops. All along, Ntikuma who was doubtful of his father's death suspected none other than his father. To find out the truth, he puts a tar-baby effigy on the farm and catches his father as the thief. The whole set of *anansesɛm* (Ananse stories) in which Ananse is either defied or caught lying or being challenged by his son Ntikuma gave rise to the expression above. Ntikuma is not being disrespectful of the father as an authority figure, but he is being skeptical and making the effort to search for what is true or false.

The Akan regards ordinary sense perception as another important basis of knowledge. However, this sensory-based knowledge is limited in its applicability, and the Akan belief about knowledge requires one to examine sensory-based as well as all knowledge critically. A critical mind is skeptical as depicted by symbols such as *saa?* (is that so? - #646), *bommokyikyie* (river fish - # 828), and *abonsam a wonim no* (the devil you know - #829). Hence, the symbol *hwehwɛ mu dua* or *ɔfamfa* (searching or measuring rod - #797-798) urges one to examine knowledge critically. It implies that the outcome of research depends on an intelligent, patient and critical examination of evidence. Knowledge must be subjected to critical enquiry.

That critical reasoning or intellectual ability - the ability to critically analyze multiple facets of a problem and to reach an informed conclusion - is valued over sensory-based, subjective, simple knowledge is depicted by several symbols. *Dwennimmɛn* (ram's horns - #332-341), *nsaa* (quality hand-woven blanket or carpet - #803-807), *kramo bɔne amma yɛanhu kramo pa* (the fake prophet or sophistry makes it difficult for the good prophet or the truth to be known - #808-812), *damedame* (checkers - #817-818), and *kuntunkantan* (egocentricism - #813-815) are examples of symbols that encode Akan views about critical reasoning and rationality. The Akan sage warns that one must be careful not to extend the claims of the power of rationality too far. This warning is encoded by the *asanturofie anomaa* (the long-tailed night jar, the bird of dilemma - #859) symbol. This bird is said to sing very beautiful songs based on what it observes in its surroundings. This bird presents a puzzling situation: when you take it home, you incur jeopardy of the bird singing about your good deeds as well as your misdeeds; when you leave it, you will miss a golden opportunity of enjoying the beautiful songs it can produce. Deciding on whether to take or leave the *asanturofie* bird entails more than rational and critical thinking. The Akan debate over whether the choice posed by the *asantrofie anomaa* is "free" or "determined."

The *bese saka* symbol (bunch of kola nuts - #703-709) that suggests the importance of critical thinking and experience. This symbol is associated with the following aphorism: *Bese pa ne konini ahahan yɛtase no ɔbanyansafoɔ* (The leaves of the white and red kola plants are very similar and it takes skill and experience to separate them - #851). This reminds one to critically examine all the possible options in dealing with problems before making decisions. It also points to the Akan view that the various sources of knowledge are complementary and not antagonistic in the search for knowledge.

Attitudes to Knowledge

Dzobo (1992a) distinguishes the following as examples of specific indigenous Akan attitudes to knowledge. One attitude to knowledge is that there is a limit to what any one individual can know, even though there is no limit to what can be known in principle. From this perspective, any one person who claims to know everything is viewed as knowing nothing. Hence, the symbol *kuntankantan* (egocentricism - #813-815) serves to remind one not to be egocentric and boastful of the little knowledge one has as depicted by the following maxim: *Nea ɔyɛ ne ho sɛ menim menim, nnim hwee* (he who knows all, knows nothing - #813-815). Also, *dwaso hantaan ne efie awerɛhoɔ* - empty boasts in public brings discredit not only to the individual, but also one's household.

Another attitude is that the individual has an active role to play in the acquisition of knowledge. Even though *nyansa* is inborn and everyone has the potential to be wise, one has to develop one's mental capacity. That is, whatever one knows is acquired through experience and through a deliberate effort on one's part to learn to know. The Akan believe that the search for knowledge is a life-long process. The symbol *nea ɔnnim sua a, ohu* (he who does not know can become knowledgeable from learning - #806) incorporates this view of learning.

The Akan regard the elderly as wise and believe that experience comes with age. This association of knowledge and wisdom with age is incorporated in the *sankɔfa* (go back and retrieve - #770-790), *kyɛmferɛ* (potsherd - #847-848), and *nyansapɔ* (wisdom knot - #794-796) symbols. The *kyɛmferɛ* (potsherd - #) symbol depicts this belief that experience and wisdom come with age by posing the question: *kyɛmferɛ se ɔdaa hɔ akyɛ, na onipa a ɔnwenee no nso nyɛ dɛn?* (If the potsherd claims it is old, what about the potter who molded it? - #847-848). However, the Akan does not necessarily consider knowledge as the preserve of a particular age group. The expression: *Akyinakyin sen anyinanyin* (the well-travelled is more experienced than the elderly who has stayed in one place all his/her life) captures this view about knowledge. In this regard the Akan views the "stay-at-one-place" elderly person as being insular and geocentric in outlook as compared with the travelled person who is said to be cosmopolitan and heliocentric in outlook.

That knowledge is not necessarily the preserve of the elderly is also illustrated by the Ananse story in which Ananse tries to collect all the wisdom and knowledge in the world to hide in a tree so that he alone would be the knowledgeable and wise one. He puts the knowledge and wisdom he has collected into a pot and hangs the pot around his neck and tries to climb the tree with the pot hanging in front of him, that is, between him and the tree. After several futile attempts by Ananse to climb the tree, his son Ntikuma, who had secretly followed his father into the bush and was supposed to have lost all his wisdom, draws Ananse's attention to the folly in attempting to climb the tree with the way the pot is hanging. Ntikuma suggests that his father should tie the pot onto his (father's) back. Ananse then realizes that his son's suggestion makes a lot of sense. Ananse gets frustrated in knowing that there is some wisdom left outside the pot in his son's head. Ananse then throws down and smashes the pot of wisdom and knowledge. Ananse's attempt, to hoard "all the wisdom of the earth" and withhold it from the public, is similar to the strategies of keepers of traditional knowledge and other trade secrets, e.g., healers and herbalists who often take their treasured knowledge with them to the grave rather than disclosing it to fellow community members who might otherwise have benefitted from it. Even when traditional knowledge-keepers decide to share their knowledge, they often resort to a welter of payments for initiation rites and impose compulsory donations to deny access to their knowledge except to some few select people. Another lesson from this *anansesɛm* is that Ananse assumes knowledge is exhaustive, but Ntikuma falsifies that assumption.

Another Akan attitude about knowledge is that knowledge is a liberator. This liberating knowledge is attained through insightful understanding of situations and the relations between things. An enlightened and insightful individual is free and creative. This view is alluded to by the symbol *kyerɛ me kwan no* (show me the way - #827). The Akan believe that knowledge must have practical bearing on the conduct of life. This is encoded in the aphorism: *Nyansa nyɛ sika na woakyekyere asie* - Wisdom is not like money which may be kept in a safe; or, one does not collect wisdom in a bag, lock it up in a box and then go to say to a friend, 'teach me something'. Knowledge must, therefore, be put to productive use.

Causality and Free Will

The Akan believes that nothing happens without a cause (*onipa mfɔn kwa* - #826). Several *adinkra* symbols such as *obi nka obi kwa* (no one should bite the other without justifiable cause - #417-423), *abɛ dua* (palm tree - #702), *sɛ anantuo kɔsene serɛ a* (if the calf is bigger than the thigh - #865) and *nipa mfɔn kwa* (one does not grow lean without a cause - #826) incorporate this belief. These symbols suggest that causality, to the Akan, is an objective reality. For example, the proverb: *sɛ mmerɛnkɛnsono si ne ti ase a, na ɛwɔ deɛ asaase reka kyerɛ no* (whenever the palm tree bends, it is because of what the soil has told it - #702), illustrates this objective reality. The palm tree is very resilient and does not bend or break easily. If a palm tree is found to be bent over, then something must have caused that.

A closer examination of the concepts *sunsum* (spirit or soul - #42-43) and *nkrabea* (destiny - #86) helps in further explaining the Akan causal theory. The Akan causal theory has it that all beings and forces act by virtue of their *sunsum*. All events are caused and are potentially explicable. In some events the causal agent is a spiritual being or force. However, not all causes are said to operate in a spiritual way. Some causes are non-spiritual such as something caused by the deliberate actions of people. In this sense, the Akan have a conception of dual causality: cause that is attributable to spiritual (e.g., *sunsum*) and divine factors such as one's *nkrabea* (destiny - #86) and cause that is attributable to one's actions. This follows from the concept of dual reality. While spiritual causality is vertical with the causal direction going from a higher spirit to a lower one, non-spiritual causality is horizontal (Gyekye, 1987).

One's misfortunes in life may be said to be caused by spirits (that is, external locus of control of causality) or one's bad character, carelessness (for example in decision-making), or lack of industry on one's part (that is, internal locus of control of causality). In this regard some illnesses are thought to be spiritually induced (*sunsum yare*). Should the illness be found to have a spiritual cause, a *musuyideɛ* ritual has to be performed to deal with the precipitating spiritual cause before any medical attempt will be made to cure the illness (Minkus, 1980). When one recovers from a long bout of illness one performs an *asubɔ* or *adwerɛ adware* (pacificatory) ceremony to sanctify one's soul. This ceremony starts with a bath of water that has been seeped in *adwerɛ* (watery shrub - #119) leaves.

The Akan say *etire nyɛ borɔferɛ na yɛapae mu ahwɛ deɛ ɛwɔ mu* (the human head - i.e., the mind - is not like the papaya fruit to be split open to determine its content - #860). This suggests that even though there exist causal laws there also exist human actions and thoughts. This must not be taken as a contradiction to the concept of destiny (*nkrabea* - #86). The Akan believe that one has the ability to choose between alternative possibilities in such a way that the choice and action are to some extent creatively determined by the conscious subject at the time. In the symbol *asanturofie anomaa* (bird of dilemma - #859), one is faced with choice between bad and good luck. When one chooses the bird, one is responsible for the bad luck one brings unto oneself by that choice. On the other hand, when one forgoes the bird and the good luck, one has to bear the responsibility associated with that choice too. The Akan use this situation of dilemma to point out that human being, as a self-conscious being, has the ability for personal initiative and response, and that within limits he/she is able to reshape himself/herself, to influence the behavior of his/her fellow beings, and to redirect the processes of the outer world. Also, self-consciousness makes reflective thinking and the sense of right and wrong possible. It enables a person to consider himself/herself as a subject and as an object of action; that is, it enables one to have freedom of choice. One, therefore, is responsible for the choice one makes.

The Akan view of causality also suggests temporal order and association. The temporal order implies direction which can be simple as well as complex. The causal agent antecedes the effect in a temporal sense. The Akan view of time is discussed further in the section on time below.

MORAL EDUCATION

The Akan consider morality in terms of right and wrong conduct (*papayɛ*) or behavior (*nneyɛeɛ*) and good and bad character (*suban*). The Akan believe that irrespective of one's capacity, one can improve upon one's morality by learning to obey moral rules. Moral education and character training in the Akan society start from infancy, and is lifelong. The various rites of passage of the society offer settings for moral and other forms of education. The child naming ceremony (*abadintoɔ*), for example, is the occasion for teaching even the young baby to distinguish between truth (*nokorɛ* - #819) and falsehood (*nkontompo*). The naming ceremony usually takes place eight days after the child is born. The officiating elder at the naming ceremony places the child on his/her lap and the child's name is called out aloud. The officiating elder dips his/her right index finger into water and let it drop onto the child's tongue. This is done three times with the saying each time: "If you say it is water, let it be water you are tasting." Then the officiating elder dips his/her right index finger into palm wine[99] for the child to taste saying, "If you say it is palm wine, let it be palm wine you are tasting." The child is then shown a black object and a white object followed each time by the saying, "If you say it is black, let it be black you are seeing and if it is white, let it be white you are seeing." By this ceremony the child receives his/her first moral instruction to speak the truth (*nokorɛ* - #19) all the time. The newborn is believed to have the ability to differentiate between sweet and non-sweet taste stimuli, and s/he is, therefore, expected to learn from this experience and grow up to be able to differentiate between truth and falsehood, and to be truthful. The vicissitude as well as the contrastive nature of the world is further reinforced by the water (representing positivity)

---

[99] In some communities, salt or lemon juice and honey were used in place of the water and palm wine. These days some people use soda pop (or any non-alcoholic beverage) or gin (or any alcoholic beverage) as a substitute for palm wine.

and the wine (representing negativity). The child is taught to see every negative situation as an opportunity for growth and learning. It can be hard to the see the silver lining when things are not going one's way. But one needs to consider that the longer one wallows in negativity, the longer it will take for things to change for the better. If one continues to focus on the bad, one will never see the good that can come of it. There is a fine line that splits one from feeling positive or negative and this starts to become a lot clearer when one becomes aware that positivity leads to enthusiasm and negativity leads to difficulties.

Let us consider an excerpt from a naming ceremony of a baby girl that was held on the in Ampia Ajumako. The child was named after the father's mother a female born on Friday. The child's full name is Afua Seguwaa Hammah. The following is what the elderly person who was performing the name ritual said:

> *Abɔfra woaba tena ase, mmɛyɛ yɛkyerɛ nkɔ. Wo maamenom ne wo papanom na ahyia ha nnɛ yi. Yɛrema wo din nnɛ. Edin a yɛde rema wo ne Afua Seguwa Hammah. Yɛbɛfrɛ wo Afua ɛfiri sɛ yɛwoo wo Efiada. Saa da yi na wo kraa pene so sɛ bra asaase yi so. Yɛde wo reto wo nana Afua Seguwaa. Ne din pa ara ne Seguwaa, ne mmarima din de Segu anaa Saigoe. Yei nti bɛbu subanpa, mmɛyɛ biribi a ɛbɛma nkurɔfoɔ anya kwan adidi wo atɛm ama ebi aka wo nana. Bio yɛde wo papa din Hammah reka wo din ho sɛdeɛ wobɛfa wo papa su na woatiatia n'anammɔn mu ayere wo ho ayɛ adwuma na woosi nkete te sɛ wo papa. Yɛka sɛ nsuo a, ka sɛ nsuo, yɛka se nsã a, ka sɛ nsã. Mfa nsuo ngyina w'ano mu nkasa nkyerɛ yɛn.*

'Baby, you are welcome to this world. Have a longer stay, just do not come and exhibit yourself and return. Your mothers and fathers have assembled here today to give you a name. The name we are giving to you is Afua Seguwaa Hammah. You are named Afua because that is the day your soul decided to enter into this world. We are naming you after your grandmother Afua Seguwaa. Her Seguwaa is the feminine form of Segu or Saigoe. In view of this, come and put up a good moral behaviour. Again we are attaching your father's name Hammah to your name. Follow the footsteps of your father and come and work hard. When we say water, let it be water, when we say drink let it be drink. Do not put water in your mouth to speak to us.'

In the past, in some farming communities, the baby boy was shown a cutlass (machete - #691) and the baby girl was for a moment covered with a basket (*kɛntɛn* - #762). The cutlass was to signify to the child that he was expected to grow up to function as a hard-working individual who will not only sustain his family, but also become a productive member of the society. The basket signified to the girl that it was the task of the woman to collect foodstuffs from the farm, carry the load home and prepare food to feed her family and others.

The eight-day-old baby may not be cognizant of what the naming ceremony is all about. The full meaning and the educational value of the ceremony are learned gradually through the years at successive ceremonies. While the rudiments (for example, differences in tastes)[100] are learned by the

---

[100] A study by Rosenstein and Oster (1988) demonstrated that within 2 hours of birth, infants with no prior taste experience differentiated sour and bitter stimuli as well as sweet versus non-sweet taste stimuli.

individual at one's own naming ceremony, added knowledge is gained at successive ceremonies at which s/he is a parent, relative, or a participant in one way or the other. In this regard the naming of one is essentially not an individual but a social learning situation. The ceremony is an educational event to inculcate in the participants the Akan values of honesty, duty, obligation, and a deep sense of and commitment to the family among other things.

The ceremony serves to teach the ancestral history as the past accomplishments and qualities of the ancestor who previously bore that name are retold. The occasion reminds the participants that as individuals each has a contribution to make to the corporate life of the group. It also serves to emphasize to the newborn that s/he belongs to a lineage with tradition and history that s/he can be proud of.[101] The ceremony also serves to teach the newborn and remind the adult participants that life is full of contrasts – occasions when living can be very "sweet" or when living can be very "bitter;" there will be ups and downs (#602-606 - zigzag), disappointments and joyous situations, and that one should not give up when the going gets tough.

Another important moral belief taught to little children centers around goodness or virtue (*papa* or *papayɛ* - #565). The Akan child is taught that God is goodness or virtue, and goodness or virtue is the first nature of God (*papayɛ yɛ Nyamesu a ɛdi kan* - #565). As Sarpong (1972, p. 40) puts it: "For it would appear that for the Akan what a man is, is less important than what a man does. To put it more concretely, a person is what he is because of his deeds. He does not perform those deeds because of what he is." From this basis, the Akan child is taught to do what is good.

Other situations used for moral education included story-telling, funeral dirges, games, quizzes and riddles (*ɛbisaa*). Games like *ɔware* and *dame dame* (checkers - #817-818) provided opportunities for teaching and learning rules important for developing children's sensibilities.

TEMPORAL AND SPATIAL KNOWLEDGE

Several adinkra symbols and the narratives linked with them indicate that social structure and social change, among the Akan, involve the organization and reorganization of time and space. In terms of agriculture, for example, the decisions people make are related to the way in which space and time are interpreted, organized, and acted upon. Also, in Akan architecture, the *fihankra* (compound house) style of building consists of a central quadrangle which is enclosed on all four sides with rooms.

The multi-room rectangular building with an open courtyard found in Akan houses, as captured by the *fihankra* symbol, marks the Akan concept of private and public space. The Akan *fihankra* building used as a home demarcates between the *fie* (inside, private) and *abɔnten* (outside, public) space.

The *fihankra* symbolizes protection, security and spirituality. When one enters the house, the open courtyard (*adiwo* in Twi; Fantse call it *paado*) represents the public space within the house. This open courtyard has multiple uses. It is usually surrounded by a verandah where guests may be received. A bigger group of guests will usually be received in the *dampan*. The *dampan* (literally, empty room) is semi-private and has multiple uses: from receiving guests, and holding court to laying the dead in state during funerals. Then, there are the private rooms: living room, bed rooms, bathrooms, etc. There is also the kitchen, which very often extends into the open courtyard. In a

---

[101] The dirges sung (or recited) by women during funerals serve similar purposes.

big Akan house, there is the women's quarters (*mmaa mu*) which will have its own open courtyard and a number of private rooms. The kitchen and the bathrooms will usually be in these quarters.

Hagan (1964) writes:

> Inevitably when identifying different domains of discourse, space and time are critical to the definition of reality. Thanks to technology, space and time can be taken in bounded units measurable from point to point. Space and time are also divisible into standard units. Thus, while technologized space is evaluated in quantitative terms, space and time are conceived traditionally as unbounded elastic continual. These contrasting notions of space and time tend to inspire characteristic attitudes toward the use of time and the dynamics of social activity. Technologized time establishes a discipline of time economy in virtue of the fact that computational time imposes a rigid frame of reference for productive activities and programs of action. The contrasting elastic notion of time is expressed in the proverbial claim, 'The dawn of the day is not in the hands of one person.' Time is a fact of collective perception and determination.

SPATIAL KNOWLEDGE

The Akan world is built of shape and space. Space, to the Akan, is more than a boundless three-dimensional extent in which objects and events have relative position and direction. It comprises *wiase*, *wimu*, and *asamando* – a spiritual and non-spiritual realm. Land (*asaase* - #29-31) is a word with much currency often utilized by the Akan to invoke responsibility, rights, sovereignty, and belonging. The word land is often used by the Akan to represent landscape, place, territory, home, or all or some of these simultaneously. There is no such thing as vacant land. All land had owners; occupied land was owned by an extended family of a community, whereas unoccupied land was managed by a chief or priest, as the case might be for members of the community – the dead, the living, and the unborn.

Several *adinkra* symbols help us to decode some of the Akan understanding of spatial and positional concepts. For example, the symbols *nsɛneɛ* (#825) and *me so nanka mentumi* (#794) encode views about weight; *sɛ apɔnkyerɛne wu a* (#656) encode views about length; *puru* (#17), *nkyinkyim* (#602-606), *obi te obi so* (#293) and *adinkrahene* (#303-310) and *sɛ nantuo kɔsene sera a* (#865) alludes to size. Several *adinkra* symbols such as *me so kɛntɛn hunu* (#762), *nsatea koro* (#12), *ahina* (#728), *namfo pa mmienu* (#205), *nsa korɔ* (#238-240), *nkyɛmu* (#823-524), and *nkorɔn* (#852-853) encode quantity. The Akan classify spatial dimensions into shape, size, height, weight, length, and width.

Furthermore, "the evocative power of the designs also facilitates the simulation of a host of ideational possibilities that could arise from contemplating these shapes even when these significations are not part of the traditional conceptions attributed to the symbols. This extrapolative possibility is demonstrated by the similarities between Classical Adikra and the mathematical technology developed by James Gates and Michael Faux, which they first named Adinkras and later Adinkrammatics[102], in recognition of the Classical Adinkra Corpus" (Abiola and Biodun, 2010).

---

[102] James Gates and a group including Charles Doran, Michael Faux, Tristan Hubsch, Kevin Iga, Greg Landweber and others have been following the geometric-physics path pioneered by Kepler and Gell-Mann. The mathematical adinkras they study are really only linked to those African symbols by name. Even so, it must be acknowledged that, like their forebears, mathematical adinkras also represent concepts that are

TEMPORAL KNOWLEDGE

Time (*bere*) is indicated by multiple temporal structures that are viewed as being natural as well as being socially constructed. Time is, in one sense, a linear continuum and is infinite, as expressed by such words as *daa, daapem, mmeresanten*, and *afeboɔ* - eternity). In yet another sense, the Akan treat time as if it were a dimension of space in the relationship of distance between locations in space and the time taken to travel between them. This space-time dimension is marked by socially constructed quantitative measures for example, hour (*dɔnhwere*) and mile (*kwansin*).

In yet another sense, time, to the Akan, is cyclical in nature. It is associated with growth, movement, life, death and destruction and renewal. Thus an aspect of the Akan's view of time is based on the cyclical and rhythmic order in nature. The seasons follow one another in an orderly manner; life and death and renewal in plant and animal life move to the rhythmic movement of nature that occurs eternally. No point in a circle is beginning, middle, or end in the absolute sense; or else all points are these simultaneously. This is encoded in the concentric circles of the *adinkrahene* symbol (king of the *adinkra* symbols - #303-310). In other words, there can never, strictly speaking, be a beginning and end of the universe; it has always moved in an infinite succession of circles and is eternal and rhythmic. When the Akan say *'abɔdeε santaann yi, obi ntenaa ase a onim n'ahyεase na obi ntena ase nkɔsi n'awieeε, gye Onyame'* (this panorama of the universe, no one has lived who saw its beginning and no one will live to see its end, except God - #3-11), they are viewing time in its infinite sense.

The Akan have a lively appreciation of time. Not, of course, of clock time. There is great moral value attached to the productive use of time. Farmers, for example, made elaborate efforts to coordinate work in the house (e.g., house repairs, cooking, tool repairs, marketing) and on the farm (e.g., planting, weeding, harvesting, storage), and to stretch nature's constraints by the skillful use of early and late varieties of crops and other time-saving devices.

Time is dynamic as indicated by the symbol *mmere dane* (time changes - #837). It is, therefore, imperative that one adapts oneself to the changing times (*mmere dane a, wo nso dane wo ho bi* - #844). The Akan regard time as fleeting and precious as indicated by the following proverb: *Bere te sε anomaa; woansɔ ne mu na otu kɔ a, worenhunu no bio* (Time is like a bird; if you do not catch it and it flies away, you will not see it again - #838). That is, time must be used productively.

Time, to the Akan, is of three dynamic dimensions: a) various constructs of the past as depicted by remote past (*tete bere*), past (*kane no*), recent past (*nnansa*); b) present (*nnε mmere, seesei, mprenmpren*); and, c) future (*ɔkyena, daakye* or *da bi*). Even as the Akan lives in the present, s/he has the ability to move to the past through memory or roam the future through imagination. The symbol *sankɔfa* (go back and retrieve - #773-793) best illustrates this ability to traverse the various time dimensions: present plans for the future are based on past experiences. The Akan believe that there must be movement with times but as the forward march proceeds, the gems must be picked from behind and carried forward on the march. The symbol *dwene hwε kan* (think ahead - #825) also is suggestive of one's ability to transcend the present to speculate the future. The following words of a popular song in Ghana make use of the various temporal structures of the Akan:

> *Mmere retwam akɔ*
> *Wobεyε biribi a, yε no prεko*

difficult to express in words. Most intriguingly, they may even contain hints of something more profound — including the idea that our universe could be a computer simulation, as in the Matrix films (Gates, 2010).

Adeɛrekye a adeɛ resa yi
Mmere ara na ɛrekɔ no
Ɔkyena wobɛka sɛ
Me huniɛ a anka
Nso na apa ho

Time is moving past
Do it now whatever you have to do
Day in day out
Time is on the move
Tomorrow you'll say
Had I known
That would be past.

In another sense, the Akan view time as periodicity or duration, and hence divide it into segments such as day (*da*), week (*nnawɔtwe* or *dapɛn*), month (*bosome*), adaduanan (forty-day cycle), and year (*afe*). The day has two main parts: *adekyeee* - day and *adesaeɛ* or *anadwo* - night (*hann ne sum* - #20-21). The *adekyeɛ* part is subdivided into seven units: *anɔpahema (daybreak), anɔpatutu* (early morning), *bɔme bosea-awia* (mid-morning), *owigyinaeɛ* (noon time), *awiaberɛ* (early afternoon), *prɛmtobere* or *mferɛtubere* (mid-afternoon), and *anwummere* (late afternoon or evening. The *adesaeɛ* or *anadwo* is subdivided into three segments: *ɔdasuo baako* (before midnight), *ɔdasuo mmienu* (around midnight), and *ɔdasuo mmiensa* (after midnight). There are also such expressions for nighttime as *anadwo dasuom* and *anadwo kɔnkɔn* and *hwanihwani* or *woyɛ hwan?* (who are you? - #123) for dawn when things appear as silhouettes.

Yet another way in which the Akan depict time is by the cyclical and seasonal climatic changes and the activities associated with these time periods: *ɔpɛ bere* (dry season), *asusuo bere* (rainy season), *ofupɛ bere*, and *bamporɔ bere* (Mensah, 1992). Towards the end of the dry season and just prior to the onset of the rainy season is the time for the preparation of the land for farming.

The Akan believe in time as a natural phenomenon as well as a social construction. The Akan view time as part of the fundamental structure of the universe. An example of natural time is indicated by the seven days of the week (*nna nsɔn*) that God is believed to have created. The Akan believe that God created the seven days, hence God is sometimes referred to as *Ɔbɔnna Nsɔn* (Creator of Seven Days). The seven days are each ruled by a planet/satellite (*okyiniwiemu*) or deity. The Akan names of the days of the week follow a regular pattern: name of deity/planet + (*a)da* – day as shown in Table #9 below[103]. Each day has its own distinct characters as follows: *Kwasiada* (Sunday), the day of *Ayisi* (*Awusi, Awisi*), is ruled by the Sun; *Dwoada* (Monday), the day of *Awo*, is ruled by the Moon; *Benada* (Tuesday) is the day of *Abena* (Mars); *Wukuada* (Wednesday) is the day of *Aku* (Mercury);*Yawoada* (*Yaada, Yawda* - Thursday) is the day of Aberao (Aberaw - Jupiter)[104]; *Fida* (Fiada - Friday) is the day of *Afi* (Venus); and *Memeneda* (Saturday) is the day of *Amene* (Saturn).

---

[103] The same patterns are to be found in English (*Mon-day, Tues-day, Wednes-day...*), in Italian (*Lune-dì, Marte-dì, Mercole-dì*) and in many other Indo-European languages: French (*Lun-di, Mar-di, Mercre-di*), German (*Mon-tag, Diens-tag, Donners-tag*), Norway (*Man-dag, Tirs-dag, Ons-dag*), and so on.

[104] Fantse fishermen along the coast refer to this as "*Aberewa na mba*" (the old lady and her children).

Table 9: Akan Names of Days of the Week

Akan Deity Name	English Name for Deity	Akan Day Name	Characteristics
Kwasi/Ayisi/Awusi/Awisi	Sun	Kwasiada	Protector
Adwo/Awo	Moon	Dwoada	Calmness/Peaceful
Abena/Bena	Mars	Benada	Compassionate
Aku/Awuku	Mercury	Wukuada	Advocate, hero
Aberao/Yao	Jupiter	Yawoada/Yaada	Aggressive/ Courageous
Afi	Venus	Fida/Fiada	Adventurer
Amene	Saturn	Memeneda	Problem-solver/ Valiant

Time and Rites of Passage

Natural time, that is, God's time, is believed to be the best (*Nyame bere ne bere pa - #* 133). Another example of the naturalness of time is depicted by the expression: *Adekyeeɛ nnyina akokɔ bɔneeɛ so; sɛ akokɔ bɛbɔn o, sɛ ɔremmɔn o, adeɛ bɛkye* - night and day are determined by nature; it is not cockcrow that changes night to day; whether the cock crows or not night will turn into day (#846-848). Natural time is not limited to the present or the past alone; it also includes futurity. This idea of future is reflected in the expression: *da bi me nsoroma bɛpue* (my star will shine one day - #845). The Akan believe that in the future God will ask each one to render an account of his or her stewardship on earth (*Daakye Onyame bɛbisa wo asɛm* - in future God will inquire something of you).

Time as natural phenomenon is also marked by the stages of human development: birth, puberty, adulthood, and death. The stages of life are, in Akan thought, circulatory in form: life in the physical world, death as a transition to life after death in the spiritual world of ancestors (*asamando*), and reincarnation from the spiritual world into the physical world. The Akan mark these time periods by various rituals: soul day (*kerada*) marked by *akradware* – soul washing ceremony, naming ceremony (*abadintoɔ*), puberty (*bragorɔ*) rites, marriage (*awareɛ* or *ayeforɔ*), and funerals (*ayie*). *Abadinto* (naming ceremony) marks the transition from the spiritual world to the physical world. The death rituals serve to mark the end of the physical aspect of human life and the beginning of spiritual life in the abode of ancestors. Time in the physical world is temporary and finite. On the other hand, time in its totality as circular natural phenomenon is infinite. The circular notion of time is also indicated in the end of year and beginning of the new year song part of which runs:

> *Afe akɔ aporɔ abɛto yɛn so bio;*
> *Adom Nyame ankum yɛn wama afe pa ato yɛn;*
> *Afenhyia pa, afe nkɔ mmɛto yɛn bio*

> The year has made its circular journey and met us again;
> The gracious God spared us our lives during the year's circular journey;
> Happy new year, may the year go round and meet us again still alive.

The Akan view of time as a social construction is seen in their concepts of work scheduling, time-budgeting, and logistic planning in which time structures are linked with activities of the people and of the state. For example, the link between time and the activities of the people is illustrated by the expression: *Sɛ ɔbaa kɔ asuo anɔpa a, ɔdom ne ho anwummerɛ* (the woman who fetches water in the morning saves time for herself in the evening - #499). Implicit in this expression is the moral imperative to use time productively.

The social construction of time is also depicted by the calendars the Akan developed. The Asante, as well as other Akan groups, developed the forty-day calendar (*adaduanan* or *adapɛn nsia*). Some of the Fantse on the coast developed a calendar based on their knowledge of the stars and lunar movements in relation to the fishing and farming seasons. In the *adaduanan* calendar system, a cycle of forty days recurring nine times (that is, nine Akwasidae ceremonies) makes a year. *Odwira* (also known as *Apafram*) or *Apoɔ*, a purificatory ceremony, was celebrated as the New Year or First Fruits festival. Some of these Akan annual ceremonies such as *Akwambɔ* and *Ahobaa* (Memorial Day) have been replaced by such Christian temporal ceremonies as Easter (*Yesu wu sɔre* - #115) and Christmas (*Buronya* - #118).

The Akan view time as having distinct characters. They believe that all the days are not equal or are not alike. This is depicted by the symbol (*nna nyinaa nsɛ* - #849). There are good or auspicious days (*nna pa*), bad or inauspicious days (*nna bɔne*), and days that are indifferent (*da hunu*). There are also *afe pa* (good year) and *afe bɔne* (bad or unlucky year). The symbol *afe bi yɛ asiane* (#839-843) also depicts this auspicious and inauspicious view the Akan have of time. The inauspicious days were used for religious rites. The days of the week have their own distinct characters as shown in Table #10 as follows:

Table 10: Days of the Week and their Characteristics

Day	Day	Name		Appellation Attribute/ Characteristic
Akan	English	Male	Female	
Dwoada	Monday	Kwadwo (Kwodwo)	Adwoa	Okoto Calmness/ Peaceful
Benada	Tuesday	Kwabena (Kɔbena)	Abenaa Araba	Ogyam Compassionate
Wukuoda	Wednesday	Kwaku (Kweku)	Akua	Ntonni Advocate, hero
Yawoada	Thursday	Yaw (Kwaw)	Yaa (Aba)	Preko Aggressive, Courageous
Efiada	Friday	Kofi	Afua (Efuwa)	Okyini Adventurer
Memeneda	Saturday	Kwame	Amma	Atoapem

		(Kwamena)	(Amba)	Valiant, problem-solver
Kwasiada	Sunday	Akwasi (Kwesi)	Akosua (Esi, Asi)	Bodua Protector

Source: Information derived from Opoku (1976), Gyekye (1987), and Mensah (1992).

MATHEMATICAL KNOWLEDGE

Various mathematical ideas are vividly portrayed in the *adinkra* writing systems. *Kente* designs, *adinkra* cloth symbols, various wood carvings, gold weights, women's hairstyles, and other things in the Akan material culture depict the application of mathematics in the lives of the Akan. Weavers, carvers, goldsmiths and crafts people perfected the ability to observe and reproduce numerical and geometrical patterns. The Akan also used these patterns in housing construction and architecture, and in games like *oware* and *dame* (#820-821). Some of these patterns are also at times geometric forms, but suggest geometries different from conventional forms. These geometries could be close to what are understood as fractal forms (Eglash, 1999). This largely non-representational character enables the *adinkra* forms and patterns to mean anything to anybody. Some of the patterns evoke the free play of the human mind in an even more radically independent way than poetry, which still operates in terms of the manipulation of socially agreed symbols represented by language.

The lines that are drawn with *dua afe* (#463-469) or *nsensan nnua* (#857) on the adinkra cloth before it is printed with various symbols are examples of Akan mathematical knowledge encoded in adinkra symbols. The numbers of lines made by the *dua afe* and *nsensan nnua* have symbolic meanings themselves. One symbolizes the indivisible, the *kra* (soul) of *Nyame*. *Nsateaa koro* (one finger - #238-240) means the same as *Gye Nyame* (except God - #3-11). Two symbolizes *Nyame* as a duality, divisible by birth. *Nsateanu* means *Mema mo mo ne yɔ me man* (I congratulate you people of my state - #633). Three symbolizes *Nyame* as the creator and ruler of the universe that is a continuum of the sky (*ewiem*), earth (*ewiase*), and the underworld (*asamando*). Four symbolizes *Nyame* as the creator and ruler of the four cardinal points of the compass and the revolving heaven. Five symbolizes *Nyame* as a Supreme Being. Six symbolizes the dialectical processes of life, death and resurrection or rebirth. It is the symbol of strength, vitality and rejuvenation. Seven is the symbol for the universe and the state. It represents the seven planets each of which presides over the seven days of the week, and the seven *abusua* that form the state. Eight symbolizes procreation, fertility and fecundity. Nine (i.e., 3+3+3) symbolizes the triad comprising *Nyame*, *Nyankopɔn*, and *Ɔdomankoma* that rules the universe (Meyerowitz, 1951; Antubam, 1963).

The lines drawn on the *adinkra* cloth are usually drawn without a ruler and, as Frutiger (1989, p. 24) points out, "the drawing of a straight line without a ruler" is an abstract idea. *Daban* (#833) is another line system in which the cloth printer uses a ruler.

The Akan systems of numeration ranged from the few number words of the ordinary person to the extensive numerical vocabulary (e.g., *apem*, *ɔpepe*, *ɔpepepepee*) of traders, astronomers and specialized public servants. An example of Akan numeration systems encoded in the adinkra symbols is given by the expression: *Woamma wo yɔnko antwa nkron a, wo nso worentwa du* - If you do not let your friend have nine you will not be able to have ten (nine - #855-856). Other *adinkra* symbols that depict the number concept include *nnamfo pa baanu* (two good friends - #205), *dua koro* (one tree - #213), *mpua anum* (hairstyle of five tufts - #357-362; #892), *nkwantanan* (hairstyle of four tufts - #363) and *koroyɛ* (unity - #187). Other examples of symbols used to indicate Akan people's views about number concepts include *ti korɔ nkɔ agyina* (one head does not constitute a council - #192-193), and *nkrɔn* (nine - #855-856). *Dame dame* (#820-821), *ɔware, ampe* and other games and quizzes provided opportunities for children to learn to count and to portray their mathematical abilities.

The *dapɛn* or *nnawɔtwe* system of counting days reflects the inclusive counting in some aspects of Akan numbering system which includes integers, fractions and operations like addition, subtraction, multiplication and division. Fractional ideas are expressed by words such as *fã* or *abunu* (half), *abusã* (third), *abunum* (fifth), and *nkotuku ano* (percentage).

Symmetry and Asymmetry of the Adinkra Symbols

The *adinkra* cloth producer, as a keen observer of things such as leaves and flowers of plants that a symmetrical and asymmetrical around him, incorporates the symmetrical nature and asymmetrical balance in his symbols. Symmetry means that one shape becomes exactly like another when it is moved in some way (that is, by a turn, flip or slide - that is through transformation). There are several kinds of symmetry to be found in a collection of adinkra symbols. One is bilateral symmetry in which an object has two sides that are mirror images of each other. The human body would be an excellent example of a living being that has bilateral symmetry. An equilateral triangle would be a geometric example of bilateral symmetry. Bilateral symmetry are found in *woforo dua pa na yepia wo* (#680).

Another kind of symmetry is radial symmetry. This is where there is a center point and numerous lines of symmetry could be drawn. The most obvious geometric example would be a circle. The *adinkrahene* symbol (#303-310) is an example of radial symmetry to be found in *adinkra*.

Examples of transformations are rotation, reflection, translation and scaling. An image has rotation when it repeats at different angles around one point. An example of rotation from adinkra symbols is *nkotimsefoɔ pua* (#370-375).

In an interview published in Garage Magazine in February 2012 Anna Craycroft talks with cyberneticist Ron Eglash about the infinite unity of thinking and doing, and he illustrated his point with the adinkra symbol *boa me na me mmoa wo* (#200) and he said:

> Using an image to try to sum it up is a great idea. Let me offer one that reminds me of what you say above but is a little more visually nuanced. Adinkra symbols are used in a stamped cloth tradition in Ghana; each symbol is associated with some aphorism. The adinkra symbol *boa me na me mmoa wo* ("Help me and let me help you" – [#200]) makes use of a geometric combination of symmetry and asymmetry: both are triangles, but one contains a white square and the other a white circle. This conveys the concept that social reciprocity contains both—you gave me a more expensive gift (asymmetry) but we treat them as if they were of equal value (symmetry). I need your help more than you need mine, but if it is a relation based on friendship, we treat the exchange of help as if the needs were equal. You can take that to a deeper level looking at the black outer circle and square—the arrow with the white square has a black circle at the end, and vice-versa for the other. So the asymmetry is created in a symmetrical fashion, a kind of higher-order symmetry. Art and science are not equally empowered in our society.

Various types of symmetry and asymmetry found in some adinkra symbols are illustrated in Table 11 below.

Table 11: Symmetry and Asymmetry Encoded in Some of Adinkra Symbols

Symbol	Type of Transformation
Bilateral symmetry ❀ ⊟ ✳	Bilateral symmetry Symmetry means that one shape becomes exactly like another when you move it in some way (turn, flip or slide – that is transformation). There are two kinds of symmetry. One is bilateral symmetry in which an object has two sides that are mirror images of each other. The human body would be an excellent example of a living being that has bilateral symmetry. An equilateral triangle would be a geometric example of bilateral symme*try.*
◎ ✺	Radial symmetry This is where there is a center point and numerous lines of symmetry could be drawn. The most obvious geometric example would be a circle. Examples from *adinkra* symbols are *adinkrahene* (on the left) and *mako nyinaa* (on the right).*
✿ 🌀	Rotation An image has rotation when it repeats at different angles around one point. For example, in the image to the left, one arm of the spiral is copied and rotated about the center point.
✣ ✳	Reflection In mathematics, an image is said to have reflection when half of the image appears to mirror across a line. For instance, the symbol to the right reflects across the X-axis, the Y-axis, and both diagonal axes. On either side of the imaginary lines, the image appears identical but opposite.

	Translation An image shows translation when it is copied and shifted horizontally or vertically. In the image to the right, one circle is repeated, moving across and vertically.
	Scaling An image shows scaling each time part of an image repeats, it becomes gradually smaller or larger. In the image to the right, the leaves of the fern gradually become smaller as the fern grows upwards.
	Asymmetry The absence of, or a violation of, symmetry (the property of an object being invariant to a transformation, such as reflection).

Measurement, geometry, symmetry (and asymmetry), and the use of patterns are just a few of the mathematical connections made with *adinkra* cloth and its symbols. Several *adinkra* symbols depict various properties of the shapes of objects the Akan encounter in their day to day activities and in their thoughts. The *adinkra* symbols incorporate forms that have more mathematical significance, and these emerge in the synergy between aesthetic forms and some mathematical principles. This correlation emerges in symmetry, one of the central aspects of aesthetic value. The forms of symmetry evident in *adinkra* include the bilateral, topological, fractal, rotational, and centripetal (Abiola and Biodun, 2010). As Abiola and Biodun further point out, "One of the most pervasive forms of symmetry evident in adinkra is bilateral symmetry, in which two parts of one form are identical. The bilateral symmetry of *kuntunkantan* (#813), for example, is realized by the spatial juxtaposition of two pairs of circles, each pair composed of one circle on top of the other, and all four circles tangent, the entire group forming a quadrilateral, with a fifth circle intersecting the other four."

Furthermore, "the evocative power of the designs also facilitates the simulation of a host of ideational possibilities that could arise from contemplating these shapes even when these significations are not part of the traditional conceptions attributed to the symbols. This extrapolative possibility is demonstrated by the similarities between Classical Adinkra and the mathematical technology developed by James Gates and Michael Faux, which they first named Adinkras and later Adinkrammatics[105], in recognition of the Classical Adinkra Corpus" (Abiola and Biodun, 2010).

---

[105] James Gates and a group including Charles Doran, Michael Faux, Tristan Hubsch, Kevin Iga, Greg Landweber and others have been following the geometric-physics path pioneered by Kepler and Gell-Mann. The mathematical adinkras they study are really only linked to those African symbols by name. Even so, it must be acknowledged that, like their forebears, mathematical adinkras also represent concepts that are difficult to express in words. Most intriguingly, they may even contain hints of something more profound — including the idea that our universe could be a computer simulation, as in the Matrix films (Gates, 2010).

TRANSMISSION OF SPECIALIZED KNOWLEDGE AND SKILLS

The Akan's appreciation and quest for knowledge led to the development of some level of formalized education in various skills and specialties such as *ahemfie adesua* (statecraft), drumming (*ayan*), hunting (*ahayɔ*), priesthood (*akɔm*), oratory, accounting (*nkontabuo*), art and crafts (*adwinneɛ*), and herbal medicine (Akuffo, 1976; McWilliam and Kwamena-Po, 1978; and Oppong, 1973). Transmission of knowledge was premised on the view that he who does not know can become knowledgeable from learning (*nea ɔnnim no sua a ohu* - #819).

The informal and formal processes of the apprenticeship system were utilized in the transmission of specialized knowledge and skills. Through informal processes the child was taught to know the history of the society (*abakɔsɛm* or *mpaninsɛm*); to show respect; to know the names of objects in the child's natural and social environment; how to count (*nkontabuo* - #211-212); and various aspects of moral values such as not to smoke, lie, or steal. The child was given a well-rounded education and training (*nimdeɛ, ntetee,* or *adwumasua amamere*). Besides the family's socialization processes, public storytelling (*Anansesɛm*- Ananse Stories),[106] games, songs,[107] drama, riddles, quizzes, and proverbs formed very important means for educating the child.

Logical reasoning, for example, is developed through riddles (*ebisaa*) and storytelling. An exercise in logical reasoning is about a man who has a fowl, a basket full of corn, and a hawk to transport across a river in a boat. The boat can carry only one of the three things at a time besides the man himself. The fowl cannot be left alone with the basket of corn, and the hawk will eat the fowl if he is not guarded. How can the man take the three things across the river? The solution lies in pairing the things that are not mutually attracted to each other, for example pairing corn and the hawk (Aggrey, 1977).

Riddles also teach one that knowledge is relative and context dependent. An example of this is in the following riddle: A man was travelling with three women - his wife, his mother and his maternal aunt. They came across a river on which was a very narrow wooden bridge. While they were crossing the river, the bridge collapsed and they fell into the river. Only the man could swim, and he could save only one woman. If you were the man, which of the three women would you rescue and why?

The Akan educational system utilizes formal and informal learning processes to stress three related goals: character, discipline, and wisdom. For example, knowing how to successfully incorporate proverbs into one's speech is a sign of wisdom and erudition; a young person who knows how to use proverbs uses them with tact, humility and modesty when in the presence of the elderly. Whether it was to achieve technical skills or moral values, the Akan educational processes never failed to stress these three related goals.

Institutionalized Knowledge and Skills

In the Asante nation, as well as the other Akan communities, various bureaucratic and other governmental functions required technical and managerial skills and expertise. The *buramfoɔ* (goldsmiths), for example, used a complex smelting process to reduce worked gold to gold dust; the *nsumankwaafoɔ* (physicians and herbalists) had knowledge of both preventive and curative

---

[106] These stories became known as Auntie Nancy Stories in the New World when the slave trade transported the people across the Atlantic Ocean. Ananse stories are a source of education, entertainment and humor. They reveal Akan social construction of reality.

[107] One song, for example, urges the indolent to go to the ant to learn its ways and be wise.

medicine from herbs and plants; and the staff of the treasury (*sannaa*) were versed in the highly intricate monetary system of weights and gold dust, and in time-keeping and collecting taxes and fines. Similarly, the hired couriers and traders (*batafoɔ, apaafoɔ* - #686-687) who plied the great roads (*akwantempɔn*) were versed in the intricate system for measuring distance, and rendering accounts after assessing and collecting tolls.

These varied skills and expertise required institutionalized knowledge. Various settings and structures were developed to disseminate broad ranges of values, attitudes, skills and various forms of specialized knowledge for the smooth functioning of the complex bureaucratic apparatus of the state. In these settings for dissemination of knowledge, the knowledge transmitted was highly institutionalized, decontextualized, deliberate and specific. The trainee was separated from home, placed under distinct authority, and put through a systematic program of instruction and curriculum where fees (e.g. *tiri nsã* - admission or initiation fee, and *mpɔnho nsã* - graduation fee) were charged in some skill areas as the specialized knowledge and skills were often protected (sometimes hoarded) by particular individuals, professional groups, or institutions.

The indigenous apprenticeship system (*adwumasua, nteteɛ* or *ɛsom*)[108] constituted a very important means for transmitting formal and institutionalized or specialized knowledge. Various initiation ceremonies and rites were performed at major points in the institutionalized learning process. These rites of passage served to accept formally the prospective trainee into the appropriate trade, to mark major transitions from one grade to another during training, and to graduate and accept formally one into the professional practice. The major goal of these institutionalized learning settings was to impart, rather than hide, knowledge and skills to accredited learners.

Schooling of the King

The Akan believe that a leader who is to teach men and present any fact of truth to man must first be taught in his subject. In this regard the king himself is required to undergo *ahemfie adesua* (palace or court training) or *amammuo ho adesua* (governance education) as depicted by the symbol *nea ɔpɛ sɛ obedi hene firi as sua som ansa* (he who wants to be a king should first learn to serve - #302). The curriculum of the *ahemfie adesua* comprises, among other things, the history and organization of the kingdom, court etiquette, drum poetry, dancing, and palace structure and administration. Learning one's history is very important to the Akan. This is because if one does not know what went on before one came into the world (past history) and what is happening at the time one lives, but away from one (current history), one will not know the world and will be ignorant of the world and mankind. Also, as encoded by the *sankɔfa* symbol, *Ɔkyena nhyehyeeɛ gyina deɛ yesua firi yɛn nkyiri; enti sɛ wo werɛfi na wosan kɔfa a, yɛnkyi* - the past serves as a guide for the future (#773-793).

The schooling of the king comprises pre-service and in-service training. Both informal and formal processes of education are employed in the socialization of one to become a king. Before one is nominated to become the king-elect, one undergoes informal training and apprenticeship. As soon as one becomes the king-elect, one is kept away from the public and formally schooled over a short period of time, usually six weeks before one is made to take the oath of office in a public ceremony as the king. Immediately after he has been sworn in, the king undergoes a more rigorous and formal on-the-job training in the palace. The continued schooling of the king takes place in

---

[108] *som* literally means to serve or service, it is used to describe apprenticeship. *Adwumasua* literally means occupational training. A trainee or an apprentice is usually referred to as *ɔsomfoɔ*. Public service was considered as *ɛsomdwuma*, which literally means work in service.

the evenings so that it may not interfere with the normal engagements of the king as it is more of the on-the-job training type. "The schooling {of the king, that is, the Asantehene], particularly in the study of the palace structure and organization, is effected with the aid of wax models of palace officials and attendants and of the items of regalia. The models are called *nkraba,* and the system of using them as visual aids for the schooling is called *nkrahene*" (Kyerematen, n.d., p. 20). The king learns from others even though he must have learned from personal experience, the Akan believe that personal experience alone is not enough for anyone to acquire all the useful knowledge of life.

Training of hunters

In other specialized areas of learning, master craftsmen and experts ordered the distribution, acquisition, and recognition of knowledge. One such expert who required training in order to acquire specialized knowledge is the hunter. The Akan say: *gye akyekyedeɛ kɔ ma agya nyɛ ahayɔ* – taking a tortoise to one's father is not a mark of good hunting skills (#221). The curriculum of the hunter, for example, included astronomy, geography, plant and animal species and their nutritional and medicinal uses, animal movements, butchery and meat preservation. As McWilliam and Kwamena-Po (1978, pp.6 and 7) write:

> A would-be hunter began his training as the apprentice of an experienced hunter, usually one who was well known for having killed the big animals, including the elephant. The new apprentice would follow his master through the woods. He would learn the use of the gun as the first step. He had to prove his ability as a first-class shot by killing a bird in flight - the hawk or any other wild bird. His course [of training] included acquiring a knowledge of edible fruits and the names of important and useful plants, particularly those for herbal use. Thus good hunters were invariably good herbalists... Similarly, the young apprentice must study the stars and know the changes in the climate and their effects on vegetation. This would enable him to predict the movement of the game and the right time to go hunting. Lastly, he must learn and understand the 'road signs' in the bush so that he could find his way back to his village after a long stay in the woods lasting several nights.

The symbol *wodu nkwanta a, gu me ahahan* (when you reach the intersection leave me a sign- #834-835) depicts the use of "road signs" (landmarks) or markers in the bush to give directions to people. The symbol also connotes time. One could tell from the freshness or dryness of the leaves or the sap from the stem of the leaf when the marker was left there. If the leaves were dry they suggested the marker was placed there long time ago. On the other hand, if the leaves looked very fresh, that suggested that the marker was left there not so long ago. One was taught these markers and their meanings.

Priesthood

Another specialized skill area that may be used to further illustrate the Akan knowledge system and how knowledge was transmitted is priesthood (*akɔm*). Training was necessary before one could assume priestly functions. In this skill area there was well demarcated initiation and graduation ceremonies at which competence and knowledge were either confirmed or tested. Entry into the ranks of priesthood of the various shrines was preceded by a period of training under the tutelage of a senior priest or priestess for three or more years. The period and type of training varied with the nature of the functions of the particular deity that the priest served. The prospective candidate for priesthood received a call either through illness or by being possessed by a deity. It was believed that refusal to obey the call would result in madness or death for the recalcitrant candidate. Relatives of the prosective candidate could intercede on his/her behalf, and if their pleas were deemed valid the possessed person would be spared by a ritual of drawing out the deity from the body of the prospective candidate.

The curriculum of the priesthood training included divination; diagnosis of diseases; prescription of cures; identification of herbs and roots and their medicinal qualities; moral lessons on respect of elders and the general public, equity of care, frugality, obedience, industry, cooperation, and chastity and abstinence; and songs and dance. Divination was based on the manipulation, usually by the casting of cowrie shells (*serewa* or *sedeɛ* - #723-728), pebbles, or some other divining devices and the recitation of specific oral texts and codes associated with particular configurations of the divining objects. Each configuration resulting from the casting of the divining devices is associated with a body of text and this text is recited after the tossing of the divining devices.

An experienced priest was able to diagnose a disease and fit it into one or more of the following principal categories of illness and disease: *honam yareɛ* (illness of the body - e.g., rheumatism, piles, boils); *nsane yareɛ* (infectious illness - e.g., yaws, measles, chicken pox)); *abusua yareɛ* (illness of the matrilineal group); *mogya yareɛ* (illness of the blood, that is, genetical disease); and *sunsum yare* (spiritually-caused illness). If the illness is not a simple bodily ailment but 'something lies behind it' then a spiritual cause is attributed to it and the priest would specify what must be done to 'remove the misfortune' (*yi mmusuo* - to propitiate the god) that is troubling the patient. All medical attempts to cure the illness would prove futile if the precipitating spiritual cause was not first dealt with and the patient released from the misfortune that was troubling him/her. The priest (and herbalist) practised both curative and preventive medicine.

Advancement after the initial entry was dependent upon "a tenacious memory, a prudent discretion, and inviolable secrecy," writes Cruickshank (1853). After training, a day was set aside for the graduation ceremony during which the graduate performed the *akɔm* dance (possession dance). It is during this time that a name is believed to be revealed to the graduate. The graduate paid a graduation fee (*mpɔnho nsã*).

WRITING IN GHANA – THE EUROPEAN INFLUENCE

The *adinkra* cloth symbols combine both pictograms (for example, *dɛnkyɛm* - #345-350 and *akokɔ* - #846-848) and ideograms (for example, *Gye Nyame* - #3-11 and *mate masie* - #802-805). Besides incorporating the ideograms and pictograms on cloth, the symbols that form part of the *adinkra* writing may also be found in woodcarving, architectural designs, and metal casting. A more recent development in the *adinkra* form of writing has been the increased use of phonological scripts based on either English or Twi language. In recent times not only letters, but also words and sentences have been incorporated. ABCD (#853) symbolizes literacy that has come to be associated with contemporary formal schooling.

Some of the phonological script is combined with the traditional ideographs and pictographs to create a whole new aesthetics. Some examples of symbols that have words wrapped around motifs include the following: *Asɛm pa asa* (the truth is gone - #823), *ɛkaa nsee nko a* (the weaver bird wishes - #595-597), *ɛkaa obi nko a* (someone wishes - #594) and *owuo sɛɛ fie* (death destroys the home - #125-127). Other symbols with words and sentences include *nipa bɛwu na sika te ase* (one will die only to leave behind one's wealth - #124), *owuo bɛgya hwan?*, (who will be spared by death - #110), and *ɛkaa obi nko a* (someone wishes - #594).

Alphabetic Writing in Ghana

The use of the Roman alphabet in Ghana dates back to the Portuguese who are believed to have introduced the phonographic writing system with the establishment of a trading post at the Elmina Castle, which was completed in 1482. In 1503 the Portuguese made their initial attempts to convert the indigenous people of Elmina to Christianity, and by 1529, a school had been set up to teach the children to 'learn how to read and write' in Portuguese ((McWilliam and Kwamena-Poh, 1975). When the Dutch routed the Portuguese out of Ghana, they did not only run schools in their castles in Ghana, the Dutch, (as well as the English, Danes and other Europeans who built castles in Ghana) sent some African children to continue their schooling in Europe. Some of these children educated in the castle schools and later in Europe helped to write the Akan language (Twi and Fantse) in the alphabetic form.

For example, between 1600 and 1602, J. P. de Marees, a Dutch traveler on the Gold Coast, was able to compile a list of vocabulary of the Fantse and Ga-Adangme languages. The Danish chaplain in one of the first Danish settlements near Cape Coast, John Mueller listed 400 Akan (Fantse) words and their Danish translations as an appendix to his book *Die Africanische Landschaft Fetu* published at Hamburg in 1675. In 1743 Jacobus Capitein, an Elmina mullato who was sent to Leyden, Holland for schooling, translated into Fantse the Lord's Prayer, the Twelve Articles of Belief, and the Ten Commandments. In 1764, Christian Protten, a mullato from Christiansborg, translated the Lord's Prayer into Fantse. He published a Ga-Twi-Danish catechism and a grammar book, *En nyttig Grammaticalsk Indledelse til Tvende hidinatil ubekiendte Sprog fanteisk ig Acraisk*. In 1785, P. E. Isert, a Danish botanist and traveller, prepared a list of Ga, Asante, and Ewe (Krepi) words and their Danish translations. The two Asante princes Owusu Nkwantabisa son of Asanthene Osei Yaw (who ruled in 1824–34) and Owusu Ansah son of Asantehene Osei Bonsu (who ruled in 1800–24) were sent to England to go to school. They also published lists of Twi words (McWilliam and Kwamena-Poh, 1975; Graham, 1976).

The Basel Mission from about 1840 modified the existing Roman alphabet to write the Akwapim Twi. This was used to translate the Bible. Rev. H. N. Riis published two books on Twi grammar. One of the two books was entitled *Elemente des Akwapim-Dialekts der Odschi-Sprache (Elements of the Akwapim Dialect of the Twi language)*. In 1854, Karl Richard Lepsius, a professor in Berlin and an Egyptologist, published *Standard Alphabet for Reducing unwritten languages and Foreign Graphic Systems to a uniform Orthography in European letter*. This rekindled interest in writing some of the Ghanaian languages using the newly standardized Roman alphabet. In 1860 Timothy Laing, a Methodist missionary published the Fantse primer, *Fante Akenkan Ahyesie*. Dan L. Carr and Joseph P. Brown published their book, *The Mfantsi Grammar* (in Fantse) in Cape Coast in 1868. In 1875, Rev. Johann Gottlieb Christaller wrote *A Grammar of the Asante and Fante Language called Tshi (Twi) based on the Akwapim Dialect with Reference to other Dialects*. In 1881 he published the *Dictionary of the Asante and Fante language called Tshi* (Twi).

Despite the improvements, the Roman alphabet system still lacked sufficient letters to transcribe many languages. One solution has been to add new letters to existing ones. Another solution has been to create a new alphabet system, for example, the Cyrillic alphabet used in writing some of the Eastern European languages. In 1888, the International Phonetic Association (IPA) created in effect a new Roman alphabet, with lower case (small) letters only through the addition of a series of new letters (Dalby, 1986).

In 1930, the Government of Ghana (then called Gold Coast) adopted an offcial national alphabet for writing the languages in the country. This alphabet system has thirty-four (34) letters. Beginning from the end of the 19ᵗʰ century, the works of Rev. R. G. Acquaah (1884–1954), J. A. Annobil, C. A. Akrofi, J. J. Addaye, F. Safori, E. J. Osew, K. E. Owusu, S. K. Otoo, A. Crakye Denteh, A. A. Opoku, E. Effa, R. A. Tabi, Efua T. Sutherland, and J. H. Kwabena Nketia have contributed immensely in developing a corpus of literary classics in Akan (Asante Twi, Akuapem Twi and Fantse). The establishment of the Ghana Broadcasting Service in 1935 created a popular platform for young Ghanaian poets and writers in various Ghanaian languages. The establishment of the Bureau of Ghana Languages in 1951 served as an important center for the development of Akan literature using the alphabetic writing system. In the 1950's and the 1960's there were several newspapers and magazines that were published in Fantse and Twi. Popular among these were *Amansuon, Nkwantabisa*, and *Dawuru*. Since then, the School of Ghana Languages of the Winneba University of Education at Ajumako, the Linguistics Department and the Language Center at the University of Ghana have contributed to the development of alphabetized writing in Akan.

CHAPTER 11

Hwehwε mu dua – Symbol of Critical examination *Wopusu nunum a na wote ne
pampan* When you shake the mint tree you realize how it smells

CONCLUSION

This book serves as an example of how the material culture of the Akan can be utilized as the context for both visual and verbal language learning. In this exploratory study, one can also discover that the links between the visual and the verbal make it possible for one to explore various themes in Akan thought and world view. It has been shown in this study that the *adinkra* symbols are more than visual representation of what the Akan verbalized. The *adinkra* symbols, when viewed as pictorial signs, ideograms, and phonograms, constitute a writing system. The symbols are linked to narratives that are drawn from the extensive Akan oral literature genres which include proverbs, stories, mythologies, poetry, funeral dirges, riddles and quizzes.

If we could exactly identify and interpret every single *adinkra* cloth symbol, every combination of symbols, and the various colors forming the background of the cloths and symbols, and the narratives that are linked to these symbols we would be able to read the *adinkra* cloth as a comprehensive "book" about the Akan of Ghana. This "book" does not only serve as a store of social knowledge and information. It also serves to record knowledge that can be viewed as progressive and dynamic rather than static in quantity and quality. By drawing on Akan verbal genres and also by appropriating symbols from other cultures the *adinkra* writing system does not only decontextualize every day interactional events.

The "book" also makes it possible for us to realize that literacy need not be associated only with formal schooling. Similarly, literacy based on writing systems that are phonetically-based is an important aspect of everyone's education in these times. However, alphabetical symbols alone have long been insufficient to record, store and convey human thoughts and knowledge. Therefore, being able to view, interpret and react to visuals such as those in the *adinkra* cloth is just as important for today's population. We live in a world that increasingly utilizes visual symbols to communicate. Manufacturers are not printing words anymore, cryptic images are the norm and many are struggling to cope with this new mode of publication. The user interfaces now have icons such as solid lines or dotted lines, singular or double lines that are used to store and disseminate information. Developing through picture, transition and phonetic, typographic symbols today embrace new evolving styles necessary for the age of globalization and mass movement of people.

In the Ghanaian society where people have limited access to books that are based on the phonetically-based writing systems, the text incorporated in the *adinkra* system of writing can serve as basis of discourse in the classroom of both the young and the old. Such discourse can contribute to knowledge and thought development. Also, in societies where phonetically-based writing is dominant, the use of ideograms and pictograms have been found useful. In the cities of Tampa, Los Angeles[109] and New York and Charlotte/Mecklenburg in the United States, for example, *adinkra* symbols have been appropriated and incorporated into public art for both the aesthetic and semantic values of the symbols. The Charlotte Area Transit System (CATS) "Art in Transit" project has its Rosa Parks Place Community Transit Center[110] enhanced with a variety of West African and *adinkra* symbols as testimony to the strength and resilience that are inherent values in her culture of origin. The Adinkra symbols sandblasted in the sidewalk are complemented with pronunciations that represent Akan proverbs that originated in Ghana. In this case, the incorporation of art is used to enhance the visual quality of the neighborhood as well as to portray its cultural diversity in a place of high pedestrian activity. In the "Public Art Program" of the city of Tampa[111], the Police Department, District III facility incorporates several *adinkra* symbols which the artist, Charles E. Humes indicates were utilized "to depict these images and serenely reflective statements in thoughtful vignettes of the plight and circumstances of people that are vital to the growth and well-being of a strong and vibrant community." Jamaican architect, Kamau Kambui, pays tribute to the Jamaican ancestors who were brought as slaves from West Africa by incorporating *adinkra* symbols in the design of the Emancipation Park[112] in Kingston, Jamaica. The symbols can be seen in various areas of the Park namely the perimeter fence, the walls at the entrance, the benches and garbage receptacles. Woodruff Park is one of Downtown Atlanta's most significant green spaces, at the heart of the city's financial, entertainment, and academic districts. The Gateway to Historic Auburn Avenue of the Woodruff Park is marked with the West African *adinkra* symbol, *sankɔfa*, meaning "learn from the past." It reads, "Know your past so that you can understand the present and direct the future."

Adinkra symbols when read as a "book" supply considerably more than information about language; they can orient one toward the ways that all book learning makes possible: linking text to text, acquiring additional symbol and word meanings as symbols and word can have multiple meanings, relying on prior knowledge (e.g., from various Akan verbal genres) to help a text make sense, and creating inferences based on information presented by a book (Smolkin and Yade, 1992, p. 439). These characteristics of learning are crucial to literacy for both school age children and adults.

Visual images are becoming the predominant form of communication across a range of learning and teaching resources, delivered across a range of media formats. Pictures exist all around us. Understanding pictures is a vital life enriching necessity. Not to understand pictures and other visuals amounts to visual illiteracy.

---

[109] See the Leimert Park Plaza - http://la.streetsblog.org/2015/07/01/leimert-park-people-st-plaza-opens-stakeholders-debate-building-a-cultural-center/

[110] See http://charlottenc.gov/cats/transit-planning/art-in-transit/completed-projects/Pages/rosa-parks.aspx

[111] See https://www.tampagov.net/sites/default/files/TeachersPacketForWeb_0.pdf

[112] See http://www.emancipationpark.org.jm/about-us/adinkra-symbols.php

What are some other educational implications of the *adinkra* system of writing? Is the knowledge encoded in the *adinkra* symbols the type of knowledge that is worth building into the formal educational curriculum of the school? The *adinkra* symbols have relevance for the work of writers and book illustrators as well as educators in general. Familiarity with these and other symbols and images of the society will play an important role in the culture's visual heritage. Writers and illustrators are recognizing that people of all ages, from toddlers to adults, enjoy and look toward illustrated books that reflect and convey the thoughts, ideals, and values of the society. School age children, for example, learn alphabets by first starting to read alphabet books most of which are picture books. As Smolkin and Yade (1992, p. 433) point out,

> children who participate in reading alphabet books are learning about at least two rather different sets of information. The first set is the "expected" set - children are learning about graphic form, how it operates and how people "talk about it." The second set may be, however, the more significant set - how people "use" books.

By reading *adinkra* symbols as an illustrated "book," educators can gain new and important insight into the value of using pictures, illustrations, and other forms of visuals to accompany discussions. Comenius, the seventeenth century Moravian bishop and educator became famous for his books *Orbis Pictus* and *Didactica Magna*, in which he astonished the educational world by suggesting that visual aids — pictures be used for instructing children in schools. This study on *adinkra* symbols have shown how in the palace school of the king visual aids are utilized.

Adinkra symbols as visual representations suggest the importance of linking visuals with various abstract verbal concepts. This is of importance to subject areas like mathematics and literature. Morris and Pai (1993, p. 84) note that

> Mathematics, as the language of quantity, is the symbol system we use in studying the physical world of nature. Mathematics may be abstract, but is certainly not vague. What mathematics does is to render symbolic the absolute precision and regularity of the cosmos we live in.

In this regard, Eglash and his students from Ronslear Institute have partnered with Ghanaian mathematics teachers and *adinkra* artists to incorporate indigenous knowledge encoded in the *adinkra* writing sytem in the mathematics curriculum of schools in the Kumase area in Ghana.

Similarly, in literature, one is not only required to read text literally, but one is also required to be able to move to the interpretive level in understanding the visual symbols in metaphors, allegories, pun, and other figures of speech in a text.

Symbols are especially significant for understanding the changing and multicultural nature of the global community. From a cross-cultural perspective, one realizes that a symbol takes on different meanings in different social context. Some of the *adinkra* symbols have been borrowed or appropriated from other cultures. It will be interesting to undertake a comparative study to see what some of the *adinkra* symbols mean in other cultures that have similar symbols. In this study, for example, we see how the ram's horns are used to symbolize strength in humility in the Akan social context. Gallant (1994, p. 704), on the other hand, makes us aware that in peasant societies in the Mediterranean region, to give a man the ram's horns "signifies the sexual conquest of his wife, thereby exposing the impotence of the husband and the power of the adulterer." That is, throwing down the ram's horns symbolizes cuckolding, and cuckolding is about loss of control and powerlessness. The white dove has been used to symbolize peace in some societies. In some

American Indian societies the smoking pipe is the symbol of peace. In this study we see that when the Akan chief sent the axe he meant peace rather than violence and/or war.

This book is just a first step in understanding the complexities of Akan and other Ghanaian symbolism. It points to the need for scholars to appreciate the importance of material culture as visual documents for research. More research is required in areas such as metal casting (particularly gold weights), wood carvings, basket weaving, and other textiles and clothing designs in order to facilitate a better understanding of the connections between verbal strategies and the visual heritage of the Akan society. For examples, the *kente* cloth designs are pregnant with mathematics that go beyond simple geometric figures, but also number series, transformations, vertices and tessellations. It is my hope, also that readers of this book and those who use African material culture in their work will be provoked to additional reflection on the interpretive possibilities these sources open up.

BIBLIOGRAPHY

Aborampah, O. M. (1999). Women's roles in the mourning rituals of the Akan of Ghana. **Ethnology**, 38 (3): 257-271.

Abraham, W. E. (1962). **The mind of Africa**. Chicago: University of Chicago Press.

Achampong, Peter. (2007). **Christian values in adinkra symbols**. Kumasi: University Press.

Ackah, C. A. (1988). **Akan ethics**. Accra: Ghana Universities Press.

Adams, Marie Jeanne. (1989). African visual arts from an art historical perspective. **African Studies Review**, 32(2): 55-103.

Adjaye, Joseph K. (1994). Editor. **Time in the black experience**. Westport, CT: Greenwood Press.

_____. (1984). **Diplomacy and diplomats in nineteenth century Asante**. Lanham, MD: University Press of America.

Agbenaza, E. (n.d.). The Ewe Adanudo. Unpublished B.A. Thesis, Arts Faculty Library, University of Science and Technology, Kumasi, Ghana.

Agbo, Adolph H. (2006). Values of adinkra and agama symbols. Kumasi: Bigshy Designs & Publications.

Aggrey, J. E. K. (1992). *Ebɔbɔ bra dɛn* 1. Accra: Bureau of Ghana Languages.

_____. (1978). *Asafo*. Tema: Ghana Publishing Corporation.

_____. (1977). *Ebisaa na abrɔme*. Accra: Bureau of Ghana Languages.

Agyeman-Duah, J. (n.d.). **Ashanti stool histories**. Accra: Institute of African Studies, University of Ghana.

_____.1962. **Ceremonies of enstoolment of Otumfuo Asantehene**. Ashanti Stool Histories, Volume 2, Series No. 33. Accra: Institute of African Studies, University of Ghana.

Aidoo, Agnes. A. (1981). Asante queen mothers in government and politics in the nineteenth century. In Filomena Steady (Editor). **The black woman cross-culturally**. Cambridge, Mass.: Schenckman.

_____. (1977). Order and conflict in the Asante Empire: A study in interest group relations. **African Studies Review**, 20(1): 1-36.

Aidoo, Thomas Akwasi (1983). Ghana: Social class, the December coup, and the prospects for socialism. **Contemporary Marxism**, 6: 142-159.

Ajei, Martin O. (2001). Indigenous knowledge and good governance in Ghana: The traditional Akan socio-political example. Accra: IEA Publication.

Akoto, Nana Baafuor Osei. (1992). **Struggle against dictatorship**. Kumasi: Payless Printing Press.

Akuffo, B. S. (1976). **Ahenfie adesua**. Accra: Ghana Publishing Corporation.

Allen, M. 1874. **The Gold Coast or A Cruise in West African Waters**. London: Hodder and Stoughton.

Allman, Jean Marie (1990). The young men and the porcupine: Class, nationalism and Asante's struggle for self-determination, 1954-57. **Journal of African History,** 31: 263-279.

Alpern, Stanley B. (1995). What Africans got for their slaves: A master list of European trade goods. **History in Africa,** 22: 5-43.

Amanor, Kojo S. (1999). Global restructuring and land rights in Ghana: Forest food chain, timber and rural livelihoods. Nordiska Afrikainstitutet Research Report 108.

Ampem, Agyewodin Adu Gyamfi (1998). *Akan mmɛbusɛm bi.* Kumasi, Ghana: University Press.

Aning, B. A. (1975). **Nnwonkoro.** Accra: Ghana Publishing Corporation.

Ansong, K. Dankyi. (2012). The influence of indigenous Akan cultural elements on Christian worship in the Kumasi Metropolitan Area. Doctoral dissertation, Depart of General Art Studies, Kwame Nkrumah University of Science and Technology, Kumasi, Ghana.

Antiri, Janet Adwoa (1974). Akan combs. **African Arts,** 8(1): 32-35.

Antubam, Kofi (1963). **Ghana's heritage of culture.** Leipzig: Kehler and Amelang.

_____. (1961). **Ghana art and crafts.** Accra: Ghana Publishing Corporation Anyidoho, Kofi. (1983). Oral Poetics and Traditions of Verbal Art in Africa. Diss. University of Texas, Austin.

_____. Ed. (1983). Cross Rhythms (Papers in African Folklore). Bloomington, Indiana: Trickster Press.Appadurai, Arjun. (1986). Introduction: Commodities and the Politics of Value. In **The Social Life Of Things: Commodities in Cultural Perspective.** Arjun Appadurai, ed. Pp. 3-63. Cambridge: Cambridge University Press.

Appiah, Kwame A. (2005). **The ethics of identity.** Princeton, New Jersey: Princeton University Press

Appiah, Michael A. (1979). Okyeame: An Integrative Model of Communication Behavior. Diss. University of New York at Buffalo.

Appiah, Peggy (1979). Akan symbolism. **African Arts,** 13(1): 64-67.

Appiah, Peggy, Kwame A. Appiah and Ivor Agyeman-Duah (2007). **Bu me bɛ: Proverbs of the Akans.** London: Ayebia Clarke Publishing.

Arhin, K. (1995). Monetization and the Asante state, in J. I. Guyer (ed.**), Money Matters: Instability, values, and social payments in the modern history of West African communities.** Portsmouth NH: Heinemann.

_____. (1994). The economic implications of transformations in Akan funeral rites. **Africa,** 64 (3): 307-322.

_____. (1990). Trade, accumulation, and the state in Asante in the nineteenth century. **Africa,** 60(4): 524-537.

_____. (1987). Savanna contributions to the Asante political economy. In Enid Schildkrout (Editor). **The Golden Stool: Studies of the Asante center and periphery.** New York: American Museum of Natural History.

_____. (1986). A note on the Asante akonkofo: A non-literate sub-elite, 1900-1930. **Africa,** 56(1): 25-31.

_____. (1983a). Rank and class among the Asante and Fante in the nineteenth century. **Africa,** 53(1): 2-22.

_____. (1983b). The political and military roles of Akan women. In C. Oppong (editor). **Female and male in West Africa.** London: George Unwin and Allen.

_____. (1968). Status differentiation in Ashanti in the nineteenth century: A preliminary study. **Research Review,** 4: 34-52.

_____. (1967a). The financing of Ashanti expansion, 1700-1820. **Africa,** 37: 283-291.

_____. (1967b). The structure of Greater Ashanti (1700-1824). **Journal of African History**, 8: 65-86.

Arhin, K. and Amissah, J. B. (1981). On Fante death rituals. **Current Anthropology** 22(2): 179-180.

Aronson, Lisa (1992). The language of est African textiles. **African Arts**, 25 (3): 36-40, 100. Arthur, G. F. Kojo (2001). **Cloth As Metaphor: (Re)Reading the adinkra cloth symbols of the Akan of Ghana**. Accra: Centre for Indigenous Knowledge Systems.

_____. (1994). Cloth as metaphor: Some aspects of the Akan philosophy as encoded in the adinkra cloth. Paper presented at the Annual Meeting of the African Studies Association, Toronto, Canada.

Arthur, G. F. Kojo and Robert Rowe. Akan Cultural Symbols Project Online. Marshall University, Huntington, W. V. (http://www.marshall.edu/akanart). 1998-2009.

Asante, M. K. (1992). **Kemet, Afrocentricity and knowledge**. Trenton, N.J.: Africa World Press. Asare-Nyarko, A. (1974). A comparison of six fungicides for the control of the black pod Disease of cocoa caused by Phytophthora palmivora (Butl.) in Ghana. Proceedings of the 4th International Cocoa Research Conference held in Trinidad.

Assimeng, J. M. (1976). **Traditional Life, Culture and Literature in Ghana**. New York: Conch Magazine.

Astley, P. (1745). **A new general collection of voyages and travels, Volumes II & III**. London: Oxford University Press cited in Fynn (1971). **Asante and its neighbours, 1700- 1807**. London: Longman.

Austin, Gareth (2012). Vent for surplus or productivity breakthrough? The Ghanaian cocoa take-off, c. 1890-1936. African Economic History Working Paper series no. 8.

Balmer, W. T. (1926). A History of the Akan Peoples of the Gold Coast. 3d impr. London: The Atlantis Press.

Bannerman, J. Yedu (1974). **Mfantse-Akan mbɛbusɛm nkyerɛkyerɛmu**. Tema: Hacquason Press.

Bauman, Richard. (1977). Verbal Art as Performance. Rowley: Newbury House.

_____. (1983a). The Field Study of Folklore in Context. In Handbook of American Folklore. Ed. Richard Dorson. Bloomington: Indiana University Press. pp. 362-68.

_____. (1983b). *Let Your Words Be Few: Symbolism of Speaking and Silence among Seventeeth-Century Quakers*. Cambridge: Cambridge University Press.

Bauman, Richard, and Joel Sherzer, eds. (1974). *Explorations in the Ethnography of Speaking*. Cambridge: Cambridge University Press.

Bellis, J. O. (1972). Archaeology and the culture history of the Akan of Ghana, a case study. Doctoral dissertation, Indiana University, Bloomington, Indiana.

Bezuidenhout, T. (1998). A discursive semiotic approach to translating cultural aspects in Persuasive advertisements. M.A. dissertation American Academy of Advertising.

Bledsoe, C. and K. Robey. (1986). Arabic literacy and secrecy among the Mende of Sierra Leone. **Man**, 21: 202-226.

Boahen, A. Adu (1977). Ghana before the coming of Europeans. **Ghana Social Science Journal**, 4(2): 93-106.

_____. (1972). Prempeh I in exile. **Institute of African Studies Research Review**, 8(3): 3-20.

_____. (1966). The origins of the Akan. **Ghana Notes and Queries**, 9: 3-10.

Boahene, K., T., A. B. Snijders, and H. Folmer, (1999), "An Integrated Socio Economic Analysis of Innovation Adoption: The Case of Hybrid Cocoa in Ghana." *Journal of Policy Modelling*, 21:2, pp. 167-84.

Boateng, Boatema, (2014). *Adinkra* and *Kente* Cloth in History, Law, and Life. *Textile Society of America Symposium Proceedings.*

Boateng, Boatema (2011). **The copyright thing doesn't happen here: Kente and adinkra cloth And intellectual property in Ghana.** Minneapolis: University of Minnesota Press.

Bodomo, A. B. (1996). On language and development in sub-Saharan Africa: the case of Ghana. **Nordic Journal of African Studies,** 5 (2): 31-53.

Borgatti, Jean. (1983). **Cloth as metaphor: Nigerian textiles from the Museum of Cultural History.** Los Angeles: Museum of Cultural History.

Bosman, W. (1705). A new and accurate description of the coast of Guinea. London cited in T. Garrard (1980). **Akan weights and the gold trade.** London: Longman.

Bowdich, T. E. (1819). **Mission from Cape Coast to Ashantee.** London: John Murray.

Bravmann, R. (1974). **Islam and tribal art in West Africa.** London: Cambridge University Press.

_____. (1968). The state sword - A pre-Ashanti tradition. **Ghana Notes and Queries,** 10: 1-4.

Brempong, Owusu (1984). *Akan highlife in Ghana: Songs of cultural transition.* Doctoral dissertation, Indiana University, Bloomington, IN.

Britwum, K. A. (1974). Kwadwo Adinkra of Gyaman: A study of the relations between the Brong Kingdom of Gyaaman and Asante from c.1800-1818. **Transactions of the Historical Society of Ghana,** 15(2): 229-239.

Busia, K. A. (1954). The Ashanti of the Gold Coast. In Daryll Forde (Editor). **African worlds: Studies in the cosmological ideas and social values of African people.** London: Oxford University Press.

_____. (1951). **The position of the chief in the modern political system of Ashanti.** London: Oxford University Press.

Camile, Michael (1996). Simulacrum. In Critical Terms for Art History, ed. Robert S. Nelson and Richard Shiff. University of Chicago Press, pp. 31 - 44.

Clanchy M. T. (2012), From memory to written record: England, 1066-1307. Third Edition. Oxford: Wiley-Blackwell

Chandler, Daniel. (2002). **Semiotics: The basics.** New York: Routledge.

Charon, Joel (1985). **Symbolic interaction: An introduction, and interpretation, an integration.** 2nd Edition. Englewood Cliffs, NJ: Prentice Hall.

Christian, Angela (1976). **Adinkra oration.** Accra: Catholic Press.

Chukwukere, I. (1982). Agnatic and uterine relations among the Fante: Male/female dualism. **Africa,** 52(1): 61-68.

_____. 1978. Akan theory of conception - are the Fante really aberrant? **Africa,** 48(2): 135-147.

Clarence-Smith, William G. (2000). Cocoa and chocolate, 1765-1914. New York: Routledge. Cohen, Abner (1979). Political symbolism. **Annual Review of Anthropology,** 8: 87-113.

Cole, H. M. and D. Ross (1977). **The arts of Ghana.** Los Angeles: UCLA.

Coronel, Michael A. (1979). Fanti canoe decoration. **African Arts,** 13(1): 54-59, 99.

Coulmas, Florian (1996). **The Blackwell encyclopedia of writing systems.** Oxford: Blackwell Publishers.

Craik, Jennifer. (2005). **Uniforms exposed: From conformity to transgression.** New York: Berg.

Cruickshank, B. (1853). **Eighteen years on the Gold Coast of Africa.** 2 Volumes. (Reprinted 1966, London: Frank Cass and Co.

Daaku, K. Y. (1970). **Denkyira.** UNESCO Research Project on Oral Traditions, No. 2. Niamey, Niger: OAU.

Dade, H. A. (1928). Economic significance of cocoa pod diseases and factors determining their incidence and control. Yearbook, Department of Agriculture, Gold Coast 23, pp. 110-128.

Dalby, David (1986). **Africa and the written word** (L'Afrique et la lettre). Paris: Karthala.

_____. 1969. Further indigenous scripts of West Africa: Manding, Wolof, and Fula alphabets and Yoruba holy–writing. *African Language Studies* 10:161–191.

_____. 1968. The indigenous scripts of West Africa and Surinam: their inspiration and design. *African Language Studies* 9:156–197.

_____. (1967). A survey of the indigenous scripts of Liberia and Sierra Leone: Vai, Mende, Kpelle, and Bassa. *African Language Studies* 8:1–51.

Dankyi D. A (2010) Tema records 75 deaths in 732 Accidents between January-September. http://newtimes.com.gh/story/tema-records-75-deaths-in-732-accidents-between-Jan - September-2010

Danquah, Francis (2004). Capsid pests as 'cocoa mosquitoes' - a study in cash crop infestation and control in Ghana, 1910-1965. *Journal of third world studies*, 21(2): 147-166.

_____. (2003). Sustaining a West African cocoa economy: Agricultural science and the swollen shoot contagion in Ghana, 1936-1965. *African Economic History*, 31: 43-74.

_____. (1991). The capsid, black pod and swollen shoot cacao diseases in Ghana, 1910-1966. Doctoral dissertation, Iowa State University, Ames, Iowa.

Danquah, J. B. (1944). **The Akan doctrine of God**. London: Lutterworth Press.

Dantzig, Albert van (1980). **Forts and castles of Ghana**. Accra: Sedco Publishing.

Danzy, Jasmine (2009). *Adinkra Symbols: An Ideographic Writing system* (Master's Thesis, Stony Brook University). Retrieved from http://dspace.sunyconnect.suny.edu/bitstream/handle/1951 /48176/000000570.sbu. pdf?sequence=2

Darkwah, Kofi (1999). Antecedents of Asante Culture. *Transactions of the Historical Society of Ghana. New Series* 3: 57-79.

Datta, Ansu (1972). The Fante asafo: A re-examination. **Africa**, 42(4): 305-315.

Datta, Ansu and R. Porter (1971). The Asafo system in historical perspective. *Journal of African History*, 12(2): 279-297.

Davis, Fred (1992). **Fashion, culture, and identity**. Chicago: University of Chicago Press. DeFrancis, John. *The Chinese Language: Fact and Fantasy*. Honolulu: University of Hawaii Press, 1984. de Graft Johnson, J. H. (1932). The Fanti Asafu. *Africa*, 5(3): 307-322.

Delaquis, E. M. N. (2013). *The Adinkra: Re-reading a Discourse within a Discourse (MA thesis)*. College of Fine Art. Ohio University. de Saussure, Ferdinand (1966). **Course in general linguistics**. New York: McGraw-Hill. de Witte, Marleen. (2003). Money and Death: Funeral Business in Asante, Ghana. *Journal of the International African Institute*. 73(4): 531- 559.

Dickson, K. B. (1971). **A historical geography of Ghana**. Cambridge: Cambridge University Press.

Dolphyne, Florence Abena and Kropp-Dakubu, M. E. (1988). The Volta-Comoe languages. In M. E. Kropp-Dakubu, editor. **The Languages of Ghana**. London: KPI, Ltd.

Domowitz, Susan (1992). Wearing proverbs: Anyi names for printed factory cloth. *African Arts*, 25(3): 82-87, 104.

Dorson, Richard, ed. 1983. **Handbook of American Folklore**. Bloomington: Indiana University Press.

Drewal, Henry John. (1996). Mami Wata Shrines: Exotica and the Construction of Self. In Arnoldi, M. J. & Hardin, K. L. (Editors). African Material Culture. Bloomington: Indiana University Press.

Drewal, Margaret Thompson. (1992). **Yoruba Ritual: Performers, Play, Agency**. Bloomington, IN: Indiana University Press.

Dseagu, S. A. (1976). Proverbs and folktales of Ghana: Their form and uses. In J. M. Assimeng (Editor). **Traditional life, culture and literature in Ghana**. New York: Conch Magazine Limited.

Dumor, E. E. K. (1975). The huza as an indigenous cooperative institution and agricultural extension work in Somanya district. Paper presented at the Ghana Sociological Association Conference in Kumasi.

Dunn, J. S. (1960). Fante star lore. *Nigerian Field*, 25(2): 52-64.

Dupuis, J. (1824). **Journal of a residence in Ashantee**. London

Dzobo, N. K. (1992a). African symbols and proverbs as source of knowledge and truth. In Kwasi Wiredu and Kwame Gyekye (editors). **Person and community: Ghanaian philosophical studies**, I. Washington, D.C.: Council for Research in Values and Philosophy.

_____. (1992b). Values in a changing society, man, ancestors and God. In Kwasi Wiredu and Kwame Gyekye (editors). **Person and community: Ghanaian philosophical studies, I**. Washington, D.C.: Council for Research in Values and Philosophy.

Edelman, Murray (1988). **Constructing the political spectacle**. Chicago: University of Chicago Press.

_____. (1971). **Politics as symbolic action**. Chicago: Markham Publishing.

_____. (1964). **Symbolic uses of politics**. Urbana, Illinois: University of Illinois Press. Efa, Edwin (1968, 1944). *Forosie*, 11th Edition. Cape Coast: Methodist Book Depot.

Eglash, R. (1999). **African Fractals: Modern Computing and Indigenous Design**. Piscataway, NJ: Rutgers University Press.

Eglash, R., & Bennett, A. (2009). Teaching with Hidden Capital: Agency in Children's Computational Explorations of Cornrow Hairstyles. *Environments, 19*(1), 58-73. Retrieved from http://www.colorado.edu/journals/cye

Eglash, R., Bennett, A., O Donnell, C., Jennings, S., & Cintorino, M. (2006). Culturally situated design tools: Ethnocomputing from field site to classroom. *American Anthropologist, 108*, 347.

Ekem, John D. Kwamena (1994). Priesthood in context: A study of Akan traditional priesthood in dialogical relation to the priest-christology of the epistle to the Hebrews, and its implications for a relevant functional priesthood in selected churches among the Akan of Ghana. Doctoral dissertation, University of Hamburg, Hamburg, Germany.

Elder, Charles and Roger Cobb (1983). **The political uses of symbols**. New York: Longman. Ellis, A. B. (1964). **The Tshi-speaking peoples of the Gold Coast of West Africa: Their religion, manners, customs, laws, language, etc**. Chicago: Benin Press.

_____. (1969). **A history of the Gold Coast of West Africa**. New York: Negro University Press.

Ephrim-Donkor, Anthony S. (1994). African personality and spirituality: The Akanfo quest for perfection and immortality. Doctoral dissertation, Emory University, Atlanta, GA.

Erlich, Martha J. (1981). A catalogue of Ashanti art taken from Kumasi in the Anglo-Ashanti War of 1874. (Doctoral dissertation, Indiana University, Bloomington, Indiana). Fabian, Johannes. (1996). **Remembering the present: Painting and popular history in Zaire**. Berkeley and Los Angeles, CA: University of California Press.

Feinstein, H. (1982). Meaning and visual metaphor. **Studies in Art Education**, 23(2): 45-55.

Finkelstein, Joanne. (1991). **The Fashioned Self**. New York, NY: Cambridge University Press

Flood, J. Guest, D, Holmes, K.A., Keane, P., Padi, B., and Sulistyowati E. (2004) Cocoa under attack. In: J. Flood and R. Murphy. (Eds.). Cocoa Futures: A source book of some important issues facing the cocoa industry. Chinchina (Colombia): CABI-EDERACAFE.

Flood, J. and Murphy, R. (Eds). (2004) Cocoa Futures: A source book of some important issues facing the cocoa industry. Chinchina (Colombia): CABI- EDERACAFE

Folomkina, S. And H. Weiser (1963). **The learner's English-Russian dictionary.** Cambridge, Mass.: MIT Press.

Fromkin, V. and R. Rodman (1978). **An introduction to language,** 2nd Edition. New York: Holt, Rinehart and Winston.

Fortes, Meyer (1950). Kinship and marriage among the Ashanti. In A. R. Radcliffe-Brown and D. Forde (Editors). **African systems of kinship and marriage.** London: Oxford University Press. Fortes, M. and E. E. Evans-Pritchard. (1967). Eds. **African political systems.** New York: KPI.

Fraenkel, Gerd (1965). **Writing Systems.** Boston: Ginn and Company.

Fraser, Douglas (1972). The symbols of Ashanti kingship. In D. Fraser and H. Cole (Editors). **African art and leadership.** Madison: University of Wisconsin Press.

_____ and H. Cole (1972). Editors. **African art and leadership.** Madison: University of Wisconsin Press.

Frutiger, Adrian (1991). **Signs and symbols: Their design and meaning.** London: Studio Editions.

Fuller, Harcourt (2010). Building A Nation: Symbolic nationalism during the Kwame Nkrumah era in the Gold Coast/Ghana. Doctoral dissertation, London School of Economics.

Fynn, J. K. (1971). **Asante and its neighbours, 1700-1807.** London: Longman. Gallant, Thomas W. (1994). Turning the horns: Cultural metaphors, material conditions, and the peasant language of resistance in Ionian Islands (Greece) during the nineteenth century. **Society for Comparative Study of Society and History,** 36(4): 702-719.

Garrard, T. F. (1980). **Akan weights and the gold trade.** London: Longman.

Gates, (2010). Symbols of power: Adinkras and the nature of reality. Physics World, 23(6): 34-39. Gaur, Albertine (1992). A history of writing. New York: Cross River Press

Gelb, I. J. (1963). A Study of Writing, Chicago: Univveersity of Chicago Press.

Gerrard, A. (1981). **African language literatures: An introduction to literary history of sub-Saharan Africa.** Harlow, Essex, England: Longman.

Gilfoy, Peggy S. (1987). **Patterns of life: West African strip-weaving traditions.** Washington, D. C.: National Museum of African Art.

Glover, Ablade (1971). Adinkra symbolism (a chart). Accra: Liberty Press.

Gockowski, J. and Sonwa, D. (2007), "Biodiversity conservation and smallholder cocoa production systems in West Africa with particular reference to the Western Region of Ghana and the Bas Sassandra region of Côte d'Ivoire." http://www.odi.org.uk/events/2007/11/19/434- paper-discussion-biodiversity-conservation-smallholder-cocoa-production-systems west africa.pdf

Gonsalves, Peter. (2012). **Khadi: Gandhi's mega symbol of subversion.** New Delhi: Sage Publications.

_____. (2010). **Clothing for liberation – A communication analysis of Gandhi's Swadeshi Revolution.** New Delhi: Sage Publications. Goody, J. (1987). **The interface between the written and the oral.** Cambridge: Cambridge University Press.

_____. (1986). **The logic of writing and the organization of society.** Cambridge: Cambridge University Press

_____. (1977). **The domestication of the savage mind.** Cambridge: Cambridge University Press.

_____. (1968). Editor. **Literacy in traditional societies.** Cambridge: Cambridge University Press.

_____ and Watt. (1963). The consequences of literacy. **Comparative Studies in Society and History,** 5: 304-345.

Goody, J. (1987). The interface between the written and the oral. Cambridge: Cambridge University Press.

___ (1986). The logic of writing and the organization of society. Cambridge: Cambridge University Press.

___ (1977). The domestication of the savage mind. Cambridge: Cambridge University Press.

____ (1968). Editor. Literacy in traditional societies. Cambridge: Cambridge University Press.

Gott, Edith S. (1994). In celebration of the female: Dress, aesthetics, and identity in contemporary Asante. Doctoral dissertation, Indiana University, Bloomington, IN.

raffenried, Charlotte V. (1992). **Akan Goldgewichte im Bernishen Historischen Museum (Akan goldweights in the Berne Historical Museum)**. Bern: Bernisches Historisches Museum.

Gyekye, Kwame (1992). The Akan concept of a person. **International Philosophical Quarterly**, 18(3): 277-287.

_____. (1987). **An essay on African philosophical thought: The Akan conceptual scheme.** New York: Cambridge University Press.

Hagan, George P. (1970). A note on Akan colour symbolism. **Research Review**, 7(1): 8-13.

_____. (1971). Ashanti bureaucracy: A study of the growth of centralized administration in Ashanti from the time of Osei Tutu to the time of Osei Tutu Kwamina Esibe Bonsu. **Transactions of the Historical Society of Ghana**, 12: 43-62.

Hau, Kathleen (1973). Pre-Islamic writing in West, Africa. **Bulletin del'IFAN**, 35(Series b, 1): 1-45.

_____. (1967). The ancient writing of Southern Nigeria. **Bulletin del'IFAN**, 29(Series b, 1-2): 150-190.

_____. (1964). A royal title on a palace tusk from Benin (Southern Nigeria). **Bulletin del'IFAN**, 26(Series b, 1-2): 21-39.

_____. (1961). _Oberi Okaime_ script, texts, and counting system. **Bulletin del'IFAN**, 23(1-2): 291-308.

_____. (1959). Evidence of the use of pre-Portuguese written characters by the Bini? **Bulletin del'IFAN**, 21: 109-154.

Hayward, Fred M. And Ahmed R. Dumbuya (1984). Political legitimacy, political symbols, and national leadership in West Africa. **Journal of Modern African Studies**, 21(4): 645-671. Henige, David (1975). Akan stool succession under colonial rule - continuity or change? **Journal of African History**, 16(2): 285-301.

Hess, Janet (2001). Exhibiting Ghana: Display, documentary, and "national" art in the Nkrumah era. **African Studies Review**, 44(1): 57-77.

Hill, Archibald (1967). The typology of writing systems. In William Austin (Editor). Papers in Linguistics in honor of LeoDostert, pp. 93-99. The Hague: Monzon.

Hill, Polly (1963). **The migrant cocoa-farmers of Southern Ghana: A study in rural capitalism.** Cambridge: Cambridge University Press.

Hopkins, A. G. (1973). **An economic history of West Africa.** New York: Columbia University Press.

Howard, Rhonda (1978). **Colonialism and underdevelopment in Ghana.** New York: AfricanPublishing Company.

Jonah, Kwesi (1999). The C. P. P. and the Asafo Besuon: Why unlike poles did not attract. **Transactions of the Historical Society of Ghana.** New Series, 3: 47-56.

Kay, G. B. (1972). **The political economy of colonialism in Ghana: A collection of documents and statistics, 1900-1960.** Cambridge: Cambridge University Press.

Kayper-Mensah, A. W. (1976). **Sank_o_fa: Adinkra poems.** Accra: Ghana Publishing Corporation.

Kent, Kate (1971). **Introducing West African cloth.** Denver: Denver Museum of Natural History.

Kiyaga-Mulindwa, D. (1980). The "Akan" Problem. **Current Anthropology**, 21(4): 503-506.

Klaeger, Gabriel (2009). Religion on the road: The spiritual experience of road travel in Ghana. In Jan-Bart Gewald, Sabina Luning and Klaas van Walraven (Editors). The speed of change: Motor vehicles and people in Africa, 1890-2000. Leiden: Brill.

Klein, A. Norman (1996). Towards a new understanding of Akan origins. **Africa**, 66(2): 248-273.

Kquofi, Steve, Peace Amate and E. Tabi-Agyei (2013). Symbolic representation and socio-cultural significance of selected Akan proverbs in Ghana. Research in Humanities and Social Sciences, 3(1): 86-98.

Kramer, Fritz W. (1984). **Notizen zur Ehnologie der Passiones**. Institut fuer Ethnologie, Berlin.

Kreamer, Chistine Mullen (2007). **Inscribing Meaning: Writing and Graphic Systems in African Art**. Smithsonian National Museum of African Art, Washington, D. C.

Kruger, Kathryn S. (2001). **Weaving the word: The metaphorics of weaving and female textual production**. Selinsgrove: Susquehanna University Press.

Kumah, J. K. (1966). The rise and fall of Denkyira. **Ghana Notes and Queries**, 9: 33-35.

Kwakye-Opong, R. (2014) Clothing and Colour Symbolisms in the Homowo Festival: A means to sociocultural development. *Research on Humanities and Social Sciences*. 4(13), 113

Kyerematen, A. A. Y. (1964). **Panoply of Ghana: Ornamental art in Ghanaian tradition and culture** New York: Praeger.

_____. (n.d.). **Kingship and ceremony in Ashanti**. Kumasi: UST Press.

_____. (1971). Interstate boundary litigation in Ashanti. In **African Social Research Documents**, Volume 14.

La Torre, Joseph R. (1978). Wealth surpasses everything. Doctoral dissertation, University of California, Berkeley, CA.

Labi, Kwame Amoah. (2009). "Reading the intangible heritage in tangible Akan Art." **International Journal of Intangible Heritage** 4: 42-57.

Labi, Kwame Amoah (1998). Fights, riots, and disturbances with 'objectionable and provocative art' among the Fante Asafo companies. **Transactions of the Historical Society of Ghana**. New Series, 2: 101-116.

Laluah, Aquah (1960). The serving girl. In Langston Hughes (editor). **An African treasury**. New York: Pyramid Books.

Lamb, Venice (1975). **West African weaving**. London: Duckworth.

Law, Robin (1995). Editor. **From slave trade to 'legitimate' commerce: The commercial Transition in nineteenth-century West Africa**. Cambridge: Cambridge University Press.

Lewin, Thomas J. (1978). **Asante before the British: The Prempean years, 1875-1900**.

Lawrence, KS: The Regents Press of Kansas.

Libby, Ron T. (1976). External Co-optation of a Less Developed Country's Policy Making: The Case of Ghana, 1969-1972. **World Politics**, 29(1): 67-89.

Liberman, I. Y. and A. M. Liberman (1992). Whole language vs code emphasis. In P. B. Gough, L. C, Ehri and R. Treiman (Editors). **Reading acquisition**. Hillsdale, NJ: Erlbaum.

Lystad, Robert A. (1958). **The Ashanti: A proud people**. New York: Greenwood Press.

Magnarella, Paul J. (2001). Assessing the concept of human rights in Africa. **Human Rights and Human Welfare**, Vol 1 & 2: 25-27.

Manuh, Takyiwaa. (1988). The Asantehemaa's court and its jurisdiction over women: A study in legal pluralism. **Research Review** (NS), 4(2): 150-166.

Mason, William A. (1928). **A history of the art of writing**. New York: McMillan Company.

Mato, Daniel (1986). Clothed in symbols - the art of Adinkra among the Akan of Ghana. Doctoral dissertation, Department of Fine Arts, Indiana University, Bloomington, IN. McCaskie, T. C. (1989). Death and the Asantehene: A historical meditation. **Journal of African History**, 30: 417-444.

_____. (1986). Komfo Anokye of Asante: The meaning, history and philosophy in an African society. **Journal of African History**, 27: 315-339.

_____. (1984). Ahyiamu – "a place of meeting": An essay on process and event in the history of the Asante state. **Journal of African History**, 25(2): 169-188.

_____. (1983). Accumulation, wealth and belief in Asante history, I: To the close of the nineteenth century. **Africa**, 53(1): 23-43.

_____. (1981). State and society, marriage and adultery: Some considerations towards a social history of pre-colonial Asante. **Journal of African History**, 22: 477-494. McGuire, Harriet C. (1980). Woyo pot lids, **African Arts**, 13(2): 54-56. McLeod, M. D. (1981). **The Asante**. London: British Museum.

_____. (1976). Verbal elements in West African art. **Quaderni Poro**, 1: 85-102.

McWilliam, H. O. A. and M. A. Kwamena-Poh (1978). **The development of education in Ghana**. London: Longman.

Mensah, K. (2009). Symbolically speaking: The use of semiotics in marketing politics in Ghana. **Identity, Culture and Politics: An afro-Asian Dialogue**, 10(1): 75-89

Mensah, J. E. (1992). **Asantesɛm ne mmɛbusɛm bi**. Kumasi, Ghana: Catholic Press.

Mensah, Owusu. 1977. Prince Owusu Ansah and Asante-British Diplomacy 1841-1884. Diss. University of Wisconsin.

Mensah-Brown, A.K. (1976). The Nature of Akan Native Law: A Critical Analysis. In *Traditional Life, Culture, and Literature in Ghana*. Ed. J.M. Assimeng. New York: Conch Magazine. Pp. 137-64.

Menzel, B. (1972). **Textile aus Westafrika, Vols. I, II, III**. Berlin: Museum fur Volkerkunde.

Meyerowitz, Eva L. R. (1962). **At the court of an African king**. London: Faber and Faber.

_____. (1952). **The Akan traditions of origin**. London: Faber and Faber.

_____. (1951). **The sacred state of the Akan**. London: Faber & Faber.

Minkus, Helaine K. (1980). The concept of spirit in Akwapim Akan philosophy. **Africa**, 50(2): 182-192. National Museum of African Art. (1997). **Adinkra: The cloth that speaks**. Washington, D.C.: National Museum of African Art.

Niangoran-Bouah, G. (1984). **L'univers Akan des poids a peser l'or, Volumes I, II, & III**. Abidjan, Cote d'Ivoire: Les Nouvelles Editions Africaines.

Ninsin, Kwame A. (1991). **The informal sector in Ghana's political economy**. Freedom Publication, Accra, Ghana.

Nketia, J. H. (1974). *Ayan*. Accra: Ghana Publishing Corporation.

_____. (1969). **Funeral dirges of the Akan people**. New York: Negro Universities Press.

Nketsia V, Nana Kobina (2009). The ancestors and nation-building: Aluta continua. Speech delivered at the Seminar on The Contemporary Relevance of Tradition I.

Obeng, Ernest E. (1988). **Ancient Ashanti chieftancy**. Tema: Ghana Publishing Corporation. Obeng, J. Pashington (1995). Asante women dancers: Architects of power realignment in Corpus Christi. Boston: African Studies Center, Boston University.

_____. (1991). Asante Catholicism: Ritual communication of the Catholic faith among the Akan Of Ghana. Doctoral dissertation, Boston University.

Ofori-Ansah, Kwaku (1978). Symbols of adinkra cloth (a chart). Washington, D.C.: Department of

Art, Howard University.

_____ (1993). Symbols of adinkra cloth (a chart). Hyattsville, MD. USA

Ollenu, L. A. A, Owusu, G. K. and Thresh, J. M. (1989) Spread of cocoa swollen shoot vim to recent plantings in Ghana. *Crop Protection* 8: 251-264.

Ollenu, N. A. (1962). **Principles of customary land law in Ghana.** London: Sweet & Maxwell.

Ong, Walter J. (1982). *Orality and Literacy: The Technologizing of the Word.* New York: Methuen

Opoku, Kofi Asare (1976). The destiny of man in Akan traditional religious thought. In J. M. Asimeng (Editor). **Traditional life, culture and literature in Ghana.** New York: Conch Magazine Limited.

_____. (1978). **West African traditional religion.** Accra: FEP International.

Oppong, Christine (1973). **Growing up in Dagbon.** Accra: Ghana Publishing Corporation.

Oroge, E. A. A. (1974). The rise and fall of the Asante. **Tarikh** 5(1): 31-45.

Ott, Albert (1968). Akan gold weights. **Transactions of the Historical Society of Ghana**, 9: 17-42.

Ott, J. Steven (1989). **The organizational culture perspective.** Chicago: Dorsey Press.

Owoahene-Acheampong, Stephen (1998). **Inculturation and Africa religion: Indigenous and Western approaches to medical practice.** New York: Peter Lang.

Owusu-Ansah, Nana J. V. (1992). **New versions of the traditional motifs.** Kumasi: deGraft Graphics and Publications.

Padi, Beatrice and G. K. Owusu (2014). Towards an integrated pest management for sustainable cocoaproduction in Ghana. http://nationalzoo.si.edu/scbi/migratorybirds/research/cocoa/padi.cfm

Padi, B., Ackonor, J. B., Abitey, M.A., Owusu, E. B., Fofie, A. and Asante E. (2000) Report on the Insecticide Use and Residues in Cocoa Beans in Ghana. Internal Report submitted to the Ghana Cocoa Board.

Padi, B., Downham, M., Farman. D. I. and Sarfo, J. E. (2001) Evidence of sex attractants in the cocoa mirids *Distanliella theobrama* (Dist) and *Sahlbergrlla singularis* Hagl. (Heteroptera: Mridae) in field-trapping experiments. In: Proceedings of the 1 3Ih International Cocoa Conference, Kota Kinabalu, Saba, Malaysia, 9-14 October2000,395-402 pp.

Padi, B., Ackonor, J. B., and Opoku I. Y. (2002) Cocoa IPM Research and Implementation in Ghana. Pages 54-62 In: J. Vos, and P. Neuenschwander, (Eds.) Proceedings of the West African Regional Cocoa IPM Workshop, Cotonou, Benin, 13-15 November 2001. Newbury (UK): CPL Press.

Patton, Sharon (1984). The Asante umbrella. **African Arts**, 7(4): 64-73, 93-94.

_____. (1980). The Asante stool. Doctoral dissertation, Northwestern University, Evanston, Illinois.

_____. (1979). The stool and Asante chieftancy. **African Arts**, 13(1): 74-77, 98.

Peirce, C. S. (1931-58): *Collected Writings* (8 Vols.). (Ed. Charles Hartshorne, Paul Weiss & Arthur W Burks). Cambridge, MA: Harvard University Press

Picton, John M. (1979). **African textiles.** London: British Museum.

_____. (1992). Tradition, technology, and lurex: Some comments on textile history and design in West Africa. In National Museum of African Art. **History, design, and craft in West African strip-woven cloth.** Washington, D. C.: National Museum of African Art.

Plass, Margaret W. (1967). **African miniatures: Goldweights of the Ashanti.** New York: Praeger.

Platvoet, J. G. (1985). Cool shade, peace and power: The gyedua (tree of reception) as an ideological instrument of identity among the Akan peoples of Southern Ghana. **Journal of Religion in Africa**, 15(3): 174-200.

Polakoff, Claire (1982). **African textiles and dyeing techniques.** London: Routledge and Kegan Paul.

Posnansky, M. (1987). Prelude to Akan civilization. In Enid Schildkrout (Editor). **The Golden Stool: Studies of the Asante center and periphery.** New York: American Museum of Natural History.

Preston, George Nelson (1973). Twifo-Heman and the Akan art-leadership complex of Ghana. Doctoral dissertation, Columbia University, New York.

Quarcoo, A. K. (1994). **The language of adinkra patterns**, 2nd edition. Legon, Ghana: Sebewie Ventures.

_____. (1972). **The language of adinkra patterns.** Legon, Ghana: Institute of African Studies.

_____. (1968). A debut of Ghanaian traditional visual art into liturgical art of the Christian church of Ghana. **Research Review**, 4: 53-64.

Ramseyer, F. A. and J. Kuhne. (1875). **Four years in Ashantee.** New York: R. Carter & Bros.

Rattray, R. S. (1969a). **Ashanti law and constitution.** New York: Negro Universities Press.

_____. (1969b). **Ashanti Proverbs.** Oxford: Clarendon Press.

_____. (1927). **Religion and art in Ashanti.** London: Oxford University Press.

_____. (1923). **Ashanti.** London: Oxford University Press.

Reindorf, C. C. (1895). A history of the Gold Coast and Asante. Basel: Basel Mission.

Renne, Elisha (1996). **Cloth That Does Not Die: The Meaning of Cloth in Bunu Social Life.** Seattle, WA: University of Washington Press.

Reynolds, Edward (1973). Agricultural adjustments on the Gold Coast after the end of the slave trade, 1807-1874. **Agricultural History**, 47(4): 308-318.

Ritzer, George (1992). **Contemporary sociological theory**, 3rd Edition. New York: McGraw Hill.

Roach, Mary Ellen, and Joan Eicher (Eds.). 1965. **Dress, Adornment, and the Social Order.** New York, NY: John Wiley.

Robertson, A. F. (1982). Abusa: The structural history of an economic contract. **Journal of Developing Studies**, 18(4): 447-478.

Robinson, Andrew. (2009). Writing and script: A very short description. Oxford: Oxford University Press.

Rosenstein, D. and H. Oster (1988). Differential facial responses to four basic tastes in newborns. **Child Development**, 59: 1555-1568.

Ross, D. H. (1998). Wrapped in pride: Ghanaian kente and African American Identity. Los Angeles: UCLA Fowler Museum of Cultural History.

_____. (1988). Queen Victoria for twenty-five pounds: The iconography of a breasted drum from Southern Ghana. Art Journal, 47(2): 114-120.

_____. (1984). The art of Osei Bonsu. African Arts, 17(2): 28-40, 90.

_____. 1982. "The Verbal Art of the Akan Linguist Staffs." *African Arts 16:1, pp. 56-67.*

_____. (1981). The Heraldic Lion in Akan Art: A Study of Motif Assimilation in Southern Ghana. Metropolitan Museum Journal, 16: 165-180.

Ross, Doran H. (1977). The iconography of Asante sword ornaments. **African Arts**, 11(1): 16-25, 90.

Rovine, Victoria (1997). Bogolan fini in Bamako: The Biography of a Malian Textile. African Arts: 30(1): 40-51, notes 94.

Rowlands, Michael (1996). The Consumption of an African Modernity. In African Material Culture. Mary Jo Arnoldi, Christraud Geary, and Kris Hardin, eds. pp. 145-166. Bloomington, IN: Indiana University Press.

Saah, Kofi. (1986). "Language Use and Attitudes in Ghana." *Anthropological Linguistics* 28. pp. 367- 77.

Sarbah, J. Mensah (1906). **Fanti national constitution.** London: William Clowes & Sons Ltd.

Sarpong, Peter (1990). **The ceremonial horns of the Ashanti.** Accra: Sedco Publishing.

_____. (1977). **Girls' nubility rites in Ashanti**. Tema: Ghana Publishing Corporation.

_____. (1974). **Ghana in retrospect: Some aspects of Ghanaian culture**. Tema: Ghana Publishing Corporation.

_____. (1972). Aspects of Akan ethics. **Ghana Bulletin of Theology**, 4(3): 40-44.

_____. (1971). **The sacred stools of the Akan**. Tema, Ghana: Ghana Publishing Corporation.

Saussure, F. de (1916 - 1983): *Course in General Linguistics* (trans. Roy Harris). London: Duckworth

Schildkrout, Enid. (1987). Editor. **The Golden Stool: Studies of the Asante center and periphery**. New York: American Museum of Natural History.

Schneider, Jane (1987). The anthropology of cloth. **Annual Review of Anthropology**, 16: 409-448.

Schneider, Jane and Annette B. Weiner (1989). Introduction. In Schneider, Jane and Annette B. Weiner (Editors). **Cloth and human experience**. Washington, D. C.: Smithsonian Institution Press.

Scribner, S. and Cole, M. (1981). **The psychology of literacy**. Cambridge, MA.: Harvard University Press.

Silver, Harry R. (1980). The culture of carving and the carving of culture: Content and context in artisan status among the Ashanti. **American Ethnologist**, 3(4): 432-446.

Simmel, George. (1957) [1904]. Fashion. The American Journal of Sociology, 62: 541-558.

Smith, Robert. (1976). Warfare and Diplomacy in Pre-Colonial West Africa. London: Methuen.

_____ (1970). The Canoe in West African History. Journal of African History, XI(4): 515-533.
Smolkin, Laura B. And David B. Yaden, Jr. (1992). O is for mouse: First encounters with the alphabet book. **Language Arts**, 69: 432-441. Spencer, Ann. (1982). In Praise of Heroes: Contemporary African Commemorative Cloth. Newark: Newark Museum.

Storm, Penny. (1987). **Functions of dress: Tools of culture and the individual**. Englewood Cliffs, NJ: Prentice Hall.

Street, B. V. and N. Besnier (1994). Aspects of literacy. In Tim Ingold (Editor). Companion Encyclopedia of Anthropology: Humanity, Culture, and Social Life. London: Routeledge.

Strother, Z. S. (1995). Invention and Reinvention in the Traditional Arts. **African Arts**, 23(2): 24-33, notes 90.

Sutherland-Addy, Esi (1998). Discourse and Asafo: The place of oral literature. **Transactions of the Historical Society of Ghana**. New Series, 2: 87-100.

Szereszewski, Robert (1966). Regional aspects of the structure of the economy. In W. B. Birmingham, I. Neustadt and E. N. Omaboe (Editors). **A study of contemporary Ghana,** I: The economy of Ghana. London: Allen and Unwin.

Tarlo, Emma. (1996). Clothing Matters: Dress and Identity in India. London:

Teal, F., Zeitlin, A. and Maamah, H. (2006) *Ghana Cocoa Farmers Survey 2004: Report to Ghana Cocoa Board*. Centre for the Study of African Economies, Oxford University.

Thompson, Robert F. (1974). **African art in motion**. Los Angeles: University of California Press.

Tordoff, William. (1965). **Ashanti under the Prempehs, 1888-1935**. London: Oxford University Press.

Tsien, Tsuen-Hsuin (1962). Written on bamboo and silk: The beginnings of Chinese books and inscriptions. Chicago: University of Chicago Press.

Tufuo, J. W. and Donkor, C. E. (1989). **Ashantis of Ghana: People with a soul**. Accra: Anowuo Educational Publications.

Van Der Geest, Sjaak (1998). *Yebisa Wo Fie*: Growing old and building a house in the Akan culture of Ghana. **Journal of Cross-Cultural Gerontology**, 13: 333-359.

Vigneri M. (2008), "Drivers of change in Ghana's cocoa sector". IFPRI-GSSP Background Paper n. 13. International Food Policy Research Institute. Vigneri M., Teal F., Maamah, H. (2004), "Coping with Market Reforms: Winners and Losers among Ghanaian Cocoa Farmer". Report to the Ghana Cocoa Board. Vogel, Susan (1988). Art/artifact. African art in Anthropology Collections. New York, NY: Center for African Art.

Wallerstein, Immanuel (1960). Ethnicity and National Integration in West Africa. **Cahiers d'Etudes Africanies** 3: 129-39.

Ward, W. E. F. (1991). **My Africa**. Accra: Ghana Universities Press.

_____. (1958). **A history of Ghana**. London: George Allen & Unwin.

Warren, Dennis M. (1990). **Akan arts and aesthetics: elements of change in a Ghanaian Indigenous knowledge system**. The Netherlands: Institute of Cultural and Social Studies.

Warren, Dennis M. (1976). Bibliography and vocabulary of the Akan (Twi-Fante) language of Ghana. Bloomington: Indiana University Research Center for language Semiotic Studies. Webster, J. B. and A. A. Boahen (1970). **History of West Africa**. New York: Praeger. Wilks, Ivor (1993). **Forests of gold: Essays on the Akan and the Kingdom of Asante**. Athens, OH: Ohio University Press.

_____. (1992). On mentally mapping Greater Asante: A study of time and motion. **Journal of African History**, 33: 175-190.

_____. (1982). Wangara, Akan and Portuguese in the fifteenth and sixteenth centuries, I. The matter of Bitu. **Journal of African History**, 23(3): 333-349.

_____. (1975). **Asante in the nineteenth century: The structure and evolution of a political order**. New York: Cambridge University Press.

_____. (1962). The Mande loan element in Twi. **Ghana Notes and Queries**, 4: 26-28.

Williams, Tracy. (2009). An African success story: Ghana's Cocoa Marketing System. IDS Working Paper 318. Institute of Development Studies, University of Sussex, Brighton, UK.

Willis, Elizabeth A. (1987). A lexicon of Igbo Uli motifs. **Nsukka Journal of the Humanities**, 1: 91-120.

Willis, W. Bruce (1998). The Adinkra Dictionary: A Visual Primer on the Language of Adinkra. Washington, DC: The Pyramid Complex.

Wingo, Ajume, (2008), "Akan Philosophy of the Person", *The Stanford Encyclopedia of Philosophy* (Fall 2008 Edition), Edward N. Zalta (ed.), URL = <http://plato.stanford.edu/archives/fall2008/entries/akan-person/>.

Wolfson, Freda (1953). A price agreement on the Gold Coast - The Krobo oil boycott, 1858-1866. **Economic History Review**, 2nd Series, 6(1): 68-77.

Yankah, Kwesi (1995). **Speaking for the chief: Okyeame and the politics of Akan royal oratory**. Bloomington: Indiana University Press.

_____. (1989a). **The proverb in the context of Akan rhetoric: A theory of proverb praxis**. Bern, Germany: Peter Lang.

_____. (1989b). Proverbs: The Aesthetics of Traditional Communication. Research in African Literatures, 20 (3): 325-346.

_____. (1985a). The Making and Breaking of Kwame Nkrumah: The Role of Oral Poetry. Journal of African Studies, 12(2): 86-92.

_____. (1985b). Risks in Verbal Art Performance. Journal of Folklore Research, 22 (2/3): 133-53.

_____. (1983). To Praise or Not to Praise the King: The Akan Apae in the Context of Referential Poetry. Research in African Literatures 14(3): 382-400.

Yarak, Larry W. (1986). Elmina and Greater Asante in the nineteenth century. **Africa**, 56(1): 33-52.

Yarwood, D. (1992). Fashion in the western world: 1500-1990. London: B. T. Batsford Limited.

Zaslavsky, Claudia (1973). Africa counts: Number and pattern in African culture. Chicago: Lawrence Hill Books.

A CATALOGUE OF ADINKRA SYMBOLS
OF THE AKAN OF GHANA

 1 2	**ABƆDE SANTANN – TOTALITY OF THE UNIVERSE** Symbol of the **TOTALITY OF THE UNIVERSE - NATURAL AND SOCIAL CREATION** From the expression: *Abɔde santaan yi firi tete, firi Ɔdomankoma; Ɔdomankoma bɔɔ adeɛ; ɔbɔɔ awia, ɔsrane ne nsoromma, ɔbɔɔ nsuo ne mframa; ɔbɔɔ nkwa, ɔbɔɔ nipa, na ɔbɔɔ owuo. Ɔte ase daa.* Literal translation: This paranoma of creation dates from time immemorial; it dates from God, the Creator; He created the sun, the moon and the stars, the rain and the wind; He created life, the human being, and He created death. He lives for ever. The symbol incorporates the eye, the rays of the sun, the double crescent moon, and the stool. The sun, the moon, and the eyes depict natural creation by a supreme being. While the stool depicts the socially created institutions and the creativity of human beings.
 3 4 5 6  7 8 9 10 11	**GYE NYAME – EXCEPT GOD** Symbol of the **OMNIPOTENCE and the OMNIPRESENCE OF GOD** From the Akan aphorism: *Abɔde santaan yi firi tete; obi nte ase a onim n'ahyease, na obi ntena ase nkosi n'awie, GYE NYAME.* Literal translation: This great panorama of creation dates back to time immemorial; no one lives who saw its beginning and no one will live to see its end, EXCEPT GOD. The symbol reflects the Akan belief of a SUPREME BEING, the CREATOR who they refer to by various names - e.g., *Ɔboadeɛ, Nyame, Onyankopɔn, Twedeampɔn.*

12	**NSATEA KORO – ONE FINGER** Symbol of the **OMNIPOTENCE OF GOD** From the expression: *Gye Nyame, mensuro obiara. Or, Nsateaa koro ntumi nkukuru adeɛ.* Literal translation: Except God, I fear no one. Or, One finger does not lift things up. This symbol has the same meaning as the *Gye Nyame* (Except God) symbol. Or one person should not be asked to bear responsibilities alone.
13	**NYAME YƐ ƆHENE – GOD IS KING** Symbol of the **MAJESTY OF GOD; SUPREMACY** and **PREEMINENCE OF GOD** From the expression: *Nyame yɛ ɔhene.* Literal translation: God is King.
14 15	**ƆDOMANKOMA – CREATOR** Symbol of the **CREATOR OF THE UNIVERSE** and **DIVINE POWER** From the expression: *Ɔdomankoma a ɔbɔɔ adeɛ ɔno na nsɛm nyinaa firi no.* Literal translation; God the Creator, all things depend on Him. This symbol is often incorporated in the pendant called *adaeboɔ* that forms part of the necklace (*ayanneɛ*) the king wears.
16	**SORO NE ASAASE – HEAVEN AND EARTH** Symbol of **INDIVISIBILITY, CONNECTEDNESS** and **UNITY** From the expression: *Asaase trɛ, na Onyame ne panin.* Also, *Nnipa nyinaa yɛ Onyame mma, obi nyɛ asaase ba.* Literal translation: Of all earth, God the Creator is the elder. Also, All people are children of the Supreme Being, God and no one is the child of the earth.
17	**PURU – CIRCLE** Symbol of the **OMNIPOTENT GOD, DIVINE POWER, ROYALTY,** and **THE SPIRIT OF GOD** From the expression: *Ɔsrane abɔ puru.* Literal translation: The moon is in full circle. The circle, with a point at the center, represents the turning universe and its pivotal point. The beginning and the end of the circle, like the creation of the universe, are only known to the **CREATOR**.

18 19	**ONYANKOPƆN ANIWA – GOD'S EYES** Symbol of **GOD'S ABILITY TO BE IN ALL PLACES, UBIQUITOUS NATURE OF GOD, EVER PRESENT GOD, and OMNIPOTENCE** From the expression: *Onyankopɔn afa boɔ sɛ ɔreto abɔ wo, wose merekɔtɛ. Also, Onyame yɛ ahuntahunii; Bɛakyihunadeɛ Nyame, onim asumasɛm biara.* Literal translation: When God attempts to throw a pebble at you, you say you are going to hide. Also, God sees all things; God the Creator is all-seeing and is everywhere. There is nothing that can be hidden from the Creator. No one can hide from God.
20 21	**HANN NE SUM – DAY AND NIGHT** Symbol of **DUALISM, ORDERLINESS, DARKNESS AND BRIGHTNESS**, and **TIME** From the aphorism*: Hann ne sum yɛ Nyame nhyehyɛɛ; adeɛkye na adeɛsa nyina na mmere na ɛkɔ ne no; wobɛyɛ biribi a, yɛ no prɛko na nimpa nte hɔ daa.* Literal translation: Day and night is part of God's order; the recurring day and night phenomenon reflects the passage of time; if you have something to do, do it now for one will not live forever. The Akan belief system has it that God's time is based on the concept of nna mere nsɔn (seven-day time). Hence another name Akan have for God is Abɔ-nna-nsɔn (Creator of Seven Days). The seven days are each ruled by a planet as follows: Kwasiada (Sunday), the day of Ayisi (Awusi, Awisi), is ruled by the Sun; Dwoada (Monday), the day of Awo, is ruled by the Moon; Benada (Tuesday) is the day of Abena (Mars); Wukuda (Wednesday) is the day of Aku (Mercury); Yoada (Yaada, Yawda – Thursday) is the day of Aberao (Aberaw - Jupiter); Fida (Fiada – Friday) is the day of Afi (Venus); and Memeneda (Saturday) is the day of Amene (Saturn*).*
22 23 24	**MMERAMUTENE – MALE CROSS** Symbol of the **SUNLIGHT, WARMTH, ENDURANCE**, and **UPRIGHTNESS**
25 26 27 28	**MMERAMUBERE – FEMALE CROSS** Symbol of **WARMTH, SUNSHINE** and **VITALITY**

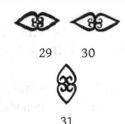 29 30 31	**ASAASE YƐ DUR - LAND IS MIGHTY** Symbol of **POWER, LIFE'S SUSTAINER, MIGHT, WEALTH, and AUTHORITY** From the maxim: *Tumi nyinaa ne asaase.* Or, *Asaase nyɛ kɛtɛ na yɛabobɔ.* Literal translation: All power emanates from land. Or, The earth is not a mat that we can fold. This symbol reflects the importance of land to the Akan. Even though land is communally owned among the Akan, land ownership by group or individuals is an important source of economic and political power. The Akan consider *asaase* (land) as the physical and feminine aspect of the dualistic nature of the universe. God, the Creator is the spiritual and masculine aspect of this duality. Hence, the Akan refer to *asaase* as **Asaase Yaa** (among the Twi-speaking Akan) or **Asaase Afua** (among the Fantse-speaking Akan), and God as **Kwame**.
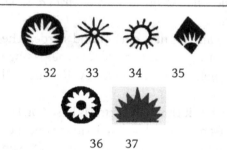 32 33 34 35 36 37	**AWIA REPUE - RISING SUN** Symbol of **VITALITY, LIFE SPARK, WARMTH, and ENERGY** From the maxim: *Ɔhene yɛ awia.* Or, *Awia repue,* Also, *Owia mu nni aduosɔn anum.* Literal translation: The king is the sun. God is king. Or, The sun is rising. Also, The sun does not have seventy-five parts. One cannot divide truth. God is referred to as **OMAWIA - SOURCE OF THE SUN'S ENERGY and VITAL FORCE.** This symbol became associated with the Progress Party in the 1969 general parliamentary elections in Ghana. To the Progress Party this symbolized the rising sun (*awia repue*) as an indication of progress.
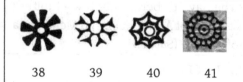 38 39 40 41	**ANANSE NTONTAN – SPIDER'S WEB** Symbol of **CUNNING, INTELLIGENCE, CRAFTINESS, CREATIVITY, SHREWDNESS,** and **SAGACITY** From the maxim: *Nyame ne Ananse Kokuroko.* Literal translation: God is the Great Spider. The spider is a principal character in Akan folk stories called Anansesɛm (Spider Stories). The stories teach that God gave Ananse the meaning of order and God taught Ananse architecture, the structure of dwellings, and the structure of life and society. This perspective is symbolized by the spider's web, which also stands for the sun and its rays and the vitality and creative powers of God. In some stories God is referred to as Ananse Kokuroko (the Great Spider). Only the spider knows the beginning and the end of its creation, the web. Similarly, only God knows the beginning and the end of His creation. God's creation may be said to have the characteristics of the spider's web: orderliness, balance, systemic, and intelligence.

42 43	**SUNSUM or NTORƆ - SOUL** Symbol of **SPIRITUAL PURITY, and CLEANLINESS OF THE SOUL** The Akan belief is that *Sunsum* is the part of ɔbɔadeɛ (God the Creator) that enters the human being at birth with the first breath. This *sunsum* is partly transmitted through the father to the child. While the male is capable of transmitting his sunsum to his offspring, the female cannot transmit her sunsum to her offspring. She transmits her blood (*mogya*) to her offspring.
44	**MEDA AYEYA – BEING IN SUPINE POSITION** Symbol of **SKEPTICISM, DISBELIEF, and UNCERTAINTY** From the proverb: *Me a meda ayeya menhu Nyame a, na wo a wubutu hɔ.* Literal translation: I lay face upwards and I couldn't see God, how much more you lying face down.
45 46	**ANYINAM NE APRANAA – THUNDER AND LIGHTNING** Symbol of the **FIRE OF THE SKY, DESTRUCTION, PURITY, FLAME, VITALITY, and RENEWAL** From the aphorism: *Sɛ anyinam te yerɛw ma apranaa bobɔ mu a, kae sɛ Onyame yɛ kɛse.* Literal translation: When it is thundering and lightning, remember God is great.

47   48

49   50

NSUO – WATER

Symbol of FERTILITY, FRUITFULNESS, VITALITY, LIFE FORCE and FECUNDITY

From the expression: *Ɔkwan atware asuo, asuo atware ɔkwan; ɔpanin ne hwan? Yɛbɔɔ kwan no ɛkɔtoo asuo; asuo no firi tete. Anaaso, Sɛ ebinom nnya nsuo nnom na wonya bi dware a, kae sɛ Onyanme yɛ hene. Anaaso, Bea a nsuo wɔ no hɔ na nkwa wɔ. Anaaso, Toturobonsu Nyame, ɔno na ɔgu ahina hunuu mu nsuo.*

Literal translation: The path crosses the river and the river crosses the path; who is the elder? When we made the path to cross the river, the river was existing already from time immemorial. Or, If some people cannot have water drink, but you have some water to take your bath with, remember God is King. Also, Where there is water there is bound to be life. Also, God the giver of rain, he fills the pot of the poor with water. One interpretation of this symbol poses the question: the river and the path which was created first? Obviously, the river as God's creation preceded the path which is a human creation. The symbol also forms part of the Akan's explanation of the origins of the universe. Water was one of God's first creations. Water is also considered the source of life and vitality and fertility. Water makes the earth fruitful, and water sustains plant and animal life. God as Rain giver (Toturobonsu) is the source of life and fertility.

51   52   53   54

HYE ANHYE - UNBURNABLE

Symbol of the **IMPERISHABILITY OF THE SELF, PERMANENCY OF THE HUMAN SOUL and TOUGHNESS**

From the expression: *Onyankopɔn nkum wo na ɔdasani kum wo a, wo nwu da.*

Literal translation: Unless you die of God, let a living person kill you, and you will not perish.

This represents the idea that GOD, the SPIRIT, never dies, or GOD lives forever. The Akan belief is that the human soul, an image of God, the Spirit, lives in perpetuity. Thus, there is life after the death of the physical part of the human being.

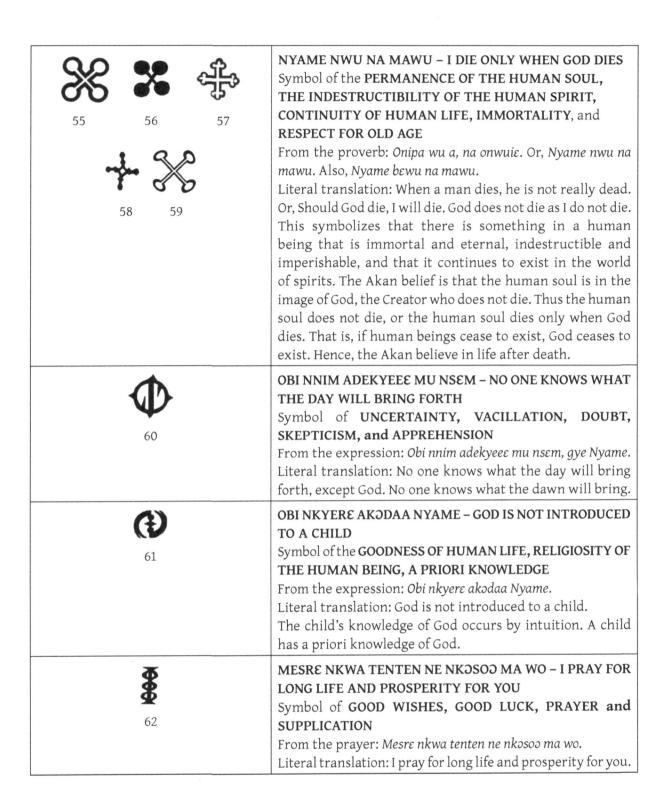

55 56 57 **58 59**	**NYAME NWU NA MAWU – I DIE ONLY WHEN GOD DIES** Symbol of the **PERMANENCE OF THE HUMAN SOUL, THE INDESTRUCTIBILITY OF THE HUMAN SPIRIT, CONTINUITY OF HUMAN LIFE, IMMORTALITY,** and **RESPECT FOR OLD AGE** From the proverb: *Onipa wu a, na onwuiε.* Or, *Nyame nwu na mawu.* Also, *Nyame bεwu na mawu.* Literal translation: When a man dies, he is not really dead. Or, Should God die, I will die. God does not die as I do not die. This symbolizes that there is something in a human being that is immortal and eternal, indestructible and imperishable, and that it continues to exist in the world of spirits. The Akan belief is that the human soul is in the image of God, the Creator who does not die. Thus the human soul does not die, or the human soul dies only when God dies. That is, if human beings cease to exist, God ceases to exist. Hence, the Akan believe in life after death.
60	**OBI NNIM ADEKYEEε MU NSεM – NO ONE KNOWS WHAT THE DAY WILL BRING FORTH** Symbol of **UNCERTAINTY, VACILLATION, DOUBT, SKEPTICISM, and APPREHENSION** From the expression: *Obi nnim adekyeeε mu nsεm, gye Nyame.* Literal translation: No one knows what the day will bring forth, except God. No one knows what the dawn will bring.
61	**OBI NKYERε AKɔDAA NYAME – GOD IS NOT INTRODUCED TO A CHILD** Symbol of the **GOODNESS OF HUMAN LIFE, RELIGIOSITY OF THE HUMAN BEING, A PRIORI KNOWLEDGE** From the expression: *Obi nkyerε akɔdaa Nyame.* Literal translation: God is not introduced to a child. The child's knowledge of God occurs by intuition. A child has a priori knowledge of God.
62	**MESRε NKWA TENTEN NE NKɔSOɔ MA WO – I PRAY FOR LONG LIFE AND PROSPERITY FOR YOU** Symbol of **GOOD WISHES, GOOD LUCK, PRAYER and SUPPLICATION** From the prayer: *Mesrε nkwa tenten ne nkɔsoɔ ma wo.* Literal translation: I pray for long life and prosperity for you.

63   64   65   66

67   68   69   70

71

NYAME DUA – GOD'S ALTAR
Symbol of the **PRESENCE OF GOD, GOD'S PROTECTION, HOLY PLACE, and SPIRITUALITY**
From the proverb: *Nyamedua yɛmpae mu.*
Literal translation: We do not split Nyamedua into two. God's presence is indivisible.
The symbol represents God's presence everywhere and every time. The Akan used to place the God's altar in front of the house as a sign of God's presence and protection.

72   73   74   75   76

77   78   79

80

KERAPA - SANCTITY
Symbol of **SANCTITY OF SELF, SPIRITUAL STRENGTH, GOOD SPIRIT, GOOD LUCK, and GOOD FORTUNE**
From the aphorism: *Kerapa yɛ Nyame ahoboa: ɔte sɛ ɔkra, okyiri fi na ɔkram fie te sɛ pete nti na Nananom de no yi mmusuo.*
Literal translation: Sanctity is part particle of the good; it is like a cat, it abhors filth; and it clears filth like the vulture does; that is why it is used to drive away evil and diseases. This symbol was woven into the bedside mat on which the king would step three times for good luck before going to bed. Every year, a cleaning ritual (**mmusuyidee**) was performed in the past. During the ceremony all streets of the townships were swept clean each morning and evening to remove mystical danger and to prevent disease or death from entering the township.

81	**MOMMA YƐMƆ MPAEƐ – LET US PRAY** Symbol of **SPIRITUAL DEVOTION, SUPPLICATION,** and **PRAYER** The ideas expressed in an Akan prayer are best captured by the following: *Yɛsrɛ wo nkwa.* *Yɛsrɛ wo adom;* *Ɛmma yɛnwu awia wuo* *Ɛmma yɛnwu anadwo wuo;* *Yɛkɔ nnae a, yɛnwo ba;* *Yɛdua aduadeɛ a, ɛnso aba pa;* *Ma asomdwoeɛ mmra wiase;* *Ma nkɔsoɔ mmra ɔman yi mu,* *Ma ɔman yi nyɛ porɔmporɔm.* Literal translation: We pray for life and pray for grace; Let not death be with us by day or by night; May we be blessed with children, And may what we plant bear good fruit, Let there be peace in the world And may there be prosperity In this land abundantly.
82	**SOM ONYANKOPƆN – WORSHIP GOD** Symbol of **DEVOTION and WORSHIP** From the expression: *Som Onyankopɔn.* Literal translation: Worship God
83	**ASƐM A ONYANKOPƆN ADI ASIE NO – WHAT GOD HAS ORDAINED** Symbol of **GOD'S EVER-ENDURING WORD** From the maxim: *Asɛm a Onyankopɔn adi asie no, onipa ntumi nnane no.* Or, *Adeɛ a Onyame ahyehyɛ no, onipa ntumi nsɛe no.* Literal translation: What God has ordained, no human being can change. The Akan have a hierarchical view of beings with God (*Nyame*) at the apex. This view implies that a lower entity cannot subvert a higher entity. While human beings make obeisance to God, human beings cannot worship lower deities that are below humans.

84	**ONYANKOPƆN, W'AHENNIE MMRA – GOD, THY KINGDOM COME** Symbol of the **SUPREMACY OF GOD, DIVINE POWER,** and **ROYALTY** From the expression: *Nyame ne hene*. Or, *Onyankopɔn w'ahennie mmra*. Literal translation: God is king. Or, God, let thy kingdom come.
85	**AGYA, ƐNA, ƆBA NE SUNSUM KRƆNKRƆN – THE FATHER, THE MOTHER, THE SON AND THE HOLY SPIRIT** Symbol of the **HOLY TRINITY** and **SPIRITUALITY** The Akan concept of TRINITY is constituted of elements from the Mother (*mogya* – blood), the Father (*ntorɔ* - spirit, personality), and God (*ɔkra* – soul). These elements combine to form the Child.
86	**NKRABEA – DESTINY** Symbol of **DESTINY, DETERMINISM, UNEQUAL DISTRIBUTION OF TALENTS, INEQUALITY** From the aphorism: *Esono onipa biara na ne nkrabea*. Or, *Onyame nkrabea mu nni kwatibea*. Literal translation: Everyone has her/his unique destiny or talents. God's destiny is not contradictory.
87	**ONYANKOPƆN BƆ YƐN HO BAN - GOD PROTECT US** Symbol of **GOD'S PROTECTION, SECURITY IN GOD,** and **PEACE** From the expression: *Onyankopɔn bɔ yɛn ho ban*. Literal translation: God protect us.
88	**ONYANKOPƆN ADOM NTI YƐTE ASE - BY GOD'S GRACE WE LIVE** Symbol of **GOD'S GRACE, GOODNESS, BENEVOLENCE, CHARITY,** and **VIRTUE** From the aphorism: *Onyankopɔn adom nti na yɛte ase*. Literal translation: By God's grace we live. Without the life-giving force from God, the human being ceases to exist.
89	**ONYANKOPƆN HYIRA YƐN ADUANE SO DAA - GOD, BLESS OUR FOOD ALWAYS** Symbol of **SUCCOR, SUSTENANCE, BLESSINGS, STRENGTH,** and **VITALITY** From the expression: *Onyankopɔn hyira yɛn aduane so daa*. Literal translation: God, bless our food always.

90	**ONYANKOPƆN, MA YƐN ADUANE DAA - GOD, FEED US ALWAYS** Symbol of **SUSTENANCE, VITALITY, ENERGY,** and **STRENGTH** From the aphorism: *Nyame na ɔgu ahina hunu mu nsuo. Or, Onyankopɔn ma yɛn aduane daa.* Literal translation: God fills the empty pot with water. Or, God, feed us always. In other words, God provides sustenance for the needy.
91	**BIRIBIARA BƐTWAM AKƆ - ALL WILL PASS AWAY** Symbol of the **PERMANENCY OF GOD'S WORD, ENDURANCE, STABILITY,** and **PERSISTENCE** From the maxim: *Biribiara bɛtwam akɔ, nanso Onyankopɔn asɛm bɛtena hɔ daa.* Literal translation: All will pass away, but not the word of God.
92	**ONYANKOPƆN DƆ WO - GOD LOVES YOU** Symbol of **GOD'S LOVE, KINDNESS,** and **CHARITY** From the expression: *Onyankopɔn dɔ wo.* Literal translation: God loves you.
93	**ONYANKOPƆN, WO PƐ NYƐ HƆ - GOD, THY WILL BE DONE** Symbol of **GOD'S WILL** From the expression: *Onyankopɔn, wo pɛ nyɛ hɔ.* Literal translation: God, thy will be done.
94	**ONYANKOPƆN NE YƐN NTENA - MAY GOD BE WITH US** Symbol of **GOD'S PRESENCE, PROTECTION,** and **COMPANY** From the expression: *Onyankopɔn ne yɛn ntena.* Literal translation: May God be with us.
95	**KAE ONYANKOPƆN ASƐM - REMEMBER GOD'S WORD** Symbol of **BELIEF, FAITH IN THE HOLY BOOK** From the expression: *Kae Onyankopɔn asɛm a ɛwɔ Twerɛ Krɔnkrɔn no mu.* Literal translation: Remember God's word in the Holy Bible.
96	**ONYANKOPƆN, TENABEA WƆ M'AKOMA MU MA WO - GOD, THERE IS ROOM IN MY HEART FOR YOU** Symbol of **DEDICATION** From the expression: *Onyankopɔn, tenabea wɔ m'akoma mu ma wo.* Literal translation: God, there is room in my heart for you.

97	**YƐDA ONYANKOPƆN ASE - WE THANK GOD** Symbol of **GRATITUDE, THANKFULNESS,** and **APPRECIATION** From the expression: *Yɛda Onyankopɔn ase.* Literal translation: We thank God.
98	**KRISTONI PAPA - GOOD CHRISTIAN** Symbol of **RELIGIOSITY, GOD-FEARING, FAITHFULNESS** and **DEDICATION** From the expression: *Kristoni papa na ɔse: Me ne Nyame nam nti mensuro.* Literal translation: The good christian says: I am not afraid for God is with me.
99	**NEA ONYANKOPƆN AKA ABƆ MU NO - WHAT GOD HAS JOINED TOGETHER** From the expression: *Nea Onyankopɔn aka abɔ mu no, mma obiara mpae mu.* Literal translation: What God has joined together, let no one separate.
100	**ASƆRE DAN - HOUSE OF WORSHIP** Symbol of **PRESENCE OF GOD, HOLY PLACE,** and **PLACE OF WORSHIP** From the expression: *Nyamesom te sɛ asɔredan mu tokuro mu ahwehwɛ; wogyina akyiri hwɛ a, ɛyɛ wo kusuu; sɛ wokɔ mu a, na wohunu ne fɛ.* Literal translation: Religion is like a church building's stained glass window which is dark when one views it from outside; one appreciates its beauty only when one enters the building.
101 102 103 104	**OWUO ATWEDEƐ - DEATH'S LADDER** Symbol of the **MORTALITY** of human beings From the expression: *Owuo atwedeɛ, ɔbaakofoɔ mforo.* Or, *Obiara bɛforo owuo atwedeɛ.* Literal translation: Death is inevitable for every person. Or, death is the ultimate equalizer. Also, death is no respecter of persons. The Akan belief is that the physical part of the human being is mortal. The **SOUL** (*SUNSUM* or *ƆKERA*), however, never dies. ***Owuo atwedeɛ eda hɔ ma obiara* – Death's ladder is there for everyone to climb.** Death is no respecter of anyone, big or small, young or old. The mighty and the low shall all die.

105	**OWUO KUM NYAME - DEATH KILLED GOD** Symbol of the **INVINCIBILITY OF DEATH, and the POWER OF GOD TO OVERCOME DEATH** From the maxim: *Nyame bɔɔ owuo na owuo kum Nyame; na Nyame na ɔte nanka aduro nti odii owuo so nkonim.* Literal translation: God created death and death killed God; yet the Eternal One also created the antidote to the venom of death, and God, therefore, overcame death. The Akan believe that The Creator created things; When He created things, He created Life; When He created Life, He created Death; When He created Death, Death killed Him; When He died, Life came into Him and woke Him up; Thereafter, He lived forever.
106	**OWUO DE DƆM BƐKƆ - DEATH WILL CLAIM THE MULTITUDE** Symbol of **DEATH AS THE EQUALIZER** and **DEATH AS THE LEVELLER** From the expression: *Owuo ne yɛn reko, ɔpatafoɔ ne hwan? Or, Owuo bɛgya hwan?* Literal translation: We are in a struggle with death, who is the mediator? Who will death leave behind?
107	**ONYANKOPƆN BƐTUMI AYƐ - GOD CAN DO IT** Symbol of **VERSATILITY OF GOD, DIVINE POWER, GOD'S SUPREMACY** From the expression: *Onyankopɔn bɛtumi ayɛ adeɛ nyinaa.* Literal translation: God can do all things.
108	**ONYANKOPƆN KA YƐN BOM - GOD, UNITE US** Symbol of **FELLOWSHIP** and **UNITY IN GOD** From the expression: *Ɔdodoɔ so Nyame a, baako nnuru akyakya. Or, Onyankopɔn ka yɛn bom.* Literal translation: When many serve God, He is not the individual person's burden. Or, God, unite us.

109	**OWUO MPƐ SIKA - DEATH ACCEPTS NO MONEY** Symbol of the **INEVITABILITY OF DEATH** for the rich as well as the poor. From the maxim: *Owuo mpɛ sika.* Literal translation: Death accepts no money. Some rich people make it seem like they can buy everlasting life with their money. This symbol suggests that no amount of money will save one from the claws of death. Death is inevitable for the poor as it is for the rich.
OWUO BƐGYA HWAN **110**	**OWUO BƐGYA HWAN? - WHO WILL BE SPARED BY DEATH?** Symbol of the **INEVITABILITY OF DEATH FOR ALL PEOPLE** From the question: *Owuo bɛgya hwan?* Literal translation: Who will be spared by death? This symbol suggests that no one will be spared by death; death is inevitable for all people.
111	**YESU WUO - JESUS' DEATH** Symbol of the **INVINCIBILITY OF DEATH and REDEMPTION** From the expression: *Nyame bɔɔ owuo na owuo kum Nyame.* Literal translation: The Eternal One created death only to be taken away by death.
112	**ASIEƐ or BANMU - MAUSOLEUM** Symbol of **SACRED GROUNDS** There are two mausoleum places for the preservation and interment of the Asante royalty: Banpanase where the corpse is embalmed in a place called Asɔnee, and Bantama where the Afenhyiasom takes place every year. After the British ransacked Kumase during the war of 1874, another place was developed at Breman as the royal mausoleum. Asiif is not only sacred grounds because that is where corpses are buried. Asieɛ also marks the place where the physical aspect of the human being is returned to the womb of Mother Earth.
113 114	**ASENNUA – CROSS** Symbol of **SUPREME SACRIFICE, REDEMPTION,** and **SELFLESSNESS** From the aphorism: *Yesu bewuu wɔ asɛnnua so bɛgyee adasa nkwa.* Literal translation: Jesus died on the cross to save mankind.

115	**YESU WUSƆRE - JESUS' RESURRECTION** Symbol of the **VICTORY OF JESUS OVER DEATH, ETERNAL LIFE, REINCARNATION, SALVATION,** and **REJUVENATION** From the expression: *Yesu wuiɛ a, woasɔre.* Literal translation: Jesus has risen from death. If God has the antidote for the venom of death, and Jesus is the Son of God, then to the Akan that Jesus would arise from death would be possible. This symbol poses the question: O Death, where is thy sting? The Akan believe that death is not the end of the human spirit, but the moment of its passage from this life to the next.
116	**MEMA WO HYƐDEN - ACCEPT MY CONDOLENCES** Symbol of **CONDOLENCE, SYMPATHY,** and **CONSOLATION** From the expression: *Mema wo hyɛden.* Literal translation: Accept my condolences.
117	**AKOKƆBEDEƐ NE KOSUA - THE HEN AND THE EGG** Symbol of the **BEGINNING OF LIFE** From the expression: *Akokɔbedeɛ ne kosua, hwan ne ɔpanin?* Literal translation: The hen and the egg, which came first? Similar expressions about the beginning of life include: Bosom po bɔtoo abɔɔ; Asase trɛ na Nyame ne panin.
118	**ABIBIREM BURONYA - CHRISTMAS IN AFRICA** Symbol of **CHRISTMAS, REBIRTH, REJUVENATION,** and **REJOICING** From the expression: *Afenhyia pa.* Literal translation: Happy new year
119	**ADWERA - WATERY SHRUB** Symbol of **PURITY, SANCTITY, CONSECRATION, CLEANLINESS, CHASTITY,** and **GOOD FORTUNE** From the expression: *Adwera nsuo, wo ne nkwansuo, nsu korogyenn a wohuru nso wonhye.* Literal translation: Water of life, you are the pure crystal clean water that boils, but does not burn. *Adwera* is a watery shrub that is used in *esubɔ* (purification) ceremony and *akradware* (soul washing) ceremony. For example, when one recovers from a long bout of illness, one performs an *esubɔ* ceremony to sanctify one's soul and appease the spirits for protecting one's life. This ceremony starts with a bath of water that has been seeped in *adwera* leaves.

120 **121**	**ANIKUM NNIM AWERƐHOƆ - SLEEP DOES NOT KNOW SADNESS** From the expression: *Anikum nnim awerɛhoɔ, anka mesi hɔ redi awerɛhoɔ a, na mereda.* Literal translation: Sleep does not know sadness otherwise I will not fall asleep when I am sad.
122	**NSORAN AKOMA – GRIEVING HEART** Symbol of **GRIEVING, SADNESS, SORROW,** and **DISTRESS** From the expression: *Me koma di yaa ne awerɛhoɔ.* Literal translation: My heart grieves; I am disheartened.
123	**WOYƐ HWAN? - WHO ARE YOU?** Symbol of **HUMAN BEING'S ESSENCE, SOCIAL STATUS** and **CLASS CONSCIOUSNESS** From the expression: *Nkonsa, woyɛ hwan? Ahemfo koraa yɛwo wɔn.* Literal translation: Nkonsa (name of a person), who are you? Even kings are born. This symbol alludes to the essential nothingness of human beings.
ONIPA BE WUNASIKA TE ASE **124**	**ONIPA BƐWU NA SIKA TE ASE - ONE WILL DIE AND LEAVE ONE'S WEALTH BEHIND** Symbol of the **RELATIVE INSIGNIFICANCE OF MATERIAL WEALTH** From the aphorism: *Onipa bɛwu na sika te ase.* Literal translation: One will die and leave one's wealth behind. The rich person cannot be saved from death by his/her wealth.
OWUO SEE FIE OWUOSEEFIE OWUO SEE FIE **125** **126** **127**	**OWUO SƐE FIE - DEATH DESTROYS THE HOUSEHOLD** Symbol of the **DESTRUCTIVE POWER OF DEATH, TRAGEDY** and **CALAMITY** From the maxim: *Owuo sɛe fie.* Literal translation: Death destroys the household.
128	**OTUMFOƆ WUO YƐ YA – DEATH IS PAINFUL** **Symbol of the AGONY OF DEATH, PAINFUL LOSS, DISTRESS, SORROW** From the expression: *Otumfoɔ wuo yɛ ya.* Literal translation: The death of the king is a sorrowful occasion. This design was carved by Kofi Nsiah to mark the passing away of Nana Opoku Ware II, the Asantehene on February 25, 1999. The passing away of Papa Kofi Nsiah in 2001 was a painful loss as his death marked the closing of a library of knowledge he stored in his head.

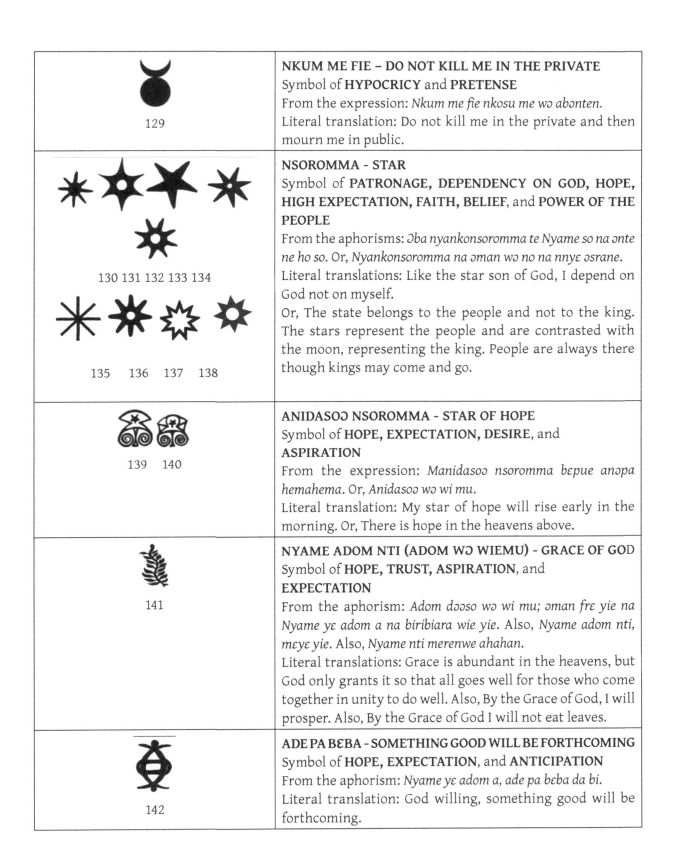

129	**NKUM ME FIE – DO NOT KILL ME IN THE PRIVATE** Symbol of **HYPOCRICY** and **PRETENSE** From the expression: *Nkum me fie nkosu me wɔ abɔnten.* Literal translation: Do not kill me in the private and then mourn me in public.
130 131 132 133 134 **135 136 137 138**	**NSOROMMA - STAR** Symbol of **PATRONAGE, DEPENDENCY ON GOD, HOPE, HIGH EXPECTATION, FAITH, BELIEF,** and **POWER OF THE PEOPLE** From the aphorisms: *Ɔba nyankonsoromma te Nyame so na ɔnte ne ho so. Or, Nyankonsoromma na ɔman wɔ no na nnyɛ ɔsrane.* Literal translations: Like the star son of God, I depend on God not on myself. Or, The state belongs to the people and not to the king. The stars represent the people and are contrasted with the moon, representing the king. People are always there though kings may come and go.
139 140	**ANIDASOɔ NSOROMMA - STAR OF HOPE** Symbol of **HOPE, EXPECTATION, DESIRE,** and **ASPIRATION** From the expression: *Manidasoɔ nsoromma bɛpue anɔpa hemahema. Or, Anidasoɔ wɔ wi mu.* Literal translation: My star of hope will rise early in the morning. Or, There is hope in the heavens above.
141	**NYAME ADOM NTI (ADOM Wɔ WIEMU) - GRACE OF GOD** Symbol of **HOPE, TRUST, ASPIRATION,** and **EXPECTATION** From the aphorism: *Adom dɔɔso wɔ wi mu; ɔman frɛ yie na Nyame yɛ adom a na biribiara wie yie. Also, Nyame adom nti, mɛyɛ yie. Also, Nyame nti merenwe ahahan.* Literal translations: Grace is abundant in the heavens, but God only grants it so that all goes well for those who come together in unity to do well. Also, By the Grace of God, I will prosper. Also, By the Grace of God I will not eat leaves.
142	**ADE PA BɛBA - SOMETHING GOOD WILL BE FORTHCOMING** Symbol of **HOPE, EXPECTATION,** and **ANTICIPATION** From the aphorism: *Nyame yɛ adom a, ade pa bɛba da bi.* Literal translation: God willing, something good will be forthcoming.

143 144 145 146 147	**BIRIBI WƆ SORO - THERE IS SOMETHING IN THE zHEAVENS** Symbol of **HOPE, EXPECTATION, and ASPIRATION** From the aphorism: *Nyame, biribi wɔ soro na ma ɛmmɛka me nsa.* Literal translation: God, there is something in the heavens, let it reach me. This symbol was hung above the lintel of a door for the king to touch three times repeating the words of the aphorism for good luck, high hope and good expectations as he went out to carry out his duties each morning.
148	**ONYANKOPƆN BƐKYERƐ - GOD WILL PROVIDE** Symbol of **HOPE** and **TRUST IN GOD** From the expression: *Onyankopɔn bɛkyerɛ.* Literal translation: God will provide.
149	**ONYANKOPƆN BƐYƐ ME KƐSE - GOD WILL MAKE ME GREAT** Symbol of **EXPECTATION, TRUST** and **CONFIDENCE IN GOD** From the expression: *Onyankopɔn bɛyɛ me kɛse.* Literal translation: God will make me great.
150 151	**ONYANKOPƆN ADOM NTI BIRIBIARA BƐYƐ YIE - BY GOD'S GRACE, ALL WILL BE WELL** Symbol of HOPE, PROVIDENCE and FATE From the expression: *Onyankopɔn adom nti biribiara bɛyɛ yie.* Literal translation: By God's grace all will be well.
152	**ABOA A ƆBƐYƐ NNAM NO - PREDATORY ANIMAL** Symbol of **LIMITATION, IMPERFECTION, BALANCE OF FORCES,** and **EQUAL PROTECTION** From the expression: *Aboa a ɔbɛyɛ nnam no, Nyame mma no mmɛn. Or, Odwan a ɔbɛyɛ asisie na Onyame ma ɔyɛ dwantorɔ.* Literal translation: The predatory animal usually has no horns. Or, It is the sheep that will be troublesome that God makes lame. This suggests the limitation in the individual. If God had not placed limitations on human beings and some wild animals they would have been utterly ruthless.
153	**NYAME TUMI SO – GOD'S POWER IS GREAT** Symbol of **GOD's POWER, OMNIPOTENCE OF GOD** From the expression: *Onyame tumi so.* Literal translation: God's power is great.
154	**ONYANKOPƆN MMERƐ NE MMERƐ PA - GOD'S TIME IS THE BEST** From the expression: *Onyankopɔn mmerɛ ne mmerɛ pa.* Literal translation: God's time is the best.

155	**ONYANKOPƆN HYIRA YƐN DAA - MAY GOD BLESS US ALWAYS** Symbol of **PRAYER** and **REQUEST** From the expression: *Onyankopɔn hyira yɛn daa.* Literal translation: May God bless us always.
156	**NYA GYIDIE - HAVE FAITH** Symbol of **FAITH, ASSURANCE,** and **BELIEF** From the expression: *Nya gyidie wɔ Onyame mu.* Literal translation: Have faith in God or Believe in God.
157 158	**AKYEMFRA - SWALLOW** Symbol of **TALENT, ABILITY, DESTINY,** and **AGILITY** From the aphorism: *Nyame amma akyemfra hwee no na ɛnyɛ ne ntware ho a.* Literal translation: If God did not give the swallow anything at all He gave it its swiftness and turning ability.
159	**NYAME SƐ AYƐYIE – PRAISE IS GOD'S** Symbol of PRAISES FOR GOD From the expression: *Nyame a ɔbɔɔ soro ne asaase, ɔbɔɔ sum bɔ owia, ɔbɔɔ ɔsrane ne nsoromma, ɔbɔɔ akɛseɛ ne nketewa sɛ ayɛyi ampa.* Literal translation: God, Creator of heaven and earth, darkness and the sun, moon and stars, the mighty and the weak, truly deserves praises.
160	**OSIADAN NYAME - GOD, THE BUILDER** Symbol of **GOD, THE BUILDER AND CREATOR** In Akan belief, God is the Supreme Creator. His creation is considered as housing construction within which He provides abode for all His creation.
161	**NYAME ƆBAATAN PA – GOD THE GOOD FATHER**
162 163 164 165 166 167	**NKƆNSƆNKƆNSƆN - CHAIN** Symbol of **FAMILY RELATIONS, UNITY, BROTHERHOOD, and COOPERATION** From the aphorism: *Yɛtoatoa mu sɛ nkɔnsɔnkɔnsɔn; nkwa mu a, yɛtoa mu, owu mu a, yɛtoa mu; abusua mu nnte da.* Literal translation: If we are linked together like a chain, in life we are linked, in death we are linked; family ties are never broken. Or, people who share common blood relations never break away from one another.

168 169 170

171 172 173 174

175 176 177

FUNTUMFUNAFU DENKYEM FUNAFU - JOINED CROCODILES
Symbol of **UNITY IN DIVERSITY, DEMOCRACY, and UNITY OF PURPOSE**

The symbol is also referred to as *ɔdɛnkyɛm mmɛmu* - Siamese twin crocodiles joined at the stomach.

From the proverb: *Funtumfunafu, dɛnkyɛmmfunafu, wɔn afuru bɔmu nso wodidi a na wɔrefom ɛfiri sɛ aduane ne dɛ ye di no mene twitwi mu.*

Literal translation: Two headed crocodiles fight over food that goes to a common stomach because each relishes the food in its throat.

This symbol stresses the oneness of humanity in spite of cultural diversity. It also emphasizes the need for unity in the family or state. Members should not quarrel or fight for selfish interests, for what each gains is for the benefit of all. It also emphasizes the reality of individuality in relation to one's membership in a society. Much as the community interests are to be pursued for the common good, individual rights, interests, passions and responsibilities cannot and must not be trampled on.

This symbol, in essence, depicts the Akan notions about the inherent difficulties of reconciling individual and group interests in a democratic system.

178 179

PEMPAMSIE or MƆMUDWAN – PREPAERDNESS or UNITY
Symbol of **STEADFASTNESS, READINESS TO SERVE, UNITY, COOPERATION, UNITY OF PURPOSE, and STRENGTH**

From the aphorism: *Pempamsie se: Bɛbirebe ahoɔden ne koroyɛ. ɔman si mpoma dua dadebo a, ɛkɔ akɔterenee.*

Literal translation: The strength of the many lies in unity. Once people are resolved in unity, nothing stops them from reaching their goal. Or, in unity lies strength.

The point being stressed by this symbol is that each link in a chain is important, and must, therefore, be strong and ready to serve. Everyone is important in their own right. No one is left over and so everyone should be ready to fill that "space" which he/she alone, but none, can occupy.

180	**ƆMANYƆ GYINA AMAMFOƆ NYINA SO – NATIONAL DEVELOPMENT IS THE RESPONSIBILITY OF ALL CITIZENS** Symbol of **PATRIOTISM, CIVIC RESPONSIBILITY,** and **NATIONALISM** From the proverb: *Sɛ ɔman myɛ yie a, yɛn nyina te mu bi.* Or, *Dodoɔ di a, dodoɔ yɔ; dodoɔ yɔ a, dodoɔ di.* Also, *Onipa bɔne baako te ɔman mu a, ne nkoa ne nipa nyinaa.* Literal translation: The prosperity of a nation benefits all citizens. Or, If many people are to eat, many people must produce; if many people produce, then many people can eat. Also, One bad citizen in a country makes slaves of the rest of the citizenry. Prosperity of a nation depends on the hard work of its citizens.
181	**ANANSE ANTƆN KASA - ANANSE DID NOT SELL SPEECH** Symbol of **FREEDOM OF EXPRESSION, FREEDOM OF SPEECH** and **HUMAN RIGHT** From the adage: *Ananse antɔn kasa.* Literal translation: The spider did not sell speech. Ananse (spider) in Akan folktales realized that speech and wisdom are accessible to all people. Speech cannot be appropriated as the property of one person as Ananse sought to do with wisdom.
182 183	**ƆKYEAME POMA – LINGUIST'S STAFF** Symbol of **AUTHORITY, LEGITIMACY, and ORATORIAL SKILLS** From the expression: *Ɔkyeame a onnim kasa na ɔse, Nana w'aso mu a.* Literal translation: The inarticulate ɔkyeame (linguist) states: Nana you heard what was said.
184 m185	**KOKUROMOTIE - THUMB** **Symbol of COOPERATION, PARTICIPATION, TEAMWORK, INDISPENSABILITY, and HARMONY** From the expression: *Yɛnsiane kokuromotie ho mmɔ pɔ.* Also, *Wode kokuromotie kɔ ayiɛ a, yɛde sotrɔ gya wo kwan.* Literal translation: One cannot make a knot without the thumb. Also, When one throws one's weight about at the funeral, one is bound to get slapped in the face. The symbol depicts the indispensability of the elderly (or chief or king) in the resolution of social problems. The elderly or king is the ultimate repository of wisdom.

211

186	**NKABOM MA YETUMI GYINA HƆ - UNITED WE STAND** **Symbol of UNITY, STRENGTH IN UNITY, and NATIONAL INTEGRATION** From the expression: *Nkabom ma yetumi gyina hɔ, mpaapaemu ma yɛhwe ase.* Literal translation: United we stand, divided we fall. Symbol emphasizes the need for united action, unity in diversity, and national unity. The Akan society comprises seven matri-clans, therefore there is need for these subgroups to unite for the good of the greater society. The Asante nation was built on the principle of nkabom that was enunciated by the legendary Ɔkomfo Anɔkye.
187	**KOROYƐ - UNITY** **Symbol of UNITY, FRATERNITY, FELLOWSHIP, and ORDER** From the riddle: *Nnomaa miɛnsa bi na won su sɛ: kyee, kaa, ne kasakranka; won ni ne hwan? Won ni ne koryɛ.* Literal translation: Three baby birds are crying: kyee, kaa, and kasakranka; who is their mother? Their mother is unity. This symbol is based on a story of three baby birds that had lost their mother. Their wailing from a tree near a farm attracted the attention of the farmer. The farmer decided to nurse the birds. The farmer became a mother to the birds. Very soon, the birds fought among themselves because each wanted their nest all to itself. Eventually two of them left to be on their own. The next day the farmer came to feed them and found out they had broken up, he urged the remaining to go and look for its siblings before the farmer would feed them together. The Asante nation was built on the principle of *nkabom (unity).*
188	**NKABOM - UNITY** **Symbol UNITY, STRENGTH IN UNITY, and NATIONAL INTEGRATION** From the expression: *Nkabom ma yetumi gyina hɔ, mpaapaemu ma yehwe ase.* Literal translation: United we stand, divided we fall.

 189 190 191	ƐSE NE TƐKRƐMA - TEETH AND TONGUE Symbol of INTERDEPENDENCE, COOPERATION, UNITY, GROWTH, DEVELOPMENT, and IMPROVEMENT From the aphorisms: Wɔnnwo ba a ɔwɔ ne se dada. Or, Tɛkrɛma wɔ hɔ a, ɛse mmɔ nkuro. Also, Ɛse ka tɛkrɛma nso wɔte bɔ mu. Literal translations: No child is born with an already developed set of teeth. Or, In the presence of the tongue, the teeth do not litigate. Also, The teeth bite the tongue sometimes, yet they continue to live in harmony. The symbol depicts the complementary nature of human beings as well as nations. Or, The tongue lying between **the two rows of teeth, literally staves off tension between the two.**
 192 193	**TIKORƆ MMPAM - ONE HEAD DOES NOT CONSTITUTE A COUNCIL** Symbol of **PARTICIPATORY DEMOCRACY, WARNING AGAINST DICTATORIAL RULE, and PLURALITY OF IDEAS** From the maxim: Ɔbakofoɔ mmu ɔman. Or, Tikorɔ mmpam. Literal translation: One person does not rule a nation. Or, One head does not constitute a council. The Akan belief is that democratic rule requires consultation, open discussion, consensus building, and coalition formation. The use of the Queen mother as a co-ruler and the Council of state or council of elders are examples of Akan forms of institutions for participatory democracy depicted by this symbol.

194	**KURONTIRE NE AKWAMU - COUNCIL OF STATE** Symbol of **DEMOCRACY, PARTICIPATORY GOVERNMENT, and PLURALITY OF IDEAS** From the aphorism: *Obakofoɔ mmu ɔman.* Or, *Ɔhene nya ahotenafo pa a, ne bere so dwo.* Literal translation: One person does not rule a nation. Or, When a king has good counselors, his reign is peaceful. In Asante, for example, the Council of State was first created by Osei Tutu just before the Asante-Denkyira War of 1700-1702. Within the Council, the Asantehene, the king, is not only the head of the nation-state, but he is also the supreme commander of the military. The Kurontirehene is the military general and deputizes as the head of the nation-state in the absence of the king. The Akwamuhene is the second in command after the Kurontirehene. Another important member of the Council of State is the Queenmother who is also a co-ruler with the king. The Council of State operates at the national (*ɔman*) level of government. A version of the Council at the lower levels of the Akan political organization is the Council of Elders at the town (*kuro*) level of government.
195	**MPUA NKRON – COUNCIL OF ELDERS** Symbol of **PARTICIPATORY DEMOCRACY, DEVOLUTION OF POWER** From the expression: *Ɔhene nya ahotenafo pa a, ne bere so dwo.* Literal translation: When a king has good counselors, his reign is peaceful.
196	WO NSA DA MU A - IF YOUR HANDS ARE IN THE DISH Symbol of PARTICIPATORY GOVERNMENT, DEMOCRACY and PLURALISM From the aphorism: *Wo nsa da mu a, wonni nnya wo.* Literal translation: If your hands are in the dish, people do not eat everything and leave you nothing.

197 198	**TUMI TE SƐ KOSUA - POWER IS LIKE AN EGG** Symbol of the **DELICACY OF POLITICAL POWER, FRAGILITY OF DEMOCRACY, and RESTRAINT** From the aphorism: *Tumi te se kosua, woso mu den a, ɛpae; na se woanso mu yie nso, ɛfiri wo nsa bɔ famu ma ɛpae.* Literal translation: Power is as fragile as an egg, when held too tightly it might break; if it is held too loosely, it might fall and break. The symbol points out the fragile nature of political power. As a symbol of democracy, it suggests the virtue of sharing political power. Power held in one hand is not safe. Power wielded by a chief is not absolute, nor is it expected to lead to tyranny. A chief is expected to exercise the power he wields cautiously and judiciously, or else he incurs the wrath of his subjects.
199	**BOA ME - HELP ME** **Symbol of COOPERATION** From the aphorism: *Boa me.* Or, *Woforo dua pa a, na yɛpia wo.* Literal translation: Help me. Or, When you climb a good tree, you are given a push. When one undertakes a good cause, one is given all the support one would need.
200	**BOA ME NA ME MMOA WO - HELP ME AND LET ME HELP YOU** **Symbol of COOPERATION, INTERDEPENDENCE** From the aphorism: *Boa me na me mmoa wo.* Or, *Benkum dware nifa na nifa so dware benkum.* Or, *Woamma wo yɔnko antwa nkron a, wonnya edu ntwa.* Literal translation: Help me and let me help you. Or, The left hand washes the right, and the right in turn washes the left. Or, If you do not allow a friend to get a nine, you will not be able to get a ten for yourself. This suggests that just as one hand cannot wash itself, so it is difficult for an individual to provide for himself/herself all that she/he may need. People and countries depend on one another for much that they require in order to survive.
201 202	**BOAFO YƐNA - THE RARITY OF A WILLING HELPER** **Symbol of SUPPORT, PATRONAGE, COOPERATION, and TEAMWORK** From the expression: *Boafo yɛ na.* Literal translation: It is hard to come by a good sponsor or patron or a willing helper.

215

203	**BOA W'ABAN - HELP YOUR GOVERNMENT** **Symbol of PATRIOTISM, NATIONALISM, CIVIC RESPONSIBILITY, GOOD CITIZENSHIP, and PARTICIPATORY GOVERNMENT** From the expression: *Ɔmampam se: Me deɛ ne sɛ merepam me man, nyɛ amambɔeɛ.* Literal translation: The monitor lizard says: Mine is to help to build up, but not to destroy my state. This symbol reflects the civic responsibility of the citizenry to participate in the democratic process to promote national development, peace and stability in the state.
204	**ƆBAAKOFOƆ – ONE PERSON** **Symbol of SOLITUDE, LONELINESS, and ALONENESS** From the expression: *Ɔbaakofoɔ nkyekyere kuro. Or, Ɔbaakofoɔ werɛ aduru a, egu. Or, Wodi wo ho wo ho a, ɛyɛ mmusuo.* Literal translation: One person does not build a town. Or, If one person goes to collect medicine, it falls to the ground. Or, If you do everything on your own, it is a taboo. Being solitary is taboo.
205	**NNAMFO PA BAANU - TWO GOOD FRIENDS** **Symbol of FRIENDSHIP, FELLOWSHIP, and COMRADESHIP** From the aphorism: *Hu m'ani so ma me nti na atwe mmienu nam daa no. Or, Adwen yɛdwen no baanu. Also, Anyankofoɔ banu goro ɔbaa koro ho a, ntoto ba.* Literal translation: The deer is always seen in pairs so that one will help the other out in case of any emergency. Or, Fruitful ideas are born when two heads come together. Also, If two friends play with one woman, it leads to misunderstanding.
206 207 208 209 210	**FAWOHODIE - INDEPENDENCE** Symbol of **FREEDOM, INDEPENDENCE, EMANCIPATION, SELF-DETERMINATION, and SELF-GOVERNMENT** From the expression: *Fawohodie ɛne ɔbrɛ na ɛnam.* Literal translation: Independence comes with its responsibilities.
211 212	**AKONTAABUO – ACCOUNTABILITY** Symbol of **ACCOUNTABILITY and TRANSPARENCY** From the proverb: *Ɛtɔ baabi a, ɛdum; ɛtɔ baabi a ɛhye nyɛ amammuo pa.* Literal translation: If fire goes out in one place and burns in another is not a mark of good government. A good leader should not display indecision.

213	**DUA KORO - ONE TREE** **Symbol of INDIVIDUALISM, PARTICULARISM, and ECCENTRICITY** From the maxim: *Dua koro gye mframa a, ebu. Also, Dua koro nyɛ kwaeɛ.* Literal translation: One tree cannot last a storm. Also, One tree does not constitute a forest.
214	**YƐREPERE ADEƐ A - WHEN WE STRIVE FOR WEALTH** **Symbol of NATIONALISM, PATRIOTISM, and SOCIAL ROLE** From the maxim: *Yɛrepere adeɛ a, yɛpere ba fie; na obi a ɔrepere adeɛ akɔ kɔtɔkɔ no, yensi no kwan.* Literal translation: When we strive for wealth, we bring it home; and we don't stop him, who strives for wealth for the land of the porcupine.
215 216 217	**ƆWƆ AFORO ADOBƐ - THE SNAKE CLIMBS THE RAFFIA PALM TREE** Symbol of **NEGOTIATION, TACTICAL MOVE, INGENUITY, and DIPLOMACY** From the aphorism: *Ɔwɔ nni nan nni nsa nso ɔwɔ foro adobɛ.* Literal translation: The snake has no limbs yet it climbs the raffia palm tree. This symbol is based on an observation of the unusual behavior of a snake in climbing a raffia palm (or any other) tree. The snake negotiates each twist and turn by a tactical anddeliberate movement. The symbol extols the importance of diplomacy and prudence as the necessary ingredients of real valor.
218	**ANOMA NE ƆWƆ - BIRD AND SNAKE** **Symbol of PATIENCE, STRATEGIC PLANNING, CALCULATION** **and TACTICAL MOVE** From the adage: *Nanka bobonya, ɔda asaase anya ɔnwam.* Or, *Wosuo ɔwɔ ti a, dea aka nyinaa yɛ ahomaa.* Literal translation: The puff adder that cannot fly has caught the hornbill that flies. Or, If you get hold of the snake's head, the rest of it is mere thread. If one succeeds in capturing the chief or the military general, then the whole state is doomed to defeat. This depicts the military strategy of destroying first a state's military base to facilitate complete conquest.

219	**NTEASE - UNDERSTANDING** **Symbol of UNDERSTANDING, TOLERANCE, PERCEPTION and DISCERNING** From the expression: *Aso pa nkyɛre asɛm ase te.* Literal translation: The good ear easily understands an issue.
220	**ADWO – PEACE** Symbol of **PEACE, CALMNESS, SPIRITUAL COOLNESS, and CONTINUITY** From the proverb: *Ɔhene nya ahotenafo pa a, ne berɛ so dwo.* Literal translation: When the king has good counselors, then his reign will be peaceful.
221	**ETUO NE AKYEKYEDEƐ - THE GUN AND THE TORTOISE** **Symbol PEACE, SKILL and DEXTERITY** From the expression: *Ɛka akyekyedeɛ ne nwaa a nka etuo nnto da wo wiram. Also, Gye akyekyedeɛ kɔ ma agya, nnyɛ ahayɔ.* Literal translation: Left with the snail and the tortoise, there would not be any gun shots in the forest. Also, Taking a tortoise to one's father is not a mark of good hunting skills.
222	**AKYEKYEDEƐ - TORTOISE** **Symbol of PEACE, STRATEGIC PLANNING, TACTFULNESS, or FUTILE ENDEAVOR** From the aphorism: *Ɛkaa akyekyedeɛ ne nwa a, ɛnka etuo rento da wo wiram. Also, Akyekyedeɛ se: Ɛhia ma adwen. Or, Huruie si akyekyedeɛ akyi a, osi hɔ kwa.* Literal translation: Left with the snail and the tortoise, there would not be any gun shots in the forest
223	**TUO ABOBA - GUN BULLETS** **Symbol of BRAVERY, MARKSMANSHIP, RESOURCEFULNESS, AND PREPAREDNESS** From the expression: *Atwereboɔ a ɛnyɛ nam no, yɛmfa nhyɛ tuo ano. Or, Atwereboɔ asa ɛnyɛ Akwawua ntoa mu a.* Literal translation: One does not load a gun with spent bullet. Or, The cartridge-belt of Akwawua has never been known to lack bullets. A resourceful and well-prepared person is never found wanting.

224	**MPABOA - SANDALS** **Symbol of PROTECTION, VALOR, VIGILANCE, ALERTNESS, and DECLARATION OF WAR** **From the ultimatum:** *Wonni atuduru a pɛ bi, wonni mpaboa a pɛ bi na me ne wɔ wɔ bi ka wɔ ɛseram. Or, Wosuro atɛkyɛ mpaboa a, wofira ne ntama.* Literal translation: Prepare for war and meet me on the battlefield. Or, If you are scared to get your feet wet in a muddy place you fall down and get your whole body wet. In the past a war parcel comprising a pair of sandals, gunpowder and a small bundle of sticks would be sent by a king to his enemy as a declaration of war. This symbol suggests the need for readiness and vigilance to use war to maintain peace and tranquility in society. The symbol is used metaphorically in this statement to express the declaration of war. There were various types of sandals the Akan people made in the past and these included *mpaboapa, nkuronnua,* and *kyaw-kyaw.*
225	**APRƐMMOƆ - CANNON** Symbol of **SUPERIOR MILITARY STRATEGY** From the expression: Literal translation: The white man brought his cannon to the bush but the bush was stronger than the cannon.
226	**BABADUA – BAMBOO SPECIE** Symbol of **RESILIENCE, STRENGTH, SELF-RELIANCE, BEING IMPENETRABLE,** and **PROTECTION** From the expression: *Babadua dɔnkɔ: onipa te n'ase a, ɔmpɛ. Or, Babadua se nyɛ ne mu apɔapɔ a, nka ɔne sibire sɛ.* Literal translation: Babadua, the slave: if a person is self-reliant, he becomes dissatisfied. Or, Babadua says that if it were not for the bumps on its stem, it would be the same as the reed. Babadua (Thalia near geniculata) – a bamboo specie, is a strong cane used in building construction and fence building. Thickets of it are extremely difficult to penetrate. It therefore symbolizes impenetrable defense system. This symbol is very prominent as umbrella finial.
227	**ASAASE ABAN - EARTH FORTRESS** Symbol of **RESILIENCE, VIGILANCE** From the expression: *Asaase aban, yɛnte gyae agye nkɔsoɔ.* Literal translation: Earth fortress, we are unrestrainable until there is progress.

228	**ETUO KORAA MENSURO NA ABAA? - EVEN THE GUN** **Symbol of BRAVERY, VALOR, DEFIANCE, CHIVALRY, and HEROISM** From the expression: *Etuo koraa mensuro na abaa?* Or, *Wokuta etuo a, womfa abaa.* Literal translation: Even the gun I fear not, how much more the stick? Or, If you carry a gun, you do not need to take a stick.
229 230 231	**FIE MOSEA - HOUSEHOLD PEBBLES** **Symbol of WARNING AGAINST THE INTERNAL ENEMY, ALERTNESS, and VIGILANCE** From the aphorism: *Fie mosea twa wo a sene sekan.* Or, *Ɔhɔhoɔ hunu dea amani aka akyerɛ no.* Literal translation: The smooth pebbles of the household when they cut they cut sharper than a knife. Or, Societal secrets are learnt by the enemy through the revelations of unpatriotic citizens. This symbol serves as warning for the need for vigilance and awareness of the enemy from within as it is more dangerous than the enemy from without. Warning that internal feuds and disloyalty can be very destructive.
232	**MPATAPƆ - PEACE KNOT** **Symbol of PEACE, PEACE PACT, PEACEFUL COEXISTENCE, NEGOTIATION, DIPLOMACY, PACIFICATION, and RECONCILIATION** From the *proverb: Bere a ntɔkwa keseku efiri ase wɔ kurotia no, na mpata abɔ pɔ keseku de rehyea no.* Literal translation: When conflict raises its ugly head at the outskirt of the town, conciliatory team gangs up to contain it. *Mpatapɔ* represents the bond or knot that binds parties in a dispute to a peaceful, harmonious reconciliation. It is a symbol of peacemaking after strife.
233	**ASOMDWOEƐ - PEACE** **Symbol of HARMONY, RECONCILIATION, PEACE and SERENITY** From the aphorism: *Wonni asomdweɛ a, woyɛ teasewu.* Literal translation: If one does not have peace, one is like the living dead.

234	**ASOMDWOEƐ FIE - HOUSE OF PEACE** **Symbol of PEACEFUL COEXISTENCE, TRANQUILITY, NON-VIOLENCE, and** From the aphorism: *Nteaseɛ ne aboterɛ tena fie baako mu a, asomdwoeɛ na ɛba.* Literal translation: When understanding and patience live together in a house, peace prevails.
235 236	**NAM PORƆ A - WHEN THE FISH ROTS** **Symbol of CORRUPT LEADERSHIP** From the aphorism: *Nam porɔ a, efiri ne ti.* Literal translation: When the fish rots, it first rots from the head. Corruption in a society starts from the leaders of the society.
237	**NEA ƆRETWA SA - THE PATH-MAKER** **Symbol of LEADERSHIP PROBLEMS, TRAILBLAZING, NEED FOR A LEADER TO HEED ADVICE** From the aphorism: *Nea ɔretwa sa nnim sɛ n'akyi akyea.* Literal translation: The path-maker or the trailblazer does not know that the path is curved behind him.
238 239 240	**NSA KORƆ - ONE HAND** **Symbol of CONCERTED ACTION, COOPERATION, and TEAMWORK; also symbol of HUMAN FRAILTY, and IMPERFECTION** From the aphorism: *Nsa korɔ ntumi nkata Nyame ani.* Literal translation: One hand is not big enough to cover the sky.
241	**APƐSƐ YƐ KƐSE A - WHEN THE HEDGEHOG GROWS FAT** **Symbol of MUTUAL BENEFIT** From the aphorism: *Apɛse yɛ kɛse a, ɔyɛ ma dufoɔkyeɛ.* Literal translation: When the hedgehog grows fat, it benefits the wet log.
242	**ƆMAN ASƐNKYERƐDEƐ - NATIONAL COAT OF ARMS (GHANA)** **Symbol of NATIONAL IDENTITY, FREEDOM AND JUSTICE, NATION-STATEHOOD, and SOVEREIGNTY** This symbol depicts the coat of arms of Ghana. This symbol incorporates other adinkra symbols such as the castle, state swords, and cocoa tree.

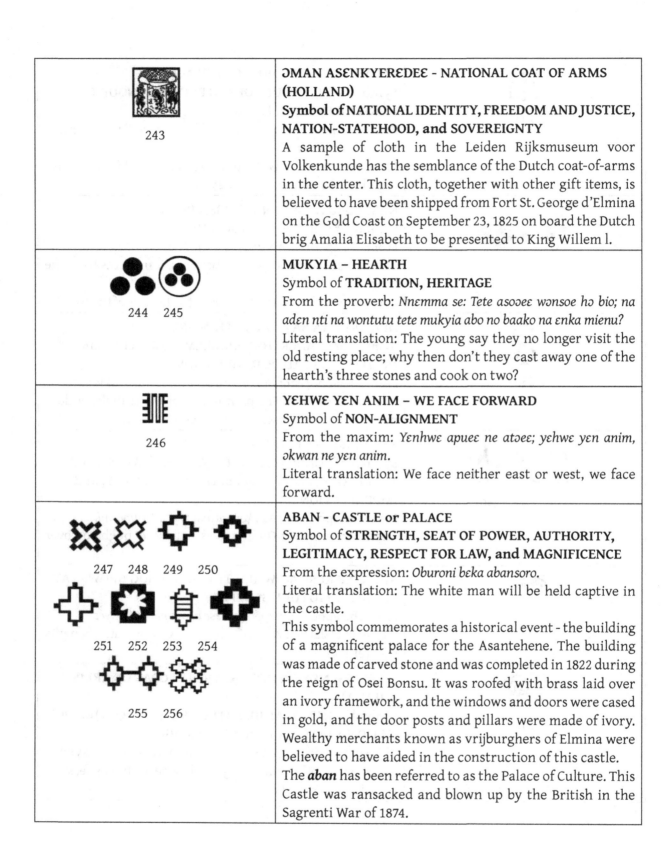243	**ƆMAN ASƐNKYERƐDEƐ - NATIONAL COAT OF ARMS (HOLLAND)** **Symbol of NATIONAL IDENTITY, FREEDOM AND JUSTICE, NATION-STATEHOOD, and SOVEREIGNTY** A sample of cloth in the Leiden Rijksmuseum voor Volkenkunde has the semblance of the Dutch coat-of-arms in the center. This cloth, together with other gift items, is believed to have been shipped from Fort St. George d'Elmina on the Gold Coast on September 23, 1825 on board the Dutch brig Amalia Elisabeth to be presented to King Willem l.
244 245	**MUKYIA – HEARTH** Symbol of **TRADITION, HERITAGE** From the proverb: *Nnɛmma se: Tete asoɔeɛ wɔnsoe hɔ bio; na adɛn nti na wontutu tete mukyia abo no baako na ɛnka mienu?* Literal translation: The young say they no longer visit the old resting place; why then don't they cast away one of the hearth's three stones and cook on two?
246	**YƐHWƐ YƐN ANIM – WE FACE FORWARD** Symbol of **NON-ALIGNMENT** From the maxim: *Yɛnhwɛ apueɛ ne atɔeɛ; yɛhwɛ yɛn anim, ɔkwan ne yɛn anim.* Literal translation: We face neither east or west, we face forward.
247 248 249 250 251 252 253 254 255 256	**ABAN - CASTLE or PALACE** Symbol of **STRENGTH, SEAT OF POWER, AUTHORITY, LEGITIMACY, RESPECT FOR LAW, and MAGNIFICENCE** From the expression: *Oburoni bɛka abansoro.* Literal translation: The white man will be held captive in the castle. This symbol commemorates a historical event - the building of a magnificent palace for the Asantehene. The building was made of carved stone and was completed in 1822 during the reign of Osei Bonsu. It was roofed with brass laid over an ivory framework, and the windows and doors were cased in gold, and the door posts and pillars were made of ivory. Wealthy merchants known as vrijburghers of Elmina were believed to have aided in the construction of this castle. The **aban** has been referred to as the Palace of Culture. This Castle was ransacked and blown up by the British in the Sagrenti War of 1874.

  257　258	**TUMI AFENA - SWORD OF POWER** **Symbol of STATE AUTHORITY, LEGITIMACY, and POWER** At the Pampafie ceremony for the installation of the Asantehene-elect, the Waree Adwumakasehene unsheathes the Bosomuru Sword and passes it on to the King-elect, repeating three times the following: *Mede wotumi ma wo* *Wo Nana Osei Tutu ne Bosommuru ɔde dii ako no ni* *Mede hyɛ wo nsa* I pass on to you your authority This is the Bosommuru Sword with which your ancestor, King Osei Tutu, waged his wars I hand it over to you To this the King-elect replies three times: *Magye* - I accept
  259	**MPOMPONSUO - RESPONSIBILITY SWORD** The ***mpomponsuo*** sword symbolizes **RESPONSIBILITY, POWER, LOYALTY, BRAVERY, and AUTHORITY.** This sword is used by the Asantehene in taking the oath of office. The other **amanhene** of Asante use this sword to swear the oath of allegiance to the Asantehene. This sword is one of the four principal state swords of the Asante. his sword was created by Asantehene Nana Opoku Ware I (r. 1731-1742), and is the foremost example of **akrafen**a.
 260　261　262　263　264  265　266　267　268　269	**AKOFENA - STATE SWORDS** **Symbol of STATE AUTHORITY, LEGITIMACY, GALLANTRY, and POWER** From the aphorism: *Konim ko di nim a, wobɔ afena hyɛ no safohene.* Literal translation: The great war hero is given a royal sword and promoted to the rank of a general. There are various state swords that are used for specific functions. Akofena is also known as NSUAEFENA as it is used to swear the oath of office and to swear allegiance to a higher authority. State swords are carried by state traders, royal messengers and ambassadors, and are used in the rituals for purifying the chief's soul and various ancestral stools. Chiefs maintain a group of sword-bearers, each of whom carries one of the various state swords on public occasions. While swords were an important military weapon in the past, their use these days is ceremonial as they have unsharpened blades.

270	**AFENANTA - DOUBLE BLADE SWORD** Symbol of **JUSTICE, FAIRNESS,** and **IMPARTIALITY** This symbol is incorporated in the state sword used by the President of Ghana as the oath of office is administered
 271 272 273 274 275	**ƆDEHYEƐ KYINIIƐ - ROYAL UMBRELLA** Symbol of **AUTHORITY, LEGITIMACY, PROTECTION and SECURITY** From the expression: *Nea kyiniiɛ si ne so ne ɔhene.* Literal translation: He who has umbrella over his head is the king.
 276 277	**ABƐNTIA - STATE HORN** **Symbol of STATE AUTHORITY, LEGITIMACY, APPELLATION, and PRAISE** From the expression: *Mmɛn na ɛma yɛhunu sɛ ɔhene wɔ hɔ.* Or, *Ntahera se: Asansa a ɔkyini aman, Akorɔma, ɔrekɔ a, ɔde nim bɛba.* Or, *Ɔmani ye ra a, yɛde ɔmani abɛn na yɛde hwehwɛ no.* Also, *Sɛ odurogya hyɛn a, yɛnsɔ gya ano.* Also, *Sɛ ɔhene wu a, na ɛmmɛntia di ahim.* Literal translation: It is the horns that make us know who is a king or a chief. Or, The horn says of the King: He is like the hawk that roams all nations; he will come home with victory. Or, When a citizen is missing, the search party looks for him with the citizen's horn. Also, When the flute is blown, we do not make fire. Also, When the king dies that is when the state horns are played continuously.

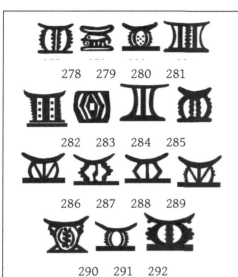

278 279 280 281

282 283 284 285

286 287 288 289

290 291 292

ƆHENE (ƆHEMMAA) ADWA – KING'S (QUEENMOTHER'S) STOOL

From the expression: *Ɔte nananom nkonnwa so.* Or, *Sɛ wobɛka me ho asɛm a, fa akonnwa na tenase.* Also, *Sɛ yɛde akonnwa kɛseɛ na ɛdi ahene a, anka nkowannwasemfoɔ yɛ ahemfo.* Or, *Sɛ ahennwa wɔ animuonyam a, na ɛnkyerɛ sɛ ɔhene a ɔte so anim yɛ nyam.*

Literal translation: He is sitting on the stool of the ancestors (i.e., He is the King). Or, If you want to talk about me, take a stool and sit down. Also, If the possession of a big stool qualified one to be chief, then stool carvers would be chiefs. Or, Even if the stool is respected it does not mean that the chief is worthy of respect.

The stool is believed to inhabit the soul of the nation. As a symbol of state power it embodies the past, present, and the future of the nation, that is, it marks continuities across generations and groups and close solidarities between the living and the dead. Through the stool, the king serves as a link between the living and the dead as well as the yet-to-be-born members of the society. The king has the responsibility to preserve the stool for posterity. The stool binds all the members of the family (and thus the nation) together. Each king decides on the symbol to be incorporated in his stool. For example, Nana Prempeh II chose the nyasapø (wisdom knot) to convey the notion that he would solve the nation's problems by sagacity rather than by the power of the sword. In the past the stool was used for gender differentiation in the society. When a successful king dies in office his stool is blackened and added to the ancestral stools in the Temple of Stools (Nkonnwafieso).

The **ɔhene** (as well as the **ɔhemmaa**) **adwa** encodes the Akan philosophical construct of state territoriality. As Preston (1973, p. 81) points out, the **ɔhene adwa** "exists only in relation to specific laws of custody of the earth [**asaase**] and this custody has its origins in prime occupancy of territory which is considered a de facto sacred act." That is, the existence of **ɔhene adwa** carries a territorial concept with it. This territory may be **kuro** (town) or ɔman (state). In essence, where there is no stool, there is no town or state.

293	**OBI TE OBI SO - SOME ONE SITS ABOVE ANOTHER** Symbol of **HIERARCHY, ORDERED STRUCTURE,** and **ORGANIZATION** From the expression: *Obi te obi so.* Literal translation: Someone is higher in authority above others.
294 295 296	**SUMPIE - PYRAMID or ROYAL DAIS** **Symbol of AUTHORITY and STATE ASSEMBLY** This is the royal dais from which the king makes public addresses. At the Asantehene's Manhyia Palace there are two such daises: *Sumpie Kumaa (Bogyawe)* and *Sumpie Kɛseɛ (Dwaberem)*.
297	**ƆBAA NE ƆMAN – WOMAN IS THE NATION** From the maxim: *Ɔbaa ne ɔman.* Literal translation: Woman is the nation. This symbol depicts the Akan belief that when a boy is born, an individual is born; but when a girl is born, a nation is born.
298 299	**ƆHENE KYƐ (ABƆTIRE) – KING'S CROWN** Symbol of **ROYALNESS** and **POWER**
300	**ƆHENE PAPA - GOOD KING** Symbol of **EXEMPLARY LEADERSHIP** From the expression: *Ɔhene dɔ wo a, ɔmma wonto ntam.* Or, *Ɔhene nya ahotenafo pa a, ne berɛ so dwo.* Also, *Sɛ ahennwa wɔ animuonyam a, na ɛnkyerɛ sɛ ɔhene a ɔte.so anim yɛ nyam.* Literal translation: The good king prevents his subjects from getting into trouble. Or, If a king has good counsellors, his reign is peaceful. Also, Even if the stool is respected it does not mean that the incumbent chief is worthy of respect. A position can remain respected even when its incumbent is unworthy.

301	**ƆHEMMAA PAPA - GOOD QUEENMOTHER** Symbol of **GOOD LEADERSHIP, HEROIC DEEDS, and BRAVERY** From the expression: *Ɔhemmaa pa Yaa Asantewaa, ɔbaabasia a ɔkura tuo ne akofena de di ako.* Literal translation: Yaa Asantewaa the good queenmother, the warrior woman who carries a gun and the sword of state to do battle. Yaa Asantewaa was the queenmother of Ïdweso (Ejisu). It was she who rallied the Asante nation to rebel against the British in 1900 after the Asantehene Prempeh I had been captured and exiled to the Seychelles Islands in the Indian Ocean. The war, Yaa Asantewaa War marked the last time a great queenmother led an army to war.
302	**NEA ƆPƐ SƐ OBEDI HENE - HE WHO WANTS TO BE A KING** **Symbol of the QUALITIES OF A LEADER, SERVICE, and LEADERSHIP SKILLS** From the expression: *Nea ɔpɛ sɛ ɔbɛdi hene daakye no, firi ase sua som ansa.* Literal translation: He, who wants to be a king in the future, should first learn to serve.
 303 304 305  306 307 308 309 310	ADINKRAHENE - KING OF THE ADINKRA SYMBOLS Symbol of GREATNESS, PRUDENCE, FIRMNESS, MAGNANIMITY, SUPREMACY and OMNIPOTENCE OF GOD From the expression: *Yede brɛbrɛ bɛkum Adinkra.* Literal translation: Slowly, but surely we will defeat Adinkra. The concentric circles signify the universe and its creator. Only the Creator of the universe, like the creator of the circle, knows its beginning and its end. This symbol is believed to have been named in memory of King Adinkra of Gyaman. King Adinkra was defeated in a war against the Asante. The Asante King at that time was Osei Bonsu. The defeat of King Adinkra was a relief for everyone. King Adinkra was authoritarian, a man of his word, and an intransigent king. This symbol is said to have played an inspiring role in the designing of other symbols. It signifies the importance of playing a leadership role.
311	**ƆBREGUO – STRUGGLING IN VAIN** Symbol of DESPONDENCY, LOSS, UNHAPPINESS, and DEPRESSION From the expression: *Ɔbreguo yɛ ya.* Literal translation: Struggling in vain is painfully depressing.

  312 313	**AKRAFOƆ-KƆN-MU – PENDANT** Symbol of PROTECTION, SPIRITUALITY
  314 315	**ADINKRAHENE NTOASO - DOUBLE ADINKRAHENE** Symbol of **GREATNESS, PRUDENCE, FIRMNESS, MAGNANIMITY,** **SUPREMACY and OMNIPOTENCE OF GOD** The concentric circles signify the universe and its creator. Only the Creator of the universe, like the creator of the circle, knows its beginning and its end. This symbol is believed to have been named in memory of King Adinkra of Gyaman
  316 317	**ADINKRA BA APAU - THE SON OF ADINKRA** Symbol of **ROYALTY, STATUS** and **AUTHORITY** Oral tradition has it that Nana Adinkra's son, Apau was captured together with other Gyamans and brought to Asokwa near Kumasi. At Asokwa Apau is believed to have introduced technological innovations in the making of adinkra cloths.
  318 319 320	**ƆHENE ANIWA - THE KING'S EYES** Symbol of **VIGILANCE, FAR-SIGHTEDNESS, INTELLIGENCE, PROTECTION, SECURITY, DEFENCE, AUTHORITY, and POWER** From the aphorism: *Ɔhene aniwa twa ne ho hyia.* Literal translation: The king's eyes are placed all around him. Or, The king sees everything. The king's sense of justice deriving from the norms and mores of the society must be constant, active and fair to all. The people are the eyes and ears of the king. The king is, therefore, said to see and hear all things that happen in the society.
  321	**ABAN PA - GOOD GOVERNMENT** **Symbol of DEMOCRATIC RULE, STABLE SOCIETY, DEVELOPMENT, and PROGRESS** From the expression: *Sɛ ɔman mu yɛ dɛ a, yɛn nyinaa te mu bi. Or, Ɔman mu yɛ dɛ a, ene wo fie.* Literal translation: If there is peace and stability in a state, we all live in it. Or, What peace and progress a society knows may be indicated by what prevails in the households in that society.

322	**ƆHENE KƆ HIA - THE KING IS GONE TO THE HAREM** Symbol of **PROTECTION, SECURITY, and WARMTH** From the expression: *Ɔhene kɔ hia.* Literal translation: The king is gone to the women's quarters (harem). Hia is where the king's wives live, that is, the female quarters. This is where the hearth is, and therefore, it is associated with warmth and food.
323 324 325 326 327 328 329 330 331	**NKURUMA KƐSE - BIG OKRA** Symbol of **GREATNESS, SUPREMACY, SECRECY, CARE-GIVER, and BENEVOLENCE** From the aphorisms: *Nkuruma kɛse, ɛbɔ ne ya hyɛ ne yam.* Also, *Amoawisi, Nkuruma kɛse a ɔwo mma aduasa nso ɔgye abayɛn.* Also, *Amoawisi a ɔwo mma aduasa nso ɔgye abayɛn.* Literal translation: The okra does not reveal its seeds through its skin; or, There is more in man's mind than shows in his face. Also, Amoawisi, the benevolent who raised thirty children of her own, yet was kind enough to raise other people's children.
332 333 334 335 33 337 338 339 340 341	**DWENNIMMƐN - RAM'S HORNS** Symbol of **STRENGTH and HUMILITY** From the proverb: *Dwenini ahoɔden ne n'ammɛn; wo pan n'ammɛn na woayi no awie.* Also, *Dwenini yɛ asisie a ɔde n'akoma nnyɛ ne mmɛn.* Literal translation: The strength of the ram lies in its horns, once they are plucked off, then it is caught in a trap. Also, The ram may bully only when it is provoked to do so.
 342 343 344	**DWENNIMMƐN NTOASOƆ - DOUBLE RAM'S HORNS** Symbol of **POWER, AUTHORITY, STRENGTH, and HUMILITY** From the proverb: *Dwenini ahoɔden ne n'ammɛn; wo pan n'ammɛn na woayi no awie.* Also, *Dwenini yɛ asisie a ɔde n'akoma nnyɛ ne mmɛn.* Literal translation: The strength of the ram lies in its horns, once they are plucked off, then it is caught in a trap. Also, The ram may bully only when it is provoked to do so.

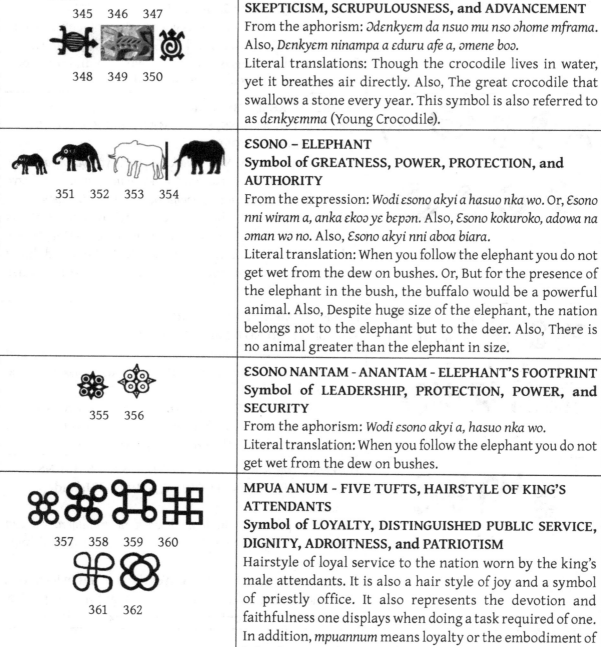

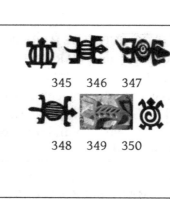 345 346 347 348 349 350	**DƐNKYƐM - CROCODILE** Symbol of **GREATNESS, POWER, ADAPTABILITY, SKEPTICISM, SCRUPULOUSNESS, and ADVANCEMENT** From the aphorism: *Ɔdɛnkyɛm da nsuo mu nso ɔhome mframa.* Also, *Dɛnkyɛm ninampa a ɛduru afe a, ɔmene boɔ.* Literal translations: Though the crocodile lives in water, yet it breathes air directly. Also, The great crocodile that swallows a stone every year. This symbol is also referred to as *dɛnkyɛmma* (Young Crocodile).
351 352 353 354	**ƐSONO – ELEPHANT** **Symbol of GREATNESS, POWER, PROTECTION, and AUTHORITY** From the expression: *Wodi ɛsono akyi a hasuo nka wo.* Or, *Ɛsono nni wiram a, anka ɛkoɔ yɛ bɛpɔn.* Also, *Ɛsono kokuroko, adowa na ɔman wɔ no.* Also, *Ɛsono akyi nni aboa biara.* Literal translation: When you follow the elephant you do not get wet from the dew on bushes. Or, But for the presence of the elephant in the bush, the buffalo would be a powerful animal. Also, Despite huge size of the elephant, the nation belongs not to the elephant but to the deer. Also, There is no animal greater than the elephant in size.
355 356	**ƐSONO NANTAM - ANANTAM - ELEPHANT'S FOOTPRINT** **Symbol of LEADERSHIP, PROTECTION, POWER, and SECURITY** From the aphorism: *Wodi ɛsono akyi a, hasuo nka wo.* Literal translation: When you follow the elephant you do not get wet from the dew on bushes.
357 358 359 360 361 362	**MPUA ANUM - FIVE TUFTS, HAIRSTYLE OF KING'S ATTENDANTS** **Symbol of LOYALTY, DISTINGUISHED PUBLIC SERVICE, DIGNITY, ADROITNESS, and PATRIOTISM** Hairstyle of loyal service to the nation worn by the king's male attendants. It is also a hair style of joy and a symbol of priestly office. It also represents the devotion and faithfulness one displays when doing a task required of one. In addition, *mpuannum* means loyalty or the embodiment of lofty duty to a desired goal.

363	**NKWANTANAN - FOUR TUFTS, HAIRSTYLE OF THE KING'S KEY BEARERS** Symbol of **LOYALTY, SECURITY, and TRUTHFULNESS** From the expression: *Aso mu nni nkwanta.* Or, *Nkwantanan, ka nokorε.* Literal translation: There are no crossroads in the ear. Or, Crossroads, tell the truth. This symbol indicates the need for a public servant to be truthful and non-contradictory. One cannot accept truth and falsehood at the same time, or no statement can be both true and false.
364 365 366	**MPUAANSA – THREE TUFTS, HAIRSTYLE OF THE COURT CRIER** Symbol of **LOYALTY, SECURITY, and TRUTHFULNESS**
367 368 369	**ƆHENE or ƆHEMMAA PAPA - THE KING'S or QUEEN'S FAN** Symbol of **PUBLIC SERVICE and LOYALTY**
370 371 372 373 374 375	**NKOTIMSEFOƆ PUA - HAIRSTYLE OF THE QUEEN'S ATTENDANTS** Symbol of **LOYALTY, DEVOTION TO DUTY, DISTINGUISHED PUBLIC SERVICE** Hairstyle of loyal service to the nation worn by the queen's female attendants. It signifies readiness to serve.
376 377	**MMƆDWEWAFOƆ PUA - HAIRSTYLE OF THE QUEEN'S ATTENDANTS** Symbol of **LOYALTY, DISTINGUISHED PUBLIC SERVICE, and PATRIOTISM**

378 379 380	**NSAFOA - KEYS** Symbol of **LOYALTY, TRUSTWORTHINESS, and DISTINGUISHED PUBLIC SERVICE** From the proverb: *Krado ne safoa mu wɔ panin.* Literal translation: Between the lock and the key, there is a senior. Keys served as the insignia of *fotosanfoɔ* or the *kotokuosanfoɔ* (treasury public servants) who carried the King's treasury bag of gold dust and gold weights. Fotoɔ was a leather bag made from the skin of a monkey. Another leather bag used in the king's treasury was called *sanaa* and this was made from the elephant's ear. Some of these treasury staff served as toll collectors in the markets and on the highways. *Nsafoa* (keys) also refer to the historic capturing of European forts by the Aka*n*.
381	**SOM PA – GOOD SERVICE** Symbol of **WORKING CONDITIONS**, and **LABOR RELATIONS** From the expression: *Wosom wo wura som pa a, ɔyi wo ayɛ.* Literal translation: If you serve your mater well, he rewards you.
383	**FA W'ANI HWƐ - JUST LOOK** Symbol of **WARNING AGAINST BEING NOSY** From the expression: *Wohunu obi ade a, fa w'ani hwɛ na mmfa w'ano nnka.* Literal translation: Just look, but do not say anything.
384 385	**DAWUROBƆNI- GONG GONG BEATER** Symbol of **ALERTNESS, LOYALTY, DUTIFULNESS, and MERITORIOUS PUBLIC SERVICE** From the proverb: *Dawurobɔni nsuro mantamu.* Literal translation: The town crier is not afraid of nooks and crannies of any neighborhood

 386　387　388	**DAWURO - GONG GONG, IRON BELL** Symbol of **ALERTNESS, LOYALTY, DUTIFULNESS, COMMUNICATION, PUBLIC ANNOUNCEMENTS, POLITICAL DISCOURSE, and MERITORIOUS PUBLIC SERVICE** From the proverb: *Dawurobɔni nsuro mantamu.* Literal translation: The town crier is not afraid of nooks and crannies of any neighborhood. The iron bell is used to announce the king's decrees and to convey messages and public announcements from the king's palace to the people. It is also used to call people to public meetings that are not of crisis nature. Iron bells are also used by priests for religious ceremonies.
 389　390　391　392  393　394　395　396	**KWATAKYE ATIKɔ - HAIR STYLE OF BRAVERY** Symbol of **BRAVERY and VALOR** This symbol is said to be a special hair style of Kwatakye, a war captain of old Asante. The symbol has come to represent bravery and fearlessness. It is also given as an earned title to any brave son of an Akan community.
 397　398　399　400　401　402　403	**AKOBƐN – WAR HORN** Symbol of **CALL TO ACTION, VOLUNTEERISM, AND MILITARY POWER** From the expression: *Kɔsankɔbi, wokasa ɔbaa ano a, Kobiri nku wo.* Also, *Sɛ ɔmani ye ra a, yɛde ɔmani abɛn na yɛde hwehwɛ no.* Literal translation: Deserter, may Kobiri (a deity) kill you if you dare speak as a man to a woman.

404   405   406   407

OHENE TUO - KING'S GUN
Symbol of **ADAPTATION, AUTHORITY, POWER, STRENGTH, PROTECTION, DEFENSE, and GREATNESS**

From the proverb: *Tuo nya otiafoɔ a, na odi abaninsɛm.*
Literal translation: It is only when a gun has a man to cock it that it performs warlike deeds.

The gun has been incorporated in Akan ceremonies such as the swearing of the king-elect into office and gun salute at funerals. In using the gun as part of the king-elect's swearing-in ceremony, it gives him the opportunity to demonstrate he is capable of carrying out his role as the commander-in-chief of the *asafo*. He fires the gun to demonstrate that he is capable of ensuring national defense and security during his rule.

At the Banpanase Installation of the Asantehene-elect the Queenmother, speaking through the Akyeamehene would say:

Wo wɔfa (nua anaasɛ nana) na odi Asantehene yi,
Ɛnnɛ ɔkɔ ne kraa akyi.
Adare bu a, yɛbɔ bi poma mu
Enti wo wɔfa (nua, nana) ne tuo na ɔhemmaa ne Kumasi Mpanimfoɔ
yɛde ma wo ahwɛ
ɔman yi so sɛnea wo wɔfa hwɛɛ ɔman yi soɔ
Ɔman yɛnto no mmradɛ;
Wose tuntum na tuntum; fufuo na fufuo
Yɛde wo wɔfa (nua, nana) tuo no ma wo
Yɛhyira wo kosɛ, kosɛ, Anɔkye komaa mu.

Your uncle (brother or grand-uncle) who has been Asantehene,
Today his soul has gone whence it came from
When the handle of an axe comes out
A new one is carved to replace it
Thus the Queenmother and Kumasi Elders pass on to you the gun of your uncle (bother or grand-uncle)
You are not to deceive the nation
Your black must be black; your white white
We present to you your uncle's (brother's or grand-uncle's) gun
We wish you well
May Anɔkye, from his sanctuary, bless you.

The Asantehene-elect later fires the ohene tuo to demonstrate that he would be capable of commanding the state's military forces on the battlefield.

234

408 **409**	**AKOO MMƆWERƐ - PARROT'S TALONS** Symbol of **SWIFTNESS, POWER, and INTELLIGENCE**
410 **411**	**ƆKƆDEƐ MMƆWERƐ - EAGLE'S TALONS** Symbol of **AUTHORITY, POWER, STRENGTH, and SWIFTNESS** From the aphorism: *Ɔkɔdeɛ se: Gye tuo, gye ɔwɔ. Or, Ɔkɔdeɛ ɔnsuro wiram aboa biara gye ɔwɔ ne tuo nko ara.* Literal translation: Except for the snake and the gun, the eagle fears nothing. Emblem of the Oyoko clan and it reflects their idea of unity and strength. The eagle is the mightiest bird in the sky, and its strength is concentrated in its talons. The Oyoko clan, one of the nine Akan clans, uses this symbol as their clan emblem.
412 **413**	**KƆTƆKƆ - PORCUPINE** Symbol of **BRAVERY, PREPAREDNESS, GALLANTRY, and POWER** From the expression: *Asante kɔtɔkɔ, kum apem a, apem bɛba. Or, Kɔtɔkɔ renko a, hwɛ n'amiadeɛ. Or, Aboa biara ne kɔtɔkɔ nni ntohyia. Or, Asante kɔtɔkɔ, monka ntoa.* Literal translation: Asante porcupine, you kill a thousand, a thousand more will come. Or, You can tell from the armament (quills) of the porcupine whether he is prepared to fight or not. Or, No animal dare meet the porcupine in a struggle. Or, Asante porcupines seize your gunpowder belts. The Asante military was likened to the porcupine's strategy of shooting its quills in barrages and would quickly it reproduce them for protection against its predators.
414 **415**	**PAGYA – STRIKES FIRE** Symbol of **BRAVERY, POWER, and VALOR** From the proverb: *Twerɛboɔ nti na tuo di abaninsɛm. Or, Etuo yɛnto no brɛɛ.* Literal translation: Thanks to the flint-stone, the gun performs warlike deeds. Or, The gun does not strike in times of peace. This was a kind of gun owned by men of valor and dexterity. It is now mostly used on ceremonial and funeral occasions.

 416	**TUO NE AKOFENA - GUN AND STATE SWORD** Symbol of **POWER, RESPONSIBILITY, AUTHORITY, LEGITIMACY, NATIONAL SECURITY, PROTECTION, and MILITARY PROWESS** From the expression: *Tuo nya otiafoɔ a, na odi abaninsɛm.* Literal translation: It is only when a gun has a man to cock it that it performs warlike deeds The gun and the sword are used in swearing a new chief into office. As a symbol, the two together, signifies the responsibility of the new ruler to continue to protect and guard the nation as did his fore bearers. The new ruler fires the gun and wields the sword to demonstrate that he is capable of performing his duties as the supreme commander of the military.
 417	**AKYƐM - SHIELD** Symbol of **BRAVERY AND HEROIC DEEDS, GLORIOUS ACCOMPLISHMENT, PERMANENCE OF DEEDS OF DISTINCTION, and DURABILITY** From the proverb: *Akyɛm tete a, ɛka ne mmeramu.* Or, *Agyan nti na yɛyɔ akyɛm.* Literal translation: When a shield wears out, the framework still remains. The good deeds of people live after them. This symbolizes bravery as well as the durability and the enduring nature of the distinguished deeds of a great person. Or, Because of the arrow, we make the shield. If it were not for aggression, defensive weapons would not be necessary.
 418	**ANKONAM BOAFOƆ NE ONYANKOPƆN - GOD IS THE HELPER OF THE LONELY** Symbol of **IMPARTIALITY, FAIRNESS, JUSTICE, ADVOCACY, and BENEFICENCE** From the expression: *Ankonam boafoɔ ne Onyankopɔn.* Or, *Aboa a ɔnni dua no, Nyame na ɔpra ne ho.* Literal translation: God is the helper of the lonely. Or, It is God who drives away the fly from the body of the animal which has no tail. This symbol points out the Akan belief that God ensures that there is justice and fairness for all, irrespective of their social class, status, or condition in life.

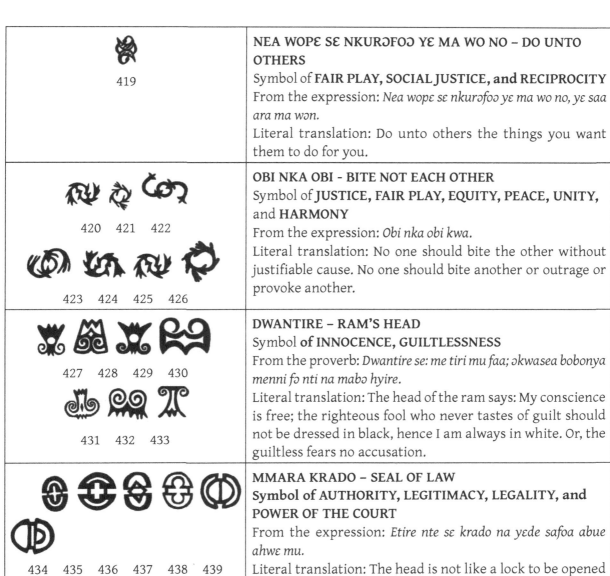

419	**NEA WOPƐ SƐ NKURƆFOƆ YƐ MA WO NO – DO UNTO OTHERS** Symbol of **FAIR PLAY, SOCIAL JUSTICE, and RECIPROCITY** From the expression: *Nea wopɛ sɛ nkurɔfoɔ yɛ ma wo no, yɛ saa ara ma wɔn.* Literal translation: Do unto others the things you want them to do for you.
420 421 422 **423 424 425 426**	**OBI NKA OBI - BITE NOT EACH OTHER** Symbol of **JUSTICE, FAIR PLAY, EQUITY, PEACE, UNITY, and HARMONY** From the expression: *Obi nka obi kwa.* Literal translation: No one should bite the other without justifiable cause. No one should bite another or outrage or provoke another.
427 428 429 430 **431 432 433**	**DWANTIRE – RAM'S HEAD** Symbol **of INNOCENCE, GUILTLESSNESS** From the proverb: *Dwantire se: me tiri mu faa; ɔkwasea bobonya menni fɔ nti na mabɔ hyire.* Literal translation: The head of the ram says: My conscience is free; the righteous fool who never tastes of guilt should not be dressed in black, hence I am always in white. Or, the guiltless fears no accusation.
434 435 436 437 438 439 **440 441 442 443 444 445**	**MMARA KRADO – SEAL OF LAW** Symbol of **AUTHORITY, LEGITIMACY, LEGALITY, and POWER OF THE COURT** From the expression: *Etire nte sɛ krado na yɛde safoa abue ahwɛ mu.* Literal translation: The head is not like a lock to be opened with a key to view the inside.

446 447 448 449	**NEA NE EPA DA WO - HE WHOSE HANDCUFF YOU WEAR** Symbol of **SERVITUDE, JUSTICE, LAW, ORDER, CONTROL** From the aphorism: *Onii a ne epa da wo no, n'akoa ne wo.* Or, *Sɛ woko kurom na sɛ hɔ ɔdekuro mantam dɛdua mu a, yemmusa sɛ kuro mu hɔ yɛ.* Literal translation: You are the subject of the one whose handcuffs you wear. Or, When you go to a town and you see the chief of the town is in handcuffs, you do not ask whether everything is alright in that town.
450 451 452	**SEPƆ - DAGGER** Symbol of **JUSTICE, CAPITAL PUNISHMENT** Knife used in executions to prevent a curse on the king. This is thrust through the victim's cheeks to prevent his invoking a curse on the king. From the proverb: *Katankranyi Ayɛboafo, ɔpimpini n'akyi ansa na wagyam.* Or, *Atɔpreɛwuo nyɛ mpatuwuo.* Literal translation: Kantankrankyi Ayɛboafo, the great executioner's sword retreats before it acts. Or, Death by torture and execution is not unexpected.
453	**OBI NKYƐ OBI KWAN MU SI – TO ERR IS HUMAN** Symbol of **FALLIBILITY, MORTALITY and IMPERFECTION** From the aphorism: *Obi nkyɛ obi kwan mu si.* Literal translation: To err is human. Sooner or later someone will stray into another person's path.
454	**ƆDƆ ANIWA – LOVE EYES** Symbol of **AFFECTION, LOVE AT FIRST SIGHT, SMILING EYES,** and **LUSTFUL LOOKS** From the expression: *Ɔdɔ foforo yɛ anifuraeɛ ne adammɔ.* Or, *Ɔdɔ mehu wo a, mebɔ m'ani asu; mefa wo a, mefa siadeɛ.* Literal translation: First love is both blinding and illogical. Or, My love, when I look at you, my eyes are sanctified; I abound in good luck when I touch you.
455 456 457 458	**FRANFRANTA – BUTTERFLY** Symbol of **BEAUTY, GRACEFULNESS, DEVOTION, CHANGE,** and **DEVELOPMENT** From the expression: *Afafantɔ se: nsa ni o, na sika a yɛde bɛtɔ.* Literal translation: The butterfly says: Here is wine, where is the money to buy with?

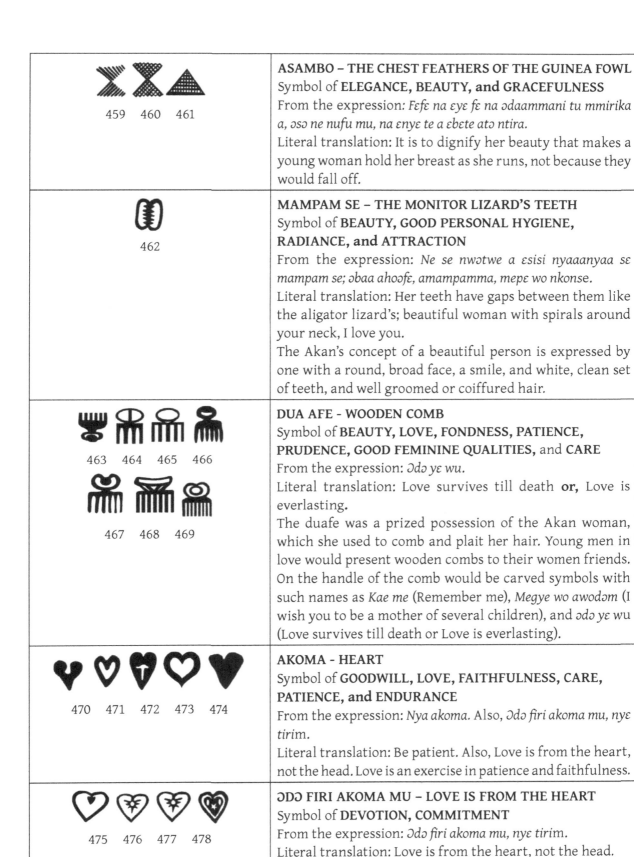

459 460 461	**ASAMBO – THE CHEST FEATHERS OF THE GUINEA FOWL** Symbol of **ELEGANCE, BEAUTY, and GRACEFULNESS** From the expression: *Fɛfɛ na ɛyɛ fɛ na ɔdaammani tu mmirika a, ɔso ne nufu mu, na ɛnyɛ te a ɛbɛte atɔ ntira.* Literal translation: It is to dignify her beauty that makes a young woman hold her breast as she runs, not because they would fall off.
462	**MAMPAM SE – THE MONITOR LIZARD'S TEETH** Symbol of **BEAUTY, GOOD PERSONAL HYGIENE, RADIANCE, and ATTRACTION** From the expression: *Ne se nwɔtwe a ɛsisi nyaaanyaa sɛ mampam se; ɔbaa ahoofɛ, amampamma, mepɛ wo nkonse.* Literal translation: Her teeth have gaps between them like the aligator lizard's; beautiful woman with spirals around your neck, I love you. The Akan's concept of a beautiful person is expressed by one with a round, broad face, a smile, and white, clean set of teeth, and well groomed or coiffured hair.
463 464 465 466 467 468 469	**DUA AFE - WOODEN COMB** Symbol of **BEAUTY, LOVE, FONDNESS, PATIENCE, PRUDENCE, GOOD FEMININE QUALITIES, and CARE** From the expression: *Ɔdɔ yɛ wu.* Literal translation: Love survives till death **or,** Love is everlasting. The duafe was a prized possession of the Akan woman, which she used to comb and plait her hair. Young men in love would present wooden combs to their women friends. On the handle of the comb would be carved symbols with such names as *Kae me* (Remember me), *Megye wo awodɔm* (I wish you to be a mother of several children), and *ɔdɔ yɛ wu* (Love survives till death or Love is everlasting).
470 471 472 473 474	**AKOMA - HEART** Symbol of **GOODWILL, LOVE, FAITHFULNESS, CARE, PATIENCE, and ENDURANCE** From the expression: *Nya akoma.* Also, *Ɔdɔ firi akoma mu, nyɛ tirim.* Literal translation: Be patient. Also, Love is from the heart, not the head. Love is an exercise in patience and faithfulness.
475 476 477 478	**ƆDƆ FIRI AKOMA MU – LOVE IS FROM THE HEART** Symbol of **DEVOTION, COMMITMENT** From the expression: *Ɔdɔ firi akoma mu, nyɛ tirim.* Literal translation: Love is from the heart, not the head.

479 480	**ƆDOFO NYERA FIE KWAN - THE LOVER WILL FIND HIS/HER WAY HOME** Symbol of **LOVE, DEVOTION, PERSISTENCE, and COMMITMENT** From the expression: *Ɔdɔfo nyera fie kwan.* Literal translation: The lover will find his/her way home.
481 482 483	**ƆDƆ NISUO – LOVE TEARS** Symbol of **LOVE, JOY, SORROW, DEVOTION, and SUFFERING** Love tears may be tears of joy or that of sorrow. Love is full of happiness and joy, or may be long suffering and full of agony.
484	**ƆDƆ BATA AKOMA HO – LOVE IS IN THE HEART** Symbol of **FAITHFULNESS, LOVE, and AFFECTION** From the expression: *Ɔdɔ bata akoma ho; sɛ ɔdɔ bɛsɔ a efiri tiri* mu. Literal translation: Love is in the heart. Love emanates from the heart but lasting love is from the head. Initial love is irrational, but lasting love is ration*al*.
485	**FA W'AKOMA MA ME – GIVE YOUR HEART TO ME** Symbol of **DEVOTION, LOVE, and COMMITMENT** From the expression: *Fa w'akoma ma me. Or, Ɔdɔfo a ɔdɔ me no na ɔde ɔdɔ nam noa aduane ma me di. Also, Sɛ mede m'akoma ma wo a, wobɛtumi asɔ mu yie?* Literal translation: Give me your heart. Or, A lover who loves me prepares food made with the love fish for me. Someone who loves you gives you the best. Also, If I give my heart to you will you handle it with care?
486	**KAE ME – REMEMBER ME** Symbol of **FAITHFULNESS, DEVOTION, and COMMITMENT** From the expression: *Kae me, ɔdɔ.* Literal translation: Remember me, love.
487	**NNAADAA ME – DO NOT DECEIVE ME** Symbol of **SINCERITY, TRUTHFULNESS, FAITHFULNESS, and COMMITMENT** From the expression: *Aware yɛdi no ɔdɔ, ɛnye anosɛm hunu; ɔdɔfo, nnaadaa me.* Literal translation: Marriage springs out of love, not empty boasts; do not deceive me my love.

488	**ME WARE WO - I SHALL MARRY YOU** Symbol of **COMMITMENT, PERSEVERANCE, DETERMINATION, and STEADFASTNESS** From the expression: *Obi ntutu mmirika nkɔdɔn aware-dan dotee. Or, Sɛ obi repɛ fie bi mu akɔ ama woawo no, na wannya hɔ ankɔ a, na ɔkɔ hɔ awareɛ.* Literal translation: No one rushes into the job of mixing the concrete for building the house of marriage. Or, If someone wishes to be born into a certain family and is unable to do so, then he will marry into the family. Marriage depends on proper and deliberate planning. The promise to marry someone carries such responsibility that one is urged not to rush into marriage as marriage is a commitment for *life*.
489	**DƐNKYƐM DUA - CROCODILE'S TAIL** Symbol of **LOVE, MARRIAGE, CONUBIALITY, MATRIMONY** From the expression: *Awareɛ ɛyɛ ayɔnkofa, ɛnyɛ abusuabɔ.* Literal translation: The contract of marriage is a contract of friendship; it is not like the bond of blood in family relationships. This symbolizes the original Mother Goddess, the Creator in whom was embodied the union of male and female; the biological union of the two opposite sex - a God who was a manifestation of the dual sexual parts present in living creatures before being separated.
490 491	**AKOMANTOASOƆ - JOINED HEARTS** Symbol of **PEACE, GOODWILL, TOGETHERNESS, UNDERSTANDING, MUTUAL RESPECT, LOVE and UNITY** From the expression: *Obi dɔ wo a, dɔ no bi.* Also, *Akoma ntoasoɔ ne ɔdɔ, anidie, ne nteaseɛ.* Literal translation: When someone loves you, show your love in return. Also, When hearts are joined together the result is love, mutual respect and understanding. This symbol signifies the joining together of the families of the couple in marriage. Marriage is a union not only of two people, but also of two families. It also stresses the need for mutual respect, understanding, and the need for concerted action or united *front*.

492 493 494 495 496 497	**ƆSRANE NE NSOROMMA - THE CRESCENT MOON AND THE STAR** Symbol of **DEVOTION, PATIENCE, LOVE, FAITHFULNESS, FONDNESS, HARMONY, CONSISTENCY, and AFFECTION** From the proverb: *Kyekye pe awaree, ɔsrane ara na obeware no.* Literal translation: *Kyekye* (the North Star) is in love; she is always waiting the return of her husband, the moon. This symbol stresses the importance of cooperation between two people in a marriage relationship.
498	**AWARE NYƐ NSA – MARRIAGE IS NOT LIKE WINE** Symbol of MARITAL PROBLEMS, THE NATURE OF MARRIAGE, From the proverb: *Awareε nyε nsafufuo na yεasɔ ahwε.* Literal translation: Marriage is not like the palm-wine to be tasted before it is drunk.
499	**AWARE MU NSƐM (AWAREƐ YƐ YA) – MARITAL PROBLEMS** Symbol of **MARITAL PROBLEMS, COMPROMISE, GIVE-AND-TAKE,** From the aphorism: *Awareε yε ya. Or, Barima mfa n'ahoɔden nware. Or, Ɔbaa kɔ nsuo anɔpa a, ɔdom ne ho anwummerε. Also, Awareε nyε nsafufuo na yεasɔ ahwε. Also, Aware foforɔ te sε kookoo ahahan, ne foforɔ mu yε frɔmfrɔm, n'awieε yε dwann.* Literal translation: Marriage is a difficult undertaking. Or, A man should treat his wife as an equal not a subservient dependent. Or, A woman who fetches water in the morning saves herself the trouble of fetching water in the evening. Also, Marriage is not like the palm-wine to be tasted before it is drunk. Also, A new marriage is like cocoa leaf, its beginnings is fine but it ends wilted. Marriage is always a trial for the partners. In order to have a successful marriage, each partner must be willing to make sacrifices and compromises.
500	**DONNO – BELL DRUM** Symbol of **ADORATION, CAJOLERY, PRAISE and RHYTHM** From the expression: *Donno bεyε dε a, εfiri amotoamu.* Literal translation: If the music of the hour-glass shaped drum will sound pleasant, it depends on the armpit. Donno is an hour glass-shaped drum. In outline the drum shows two triangles that meet at the apex, the symbol of the bisexual Mother God as the ruler of the sky, earth, and the underworld. The Donno is one of the very few drums females are allowed to play in the Akan society. Young women use the donno to sing the praises and appellations of a young woman when celebrating her puberty rites (*bragorɔ*).

501 502 503 504 505 506 507 508 509	**DONNO NTOASO - JOINED BELL DRUM** Symbol of **PRAISE, ADULATION, UNITED ACTION, UNITY, and JUBILATION** From the expression: *Ɔbaawarefoɔ ahoɔfɛ gyam ne kunu te n'anim.* Literal translation: The good appearance or beauty of the married woman is a credit to her husband to whom it sings praises.
510	**AWARE PAPA – GOOD (SUCCESSFUL) MARRIAGE** Symbol of **SUCCESSFUL MARRIAGE, MARITAL BLISS** From the expression: *Ɔbaa nya aware pa a, ɛyɛ animuonyam ma ɔno ne n'abusuafoɔ.* Or, *Aware pa gyina aboterɛ afuo mu.* Literal translation: Good or a very successful marriage is beneficial for the woman as well as her family. Or, Marriage prospers only in the farm of patience.
511	**AWARE BƆNE – BAD MARRIAGE** Symbol of **BAD MARRIAGE, DIFFICULTIES IN MARRIAGE, and UNSUCCESSFUL MARRIAGE** From the expression: *Aware bɔne tete ɔbaa pa.* Or, *Me ne m'aware bɔne; meso kɛntɛn hunu na worehwehwɛ mu.* Also, *Kɔ aware te adwerɛ, na mereyɛ no dɛn ni o?* Also, *ɔbaa a ɔbɛbɔ adwoman nnim sɛ wakɔ aware pa.* Literal translation: Bad treatment in marriage destroys or corrupts a good woman. Or, Me and my disastrous marriage; I am carrying an empty basket and you are searching through it. Also, What am I to do with an ill-fated marriage that always requires propitiatory rituals? Also, If a woman is going to commit adultery, it does not matter that she has good marriage.
512	**YERENOM BEBREE AWAREƐ – POLYGAMY** Symbol of **WARNING AGAINST POLYGAMY, GENDER EXPLOITATION**, and **MALE DOMINATION** From the proverb: *Wopɛ akasakasa a, na woware yerenom bebree.* Or, *Mmaa dodoɔ awareɛ mu nni biribi sɛ ohia.* Literal translation: If you like frequent quarrels then you marry many wives. Or, To marry many women is nothing but poverty.

513	**KƐTƐ PA - GOOD BED** Symbol of **GOOD MARRIAGE, SUCCESSFUL MARRIAGE, GOOD CARE** From the expression: *Ɔbaa kɔ aware pa a, na yɛde no to kɛtɛ pa so.* Literal translation: A successful or good marriage begins with the good bed on which the wife sleeps in her marital home.
514 515	**ƆBAATAN – MOTHERLINESS** Symbol of **DOUBLE LIFE, PREGNANCY, REPRODUCTIVE POWERS,** and **MOTHERLINESS** From the aphorism: *Ɔbaatan na onim deɛ ne ba bɛdie.* Also, *Eno ɔbaatan pa, nkuruma kɛse a ne yam abaduasa na ɔmmoa.* Also, *Eno, woyɛ sɛn kɛseɛ a wogye adididodoɔ.* Or, *Wo nuabaa aserɛ so a, wonna so.* Literal translation: The mother knows what her child will eat. Also, Good mother, the okra full of the seeds of many issues and proven. Also, Mother, you are the big cooking pot that feeds many people. Or, If your sister has big and beautiful thighs, you do not sleep there. A pregnant woman is said to have a DOUBLE LIFE: her's and the baby's.
516	**YAFUN YƐ AKWANTEN – THE WOMB IS LIKE THE HIGHWAY** Symbol of **MOTHERHOOD** From the expression: *Yafun yɛ akwaten, dea yɛ ne dea ɛnyɛ nyina fa mu.* Literal translation: The stomach (i.e. the womb) is like the throughfare, the good and the ugly all pass through.
517	**MMƆFRA BƐNYINI – THE YOUNG SHALL GROW** Symbol of **GROWTH, MATURATION, DEVELOPMENT, RESPONSIBILITY,** and **PARENTAL CARE** From the aphorism: *Obi hwɛ wo ma wo se fifiri a, wo nso hwɛ no ma ne deɛ tutu.* Or, *Ɔba nyini ɔse fie, nanso ɔnka hɔ, ɔwɔ abusua.* Literal translation: When one takes care of you as you grow your teeth, you return one's favor by taking care of one during one's old age when one's teeth begin to fall out. Or, A child grows up in its father's house, but he does not stay there, it has a matriclan.

518 519	**ƆBAATAN AWAAMU – THE WARM EMBRACE OF A MOTHER** Symbol of **MOTHERHOOD, PARENTAL CARE, WARM EMBRACE,** and **LOVE** From the aphorism: *Ɔbaatan pa na ɔnim deɛ ne mma bɛdi.* Or, *Wo nuabaa aserɛ so a, wonna so.* Literal translation: The good mother knows what her children will eat. Or, If your sister has big and beautiful thighs, that should not give you a reason for you to sleep on her thighs.
520 521 522 523 524 525 526	**AKOKƆ NAN – HEN'S FEET** Symbol of **PARENTAL DISCIPLINE, DISCIPLINE, PROTECTION, PARENTHOOD, CARE,** and **TENDER LOVING CARE** From the proverb: *Akokɔ nan tia ne ba so a, ɛnku no.* Literal translation: When the hen treads on its chicken, she does not mean to kill them. Or, Parental admonition is not intended to harm the child. This represents the ideal nature of parents, being both protective and corrective. An exhortation to nurture children, but a warning not to pamper them.
527	**EBAN - FENCE** Symbol of LOVE, SAFETY, PRIVACY and SECURITY From the proverb: *Ɛban kata asɛm so.* Literal translation: The fence round the house conceals its secret. The home to the Akan is a special place. A home which has a fence around it is considered to be an ideal residence. The fence symbolically separates and secures the family from the outside. Because of the security and the protection that a fence affords, the symbol is also associated with the security and safety one finds in love.

 528 529 530  531 532 533	**FIHANKRA - COMPOUND HOUSE** Symbol of **SAFETY, SECURITY, SOLIDARITY, UNITY, SPIRITUALITY, PROTECTION, CLOSE FAMILY TIES,** and **BROTHERHOOD** From the expression: *Yɛbisa sɛ kyerɛ me osimasi ne fie, nyɛ ne sika dodoo a ɔwɔ.* Literal translation: We ask to be shown one's house, not how much money one has. The symbol reflects the Akan's organic conception of a family. This symbol depicts a kind of architecture which is highly regarded by the Akans. It is a kind of house in which there is a central quadrangle with rooms on each of the four sides. *Fihankra* symbol depicts the Akan family house which is rectangular in shape and has a central courtyard. It is a symbol of protection, security and spirituality. The open courtyard within the house serves as the center of activities in the household.
 534 535 536	**MFRAMADAN - WELL VENTILATED HOUSE** Symbol of **HOSPITALITY, FORTITUDE, SAFETY, RESILIENCE,** and **SHELTER** The Akan house is not only well ventilated, it is resilient and can withstand the hazards of storms, rainfall and the tropical hot weather. This is encoded in the symbol *mframadan* - well ventilated or breezy house. This symbol suggests a reinforced or well-built home — one built to withstand windy and treacherous conditions. It reflects in Asante history a clause in the unwritten constitution of the Golden Stool. Oral accounts say that according to that clause, mud houses in Kumasi must be reinforced with turf. This reinforcing would cause the house to be sturdier and resistant to unfavorable weather conditions.
 537 538 539  540 541 542 543	**BLƆK DAN - BLOCK HOUSE** Symbol of **PROTECTION, SECURITY, WEALTH** and **PROSPERITY** From the expression: *Wonni sika a wontwa blɔk.* Literal translation: One builds a cement or cinder block house when one has the money.

544 545 546	**FIE NE FIE – THERE IS NO PLACE LIKE HOME** Symbol of **SECURITY, COMFORT, PROTECTION, WELCOME** and **BEING ACCEPTED** From the expression: *Fie ne fie, fie nte sɛ wiramu.* Literal translation: There is no place like home; being home is not like being in the bush.
547	**ABIREKYI MMƐN NE ƆDƆ – RAM'S HORNS AND LOVE** Symbol of **LOVE, HAPPINESS, MARITAL BLISS** From the expression: *Mmaa pɛ dɛ, kyiri ka.* Or, *Sokoo na mmaa pɛ.* Or, *Kwakye adeɛ yɛ fɛ, nso yɛde sika na ɛtɔ.* Litral translation: Women tend to enjoy the assets, but not the liabilities that flow from a relationship with a man.
548	**ABUSUAFOƆ HO TE SƐN – HOW IS THE FAMILY** Symbol of **FRATERNAL GREETINGS** From the expression: *Abusuafoɔ ho te sɛn?* Literal translation: How is the family? This greeting is exchanged between family members when they meet away from home.
549	**TENA FIE – STAY AT HOME** Symbol of **FAMILY RESPONSIBILITY** From the expression: *Tena fie. Or, Wonam nam a, hyia na wohyia; aboa antenna fie a, ɔgye abaa. Also, Ɔbadueduefoɔ nto oni funu.* Literal translation: Stay at home. Or, When one does not stay at home one gets into trouble, the animal that roams is often beaten as it is always falling into troubles. Also, The wandering child does not meet with his mother's corpse.
550	**ABUSUA PA – GOOD FAMILY** Symbol of **FAMILY UNITY, KINSHIP TIES, FAMILY SUPPORT** From the expression: *Abusua pa mu na adɔyɛ ne koryɛ wɔ.* Literal translation: Love and unity abound in a good family.
551	**ABUSUA BƆNE – MALEVOLENT FAMILY, also DEPRAVED FAMILY** Symbol of **FAMILY DISUNITY, BLAMING ONE'S FAMILY** From the expression: *Wontumi wo ho a, na wose abusuafoɔ anhwɛ me.* Or, *Oyoko ne Dako, abusua dapaafo kwabusufoɔ a wɔware wɔn ho.* Literal translation: The lazy person always blames it on his/her family. Or, Oyoko and Dako clans are depraved for they inter-marry even though they are related. This is also said of the Amoakare and Adaa clans. Amoakare, Adaa and Aberade are branches of the same Aduana family. Similarly, Oyoko and Dako are branches of the same family. It is a taboo for one to marry one's family member.

552	**ABUASUA HWEDEƐ – FAMILY DISPUTE** **Symbol of DISUNITY WITHIN A FAMILY, FAMILY DISPUTE, and FAMILY IN CRISIS** From the expression: *Abusua hwedeɛ gu nkuruwa, me nko me deɛ na egya da mu.* Literal translation: Every family has its internal crisis or dispute that may be simmering, mine is ablaze. *Hwedeɛ* is a species of grass that grows scattered in little tufts. In this symbol the *abusua* is seen like this grass, and like grass it burns in the typical wildfire manner when set ablaze by family disputes. The *abusua* is made up of clusters of sisters and their children. Sibling rivalry, family disputes, and petty jealousies can set sisters apart as if they are enemies, not family members.
553 554 555	**ABUSUA TE SƐ KWAEƐ – THE FAMILY IS LIKE A FOREST** Symbol of **UNITY IN DIVERSITY, FRATERNITY, VARIATION, and HETEROGENEITY** From the aphorism: *Abusua te sɛ kwaeɛ, wokɔ mu a, na wobɛhu deɛ ɛwɔm. Or, Abusua te sɛ kwaeɛ, wokɔ mu a, na wohu sɛ nnua a ɛwɔm no sisi mmaako mmaako.* Literal translation: The family is like the a forest, it is when you have entered it that you will see what is inside. Or, The family is like forest, if you view it from far away, the trees appear to be together, but when one gets closer to it one sees that each tree has a specific location or that each tree stands alone as individuals.
556	**ABUSUA PANIN KYERƐ WO DƆ - FAMILY HEAD SHOW YOUR AFFECTION** Symbol of **KINDNESS, BENEVOLENCE, HOSPITALITY, SYMPATHY, GENEROSITY, and PARENTAL LOVE** From the expression: *Agya a woyɛ mmɔfra ni. Or, Woyɛ damprane a ase yɛ nwunu; abusua panin kyerɛ wo dɔ.* Literal translation: A father who is a mother to children. Or, You are like the giant shade tree in the desert; family head assert your affection.
557	**WO NA WU A – WHEN YOUR MOTHER DIES** From the proverb: *Wo na wu a na w'abusua asã.* Literal translation: When your mother dies, that is the ned of your family.

558 559 560 561 562	**ABUSUA DƆ FUNU – THE FAMILY LOVES THE DEAD** Symbol of **FAMILY UNITY, SOLIDARITY,** and **FAMILY RESPONSIBILITY** From the expression: *Abusua dɔ funu.* Literal translation: The family loves the corpse. Funeral is an occasion on which the unity and solidarity of the lineage receive public expression as funeral expenses are shared among adult members of the lineage.
563	**AYIE FƐ - BEAUTIFUL FUNERAL** Symbol of **CONSPICUOUS CONSUMPTION, OSTENTATIOUS DISPLAY, PROFLIGACY,** and **EXTRAVAGANCE** From the proverb: *Ayie fɛ ne ka.* Literal translation: An extravagant funeral spells debt.
564	**BOA W'AWOFOƆ - HELP YOUR PARENTS** **Symbol of FAMILY SUPPORT, INTERDEPENDENCE OF FAMILY MEMBERS, RECIPROCAL FAMILY OBLIGATIONS, and FAMILY BONDS** From the expression: *Boa w'awofoɔ.* Literal translation: Help your parents.
565	**BOA MPANIMFOƆ - HELP THE ELDERLY** Symbol of **SUPPORT FOR THE ELDERLY, RESPECT FOR OLD AGE,** and **SECURITY AND WELFARE OF THE ELDERLY** From the expression: *Boa mpanimfoɔ.* Literal translation: Help the elderly.
566	**WOYƐ ABOFRA A – WHILE YOU ARE YOUNG** Symbol of **RESPECT, TOLERANCE OF DIVERSITY, and VENERATION** From the expression: *Woyɛ abɔfra a, nsere akwatia.* Literal translation: While you are young, do not laugh at a short person for you never can tell how you will look in your old age.
567	**MOMMA YƐNNODƆ YƐN HO – LET US LOVE ONE ANOTHER** Symbol of **UNITY, LOVE, FRATERNITY, and FELLOWSHIP** From the expression: *Obi dɔ wo a, dɔ no bi.* Also, *Momma yɛnnodɔ yɛn ho na nipa nkyɛre na wamia.* Literal translation: When someone loves you, show your love in return. Also, Let us love one another for the individual is insufficient unto himself/herself

568	**YƐ PAPA – DO GOOD** Symbol of **VIRTUE, GOODNESS**, and **SELFLESSNESS** From the aphorism: *Woyɛ papa a woyɛ ma wo ho, woyɛ bɔne nso a, woyɛ ma wo ho. Also, Onipa yɛ wo yie a, mfa bɔne nyɛ no.* Literal translation: When you do good, you do it unto yourself. Also, To him who is good to you, do him no evil.
569	**BU WO HO – RESPECT YOURSELF** Symbol of **SELF RESPECT** From the expression: *Bu wo ho. Or, Yɛdi wo ni a, di wo ho ni.* Literal translation: Respect yourself. Or, If you are respected, you respect yourself.
570	**MA W'ANI NSƆ NEA WOWƆ - BE CONTENT WITH YOUR LOT** Symbol of **CONTENTMENT, GRATIFICATION,** and **SATISFACTION** From the aphorism: *Nsuo anso adwareɛ a, ɛso nom. Or, Wo tiri sua na wotete dɔteɛ tetare ho sɛ wo rema no ayɛ kɛse a, nsuo tɔ fɔ no a, ɛtete gu. Also, Ma w'ani nsɔ nea wowɔ.* Literal translation: If a quantity of water does not suffice for a bath, it will at least be sufficient for drinking. Or, If you have a small head and you try to increase the size by adding layers of mud onto your head, when it rains such layers will be washed off. Also, Be content with your lot.
571 572 573 574 575 576 577 578 579 580 581	**ANI BERE A, ƐNSƆ GYA - FIRE IS NOT SPARKED IN EYES RED WITH ANGER** Symbol of **PATIENCE, SELF-CONTROL, SELF-DISCIPLINE, and SELF-CONTAINMENT** From the proverb: *Ani bere a, ɛnsɔ gya. Or, Ɛnyɛ obiara a ne bo afu na omuna.* Literal translation: No matter how flaming red one's eyes may be, fire is not sparked in one's eyes. Or, Every frowned face does not necessarily depict anger.
582	**NYA ABOTERƐ - BE PATIENT** Symbol of **PATIENCE, DILIGENCE, SELF-CONTROL, TOLERANCE,** and **FOREBEARANCE** From the aphorism: *Aboterɛ tutu mmepɔ. Or, Nya aboterɛ. Or, Wofa nwansena ho abufuo a, wobere wo kuro.* Literal translation: Patience moves mountains. Or, Have patience. Or, If you get annoyed with the housefly, you bruise your sore.

583	**NYƐ AHANTAN – DO NOT BE ARROGANT** Symbol of **WARNING AGAINST ARROGANCE** From the expression: *Nyɛ ahantan.* Literal translation: Do not be arrogant.
584	**NNI AWU – DO NOT KILL** Symbol of **RESPECT FOR HUMAN LIFE, WARNING AGAINST MURDER** From the expression: *Nni awu na nkwa yɛntɔn.* Literal translation: Do not kill for life cannot be purchased. This symbol depicts the high value Akans place on human life. Human life is too precious to be wasted by senseless killing.
585	**DI MMRA SO – OBSERVE OR OBEY THE RULES** Symbol of **BEING LAW ABIDING, CONFORMITY, RESPECT FOR THE LAW** From the expression: *Nipa ho antɔ no a, na ɛfiri n'asɛm.* Or, *Di mmra so.* Literal translation: If one is not happy, one's conduct is the cause. Or, Obey the rules.
586	**MMƆ ADWAMAN - DO NOT FORNICATE** Symbol of **CHASTITY, DECENCY, CONTINENCE, SELF CONTROL**, and **ABSTINENCE** From the expression: *Wo nuabaa asrɛ so a, wonna so.* Or, *Wodidi abɔntene so a, yɛbɛbɔ wo didi-dawuro.* Literal translation: If your sister has beautiful thighs, that would not be where you sleep. Or, If you have sex outside the house, you are ridiculed in public to the accompaniment of a gong-gong.
587 588 589	**MFOFOO ABA - SEED OF THE MFOFOO PLANT** Symbol of **WARNING AGAINST JEALOUSY, INTOLERANCE,** and **ENVY** From the proverb: *Deɛ mfofoo pɛ ne sɛ gyinantwi abɔ bidie.* Literal translation: What the fofoo plant always wishes is that the gyinatwi seeds should turn black. The symbol reminds one that jealousy and covetousness are unbecoming of a good citizen.
590 591	**KATA WO DEƐ SO – COVER YOUR OWN** Symbol of **JEALOUSY, BICKERING, GOSSIP**, and **SLANDER** From the expression: *Kata wo deɛ so na bue me deɛ so.* Also, *Gyae me ho nkontabuo na pɛ wo deɛ.* Literal translation: Cover your own shortcomings and expose mine. Also, Stop all this slanderous accounts about me and put your time to productive work.

592 593	**ATAMFOƆ REBRƐ - ADVERSARIES ARE SUFFERING** Symbol of **ENVY, ENEMITY,** and **JEALOUSY** From the expression: *Wotiatia obi deɛ so hwehwɛ wo deɛ a, wonhu.* Literal translation: If you trample upon what belongs to someone in the hope of finding what belongs to you, you never find it.
594	**ƐKAA OBI NKO A – SOMEONE WISHES** Symbol of **PETTY JEALOUSY, ENVY, MALICE,** and **RESENTMENT** From the expression: *Ɛkaa obi nko a, nka mawu.* Literal translation: Someone wishes I was dead.
595 596 597	**ƐKAA NSEE NKO A – THE WEAVER BIRD WISHES** Symbol of **PETTY JEALOUSY, ENVY, MALICE,** and **RESENTMENT** From the expresion: *Ɛkaa nsee nko a, anka onyina dua awu.* Literal translation: The woodpecker wishes the onyina (silk cotton) tree were dead.
598	**ƐNNI NSEKUO – DO NOT GOSSIP** Symbol of **WARNING AGAINST SLANDER, GOSSIP,** and **IDLE TALK** From the expression: *Ɛnni nsekuo. Or, Ɔtope se, akyekyedeɛ nka nkyerɛ anwonomo na anwonomo nso nka nkyerɛ mmatatwene, na mmatatwene nka nkyerɛ ɔman, ɛfiri se yɛse, yɛse na ɛma asɛm trɛ.* Literal translation: Do not gossip. Or, The big snail tells the tortoise to tell the thatching reed, so that the thatching reed may tell the liana, for the liana to tell the state because, "we say, we say" (gossip) makes news spread.
599	**WOAYƐ AFƐRE – YOU HAVE PERSISTED AND ENDED IN DISGRACE** Symbol of **DISHONOR, DISGRACE, SHAME,** and **HUMILIATION** From the expression: *Fɛdeɛ ne owuo, fanyinam owuo. Or, Woayɛ afɛre. Or, Ne tiboa abu no fɔ. Or, Pae mu ka yɛ fɛre na nso ɛyɛ ahodwo.* Literal translation: Death and dishonor, death is preferable. Or, You have persisted and ended in disgrace. Or, One's conscience has judged one guilty. Or, Owning up to the truth openly may be embarrassing, but it brings peace and contentment.

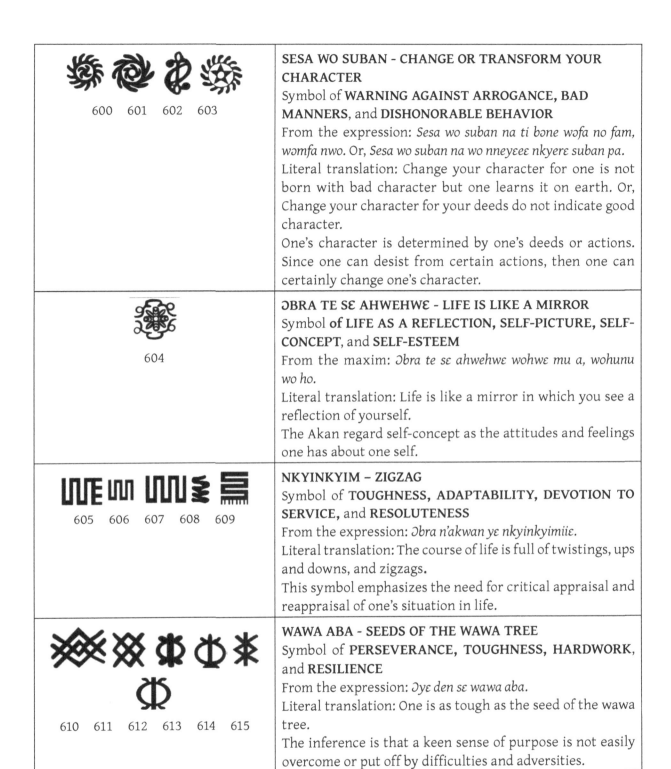

600 601 602 603	**SESA WO SUBAN - CHANGE OR TRANSFORM YOUR CHARACTER** Symbol of **WARNING AGAINST ARROGANCE, BAD MANNERS,** and **DISHONORABLE BEHAVIOR** From the expression: *Sesa wo suban na ti bɔne wɔfa no fam, wɔmfa nwo.* Or, *Sesa wo suban na wo nneyɛeɛ nkyerɛ suban pa.* Literal translation: Change your character for one is not born with bad character but one learns it on earth. Or, Change your character for your deeds do not indicate good character. One's character is determined by one's deeds or actions. Since one can desist from certain actions, then one can certainly change one's character.
604	**ƆBRA TE SƐ AHWEHWƐ - LIFE IS LIKE A MIRROR** Symbol **of LIFE AS A REFLECTION, SELF-PICTURE, SELF-CONCEPT,** and **SELF-ESTEEM** From the maxim: *Ɔbra te sɛ ahwehwɛ wohwɛ mu a, wohunu wo ho.* Literal translation: Life is like a mirror in which you see a reflection of yourself. The Akan regard self-concept as the attitudes and feelings one has about one self.
605 606 607 608 609	**NKYINKYIM – ZIGZAG** Symbol of **TOUGHNESS, ADAPTABILITY, DEVOTION TO SERVICE,** and **RESOLUTENESS** From the expression: *Ɔbra n'akwan ye nkyinkyimiiɛ.* Literal translation: The course of life is full of twistings, ups and downs, and zigzags. This symbol emphasizes the need for critical appraisal and reappraisal of one's situation in life.
610 611 612 613 614 615	**WAWA ABA - SEEDS OF THE WAWA TREE** Symbol of **PERSEVERANCE, TOUGHNESS, HARDWORK,** and **RESILIENCE** From the expression: *Ɔyɛ den sɛ wawa aba.* Literal translation: One is as tough as the seed of the wawa tree. The inference is that a keen sense of purpose is not easily overcome or put off by difficulties and adversities.

  616 617	**TABONO – PADDDLE** Symbol of **STRENGTH, PERSISTENCE, PERSEVERANCE, UNITY OF PURPOSE,** and **HARD WORK** From the aphorism: *Ɛhyɛn wɔka no afanu a, na ɛkɔ akɔtenee.* Literal translation: The canoe must be paddled on both sides to make it go straight. Steady paddling inspires confidence and industry. Or, Unity is strength. Tabono is also used as a bait in fishing, or it is the spatula that gold weight-casters use.
  618 619 620 621	**ƆSRANE - MOON OR ƆSRANEFA – CRESCENT MOON** Symbol of **FAITH, PATIENCE, DETERMINATION, PERSEVERANCE** From the aphorism: *Ɔsrane mfiti prɛko pɛ ntware ɔman.* Literal translation: The moon does not go round the nation at one go. Or the moon does not form a circle hastily.
622 623 624 625 626 627 628 629 630 631 632	**AYA – FERN** **Symbol of INDEPENDENCE, PERSEVERANCE, AUTONOMY, ENDURANCE, DEFIANCE AGAINST OPPRESSION,** and **RESOURCEFULNESS** From the expression: *Mensuro wo.* Literal translation: I am not afraid of you. I am independent of you. The *aya* (fern) plant grows in very hardy conditions and the symbol reflects endurance and defiance of difficulties.
  633	**MO NO YƆ – CONGRATULATIONS** Symbol of **PRAISE, REWARD, HONOR** and **RECOGNITION** From the expression: *Mema mo mo-no-yɔ, me man. Also, Ɔbrane twa apɔ a, yɛma no mo.* Literal translation: I congratulate you my people. Also, When one performs a good deed, one is recognized and praised.
  634	**PAGYA WO TI NA GYE ASEDA – RAISE YOUR HEAD AND ACCEPT THANKSGIVING** Symbol of **GRATITUDE, BENEFICENCE,** and **THANKFULNESS** From the expression: *Ɔkanni kyɛ adeɛ a, ɔgye aseda.* Literal translation: If an Akan makes a present he accepts thanks.

635 636	**WOYƐ ƆHƆHO PAPA A – WHEN YOU DO GOOD FOR A STRANGER** Symbol of **INGRATITUDE** and **UNGRATEFULNESS** From the expression: *Woyɛ ɔhɔhoɔ papa a, ɔde wo ti bɔ dua.* Also, *Ɔhɔhoɔ annya wo adeɛ a, ɔgya wo ka.* Also, *Ɔhɔho nni nkɔ yɛ ɔmanni mfɔneɛ.* Literal translation: If you show kindness to a stranger, he may repay you with ingratitude. Also, If your visitor does not leave you in wealth, he leaves you in debt. Also, Let the stranger enjoy it na go means, often, the citizen starving.
637	**W'ANO PƐ ASƐM – YOU ARE NOSY** Symbol of **BEING NOSY, INQUISITIVE,** and **MEDDLESOME** From the expression: *Asɛm mpɛ nipa, nipa na ɔpɛ asɛm.* Also, *Onipa ho antɔ no a, na ɛfiri n'asɛm.* Or, Ano kokuroko twa ne ho adafi. Literal translation: Trouble does not seek out a trouble-maker, the trouble-maker courts trouble. Also, If one is unhappy, one's conduct is the cause. Or, A chattering mouth is its own traitor (it betrays itself).
638	**NTWITWA WO HO NKYERE ME – DO NOT BOAST** Symbol of **WARNING AGAINST ARROGANCE, HAUGHTINESS** and **POMPOSITY** From the expression: *Ntwitwa wo ho nkyerɛ me.* Literal translation: Do not be boastful to me.
639 640 641 642	**ANI HUNU YEA A – THE EYES SEE SUFFERING** Symbol of **PAIN, FORTITUDE, FOREBEARANCE,** and **LONG-SUFFERING** From the expression: *Ani hunu yea a, ɛtim deɛ ɛtim.* Literal translation: The eyes see all pain and suffering, yet they remain in their place.
643	**AKA M'ANI - ONLY MY EYES** Symbol of **PATIENCE** From the expression: *Aka m'ani na mede hwɛ woɔ.* Literal translation: I have nothing but my eyes to look at you.
644	**MEKYIA WO – I SALUTE YOU** Symbol of **GREETINGS, RECOGNITION,** and **RESPECT** From the expression of greetings: *Mekyia wo.* Literal translation: I salute you. When the Akan meet, they exchange greetings first before they carry out any conversation. Greetings are not just exchange of handshake or words, but recognition of a fellow human being.

645	**MAHU WO DADA – I HAVE SEEN YOU ALREADY** Symbol of **SURPRISE, EXCITEMENT,** and **WELCOME** From the expression: *Mahu wo dada.* Literal translation: I have already seen you.
646	**AKWAABA – WELCOME** Symbol of **HOSPITALITY, GREETING,** and **RECEPTION** From the expression of welcome greetings: *Akwaaba.* Literal translation: Welcome.
647	**WO HO TE SƐN? – HOW ARE YOU?** Symbol of **GREETINGS, RECOGNITION,** and **FRIENDLINESS** From the expression of greetings: *Wo ho te sɛn?* Literal translation: How are you?
648	**WOASESA – YOU HAVE CHANGED** Symbol of **ADMIRATION, SURPRISE,** and **WONDER** From the expression of greetings: *Woasesa!* Literal translation: You have changed!
649	**SAA? – IS THAT SO?** Symbol of **DOUBT, ENQUIRY,** and **SKEPTICISM** From the question: *Saa?* Literal translation: Is that so?
650	**GYE W'ANI – ENJOY YOURSELF** Symbol of **THE JOY OF LIVING, REJOICING, MERRY-MAKING, HAPPINESS,** and the **WORTH OF LIVING** From the maxim: *Onua gye w'ani na nipa nkwa yɛ tia.* Literal translation: Enjoy life for one has a short stay in this world. This means more than having fun. This urges one to make the best out of life.
651	**FIRI HA KO – GO AWAY** Symbol of **BEING UNWELCOME** From the expression: *Firi ha kɔ.* Or, *Menyɛ nanabene na woaka akyerɛ me sɛ firi ha kɔ.* Literal translation: Go away. Or, I am not a stranger for you to ask me to leave.
652 653	**YƐBƐHYIA BIO – WE WILL MEET AGAIN** Symbol of **FAREWELL** From the expression of parting greetings: *Yɛbɛhyia bio.* Literal translation: We'll meet again.

654	**ƆKWAN NI HƆ - NO WAY** Symbol of **PESSMISM, LACK OF OPPORTUNITY,** and **CLOSURE** From the expression: *Ɔkwan nni hɔ.* Literal translation: There is no way.
655	**NANTE YIE – GOODBYE** Symbol of **FAREWELL, GODSPEED,** and **SAFE JOURNEY** From the expression of farewell or parting greetings: *Nante yie.* Literal translation: Goodbye or farewell.
656 657	**AHOƆFƐ NTUA KA – BEAUTY DOES NOT PAY** Symbol of **GOOD MANNERS, MODESTY** and **BEAUTIFUL CHARACTER** From the maxim: *Ahoɔfɛ ntua ka, suban pa na ɛhia. Or, Akyem prosi se" Sɛ ahoɔfɛ tua ka a, anka wanya ne ho.* Literal translation: Beauty does not pay; it is good character that counts. Or, The red-headed weaver bird says; If beauty were profitable, then he would become rich.
658	**EHURU A ƐBƐDWO – IT WILL COOL DOWN AFTER BOILING** Symbol of **HUMILITY, MODESTY,** and **WARNING AGAINST ARROGANCE** From the maxim: *Kuta wo bɔdɔm na ɛhuru a, ɛbɛdwo.* Literal translation: Slow down for it will cool down after boiling.
659	**APƆNKYERƐNE WU A – WHEN THE FROG DIES** Symbol of **SIGNIFICANCE, VALUE,** and **IMPORTANCE** From the maxim: *Aponkyerɛne wu a, na yɛhunu ne tenten.* Literal translation: It is when the frog dies that we see its full measure. One is often valued when one is no more.
660	**ATAMFOƆ ANI AWU – ADVERSARIES ARE ASHAMED** Symbol of **SHAME, REMORSE** and **GUILT** From the expression: *Atamfoɔ ani awu. Or, Wotan me a, kata w'ani.* Literal translation: Adversaries are ashamed. Or, If you hate me, cover your eyes.

661	**ƆBRA YƐ BONA – LIFE IS A STRUGGLE** Symbol of the **VICISSITUDES OF LIFE, PERSISTENCE,** and **DETERMINATION** From the expression: *Ɔbra yɛ bɔna. Also, Ɔbra ne dea wo ara woabɔ. Also, Nsuo tɔ hwe wɔn a owia fi hye wo a, na wohu sɛ ɔbra ne bɔ yɛ ya.* Literal translation: Life is a struggle. Also, Life is what you make of it. Also, When you get soaked by the rain and then scorched by the sun you experience the vicissitudes of life.
662	**ADASA PƐ MMƆBORƆ – SOME PEOPLE DELIGHT IN THE FALL OF OTHERS** Symbol of **JEALOUSY, ENVY** and **SELFISHNESS** From the expression: *Adasa pɛ mmɔborɔ.* Literal translation: Some people delight in the fall of others.
663	**NNYEGYEƐ – FESTTER or DOOR BELL** Symbol **of ANNOYANCE, IRRITATION, PESTERING, BOTHER or SYMBOL OF KNOCKING** From the expression: *Nipa gyegyefoɔ sen ɔbonsam. Or, Ɔbosom ankɔda a, na ɛfiri nnyegyesoɔ.* Literal translation: The pester is worse than the devil. Or, If the priest does not go to sleep, it is because of flattery. Door-bell of the rattling or mobile type was hung in front of the main door of a house or the bedroom to announce the entry of a person.
664	**ANI NE ANI HYIA – WHEN EYES MEET** Symbol of **AGREEMENT, HARMONY, ACCORD, CONFLICT RESOLUTION,** and **COMPROMISE** From the aphorism: *Ani ne ani hyia a, ntoto mma.* Literal translation: When two people see eye to eye, there is bound to be no discord.
665	**ATAMFOƆ ATWA ME HO AHYIA – ADVERSARIES ARE ALL AROUND ME** Symbol of **JEALOUSY, ENVY, ENMITY,** and **MALICE** From the expression: *Yɛkyiri me, yɛnnɔ me, ɛfiri tete. Also, Atamfoɔ atwa me ho ahyia.* Literal translation: They hate me; they don't love me, dates from time immemorial. Also, Adversaries are all around me.

666	**WO NSA AKYI -THE BACK OF ONE'S HAND** Symbol of **SELF-DETERMINATION, PERSEVERANCE, and TENACITY** From the proverb: *Wo nsa akyi bɛyɛ wo dɛ a, ɛnnte sɛ wo nsa yamu.* Literal translation: The back of one's hand does not taste as good as the palm does.
667	**NYA AKOKODURO – HAVE COURAGE** Symbol of **COURAGE, FORTITUDE, DETERMINATION** and **VALOR** From the expression: *Nya akokoduro.* Literal translation: Have courage.
668	**HWƐ YIE – BE CAUTIOUS** Symbol of **CAUTION, CAREFULNESS, VIGILANCE**, and **ALERTNESS** From the aphorism: *Nipa bɛhwɛ yie na ɛfiri deɛ wahunu.* Literal translation: From experience one learns to be cautious.
669	**BƆ WO HO BAN – PROTECT YOURSELF** Symbol of **PROTECTION, SAFEGUARD**, and **PRECAUTION** From the adage: *Bɔ wo ho ban.* Literal translation: Protect yourself; be on your guard.
670	**HWƐ W'AKWAN MU YIE – BE CIRCUMSPECT** Symbol of **CIRCUMSPECTION, PRUDENCE**, and **ALERTNESS** From the expression: *Hwɛ w'akwan mu yie.* Literal translation: Be circumspect.
671	**BRƐ WO HO ASE – BE HUMBLE** Symbol of **HUMILITY, MODESTY**, and **SIMPLICITY** From the adage: *Brɛ wo ho ase.* Literal translation: Be humble.
672	**GYE ME DI – TRUST ME** Symbol of **TRUST, FAITH, ASSURANCE**, and **BELIEF** From the expression: *Gye me di.* Literal translation: Trust me.
673	**MENSURO WO – I AM NOT AFRAID OF YOU** Symbol of **BRAVERY, COURAGE**, and **VALOR** From the expression: *Mensuro wo.* Literal translation: I am not afraid of you.

674	**ƆBRA TWA WO A – LIFE'S AGONIES** Symbol of **DETERMINATION, PERSEVERANCE, and RESILIENCE** From the aphorism: *Ɔbra twa wo a, ɛsene sradaa.* Literal translation: The agonies of life cut sharper than saw.
675 676	**DWEN WO HO - THINK ABOUT YOURSELF** Symbol of **SELF EXAMINATION** From the aphorism: *Dwen wo ho.* Literal translation: Think about yourself.
677	**DWENE WO HO – THINK ABOUT YOURSELF** Symbol of **SELF EXAMINATION** From the aphorism: *Dwen wo ho.* Literal translation: Think about yourself.
678	**ANYI ME AYƐA – IF YOU WILL NOT PRAISE ME** Symbol of INGRATITUDE, UNGRATEFULNESS and BOORISHNESS From the expression: *Anyi me ayɛ a, nsɛe me din.* Literal translation: If you will not praise me, do not undermine my intergrity.
679	**DADEƐ BI TWA DADEƐ BI MU - ONE PIECE OF IRON MAY BE STRONGER THAN ANOTHER**
680	**WOFORO DUA PA A - WHEN YOU CLIMB A GOOD TREE** **Symbol of SUPPORT, COOPERATION AND ENCOURAGEMENT** From the expression: *Woforo dua pa a, na yepia wo.* Literal translation: When you climb a good tree, you are given a push. More metaphorically, it means that when you work for a good cause, you will get support.
681	**AKOSOMBO NKANEA – AKOSOMBO LIGHTS** Symbol of **NATIONAL DEVELOPMENT, INDUSTRIALIZATION, ELECTRICAL POWER** From the expression: *Akosombo nkanea de adwuma aba yɛn man yi mu.* Literal translation: The Akosombo electric power project has brought industrial development to our country.
682	**TEFRƐ - COCKROACH** Symbol of **HOSTILITY** From the proverb: *Tɛfrɛ tɔ nkokɔ mu a, sesɔ na wɔn sesɔ no.* Literal translation: When a cockroach falls into the midst of chicken, they do not spare it.

683	**AYEFARE SIKA – ADULTERY FEES** Symbol of **WARNING AGAINST BOASTING ABOUT SHAMEFUL ACT,** From the proverb: *Ayefare sika ntwa poa.* Literal translation: Adultery fees cannot be used for boasting.
684	**APASO – PAIR OF SCISSORS** From the proverb: *Wontɔn apaso so wo ti afu. Or, Woankasa wo tiri ho a, yɛyi wo ayi bɔne.* Literal translation: You sell pairs of scissors, yet your hair is over-grown. Or, If one does do not speak out one's views, one is given a bad hair cut.
685	**NSUO NTƆ NGYAE ANSA YƐAKƆSƆ NSUO – WE COLLECT RAINWATER AS IT IS RAINING** Symbol of **PLANNING AHEAD, WARNING AGAINST PROCRASTINATION** From the proverb: *Nsuo ntɔ ngyae ansa yɛakɔsɔ nsuo.* Literal translation: One does not wait till it stops raining before one goes to collect rainwater. Make hay while the sun shines.
686 687	**ƆPAANI APADIE – LABORER** Symbol of **WORKING CONDITIONS, CONDITIONS OF SERVICE, and LABOR RELATIONS** From the expression: *Ɔpaani hwease a, okonkoni abɔ fam.* Literal translation: If a hired laborer falls down, then the rich trader has fallen. A rich trader's prosperity depends on his/her workers.
688	**NYA ASƐM HWƐ – GET INTO TROUBLE AND YOU WOULD SEE** From the proverb: *Nya asɛm hwɛ, hɔ na wobehu w'atamfo.* Literal translation: Get into trouble, it is then you would see who your enemies are.
689	**ƆDƆ YƐ FƐ SEN SIKA – LOVE IS MORE BEAUTIFUL THAN WEALTH** From the expression: *Ɔdɔ yɛ fɛ sen sika.* Literal translation: Love is more beautiful than wealth.
690	**KƆTƆ REWEA – THE CRAB IS CRAWLING** From the expression: *Kɔtɔ rewea, ne ba so rewea; hwan na ɔbɛgye ne nyanko taataa?* Literal translation: The parent crab is crawling, the baby crab is crawling; who will assist the other to learn to walk upright?

691 692	**KUROTWIAMANSA – LEOPARD** From the expression: *Kurotwamansa tɔ nsuo mu a, ne ho na ɛfɔ, ne ho nsensane de ɛhɔ daa.* Or, *Kurotwiamansa hunuu nifa to a, anka aboa biara nka wiram.* Literal translation: The leopard gets wet in water, but its stripes still remain unchanged. Or, If the leopard knew how to spring upon its prey from the right then no other animal would survivie in the bush.
693	**DWA SO HANTAN – PUBLIC PRIDE** Symbol of **HAUGHTINESS, SELF-IMPORTANCE** and **POVERTY** From the maxim: *Dwa so hantan ne fie awerɛhoɔ, mienu nyinaa yɛkyiri.* Literal translation: Public pride and grief in the home are both abhorred (Public gentility, home cry are both abhorred).
694	**ASɔ NE AFENA – THE HOE AND THE MATCHETE** Symbol **of HARDWORK, ENTREPRENEURSHIP, INDUSTRY,** and **PRODUCTIVITY** From the expression: *Mmirikisie a yɛantumi annɔ no na yɛfrɛ no nsamampɔ.* Or, *Woansɔ w'afena ne w'asɔtia mu annyɛ adwuma a, ɔkɔm bɛde wo.* Literal translation: The farm that is not tended is referred to as a sacred burial ground. Or, One must work to live. In the past in farming communities, as part of the naming ceremony for a child, the male child was given a matchete in accordance with the gender division of labor to signify to the child that he should grow up to assume the responsibility of the man to clear the land to make a farm to raise food for his family.

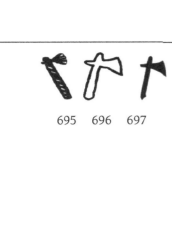 695 696 697	**AKUMA – AXE** Symbol of **POWER, HARDWORK, CONFLICT RESOLUTION, WISDOM and PEACE** From the expression: *Odupɔn biara nni hɔ a akuma ntumi ntwa mu.* Also, *Adare bu a, yɛbɔ bi poma mu.* And, *Sɛ adere tumi kwaeɛ a, anka yɛankɔbɔ akuma.* And, *Ɔpanin tiri mu ha yɛhɔn akuma.* Or, *Dua biara nni hɔ a ɛyɛ den sɛ akuma ntumi ntwa, nanso asɛm biara yɛ den a, yɛmfa akuma na ɛtwa, na yɛde yɛn ano na ɛka ma no twa.* Literal translation: There is no tree which cannot be felled by an axe. Also, When the handle of an axe breaks, a new one is carved to replace it. And, If the knife could clear the forest, the axe would not have been manufactured. And, It is from the head of the elederly that one removes the axe-head. Or, There is no tree that is so hard that it cannot be felled with an axe; however, no matter how intractable a case may be, it must be settled by counseling and negotiations, not with an axe. The symbol is used to connote the view that there is no issue or problem so difficult that it cannot be resolved by peaceful means. The lumberjack tackles all trees, small and big, by tact and diplomacy so that the tree does not fall on him to kill him. The axe is one of the essential farming tools. It is used to fell trees in the preparation of land for farming.
 698	**OKUAFOO PA - GOOD FARMER** Symbol of **HARD WORK, ENTREPRENEURSHIP, INDUSTRY, and PRODUCTIVITY** From the expression: *Okuafo pa ne obi a ɔyɛ nsiyɛfoɔ, ɔno na ɔse: W'afuo so a, woyɛ ne nyinaa.* Literal translation: The good and industrious farmer says: No matter how big your farm is, you tend it all.
 699 700 701 702	**AFA – BELLOWS** Symbol of **BEING INDUSTRIOUS, ASSIDUOUS, HARDWORKING, TENACIOUS, and EFFICIENT** From the expression: *Afa na ɔboa odwumfoɔ ma ne tono, anka odwumfoɔ nni ahoɔden.* Literal translation: It is the bellows that help the blacksmith (or goldsmith) to forge, without them he would be helpless.

 703	**KOOKOO DUA - COCOA TREE** Symbol of **WEALTH, PROSPERITY and CONSPICUOUS CONSUMPTION** From the expression: *Kookoo dua yɛ sika dua; kookoo sɛɛ abusua, paepae mogya mu.* Literal translation: Cocoa is a money tree; yet cocoa ruins the family, and divides blood relations. Cocoa was introduced into Ghana in the late nineteenth century as a cash crop. Within a decade or so after its introduction, it became Ghana's number one foreign exchange earner. As a new source of wealth, it has brought in its wake changes in land ownership and tenure, and has contributed to the increasing intensification of social stratification. It has been a source of political upheavals and family disputes over land ownership. It has helped to create a situation of landlessness in some rural areas.
 704	*SANKONU W'ABɛ* **- GO BACK AND TEND YOUR PALM TREE** Symbol of **PLANT DISEASE, OCCUPATIONAL HAZARD, RISK, LOSS and DESPERATION** From the maxim: *Sɛ woyɛ kookoo na annyɛ yie a, sankonu w'abɛ.* Literal translation: When cocoa farm fails, you may as well go back and tend your oil palm farm. In Ghana, cocoa mirids have been known as serious pests since 1908 and because of their devastating effects, the local farmers called them "Sankonu w'abe" which literally means "go back to the planting of oil palm", reflecting the situation before the introduction of cocoa. This maxim is associated with the devastating effect of a plant disease that afflicted cocoa farms from as far back as 1908, but efforts to eradicate the disease came to a head in the 1940s and 1950s in Ghana. The disease proved to be an economic disaster for farmers as their cocoa farms were destroyed. The devastating plant disease made farmers resort to the growing of oil palm trees. Interestingly, the Ghanaian cocoa farmer has no domestic use of the cocoa, but the Ghanaian farmer has several domestic uses for the products from the oil palm tree - food (as cooking oil and/or soup), soap making, basket weaving, brooms, fences, palm wine, active charcoal used by blacksmiths - even the dead palm tree is a source of a mushroom delicacy and the nutritious, high protein *akɔkon.*

 705	**ABƐ DUA - PALM TREE** Symbol of **SELF-SUFFICIENCY, RESILIENCE, VITALITY, WEALTH,** and **CAUSATION** From the proverb: *Nipa nyɛ abe dua na ne ho ahyia ne ho.* Or, *Se mmerɛnkensono si ne ti ase a, na ɛwo dea asaase reka kyerɛ no.* Also, *Nnua nyinaa bewu agya abɛ.* And, *Sɛ biribia anka papa a, anka ɛngye grada.* Literal translation: The human being is not a palm that she or he should be self-sufficient. Or, Whenever the palm tree bends down it is because of what the earth has said to it. Also, All trees will wither but the palm tree. And, If nothing rustles the dry palm fronds, they would not have made sound. The first analogy is based on the unique qualities of the palm tree as a source of various products like oil, wine, yeast, broom, soap, mat, and roofing material. Metaphorically speaking, the power of the king is evergreen and does not diminish with time and circumstances. In the second and fourth proverbs talk about cause and effect. There is no smoke without fire.
 706 707 708 709  710 711 712	**BESE SAKA - BUNCH OF COLA NUTS** Symbol of **AFFLUENCE, POWER, ABUNDANCE, PLENTY, TOGETHERNESS AND UNITY** From the aphorism: *Bese pa ne konini ahahan yɛtase no ɔbanyansafoɔ.* Also, *Nhohoɔ a ɔtare bese ho; ɔno a ɔnte nwe nso ɔnte ntɔn.* Literal translation: The leaves of the two kinds of kola are distinguished from one another with wisdom. The leaves of the white and red kola plants are very similar and it takes skill and experience to separate them. One has to take care in dealing with problems, and separate them carefully. Also, the red ant on the pod of kola nuts does not pluck the kola nuts to eat or sell. The meaning of the symbol alludes to the dog in the manger attitude that some people have towards economic resources. The cola nut played an important role in the economic life of Ghana. A widely-used cash crop, it is closely associated with affluence and abundance. This symbol also represents the role of agriculture and trade in bringing peoples together.

713	**NKATEHONO – GROUNDNUT (PEANUT) SHELL** Symbol of **RESOURCEFULNESS, CONTINUOUS GROWTH** From the aphorism: *Wobɛdua biribi ama me a, dua nkateɛ nnua aburoo. Or, Aware te sɛ nkateɛ, wommɔeɛ a, wonhunu deɛ ɛwɔ mu.* Literal translation: If you want to grow something for me, plant groundnuts (peanuts) not corn. Or, You can't tell what marriage is like until you have tried it. Peanuts reproduce themselves without being planted and thus symbolize continuous growth or permanent relationship. This symbol depicts the idea of bequeathing a legacy that is self-perpetuating and self-generating rather than a one-shot gift of temporary use. Or it signifies that marriage must be entered into on permanent basis.
714	**APA – DRYING MAT** Symbol of **PRESERVATION** and **SECURITY** From the maxim: *Putuo hye a, yɛdi dwo.* Literal translation: When the yam barn catches fire, that may be the occasion to enjoy a yam meal. A bad situation may be a blessing in disguise. This drying mat is used in food preservation through drying in the sun. The mat is spread either on the ground or on an elevated platform or skid in the sun to dry fruits (e.g. cocoa and coffee beans) and food items such as pepper, fish plantain and cassava. The mat is also used to store food or to partition rooms, ceiling, and as a fence. A special kind of *apata* for storing and preserving yams is called *putuo* (yam barn).
715 716 717	**SITIA BƐKUM DORƆBA – THE STEERING WHEEL MAY KILL THE DRIVER** Symbol of **OCCUPATIONAL HAZARDS, INDUSTRY**, and **HARDWORK** From the expression: *Sitia na ɛbɛkum dorɔba.* Literal translation: The driver may die at the steering-wheel of his vehicle.
718 719	**ƆBOHEMAA – DIAMOND** Symbol of **PECIOUSNESS, GEM**, and **TREASURE** From the maxim: *Wode wo sika tɔ aboɔ a, wowe.* Literal translation: When you waste your money in buying non-precious stone, you eat it.

720 721 722	**ƆKƆTƆ – CRAB** Symbol of **INDUSTRIOUSNESS, HARDWORK, WEALTH,** and **SOCIAL CLASS** From the expression: *Nwaanwaa kɔtɔ, wo na wonim mpɔ daberɛ.* Also, *Sika te sɛ hwene mu nwii, wotu a, na woresu. Or, Kɔtɔ nwo anomaa. Or, Ayɔnkogorɔ dodoɔ nti na ɔkɔtɔ annya tire.* Literal translation: The skilled and crafty crab, you know the hiding place of alluvial gold nuggets. Also, Digging for gold is like pulling hair from the nose; it makes one cry. Or, The crab does not give birth to a bird. Or, Playing around too much with friends cost the crab its head.
723 724 725 726 727 728	**SEREWA (SEDEƐ) – COWRIES** Symbol of **AFFLUENCE, WEALTH, FINANCIAL RESOURCES, ENTREPRENEURSHIP, INFLUENCE,** and **POWER** From the expression: *Wonhyɛ sika pɛtea a, wokasa a, yɛmmu wo.* Or, *Wodidi bata anim a, edwa bɔ wo.* Literal translation: The views of one not wearing gold finger ring are not respected. Or, If you consume your financaila resources in advance, your business becomes unsuccessful.
729	**SIKA TU SE ANOMMAA - MONEY FLIES LIKE A BIRD** Symbol of **FRUGALITY, ENTREPRENEURSHIP,** or **EXTRAVAGANCE** From the maxim: *Sika tu se anommaa.* Literal translation: Money flies like a bird. Money not properly handled will be lost. Bad investment decisions will cause one to lose one's money.
730	**TOA – BOTTLE or GOURD** Symbol of **STORAGE, MEASUREMENT, DIMENSIONALITY** From the expression: *Mpanimfoɔ se mobae a, mo nsa ntoa mienu.* Or, *Toa na ɔpɛ na ahoma hyɛ ne kɔn.* Also, *Toa mu wɔ adeɛ a, Amakye na ɔnim.* Literal translation: The elders present you with two bottles of drinks as their indication of welcoming you. Or, The bottle must like it that there is rope tied around its neck. Also, If there is anything profitable in gourd, then Amakye knows about it.
731	**AHINA – POT** Symbol of **STORAGE, MEASUREMENT, DIMENSIONALITY** From the expression: *Woyi w'ahina ayɛ pii a, ɛbɔ. Or, Yɛntɔ ahina mono ngu no hyɛ.* Literal translation: If you praise your water pot too much, it breaks. Or, We do not buy a new drinking pot and then weld it.

 732	**YEBƐDAN AGYA – WE SHALL LEAVE EVERYTHING** Symbol of the **RELATIVE INSIGNIFICANCE OF MATERIAL WEALTH** From the expression: *Yebɛdan agya*. Or, *Onipa ne asɛm; wofrɛ sika a, sika nnye so, wofrɛ ntama a, ntama nnye so, onipa ne asɛm.* Literal translation: We shall leave everything behind. Or, It is human being that counts; you call upon gold, it answers not; you call upon clothing, it answers not; it is human being that counts. Material things are not as important as the human being. Material wealth will be left behind when one dies. At the point of death it is only human being that will answer one's cry of desperation.
 733 734 735	**EBI TE YIE - SOME PEOPLE ARE BETTER SEATED** Symbol of **EXPOLITATION, WEALTH, UNEQUAL TREATMENT, SOCIAL CLASS,** and **SOCIAL INEQUALITY** From the expression: *Ebi te yie ma ebi so nte yie koraa. Or, Obi akabɔ yɛ obi ahonya, obi amiadie yɛ obi nso nkwa, na obi ahohia ne obi ahotɔ.* Literal translation: Some people are better seated, yet others are not. Or, The prosperity of one person depends on another person's poverty. This symbol alludes to the unequal economic relations and unequal political power relations in the society. This symbol gained popularity in the late 1960s and early 1970s when Ampadu and his African Brothers Band recorded a song with the title, *Ebi te yie.*
 736	**GYE KƆDIDI – TAKE THIS FOR SUBSISTENCE** Symbol of **POVERTY, UNDERPRIVILEGED,** and **INDIGENCE** From the expression: *Ohia na ɛmaa adoee wee mako. Or, Gye kɔdidi ma ohia yɛ animguase. Or, Srɛsrɛ bi di nyɛ akorɔnobɔ.* Literal translation: Poverty forces the monkey to eat pepper. Or, Take this for subsistence makes it a disgrace to be poor. Or, To beg here and there for something to eat does not constitute stealing.

737	**ASETENA PA – GOOD LIVING** Symbol of **CONSPICUOUS SPENDING, INDULGENCE, WEALTH, UPPER SOCIAL CLASS** From the expression: *Asetena pa yɛ awerɛfiri.* Or, *Ateyie yɛ awerɛfiri.* Also, *Adididaa na ɛyɛ, na nyɛ adididaakoro.* Literal translation: Good living makes one forget one's humble beginnings. Or, Daily satisfaction is better than one day's indulgence. Good living makes one forget the inevitability of death for the poor as well as the rich.
738 739	**VW – VW** Symbol of **SOCIAL CLASS, STATUS, WEALTH, and PRESTIGE**
740 741	**BENZ – MERCEDES BENZ** Symbol of **SOCIAL CLASS, STATUS, WEALTH**, and **PRESTIGE** From the expression: *Mehunu wo no na woabenze.* Literal translation: When I saw you, you were riding in a Mercedes Benz.
742 743	**TOYOTA – TOYOTA** Symbol of **RISKS OF AUTOMOBILE TRANSPORTATION, ROAD HAZARDS, and NEED FOR ROAD SAFETY** From the expression: *Toyota na ekae yɛn akwantu mu mmusuo.* Literal translation: Toyota reminds us of the hazards of travelling. This is in remembrance of an automobile accident at Kasoa in the early 1970s in which twenty-two perished on the spot after a Toyota mini-van somersaulted.
744 745 746	**FOON – TELEPHONE** Symbol of **COMMUNICATION, STATUS, PRESTIGE, FREEDOM OF SPEECH, and MODERNIZATION** From the expression: *Migyina abɔten na merekasa yi wɔ me mobitɛl so. Anaa sɛ, ɛyɛ a twa me kɛkɛ.* Literal translation: I am in the streets talking to you on my Mobitel phone. Also, Call me. The symbol represents the freeing up of the telephone communication system in the late 1990s in Ghana. Mobitel was one the first private company to break the monopoly of the state-owned telephony system.

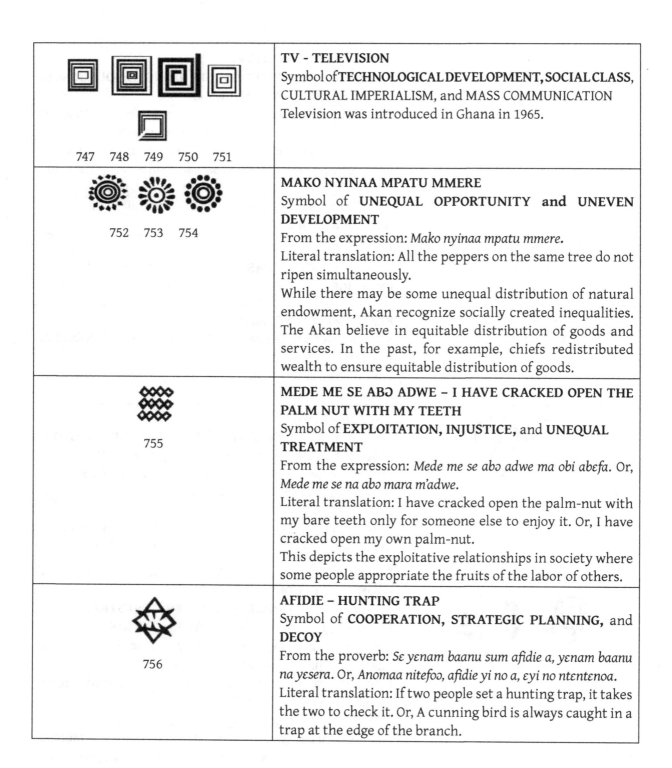747 748 749 750 751	**TV - TELEVISION** Symbol of **TECHNOLOGICAL DEVELOPMENT, SOCIAL CLASS, CULTURAL IMPERIALISM,** and **MASS COMMUNICATION** Television was introduced in Ghana in 1965.
752 753 754	**MAKO NYINAA MPATU MMERE** Symbol of **UNEQUAL OPPORTUNITY and UNEVEN DEVELOPMENT** From the expression: *Mako nyinaa mpatu mmere.* Literal translation: All the peppers on the same tree do not ripen simultaneously. While there may be some unequal distribution of natural endowment, Akan recognize socially created inequalities. The Akan believe in equitable distribution of goods and services. In the past, for example, chiefs redistributed wealth to ensure equitable distribution of goods.
755	**MEDE ME SE ABƆ ADWE – I HAVE CRACKED OPEN THE PALM NUT WITH MY TEETH** Symbol of **EXPLOITATION, INJUSTICE,** and **UNEQUAL TREATMENT** From the expression: *Mede me se abɔ adwe ma obi abɛfa.* Or, *Mede me se na abɔ mara m'adwe.* Literal translation: I have cracked open the palm-nut with my bare teeth only for someone else to enjoy it. Or, I have cracked open my own palm-nut. This depicts the exploitative relationships in society where some people appropriate the fruits of the labor of others.
756	**AFIDIE – HUNTING TRAP** Symbol of **COOPERATION, STRATEGIC PLANNING,** and **DECOY** From the proverb: *Sɛ yɛnam baanu sum afidie a, yɛnam baanu na yɛsera.* Or, *Anomaa nitefoɔ, afidie yi no a, ɛyi no ntɛntɛnoa.* Literal translation: If two people set a hunting trap, it takes the two to check it. Or, A cunning bird is always caught in a trap at the edge of the branch.

757	**MESO NANKA MENTUMI – I CANNOT EVEN CARRY THE PUFF ADDER** Symbol **EXPLOITATION, BEING OVER-BURDENED WITH WORK** From the proverb: *Meso nanka mentumi a, wose menkɔfa enini mmɔ kahyire.* Literal translation: I cannot even carry the puff adder, yet you want me to use the python as the carrying pad.
758 759	**ABETEƐ NTEMA – PORTIONING ABETEƐ MEAL** Symbol of **DISTRIBUTION OF RESOURCE, EQUITABLE DISTRIBUTION,** and **ECONOMIC JUSTICE** From the expression: *Yɛretete abeteɛ na ne kyɛ ara ne no.* Literal translation: As we portion out the abeteɛ meal, that is its distribution.
760	**UAC NKANEA – UAC LIGHTS** Symbol of **ECONOMIC DOMINATION AND ECONOMIC (UNDER) DEVELOPMENT; SHADY ECONOMIC DEALS, PRICE FIXING** From the expression: *UAC nkanea dwann mma yenhunu awam adwadifoo.* Literal translation: The bright UAC lights make it difficult to expose the colluding merchants. UAC stands for United Africa Company. This Company is a subsidiary of the giant multinational corporation, UNILEVER. The first street lights in Kumasi were placed in front of the UAC Store in the Adum section of the city. Some people, therefore, claim that the symbol represents this historical event. Some other people also claim the ideograph represents the floodlighted-Kumasi Sports Stadium that UAC presented to Ghana to commemorate Ghana's independence in 1957. The verbal expression that goes with the ideograph depicts the ubiquitous presence and the dominant influence of the UAC Group of Companies in Ghana. The UAC presence in Ghana dates back to when Lever Brothers entered the West African market to buy slaves and palm oil for soap manufacture. In the 1930s and 1940s UAC spearheaded a ring of European trading companies, Association of West African Merchants (AWAM), that controlled the market for imported items and the exporting of agricultural produce, especially palm oil and cocoa. The price fixing rings led to violent protests and cocoa hold-ups by Ghanaian farmers. The machinations of these companies gave rise to the word AWAM which has come to mean shady dealings, price fixing, or corruption in many Ghanaian languages.

271

761	**NNOMAA NE DUA – BIRDS ON A TREE** Symbol of **SOCIAL CLASS, CLASS CONSCIOUSNESS, AND EQUITABLE DISTRIBUTION OF WEALTH** From the maxim: *Nnomaa goro atipεn atipεn. Anomaa nua ne nea ɔne no da dua koro.* Or, *Duapa so aba bere a, nnomaa nyina di bi.* Literal translation: Only birds of the same species or class play together on the same tree. Or, When a good tree bears fruit all birds eat from it.
762	**WOBU KɔTɔ KWASEA A – WHEN YOU FOOL THE CRAB** Symbol of **EXPLOITATION, UNFAIRNESS** From the proverb: *Wobu kɔtɔ kwasea a, Nyame hunu w'akyi.* Literal translation: When you fool the crab, God sees your rear end.
763	**ASAAWA – SWEET BERRY or MIRACLE BERRY** (*Synsepalum dulcificum*) Symbol of **SWEETNESS, SWEET TASTE, PLEASURE**, and **HEDONISM** From the proverb: Asaawa se: *Ɔdε nka anomu.* Literal translation: Yhe miracle berry says: Sweetness does not last forever. A thing of joy does not last forever. Once the fleshy, tasteless pulp coats your tongue, everything you eat for the next few hours or so will taste sweet. Bite into a lemon or a lime and the distinctive flavors of these fruits will be enjoyed, but their sourness will not pucker your mouth. Even a sip of straight vinegar will taste sweet. The basis for this reaction is the presence of miraculin in the fruit of this species. This taste modifying protein does not actually taste sweet, but apparently it binds to receptors of the taste buds, temporarily changing their function. While the taste modifying capabilities of the fruits have been known for over a century, miraculin was only isolated in the early 1970's. The exact mechanism of action has yet to be elucidated, but is the subject of research, especially for its potential use as an "artificial sweetener".
764	**AKWANNKYεN BORɔDEWA - ROADSIDE PLANTAIN TREE** Symbol of **HARRASSMENT, EXPLOITATION** and **INEQUALITY** From the proverb: *Akwannkyεn borɔdewa se, Nwaawaeho amma me anyε yie.* Literal translation: The plantain tree by the roadside says: The stripping off of my leaves does not allow me to flourish.

765

MENSO WO KENTEN - I DO NOT CARRY YOUR BASKET
Symbol of **INDUSTRY, SELF-RELIANCE** and **ECONOMIC SELF-DETERMINATION**

From the expression: *Menso wo kɛntɛn. Or, Akɔkora wɔammɔ ne bra yie, na ɔsoa ne kɛntɛn.*

Also, *Me ne m'aware bɔne, meso kɛntɛn hunu kora a na worehwɛhwɛ mu.*

Literal translation: I do not carry your basket. Or, The old man who has nothing carries his own basket.

Also, Me and my bad marriage, even when I carry an empty basket you search through it.

The symbol implies the economic self-determination of one, especially a woman. Baskets are used to carry food items from the farm to the house, to store things and to decorate rooms. In the past, as part of the naming ceremony, the female child was momentarily covered with a basket to signal to her that she should grow up into an industrious woman whose responsibility would be to collect foodstuff from the farm, carry it home to prepare food for the husband and children

766   767

KOFORIDUA FRAWASE - KOFORIDUA FLOWERS
Symbol of **URBANIZATION, ECONOMIC PROSPERITY, and CONSPICUOUS CONSUMPTION**

From the expression: *Koforidua nhwiren, dea mede wo reye!*
Literal translation: Koforidua flowers, what use do I have of you!

The ideograph stems from the conspicuous consumption by some rich people during the rapid urbanization of Koforidua following the success of the cocoa industry, and later the diamond mining industry in the Eastern Region of Ghana at the turn of the nineteenth century.

768   769   770   771

SENCHI BRIDGE – SENCHI BRIDGE
Symbol of **ECONOMIC DEVELOPMENT, NATIONAL INTEGRATION,** and **PROGRESS**

From the expression: *Ghana abue; onua tu kwan kɔhwɛ Senchi bridge.*
Literal translation: Ghana has progressed; brother, travel and see the Senchi bridge.

 772	**KOMFOAKU – STRENGTH AND PRIDE OF LABOR** Symbol of **DIGNITY OF LABOR, PRIDE OF LABOR,** and **STRENGTH OF LABOR, LABOR PRODUCTIVITY** From the expression: Komfoaku se: *Adwuma den and ne nkisi na ɛde mpontuo ba ɔman mu.* Literal translation: Komffoaku says: Hard work and pride of labor are necessary for national development.
 773 774 775 776  777 778 779 780  781 782 783 784  785 786 787 788  789 790 791 792 793	**SANKOFA - GO BACK AND RETRIEVE** Symbol of **WISDOM, KNOWLEDGE, and the PEOPLE'S HERITAGE** From the aphorism: *Sɛ wo werɛ fi na wosan kɔfa a, yenkyi.* Literal translation: There is nothing wrong with learning from hindsight. The word SANKƆFA is derived from the words SAN (return), KƆ (go), FA (look, seek and take). This symbolizes the Akan's quest for knowledge with the implication that the quest is based on critical examination, and intelligent and patient investigation. The symbol is based on a mythical bird that flies forwards with its head turned backwards. This reflects the Akan belief that the past serves as a guide for planning the future, or the wisdom in learning from the past in building the future. The Akan believe that there must be movement with times but as the forward march proceeds, the gems must be picked from behind and carried forward on the march. In the Akan military system, this symbol signified the rearguard, the section on which the survival of the society and the defense of its heritage depended.
 794 795 796	**TETE WƆ BI KA – THE ANCIENTS HAVE SOMETHING TO SAY** Symbol of **HERITAGE, CANON** From the expression: *Tete wɔ bi ka, tete wɔ bi kyerɛ.* Literal translation: The ancients have something to offer posterity. This symbol combines sankɔfa with adwa or hwehwɛ mu dua to encode the view that the heritage must be passed on.

 797 798 799	NYANSAPƆ - WISDOM KNOT Symbol of WISDOM, INGENUITY, INTELLIGENCE, CULTURAL HERITAGE, and CRITICAL REASONING From the proverb: *Nananom nyansapɔ, yɛsiane no ɔbanyansafoɔ.* Literal translation: It takes the wise one to untie the knot of wisdom to discern the wisdom bequeathed by one's heritage. An especially revered symbol of the Akan, this symbol conveys the idea that a wise person has the capacity to choose the best means to attain a goal. Being wise implies broad knowledge, learning and experience, and the ability to apply such faculties to practical ends.
 800 801	HWEHWɛ MU DUA - MEASURING STICK **Symbol of CRITICAL EXAMINATION, EXCELLENCE, PERFECTION, RATIONALITY, KNOWLEDGE, and QUALITY CONTROL** **From the aphorism:** *Wɔse fa na w'amfa a, worenhu mu; wohwehwɛ mu a, na wohu mu; wopusu no a, na wote ne pampan.* **Literal translation: You miss the opportunity to know when you refuse to take it upon request; you know what it entails when you examine it critically; you know the smell only when you shake it. Knowledge must be subjected to critical enquiry.** **This symbol stresses the need to strive for the best quality, whether in production of goods or in human endeavors.**
 802 803 804 805	MATE MASIE - I HAVE HEARD AND KEPT IT Symbol of **WISDOM, PRUDENCE, KNOWLEDGE, and LEARNING** From the aphorism: *Nyansa bunu mu ne m'ate m'asie. Or, Tete ka aso mu a, na efiri kakyerɛ.* Literal translation: In the depth of wisdom abounds knowledge and thoughtfulness. I consider and keep what I learn. Or, Preservation of a people's culture has its basis in oral tradition. Knowledge is divine. To have a good ear and to retain everything heard from the master is a mark of excellence in learning. The symbol reflects the Akan's love of and quest for knowledge, and also respect for the wise person. It originates from the Akan belief that a people without knowledge of their history is like a tree without roots. The symbolism of *Mate Masie* (*Ntesie*) is borne out, for example, during story-telling sessions and ceremonial occasions such as naming ceremony (**abadint**o) when moral lessons and social values of the community as well as community and family histories are articulated.

  806 807 808 809 810	**NSAA – HORSE OR CAMEL HAIR BLANKET** Symbol of **EXCELLENCE, GENUINENESS,** and **AUTHENTICITY** From the proverb: *Nea onim nsaa na ɔtɔ n'ago.* Literal translation: He who cannot recognize the genuine camel-hair (or horse-hair) blanket buys its fake. Or, the untutored accepts sophistry as science. This symbol extols excellence and eschews satisfaction with mediocrity.
 811 812 813 814 815	**KRAMO-BƆNE – QUACKERY (FAKE MOSLEM)** Symbol of the **NEED FOR CRITICAL INQUIRY, WARNING AGAINST QUACKERY, SOPHISTRY, DECEPTION,** and **HYPOCRISY** From the expression: *Kramo-bɔne amma yanhu kramo-pa.* Literal translation: We cannot tell a good Moslem from a bad one. The fake and the genuine look alike because of hypocrisy. Or, To the uneducated sophistry is science.
  816 817 818	**KUNTANKANTAN – EGOCENTRICISM** Symbol of **WARNING AGAINST INFLATED PRIDE, EGOCENTRICISM, ETHNOCENTRICISM,** and **ARROGANCE** *From the aphorism: Nea ɔyɛ ne ho sɛ menim menim, nnim hwee. Or, Nim-nim, nnim.* Literal translation: The one who claims to know all, knows nothing. Or, Know-it-all knows nothing. The symbol *kuntankantan* (egocentricism) serves to remind one not to be egocentric and boastful of the little knowledge one has. If you pride yourself on your wisdom, it is a sign of ignorance.
819	**NEA ONNIM - THE ONE WHO DOES NOT KNOW** Symbol of **KNOWLEDGE, LIFE-LONG EDUCATION, and CONTINUED QUEST FOR KNOWLEDGE** From the maxim: *Nea onnim sua a, ohu; nea ɔdwen sɛ onim dodo no, sɛ ogyae sua a, ketewa no koraa a onim no firi ne nsa. Also, Nim-nim, nnim.* Literal translation: He who does not know can become knowledgeable from learning; he who thinks he knows and ceases to continue to learn will stagnate. Also, Know it all knows nothing. To grow is to live, to stagnate is to die. Only as one continues to search for knowledge will one grow wiser. Education is a life-long process.

820 821	**DAME DAME - CHECKERS** Symbol of **STRATEGIC PLANNING, ADROITNESS, DEXTERITY, CRITICAL THINKING, and GAMESMANSHIP** From the aphorism: *Kwasea ani te a, na agorɔ agu. Or, Mepɛ kwasea bi ne no ato dame.* Literal translation: When the fool learns to understand the rules of a game, the game ends. Or, I will like to play a game of checkers with some fool. This symbolizes that knowledge is accessible even to the fool.
822	**NOKORɛ – TRUTH** Symbol of **HONESTY, VALIDITY, AUTHENTICITY,** and **VERACITY** From the proverb: *Nokorɛ nsuma. Or, Nkontompo ama nokorɛ boɔ ayɛ den. Or, Nokorɛ mu nni abra. Also, Nokorɛ nya ahe na wotwa mu nkontompɔ.* Literal translation: Truth does not hide. Or, Hypocrisy makes truth have a high price. Or, There is no contradiction in truth. Also, Truth is not much to lie in it.
823	**ASɛM PA ASA – THE TRUTH IS GONE** From the expression: *Asɛm pa asa.* Literal translation: The truth is gone. This symbol depicts the Akan view of knowledge as being unchanging and absolute.
824	**GYINA PINTINN – STAND FIRM** Symbol of **BEING PRINCIPLED, DISCIPLINE, RESOLUTENESS, and UNDAUNTEDNESS** From the expression: *Gyina pintinn.* Literal translation: Stand firm; be principled.
825	**DWENE HWɛ KAN - AIM HIGH** Symbol of **FORETHOUGHT, PLANNING AHEAD,** and **ORGANIZATION** From the aphorism: *Dwene hwɛ kan.* Literal translation: Aim high or think ahead.
826 827	**NKYɛMU – DIVISION, ALLOTMENT, DISTRIBUTION** Symbol of **PRECISION, PROPORTIONALITY,** and The divisions done onto the plain cloth before the stamping is done.

828	**NSƐNEƐ – SCALES** Symbol of **MEASUREMENT, BALANCE, PRECISION, QUANTIFICATION, WEALTH, FRUGALITY, COMMERCE and TRADE** From the proverb: *Wodi wo sika a, wose wo nsɛneɛ mu nyɛ den. Or, Wokeri sika kɔtɔ boɔ a, wo we.* Literal translation: When one is being wasteful of one's money, one tends to blame it on a defect in one's scale. Or, When you weigh gold dust to buy a piece of rock, you eat it. The scale was used to weigh gold dust which served as money. Special weights (*mmramoɔ*) were designed and used as counterweights in measuring the gold dust in various financial and monetary transactions. One who tends to spend one's gold dust on frivolities was considered a spendthrift, but such a person usually tended to blame his/her extravagance on some perceived defect in the measuring scales.
829	**NIPA MFɔN KWA - ONE DOES NOT GROW LEAN WITHOUT A CAUSE** Symbol of **CAUSE AND EFFECT, CAUSALITY, and PRINCIPLE OF DETERMINISM** From the expression: *Nipa mfɔn kwa. Or, Sɛ anantuo kɔsene srɛ a, na yadeɛ wɔ mu.* Literal translation: One does not grow lean without a cause. Or, If the calf grows bigger than the thigh, then it must be diseased.
830	**KYERƐ ME KWAN NO – SHOW ME THE WAY** Symbol of **MENTORING, GUIDANCE, APPRENTICESHIP** From the expression: *Kyerɛ me kwan no ma menhu.* Literal translation: Show me the way so that I can know (learn).
831	**BOMOKYIKYIE – THE RIVER FISH (MUDFISH or CATFISH)** Symbol of **INCONTROVERTIBLE EVIDENCE, EYEWITNESS ACCOUNT** From the proverb: *Sɛ bomokyikyie firi nsuoase bɛkã sɛ ɔdɛnkyɛm awu a, yɛnnye no akyinnie.* Literal translation: When the mudfish (catfish) comes from the bottom of the river to say that the crocodile is dead, we do not doubt it.

832	**ƆBONSAM A WONIM NO - THE DEVIL YOU KNOW** **Symbol of AWARENESS, ALERTNESS, KNOWLEDGE** From the proverb: *Ɔbonsam a wonim no ye sen ɔsoro bɔfoɔ a wonni no.* Literal translation: The devil you know is better than the angel you do not know.
833	**DABAN – A MEASURE, SURETY or IRON BAR** Symbol of **MEASUREMENT, GUARANTEE, IRON SMELTING** From the expression: *Daban da hɔ a, ɛda asɛm so. Or, Daban da aburokyire a, ɔtomfoɔ dea.* Literal translation: A promissory note or surety has to be honored. Or, The blacksmith owns the iron ore that is discovered abroad.
834 835	**WODU NKWANTA A – WHEN YOU REACH THE INTERSECTION** Symbol of **WARNING, SIGNAL, MARK, BEACON, GUIDE, INDICATOR** From the expression: *Wodu nkwanta a, gu me ahahan.* Literal translation: when you reach the intersection (or crossroads), leave me an indicator or sign.
836	**FRANKAA – FLAG** Symbol of **WARNING, SIGN, IDENTIFICATION** From the expression: *Asɛm kɛseɛ reba a, frankaa nsi so.* Literal translation: Crisis occurs without prior warning.
837	**MMERE DANE - TIME CHANGES** **Symbol of** CHANGE, LIFE'S DYNAMICS, DIRECTION, **and** MOTION **From the expression:** *Mmere dane.* **Literal translation: Time changes.**
838	**MMERE TU SƐ ANOMAA – TIME FLIES LIKE A BIRD** Symbol of **MOTION and WARNING AGAINST PROCRASTINATION** From the maxim: *Mmere tu sɛ anomaa, na wobɛyɛ biribi a, yɛ no prɛko. Or, Mmere te sɛ anomaa, ɔtu a worenhu no bio.* Literal translation: Time flies like a bird; do what you have to do now. Or, Time is like a bird, it flies and you see it no more.

839 840 841 842 843	**AFE BI YE ASIANE - INAUSPICIOUS YEAR** Symbol of **MISFORTUNE, BAD LUCK, and IINAUSPICIOUS TIMES** From the expression: *Afe bi ye asiane.* Literal translation: **Some years are inauspicious or unlucky.**
844	**MMERE DANE A – WHEN TIME CHANGES** Symbol of **TIME, GROWTH** and **ADAPTABILITY** From the expression: *Mmere dane a wo nso dane wo ho bi. Or, Mmerɛ di adannee.* Literal translation: When time changes, adapt yourself to the times. Or, Times change.
845	**DA BI ME NSOROMMA BEPUE – MY STAR WILL SHINE ONE DAY** Symbol of **HOPE, TRUST, EXPECTATION, and OPTIMISM** From the expression: *Da bi me nsoromma bɛpue.* Literal translation: My star will shine (rise) one day.
846 847 848	**AKOKƆ – FOWL (ROOSTER)** Symbol of **TIME, GENDER DIVISION OF LABOR, WARNING AGAINST HAUGHTINESS** From the expression: *Adekyeeɛ nnyina akokɔbɔneeɛ so; sɛ akokɔ bɛbɔn, sɛ ɔremmɔn o, adeɛ bɛkye. Or, Akokɔbedeɛ nim adekyeeɛ nso ɔtie onini ano. Also, Akokɔnin gya aho hɔhoa yi na yɛn nyina fi kosua mu.* Literal translation: Cockerel should stop boasting for it came from an egg just like the hen.
849	**NNA NYINAA NSƐ – ALL DAYS ARE NOT EQUAL** Symbol of **INEQUALITY, UNEQUAL OPPORTUNITY, TIME** From the expression: *Nna nyinaa nsɛ.* Literal translation: All days are not equal.
850 851	**KYƐMFERƐ - POTSHERD (BROKEN POT)** Symbol of **KNOWLEDGE, EXPERIENCE, SERVICE, KEEPSAKE, ANTIQUITY, RARITY, and HEIRLOOM** From the proverb: **Kyɛmferɛ se ɔdaa hɔ akyɛ, na onipa a ɔnwenee no nso nyɛ dɛn?** *Or, Obi afa me kyɛmferɛ na ɔkye mu nkateɛ. Also, Awisiaa deɛ ne kyɛmferɛ.* Literal translation: The potsherd claims it is old, what about the potter who molded it? Or, Someone is using my potsher to roast his/her groundnuts (peanuts). Also, An orphan's possession is a broken pot.

852	**ADWUMA AMAMMRA – ORGANIZATIONAL CULTURE** Symbol of **ORGANIZATIONAL CULTURE, TRADE SECRETS, PROFESSIONAL CODE OF CONDUCT, ORGANIZATIONAL RULES AND REGULATIONS, and ORGANIZATIONAL ETHICS** From the maxim: *Adwuma biara wɔ mu amammra. Or, Adwadie wɔ mu amaneɛ.* Literal translation: Every organization or profession has its own customs. Or, Trading has its customs.
AB CD **853**	**ABCD – THE ALPHABET** Symbol of **BEING LETTERED, BEING KNOWLEDGEABLE, FORMAL EDUCATION** From the aphorism: *Sukuu nko na nyansa so nko. Or, Mia w'ani yɛ ɔsetie na nimdeɛ wɔ hɔ yi, yɛfa no obi ano.* Literal translation: Knowledge can be independently gained outside the formal school system. Book knowledge and wisdom are two separate things. Or, Learn to be a good listener, for much knowledge may be gained from others.
854	**AHAHAN – LEAVES** Symbol of **KNOWLEDGE, MARK OF DISTINCTION also CO-OPERATION, UNITED ACTION** From the expression: *Kɔnini ahahan ne besehene ahahan yɛtase no ɔbanyansafoɔ. Also, Yɛnkɔte aduro a, ɛne ahahan. Or, Wodu nkwanta a, gu me ahahan. Or, Nhaha-ata mmienu kabɔm a, ɛyɛ pepe.* Literal translation: It takes the wise and skilled person to distinguish between the leaves of the red and white cola trees. Also, One does not go and pluck any leaf and call it medicinal. Or, When you reach the intersection (or crossroads) leave me an indicator or sign. Or, When two leaves are placed together they are hard to break. United we stand, divided we fall.
855 856	**NKORɔN – NINE** From the proverb: *Woamma wo yɔnko antwa nkrɔn a, won so worentwa du.* Literal translation: If you do not let your friend have nine, you will not be able to have ten.
857	**NSENSAN DUA – LINE MAKING INSTRUMENT** First the printer makes a grid pattern with dye on the cloth using a comb-like tool or a long ruler. Then it is decorated by stamping the squares with shapes and symbols with special meanings.

858 859 860 861	**NSENSAN – LINES** Symbol of **NUMBERING, COMPUTATION, and ACCOUNTING** Lines are drawn with *dua afe* or *nsensan nnua* on the cloth before printing of various symbols. The dua afe or nsenan nnua has two, three to ten "teeth." The numbers of lines made have symbolic meanings themselves. San dan ho (make a mark on the wall), a system of credit in which lines of various colors are utilized, is sed by entrepreneurs to extend credit to customers.
862	**ASANTUROFI ANOMAA – THE BIRD OF DILEMMA (THE LONG-TAILED NIGHTJAR)** Symbol of **DILEMMA; BEING IN A QUANDRY; IMPASSE, and PREDICAMENT** From the aphorism: *Asanturofi anomaa, wofa no a, woafa mmusuo; wogyae no nso a, woagyae siadeɛ.* Also, *Abusuasɛm nti na yɛmfa asanturofie mma fie.* Literal translation: The long-tailed nightjar, the bird of dilemma; when you capture it you incur jeopardy; when you let it go you will a golden opportunity. Also, It is because of the taboo against it that the nightjar is not brought into the house.
863	**NIPA TIRE NYƐ BƆFERƐ - THE HUMAN MIND IS NOT LIKE THE PAPAYA FRUIT** Symbol of **IMPREGNABILITY OF THE HUMAN MIND** From the proverb: *Nipa tire nye bɔferɛ na yɛapaa mu ahwɛ dea ɛwɔ mu.* Literal translation: The human mind is not like the papaya fruit to be split open to see what is on the inside.
864	**MEWƆ HA – I AM HERE** Symbol of **PRESENCE, DEPORTMENT, and ALERTNESS** From the expression: *Mewɔ ha.* Literal translation: I am here.
865	**ABURUBURO KOSUA – DOVE'S EGG** Symbol of **DESTINY, FATE, and DETERMINISM** From the aphorism: *Aburuburo kosua, adeɛ a ɛbɛyɛ yie nsɛe da.* Literal translation: Dove's egg, what has been destined to prosper can never be destroyed.

866	**KWADU HONO – BANANA PEEL** Symbol of **PROOF, TESTIMONY** and **EVIDENCE** From the maxim: *Da bi asɛm nti na yɛdi kwadu a yɛgya ne hono.* Or, *Da bi asɛm nti na yɛdɔ kɔto kwadu a, yɛgyam ho.* Literal translation: When we eat banana we leave its peel to be used as evidence. Or, For future need we clear around the banana tree to help it flourish.
867	**ANANTUO – CALF** Symbol of **CAUSALITY, SKEPTICISM** From the proverb: *Sɛ anantuo kɔsene serɛ a, na yadeɛ wɔ mu.* Literal translation: If the calf gets bigger than the thigh, then it is diseased.
868	**SE ANTIE YE MMUSUO – DISOBEDIENCE CAN BE DISASTROUS** Symbol of **WARNING AGAINST DISOBEDIENCE, RESPECT, OBEDIENCE and DISASTER** From the proverb: *Se antie yɛ mmusuo.* Literal translation: Disobedience can have disastrous results.
869	**AKYIN-AKYIN – THE TRAVELLED** From the Proverb: *Akyin-akyin sen anin-anin.* Or, *Akyinakyin ama mahunu nnɔma na ama mate nsɛm.* Literal translation: The travelled is more cosmopolitan and worldly than the aged who is stuck in one place. Or, Travelling has given me a better exposure to more opportunities.
870	**OSOHOR – OSTRICH** Symbol of SEARCHING, INQUIRY and DISCOVERY
871 872	**AHINANSA – TRIANGLE** Symbol of **PRIDE OF STATE** and **UNIVERSE** The triangle represents God as the ruler of the universe which is a continuum of sky (*ewimu*), the earth (*asaase*), and the underworld of spiritual beings (*asamanase*). The symbol also represents *adaeboɔ* - the pendant worn by the king.

873	**KOTEPOMPONINI AHAASA – THREE HUNDRED AGAMA LIZARDS** Symbol of **DETERMINISM** From the proverb: *Sɛ wotoatoa kotepomponini ahaasa ma wɔne prammire tenten yɛ pɛ a, wɔn ano borɔ nto prammire ano borɔ.* Literal translation: If you line up three hundred agama lizards to be as long as a cobra, they cannot be as poisonous as a cobra. You cannot make a person what she/he is not, no matter how you treat her/him.
874	**HUHU HUHU – RUMORS** Symbol of **MISINFORMATION, RUMOR MONGERING, DISINFORMATION, KNOWLEDGE AS COUNTER TO IGNORANCE** From the expression: *Huhuhu nyɛ me hu.* Literal translation: Rumors do not scare me. The well informed person is not bothered by unfounded rumor.
875	**ANYANSAFOƆ MIENU – TWO WISE PEOPLE** From the proverb: *Anyansafoɔ mienu kyɛ nwa miɛnsa a, asisie ba.* Literal translation: If two wise people share three snails, there is bound to be cheating.
876	**TƆNTƆNTE NETETƆNTE – THE BLIND AND THE LAME** Symbol of **FORESIGHT, SOBER REFLECTION,** and **PLANNING AHEAD** From the proverb: *Tɔntɔnte ne Tetɔnte se: Yɛrenom nsa na yɛrefa adwen.* Literal translation: The blind and the lame say: As we are drinking, we are planning ahead. Also, in a seemingly light moment, we can slowly make progress on other important issues.
877	**SAPƆFO – OLD SPONGE** Symbol of **USEFULNESS; RECYCLING OF USED OBJECTS** From the proverb: *Sapɔfo, yɛfa no da hia da.* Literal translation: The discarded old sponge is found useful when the need arises.

878	**PESEMENKOMENYA – SELFISHNESS** Symbol od SELFISHNESS, SELF-CENTEREDNESS, SELF-CONCEIPT and INDIVIDUALISM From the expression: *Pesemenkomenya see oman.* Literal translation: Selfishness destroys a nation.
879 880	**AKYEM - SHIELD** Symbol of **BRAVERY AND HEROIC DEEDS, GLORIOUS ACCOMPLISHMENT, PERMANENCE OF DEEDS OF DISTINCTION, and DURABILITY** From the proverb: *Akyem tete a, eka ne mmeramu.* Or, *Agyan nti na yeyo akyem.* Literal translation: When a shield wears out, the framework still remains. The good deeds of people live after them. This symbolizes bravery as well as the durability and the enduring nature of the distinguished deeds of a great person. Or, Because of the arrow, we make the shield. If it were not for aggression, defensive weapons would not be necessary.
881	**GYA TIA DADA– OLD FIRE-BRAND** From the expression: *Gya tia dada ano nye sona.* Literal translation: The old fire-brand's end is not difficult to light up. Or, it is easy to rekindle an old flame, or an old love.
882	**AHWEDEE – SUGARCANE** Symbol of **IMPERFECTION, LIMITATION and INADEQUACY** From the expression: *Ahwedee Abena se, me de nkosi me nkon mu.* Literal translation: Sugarcane Abena says, I have my limitations, my sweetness ends at the fronds.
883	**ATUMPAN TWENE – TALKING DRUMS** Symbol of COMMUNICATION, MUSIC, RHYTHM, and APPELLATION From the expression: *Yenka nni wakyi a wose agoro ye de.* Literal translation:
884	**HWIMHWIM ADEE – A THING EASILY GAINED** Symbol of HURRIEDNESS, HASTE, From the proverb: *Hwimhwim adee ko sorosoro.* Literal translation: A thing easily gained goes quickly. Easy come, easy goes.

885	**PROPROBINSIN – GRUB (SCARAB)** Symbol of **USEFULNESS, RESOURCEFULNESS, ROLE PLAYING.** **PROTECTION FROM EVIL, RESOURCE MANAGEMENT,** and **WASTE MANAGEMENT** From the expression: *Aproprobinsin koraa ho wɔ mfasoɔ.* Literal translation: Even the grub performs a useful role.
886	**BƆNE FAFIRI – EXCULPATION, ATONEMENT** and **FORGIVENESS** Symbol of **ATONEMENT, EXCULPATION and FORGIVENESS** From the Christian prayer: *Fa yɛn bɔne fir yɛn* Literal translation: Forgive us our trespasses.
887	**HERITAGE** **Symbol of HERITAGE, TRADITION** and **CULTURE** From the proverb: *Wokɔ kurow bi mu a, dwom a ɛho mmɔfra to no, wɔn mpaninfoɔ na ɛto gya wɔn.* Literal translation: When one goes to a village, the song the children there would be singing is the song their elders once sang. Tradition is handed down.
888	**KANEA – HURRICANE LAMP** Symbol of **BRIGHTNESS, LIGHT, PROGRESS, CLARITY, TRANSPARENCY, ENLIGHTMENT** and **ILLUMINATION** From the proverb: *Yɛsɔ kanea si kaneadua so, yɛmfa nkosuma pono ase.* Literal translation: A lamp is lighted to be placed on a lamp post rather than being hidden under a table.
889	**WODI ASƐMPA A - IF YOU DO WHAT IS JUST** From the proverb: *Wodi asɛmpa a, wonyin kyɛ.* Literal translation: If you do what is just (good), you live long. The pursuit of justice brings long life and peace of mind.
890	**ƆBRAKWAN ATWEDEƐ – LIFE'S SOCIAL LADDER** Symbol of the **SOCIAL LADDER** From the adage: *Ɔbrakwan atwedeɛ, obi reforo kɔ sor no, na obi so resane, na obi so deɛ, ogyina na ogyina.* Literal translation: The social ladder is such that some people move up, some people move down, and other people stay in the same position. In society, some individuals and families experience drastic changes in social status and lifestyle. Vertical social mobility refers to moving up or down the so-called social ladder.

891	**KONKRON – IMPETUOUS** Symbol of being **IMPETUOUS, RASH, IMPULSIVE, ARROGANCE** and **BAD MANNERS** From the aphorism: *"Agya, gyae na menka," wokyi.* Literal translation: "Father, let me say it" is forbidden (ie, bad manners is improper behavior). It is unbecoming (improper) for a child (junior person) to say what should be said by the father (or his senior). This proverb seeks to guide children to refrain from being arrogant in society, hence have respect and honor for the elderly in society.
892	**MPUA ANUM - FIVE TUFTS, HAIRSTYLE OF KING'S ATTENDANTS** Symbol of **LOYALTY, DISTINGUISHED PUBLIC SERVICE, DIGNITY,** **ADROITNESS, and PATRIOTISM** Hairstyle of loyal service to the nation worn by the king's male attendants. It is also a hair style of joy and a symbol of priestly office. It also represents the devotion and faithfulness one displays when doing a task required of one. In addition, mpuannum means loyalty or the embodiment of lofty duty to a desired goal."
893	**ƆBOƆ PAYEƐ – SPLIT STONE** Symbol of FUTILITY, POINTLESSNESS From the proverb: *Ɔboɔ payeɛ a, yɛmpam.* Literal translation: When a stone splits it cannot be sewn together
894	**OTUMFOƆ – THE POWERFUL ONE** Symbol of **AUTHORITY, POWER**, and **SUPREMACY** From the maxim: *Otumfoɔ worɔ ne kawa a, ɔworɔ fa n'abatir.* Literal translation:When the powerful one removes a ring from his finger, he removes it through his shoulder
895	**TUMI – POWER** Symbol of **POWER, INFLUENCE, AUTHORITY** and **CCONTROL** From the aphorism: *Nyame tumi so.* Also, *Ɔhene na ɔwɔ tumi.* Literal translation: God is all powerful. Also, The King is entrusted with power.

  896	**Bɔ WOHO BAN – PROTECT YOURSELF** Symbol of **HIV/AIDS AWARENESS, PROTECTION, and PREVENTION** From the aphorism: *Nnɛ yareɛ aba, nti ɛyɛ a na w'abɔ ho ban.* Also, *Wobedi ɔdɔ a, bɔ woho ban na hwɛ yie.* Literal translation: STDs abound, protect yourself, Also, Be careful who you make love with.
  897	**MENSAN NKɔFA ME RɔBA – LET ME GO BACK FOR MY RUBBER** Symbol of **HIV/AIDS AWARENESS, PROTECTION, and PREVENTION** From the expression: *ɔdɔ, ma mensan nkɔfa me rɔba nhyɛ.* Literal translation: My love, let me go back for my rubber (condom).
  898	**DEA ƐKɔ SORO – WHAT GOES UP** Symbol of **INEVITABILITY, INEXORABLENSS, CERTAINTY** From the maxim: *Dea ɛkɔ soro biara ba famu.* Literal translation: Whatever goes up will eventually come down.
  899	**WONNI PANIN A – IF YOU DO NOT HAVE AN ELDERLY PESON** Symbol of **RESOURCEFULNESS, CHERISHED HERITAGE** From the aphorism: *Wonni panin a, due.* If you do not have an old person (man or woman), pity on you. To have an elderly person in one's home is to have a source of reference and knowledge based on experience, and the person who does not have this source of reference deserves to be pitied.
  900	**EFIE NE ABɔNTEN – HOME AND OUTSIDE** Symbol of **MORALITY, MORALS, NORMS and DECENCY** From the maxim: *Dea ɛwɔ fie so biara na ɛwɔ abɔnten so.* Literal translation: Whatever exists in households exists also outside. What norms exist in a society are what may be found in the households.
  901	**ɔKɔMFO KÃ NE NKONIMDIE – THE PRIEST BOASTS OF HIS ACCOMPLISHMENTS** Symbol of **DUPLICITY, FRAUDULENCE and DECEIT** From the aphorism: *ɔkɔmfo kã ne nkonimdie na ɔnkã ne nkoguo.* Literal translation: The fetish priest tells of his victories but not his defeats. The fetish priest boasts of his successful prophecies but says nothing about the unfulfilled ones.

902	**AHWENE PA NKASA – PRECCIOUS BEADS DO NOT JINGLE** Symbol of **HONOR, DIGNITY, NOT BEING A BRAGGADOCIO, NOT BEING BOASTFUL, WARNING AGAINST BEING CONCEITED** From the aphorism: *Ahwene pa nkasa.* Literal translation: Precious beads do not jingle. In a polygamous relationship, proverbial textile prints such as *Ahwene pa nkasa* ("Precious beads do not jingle") cloth may be worn by a teasing "senior wife" who might well feel like proclaiming loud and clear, to the hearing of her co-wives, that "A man is not a pillow upon which to rest one's head." Empty barrel makes the most noise.
903	**DƆ ME NA ME NNƆ WO BI – LOVE ONE ANOTHER** Symbol of **FRATERNITY, COOPERATION** From the aphorism: *Dɔ me na me nnɔ wo bi.* Literal translation: Love one another. Scratch my back and I will scratch yours.
904	**NAMMA – SIBLINGS** Symbol of **FAMILY RELATIONS, BIRTHRIGHT,** and **INHERITANCE ORDER** From theaphorism: *Nãmma nsae a, wofase nni ade.* Literal translation: When one's siblings (mother's children) are alive (or do exist), a nephew does not inherit.
905	**WANSENA NNI BI MPO A – EVEN THE FLY THAT HAS NOT MUCH TO OFFER** Symbol of **GENUINE GENEROSITY, KINDNESS, SINCERE APPRECIATION** and **THANKFULNESS** From the aphorism: *Wansena nni bi mpo a, wɔposa ne nsa mu.* Literal translation: Even the fly that has not much to offer, it rubs its hands together.
906	**YƐNTENA NSERE – LET US LIVE IN HARMONY** Symbol of **HARMONY, CONCORD, AGREEMENT.** From the expression: *Hom mma yɛntena nsere.* Literal translation: Let us live in harmony.
907	**AFA ME NWA – YOU HAVE PICKED ME EASILY AS A SNAIL** Symbol of **PEACE, HARMONY** and **TRANQUILITY** From the aphorism: *W'afa me nwa. Or, Nwa de ne ho sie yie a, na wɔfrɛ no otope.* Literal translation: You have picked me easily as a snail. Or, When a snail takes care of itself well when it is taken it is taken as a big snail.

908	**ƆBAA PA – GOOD (PERFECT) or IDEAL WOMAN** Symbol of IDEAL WOMAN, MODEL WOMAN, WELL-MANNERED WOMAN From the naxim: *Ɔbaa pa de oni na ɛkɔ aware.* Literal translation: The ideal woman models her mother in marriage
909	**ASETENA PA – GOOD LIVING** Symbol **of COMPLACENCY, SMUGNESS and HAUGHTINESS** From the maxim: *Asetena pa ma awerɛfiri.* Literal translation: Ostantacious living creates complacency.
910	**ABOSOMAKOTERƐ - THE CHAMELEON** Symbol **of LIMITATION, CONSTRAINT, INADEQUACY, DEFICIENCIES, INADEQUACY and CONSTRICTION** From the proverb: *Abosomakoterɛ nim adanedane a, nyɛ dea ɛwɔ adaka mu.* Literal translation: If the chameleon can change colors, it can not change to the color of what is inside a box.
911	**PANIN NE MMƆFRA – THE ELDERLY AND THE YOUNG** From the maxim: *Ɔpanin hu sɛ deɛ ɔne mmɔfra nante a, wɔsoa n'adwa.* Literal translation: When the elder learns to walk with the young, they carry his stool. Being an elder does not automatically confer privileges on a person, for the person must behave in a responsible way in order to earn the respect, authority and the service due elders.
912	**ABƆFRA HURI – WHEN A CHILD JUMPS** Symbol of **RESPECT FOR THE ELDERLY,** and **VENERATION OF THE ELDERLY** From the maxim: *Se abofra yɛ sɛ obehuru atra ne panin a, ɔkyere no siaw ne kɔn ho.* Literal translation: If a child attempts to jump over an elder, he gets caught in the elder's armpit.
913	**APRUKUMA – A MEDICINAL SEED** From the proverb: *Aprukuma egu nhyirene mpo na ekum akwaduo yi, na ebegu ebibra.* Literal translation: If the flower from the *aprukuma* kills the baboon, what about the hard seed? Aprukuma is a seed with a very hard shell. If the falling petals of its flowers can kill the baboon, what about the seed itself? The hard shell is ground to cure boils, severe headache and other illnesses.

914	**ADU HWAM – FRAGRANCE** Symbol of **SWEET SMELL, FRAGRANCE, POWERFUL AROMA** From the proverb: *Pɛrɛkɛse Gyamadu, ofiti kurotia a, na he ho bɔn afie mu.* Literal translation: The strong aroma of the **perekese** precedes it into all households even when it is at the outskirts of the town. The **pɛrɛkɛse** (*Tetrapleura tetraptera*) is used here symbolically to represent the king. The king's authority and power is felt in all households in his kingdom. *Tetrapleura tetraptera* is a species of flowering plant in the pea family native to West Africa. The fruit is conventionally used as spice and as a natural multivitamins. It is rich in protein, lipids, potassium, iron, magnesium, phosphorous, and vitamin C. In Nigeria, it is cooked in soup and fed to mothers to prevent post-partum contraction. In Ghana, *prɛkɛsɛ* has been used to flavor soft drinks. The drink has been approved by the Food and Drugs board, and is marketed to reduce hypertension, decrease the severity of asthma attacks, and promote blood flow. Studies indicate that *prɛkɛsɛ* extract reduces the risk of certain types of ulcer. It can also inhibit the growth of bacteria. Dried fruits have been powdered and combined in soap bases to include anti-microbial properties. Moreover, the fruit extract can reduce convulsions with its ability to slow down the central nervous system.
915	**AWURADE NE YƐN KANEA – THE LORD IS OUR LIGHT** Symbol of **SALVATION, FEARLESSNESS, DIVINE LIGHT, DELIVERANCE** From the aphorism: *Awurade ne yɛn kanea, yɛnsuro.* Also, *Awurade, Wo ne kanea yɛde hwɛ yɛn akwan mu.* Literal translation: The Lord is our light, we are not afraid. Also, Lord, You are the light that guide us on our pathways.
916	**M'AKOMA – MY HEART** Symbol of **DEVOTION, COMMITMENT, DEVOUTNESS, RELIGIOUS FERVOR and PIETY** From the expression: *Awurade, m'akoma yɛ wo de.* Literal translation: Oh Lord, my heart belongs to you.

917	**NYAME ƆBAATANPA – GOD THE GOOD PARENT** Symbol of the MOTHERLINESS, PARENTAL CARE, PARENTHOOD From the expression: Nyame ɔbaatanpa; ne adɔyɛ dɔɔso. Literal translation: God the great parent; his love knows no bounds.
918	**ODURUYƐFO – THE MEDICINE PERSON** **Symbol of PERSONAL RESPONSIBILITY, DUTY, OBLIGATION and ACCOUNTABILITY** From the maxim: *Oduruyɛfo nnom aduro mma oyarefoɔ.* Literal translation: The medicine person does not the medication on behalf of the sick person. The responsibility for taking medication lies with the sick person.
919	**DUFƆKYEƐ – WET LOG** **Symbol of CONSEQUENCES and COSTS** From the proverb: *Sɛ wotena dufɔkyeɛ so di bɔferɛ a, woto fo, na w'ano so fo.* Literal translation: If one sits on a wet log to eat pawpaw (papaya), one's bottom gets wet and one's mouth gets wet too. The wet log may be a comfortable place to sit and pawpaw may be a nice fruit to eat. Hence this proverb metaphorically points out two pleasant activities that one can engage in, but they come at cost. One cannot expect to have all things to be rosy all the time.
920	**OBI NTUTU ANOMAA HO – ONE DOES NOT PLUCK THE FEATHERS OFF A BIRD** **Symbol of TRANSPARENCY, OPENNESS, FREE FROM PRETENSE OR DECEIT and ACCESSIBILITY OF INFORMATION** From the maxim: *Obi ntutu anomaa ho na ɔmfa nkyerɛ ɔpanin sɛ anomaa bɛn ni.* Literal translation: One does not pluck the feathers off a bird and takes to ask his elder what bird is it. Asking someone to name a featherless bird smacks of deceit and/or lack of transparency.

APPENDIX A

ADINKRA CLOTH COLLECTED BY BOWDICH
IN 1817 – BRITISH MUSEUM

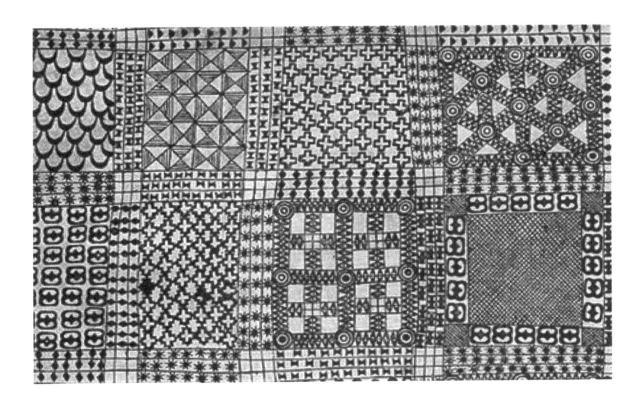

APPENDIX B

ADINKRA CLOTH SENT TO HOLLAND TO KING WILLIAM I IN 1825 FROM THE ELMINA CASTLE

Used with Permission from **"Collection Nationaal Museum
van Wereldculturen. Coll.no. RV-360-1700"**

APPENDIX C

ADINKRA CLOTH BELIEVED TO BELONG TO ASANTEHENE PREMPEH I CAPTURED IN 1896

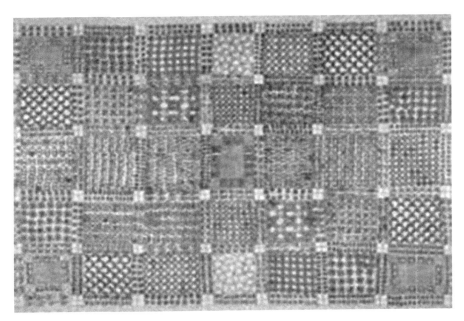

Used with permission from the National Museum of African Museum, Smithsonian Institution

Wrapper *(adinkra)*
Asante artist
Ghana
Mid-late 19th century
Imported cotton cloth, black pigment
H x L: 194.5 x 285.6 cm (76 9/16 x 112 7/16 in.)
Framed: 210.8 x 302.3 x 5 cm (83 x 119 x 1 15/16 in.)
Museum purchase
83-3-8
Photograph by Franko Khoury
National Museum of African Art

APPENDIX D

THE ADINKRA SYMBOLS IDENTIFIED
BY RATTRAY IN 1927

Rattray failed to identify about seven symbols that were in
the *adinkra* cloth collected by Bowdich in 1817.

APPENDIX E

INCULTURATION ADINKRA SYMBOLS CATHOLIC CHURCH OF GHANA

M'akoma ye wo dea.

Nyame Tumi So (1)

Nyame Kaatan pa

Odo Nsa Christ Mu.

Ahunanyankwa

Food for life (1)

Christ mu ab‸wanifua, obea di mrma na anani.

Abusuabo wo Christ mu

Nhyira nka Ghanaman No 1

Jesus le ase dea

Apampa

Me man ne Jesus nti

Aurade ne yen kanea (2)

Bone fafiri ye

Dom yen nyansa

Inculturated Symbols

297

APPENDIX F

ADINKRA SYMBOLS IN SOME OF THE CORPORATE LOGOS IN USE IN GHANA

INDEX

Printed in the United States
By Bookmasters